Advances in Simulation

Volume 5

Series Editors:

Paul A. Luker
Bernd Schmidt

Advances in Simulation

Paul A. Fishwick   Paul A. Luker
Editors

Qualitative Simulation Modeling and Analysis

With 121 Figures

Foreword by
Herbert A. Simon

Springer-Verlag
New York Berlin Heidelberg London
Paris Tokyo Hong Kong Barcelona

Editors:

Paul A. Fishwick
Computer and Information
  Sciences Department
University of Florida
Gainesville, FL 32611-2024
USA

Paul A. Luker
Department of Computer Science
California State University, Chico
Chico, CA 95929-0410
USA

Series Editors:

Paul A. Luker
Department of Computer Science
California State University, Chico
Chico, CA 95929-0410
USA

Bernd Schmidt
Institut für Informatik
Universität Erlangen-Nürnberg
Erlangen
FRG

Library of Congress Cataloging-in-Publication Data
Qualitative simulation modeling and analysis/Paul A. Fishwick. Paul
  A. Luker, editors; foreword by Herbert A. Simon.
     p.   cm.—(Advances in simulation; v. 5)
  Includes bibliographical references and index.
  ISBN 0-387-97400-8 (USA).—ISBN 3-540-97400-8 (EUR)
  1. Computer simulation. I. Fishwick, Paul A. II. Luker, Paul A.
III. Series.
QA76.9.C65Q35   1991
003′.3—dc20   90-25822

Printed on acid-free paper.

© 1991 Springer-Verlag New York, Inc.
All rights reserved. This work may not be translated or copied in whole or in part without the
written permission of the publisher (Springer-Verlag New York, Inc., 175 Fifth Avenue, New
York, NY 10010, USA), except for brief excerpts in connection with reviews or scholarly analysis.
Use in connection with any form of information storage and retrieval, electronic adaptation,
computer software, or by similar or dissimilar methodology now known or hereafter developed
is forbidden.
The use of general descriptive names, trade names, trademarks, etc., in this publication, even if
the former are not especially identified, is not to be taken as a sign that such names, as understood
by the Trade Marks and Merchandise Marks Act, may accordingly be used freely by anyone.

Typeset by Asco Trade Typesetting Ltd., Hong Kong.
Printed and bound by Edwards Brothers, Inc., Ann Arbor, Michigan.
Printed in the United States of America.

9 8 7 6 5 4 3 2 1

ISBN 0-387-97400-8 Springer-Verlag New York Berlin Heidelberg
ISBN 3-540-97400-8 Springer-Verlag Berlin Heidelberg New York

Foreword

The use of qualitative models of phenomena must go back to the beginnings of human thought. If you overshoot the target, bring the bow a little lower the next time. Of course, you must be careful to make moderate adjustments, to keep the system homing on a stable equilibrium. This seems to us a very natural way of thinking, and it hardly occurs to us to ask whether it can be formalized or what are its limits.

With the advent of abstract mathematics, these questions arise in a new form. Sometimes, we know the shape of the equations that govern the phenomena of interest, but we do not know the numerical values of parameters—perhaps, at most, we know their signs. Can we draw any conclusions about the system behavior? Examples abound in economics and thermodynamics, just to mention two domains. Experience tells us that, if the price of a commodity is raised, the amount demanded will decrease, but the amount offered by producers will increase. What will happen to the amount bought and sold, and to the price, if a sales tax is imposed? Reason (qualitative reason) tells us that less will be bought and sold than before, and that the price will rise, but by less than the amount of the tax. What is the mechanism of the reasoning that reaches these conclusions?

Or we look at the p-v diagram of a steam cycle, and notice that the volume of the system increases at high pressure and then returns to its original value at low pressure, so that the integral of pdv along the path is positive. We conclude that work has been done around the cycle. What is the basis for our conclusion?

Now it has been known for many years that such reasoning has a sound mathematical foundation. In the economics example, for example, if we write out the equations symbolically and shift the cost curve by the amount of the tax, we can compute the new equilibrium values of price and quantity symbolically. Then, by taking account of the signs of certain partial derivatives (the slopes of the supply and demand curves) *and* by assuming that the equilibrium is stable (equivalent, again, to assumptions about the signs of certain expressions), we can infer that the change in price will be positive, that the change in quantity will be negative, and even that the change in price will be less than the tax. This computation is called by economists "the method of comparative statics." Le Chatelier made use of essentially the same method in his work on shifts in chemical equilibrium, leading to the famous "Le Chatelier Principle."

Since the results depend only on the signs of certain quantities and since these signs do not change if an arbitrary monotonic transformation is made in the scales on which each of the variables is measured, it becomes clear that these matters can be dealt with by the mathematics of monotonic transformations, or, what is nearly the same thing, the mathematics of ordinally measured quantities.

Surprisingly (at least it seems surprising to me), these matters do not receive extensive treatment in the mathematical literature or in the curriculum in elementary mathematics. Perhaps mathematicians find them too elementary to be worthy of attention. At any rate, virtually every field of applied mathematics that stands to benefit from the use of qualitative reasoning has had to reinvent these techniques for itself. As a result, their notations, their methods of modeling, and their vocabularies form a cacophony of voices that communicate poorly. Knowledge about qualitative reasoning that is won in one discipline does not migrate rapidly and easily to others.

This volume brings together a number of these voices and their vocabularies, in order to allow them to be compared and understood. Most of them are built upon the structure of ideas that I have suggested above—on notions of the behavior of ordinally measured quantities—although the reader may sometimes have to work a bit to make the connections.

But, as well as similarity, diversity deserves attention. We want to develop qualitative reasoning as a working tool, which we can apply to various domains and to problems with all kinds of structures. We can learn a great deal from the examples in this book about the conditions under which particular notations and computational schemes may be advantageous. Until the mathematicians provide us with a suitable textbook on qualitative reasoning with ordinal variables, perhaps we can use this volume as a textbook. And even after the systematic textbook appears, we will want to see how the theory applies to examples, of which quite a number are supplied here.

Formal treatments of qualitative reasoning and qualitative models of dynamic systems are relatively new products. Even if it turns out that the mathematics underlying them is relatively simple, new and interesting complexity will no doubt emerge when we apply them to real problem domains. The techniques described in this book seem to me highly promising for exploring the problem of complexity, and I would hope that its publication will stimulate new research interest in this field, as well as new applications of the techniques already developed.

Finally, as we think about qualitative reasoning, it is not too soon to explore the new problems that arise when we try to apply our methods to domains that are characterized by chaos (in the contemporary technical meaning of that term). When we enter the world of nonlinear phenomena, and especially when we leave the domain where our systems tend toward stable equilibria or stable limit cycles, what can we say about them? Even though we know that detailed prediction of the future paths of chaotic systems is intrinsically impossible, we need not give up trying to characterize their behavior qualitatively. Already, we know, from the work of Mitchell Feigenbaum and others, that bifurcation can be predicted on qualitative grounds, and that the shapes of the strange attractors that replace equilibria in such systems can often be inferred.

I do not suggest that the papers in this volume, which are directed at the modeling of classical, nonchaotic systems, will provide answers to these questions. I do suggest that an understanding of qualitative reasoning in this "classical" domain may be a first step toward understanding how we can reason qualitatively about chaos—about systems, for example, whose behavior diverges with the slightest shift in initial conditions.

But the study of the healthy, robust organism must precede the study of pathology. In this volume, you will find a substantial body of analysis of systems that can be treated in terms of basic concepts of equilibrium, steady state and disequilibrium, and of stability and instability. It provides plenty of food for qualitative thought.

Pittsburgh, Pennsylvania   Herbert A. Simon

Series Preface

To most people, simulation is, almost by definition, quantitative. At the heart of many simulations are variables that take values in some continuous numeric range. The subject of this volume, qualitative modeling and simulation, permits a view of the world that has, until recently, been ignored in simulation. There are many situations in which it is not possible to quantify the attributes in a way that has any meaning or validity. In other situations, although quantification is possible, it is not appropriate for the particular study. The "art" of simulation, if there is one, is to produce a model that is appropriate for the task in hand. Qualitative modeling provides us with techniques that enable the modeler to concentrate on what is known about the system being modeled—our knowledge of this system is the key.

Qualitative modeling has developed from a number of roots. One of the prominent ones is naive physics, in which relationships between real-world objects are subjected to "commonsense" reasoning. Even more important, perhaps, has been the influence of causal reasoning. Qualitative modeling therefore has strong roots in artificial intelligence, for which the crucial component is the representation and manipulation of knowledge. The reader will find this relationship quite evident, in a number of different ways, in the chapters of this book. At the same time, it is interesting to note the breadth of the collection as a whole.

I would like to thank the authors of the individual chapters in this book. A special "thank you" goes to the coeditor of the volume, Paul A. Fishwick, who took on greater than his fair share of the burden. I hope he reaps greater than his fair share of the rewards.

I am very grateful to Gerhard Rossbach of Springer-Verlag for his endless patience and for his faith in and commitment to the series.

As the complexity of our world increases, our dependence—that is not too strong a word—on simulation also increases. Consequently, we are ever more demanding of our simulations, or in other words, we are constantly seeking *Advances in Simulation*. It was from a desire to document, share, and encourage these advances that this series was created. We would like to cover all aspects of advances in simulation, whether theoretical, methodological, or hardware- or software-related. An important part of the publication of material that constitutes an advance in some discipline is to make the material available while it is still of considerable use. Gerhard and the production staff at Springer-Verlag see to it that this is the case. I urge anybody who is eager to share their advances in simulation to contact Bernd Schmidt or myself. We would love to hear from you.

Chico, California   Paul A. Luker

Preface

Qualitative simulation can be defined in a number of ways, from a variety of perspectives. In general terms, it can be defined as a classification of simulation and modeling methods that are primarily nonnumerical in nature. The "qualitative" characterization of systems can apply itself to simulation input, output, model structure, and analysis method. Our study of qualitative methodology does not preclude quantitative approaches; instead, we suggest that qualitative approaches can augment traditional quantitative approaches by making them more amenable to a wide range of simulation users with differing levels of expertise, in both simulation methodology and the problem domain. For instance, suppose that the knowledge available for a particular simulation is not in numerical form; instead, it may be in linguistic form. Somehow we must translate the natural language text into an intermediate form acceptable by the simulation program. How do we accomplish this translation effectively? This is just one instance where simulation input is not in numerical form. Another instance relates to the kind of information expressed in expert systems. Expert system knowledge is chiefly symbolic and linguistic since human decision making is based largely on this type of information. The study of how one can utilize symbolic forms in simulation modeling is a key concern of qualitative simulation. Pictorial methods are also very important in simulation modeling, since these methods allow users to create system analogies by using graph-based techniques.

Studies in qualitative simulation are prompted by the following concerns:

1. Knowledge and data are sometimes symbolic or linguistic in form. How are these forms integrated into simulation programs?
2. How are simulation models created over time? We term this process *simulation model engineering* and suggest that studies in qualitative methods can enable us to take a step toward automating the simulation model construction procedure.
3. We need to make the user interface between man and machine better. Humans inherently think and reason in qualitative terms. Even though a simulation model is quantitative, we need better man–machine interfaces,

and translation methods from qualitative to quantitative knowledge and vice versa.

4. Humans think about dynamic systems (and, in general, the world around them) by using "mental models" of those systems. We can build qualitative simulation models that can be validated against cognitive models of systems. In this way, qualitative simulation can serve as a vehicle for creating cognitive models in artificial intelligence.

During our research of the choice of chapter authors for this book, we found substantial evidence of qualitative methodology in a wide variety of disciplines, from ecological system modeling to power flow modeling in mechanical engineering. We believe it important to have a book that encapsulates many of the common methodologies inherent in all of the discipline-specific models. In this sense, this book tries to bring together many otherwise disparate sources under the umbrella of qualitative simulation and analysis. The study of qualitative simulation, like simulation in general, is highly interdisciplinary, and so qualitative methods as described within each chapter will have a wide range of utility to those who are seeking more comprehensive and flexible simulation methods.

We are very excited about this book and feel that much future work lies ahead in the qualitative simulation area. In the future we would like to see more simulation textbooks cover more aspects of model building, evolution, and methodology with the aid of qualitative approaches. One of us (Paul Fishwick) would like to thank the National Science Foundation (Award IRI-8909152) for partial support during this research period. Most of all, the editors are indebted to each and every chapter author for their contribution to this field, and to Herb Simon for setting the scene so well.

Gainesville, Florida   Paul A. Fishwick
Chico, California   Paul A. Luker

Contents

Contributors

Ralph H. Abraham, Department of Mathematics, University of California, Santa Cruz, CA 95064, USA.

Wanda H. Austin, Aerospace Corporation, 2350 East El Segundo Boulevard, El Segundo, CA 90245, USA.

Howard W. Beck, Department of Agricultural Engineering, University of Florida, Gainesville, FL 32611, USA.

François E. Cellier, Department of Electrical and Computer Engineering, University of Arizona, Tucson, AZ 85721, USA.

Paul A. Fishwick, Computer and Information Sciences Department, University of Florida, Gainesville, FL 32611, USA.

Leo C.M.M. van Geffen, Faculty of Mechanical Engineering, Engineering Design Section, University of Twente, 7500 AE Enschede, The Netherlands.

Clark Glymour, Department of Philosophy, Carnegie Mellon University, Pittsburgh, PA 15213, USA.

Peter M.A.L. Hezemans, Faculty of Mechanical Engineering, Laboratory for Power Transmissions, 5600 MB Eindhoven, The Netherlands.

Yumi Iwasaki, Knowledge Systems Laboratory, Stanford University, Palo Alto, CA 94304, USA.

Behrokh Khoshnevis, Department of Industrial and Systems Engineering, University of Southern California, Los Angeles, CA 90089, USA.

George J. Klir, Department of Systems Science, Thomas J. Watson School of Engineering, State University of New York, Binghamton, NY 13901, USA.

Richard Levins, Department of Population Science, Harvard School of Public Health, Boston, MA 02115, USA.

Charles J. Puccia, Department of Population Science, Harvard School of Public Health, Boston, MA 02115, USA.

George P. Richardson, The Rockefeller College, State University of New York at Albany, Albany, NY 12222, USA.

Richard Scheines, Department of Philosophy, Carnegie Mellon University, Pittsburgh, PA 15213, USA.

Peter Spirtes, Department of Philosophy, Carnegie Mellon University, Pittsburgh, PA 15213, USA.

Jean U. Thoma, Department of Mechanical Engineering, University of Waterloo, Waterloo, Ontario N2L 3G1, Canada.

CHAPTER 1

Invariance and Nominal Value Mapping as Key Themes for Qualitative Simulation

Paul A. Fishwick

Abstract

We discuss the purpose of qualitative studies in simulation modeling and analysis. The notions of invariance (with regard to system structures, input, and output) and nominal value mapping are seen as central concepts (or "themes") to the variety of qualitative methods that currently exist in simulation. Thus, our purpose is to try to help unify the study of qualitative methods by relating them to each other using the key themes. In our work we have found that many different scientific and engineering disciplines have been doing simulation using qualitative methodology; our purpose, then, is to illustrate that these efforts are connected and that the collective concepts and methodology can be potentially utilized as a set of interdisciplinary tools. The thrust in qualitative methods is seen as a step toward making quantitative methods more accessible and usable by many different types of researchers and project managers. However, as we emphasize in the text, we must be extremely careful that qualitative approaches are carefully studied so that we do not fall into the trap of using ambiguous input to generate purely ambiguous results; results must, in the long term, be directly useful to decision makers that rely on simulation (among other tools) to make well-informed decisions. We also stress that the choice of which input, output, and model to use depends on the specific goals of the analyst. It is too easy, sometimes, either to create qualitative solutions that have no utility or to make qualitative an expression that has a more powerful quantitative equivalent.

1. Introduction

Most of the qualitative methods that we will delineate involve discussions about natural language system descriptions and pictorially oriented methods for system understanding. Text and pictures, therefore, are essential for qualitative simulation modeling and analysis. But, if we are to look further to see

Reprinted with permission from the *Transactions of the Society for Computer Simulation* (SCS) 7, 4 (Dec. 1990), pp. 339–361. © Simulation Councils, Inc.

why qualitative methods are useful in simulation, we frequently come across the central notion of *invariance* in systems. The clearest example is the study of analogy in systems science: If one system is mapped to another system via a behavior-preserving homomorphic mapping [17, 56, 61, 64], then we can see that the original system is invariant under the mapping function. Furthermore, this implies that both systems (the original and the mapping) remain in the same equivalence class. Bond graph modeling [28] has been shown to be a useful method for graphically modeling systems while considering invariance with respect to a scientific domain and the generic concepts of generalized "effort" and 'flow" in systems. Systems can, therefore, be placed into classes each of which is identified by a particular quality or set of qualities [22].

Certain variances in quantitative structure will not change the qualitative structure of a set of inputs, a model, or a collection of simulation output data. It is these invariant classifications that act to justify qualitative simulation as a viable scientific method. Consider examples of invariance. When studying graphical phase-plane output we want to know when a system changes its basic qualitative nature; for instance, when does a system based on a differential equation set undergo qualitative changes? We can generally look at two types of numbers that characterize fundamental qualitative change in many systems: parameter values and eigenvalues. When these numbers cross a threshold (or bifurcation point) then the system fundamentally changes its behavior, that is to say that the qualitative system nature is *invariant* to minor quantitative changes in parameter values. It is only when a parameter or eigenvalue reaches a given numeric threshold (such as zero) that we are willing to assign a different *quality* to the system. Another example of invariance relates to energy modeling [41, 42, 49, 53]. A bond graph, for instance, stresses relationships between components in terms of energy flow. Let us consider a bond graph that is composed of a single graph node with a source effort in-arc and out-arcs for resistance and capacitance. This simple graph describes many systems such as an electronic RC circuit and the harmonic motion of a pendulum swing. The bond graph is, then, invariant to many discipline-specific changes. In particular, a bond graph is invariant to certain variable name and structural changes in a system of equations for any given energy-based discipline such as electrical engineering or fluid mechanics. Other qualitative methods are associated with mapping name space to quantity space, or *nominal value mapping*. For instance, the quality of the natural language expression "fast moving" could conceivably map to a variety of quantities. Various methods such as interval arithmetic and fuzzy set theory [35, 57] directly address this problem. Also, in artificial intelligence, researchers in qualitative simulation [37] and qualitative reasoning [54] are concerned with characterizing all possible system behaviors through "envisionment." The work in qualitative physics and reasoning will have an important impact in computer-aided instruction since people construct mental models of physical devices and system behaviors to overcome inherent human difficulties in real-time, intensive computation (i.e., solving a set of linear equations). In terms of fuzzy methods, a special instance of a fuzzy set that is both normal and convex (called a "fuzzy number") can be defined over a confidence region; there have been significant amounts of mathematics [33] generated on fuzzy arithmetic and algebra and some recent work applying fuzzy arithmetic to discrete event simulation [40]. Zadeh's concept of a linguistic variable [58–60] plays a central role in nominal value mapping.

The concept of turbulence is a qualitative concept; however, the Reynolds number provides a metric that allows us to map quality to quantity—higher Reynolds numbers mean a move from laminar to turbulent flow. Adjectives such as *laminar* and *turbulent* characterize the qualitative nature of the flow; we often associate mental models and mnemonic visual icons or patterns [36] for purposes of quick association and recall. Many other examples can be given, but it suffices to say that qualitative simulation involves the study of system invariance and formal mappings with respect to text and pictorials. The notion of studying qualitative methods, in general, is not new; we may find ample evidence of qualitative theories for fields such as the qualitative theory of differential equations, qualitative methods in chemistry, and qualitative methods in economics. Our efforts, here, are to elaborate on what kinds of qualitative studies are appropriate to computer simulation.

At first sight, it might seem that the terms *natural language* and *pictures* should not be formally discussed when talking about computer simulation; topics such as natural language may be seen as being "too high level," "too informal," or "ambiguous." It is our claim, though, that the use of natural language and pictures in simulation is not only a desirable aspect of a simulation system, but it is also essential if, as human analysts, we are to understand what kinds of results that we are getting from the simulation after it has executed on given input data. Pictorials and natural language text are, indeed, informal methods for describing and analyzing processes; however, they are informal methods that are, nevertheless, used frequently. We need to find good ways of mapping from qualitative inputs to quantitative inputs and models, and then perform an inverse mapping from quantitative results to qualitative results when the simulation is finished and the analysis begins. These "mappings" must be unambiguously defined since they are the cornerstone upon which qualitative methods can be constructed. When we discuss qualitative methods in simulation modeling and analysis, we are not advocating qualitative methods *instead* of quantitative methods, but rather qualitative methods as an *augmentation* to quantitative methods.

Let us examine some simple scenarios. Imagine that analysts are simulating the traffic flow associated with a busy intersection. They gather data and statistics, and formulate models. Why, though, are they doing simulation at all? To answer this, we must back up a step and imagine two engineering managers (overseeing the analysts in their job positions) discussing the problem with the intersection at rush hour; they say that the cars are far too backed up and there need to be better response times to ease the "burden of waiting" on the car occupants. The reason, then, that the analysts are doing simulation is in direct response to problem statements made in natural language. The problem of "there needs to be better response times" has been translated into a specific solution such that "we should run multiple simulations to gather statistics; then we will modify the traffic light positions and timings to satisfy the constraint that the mean flow through the intersection will be no greater than 20 cars/minute." This traffic example points to the concept that many simulations are conducted as the result of having asked direct questions in natural language. The notion of an intersection being "too busy" has been translated into an intersection with "a mean flow rate no greater than 20 cars/minute."

A scenario involving analysts using dynamic finite-element analysis (i.e., simulation) on a bridge structure suggests to us that the initial question asked might have been "I wonder if this bridge will fall down in strong winds?" The solution involves computer simulation; however, one must translate terms such as *bridge* into a specific structure, and one must translate terms such as *fall down* and *strong wind* into quantitative equivalents such as "$d^2H/dt^2 = -9.8$ ft/s^2" and "$dW/dt \geq 100$ mph," respectively. Normally, the interface between natural language and simulation is left up to the analyst. That is, analysts do not get any help from the simulation system as to what *strong winds* mean. The study of natural language in simulation [8–10, 19] can be seen as adding a "qualitative" component to a simulation system. People are not interested primarily in whether an arbitrary variable δ is minimized; they are interested in whether or not the bridge structure will fail its task. The natural language components of a simulation are the closest to what an analyst is seeking; the quantitative structures are there to solve the problem using quantitative measures. The real problem is that humans simply do not often think quantitatively. By this statement, we do not mean that humans are incapable of computation, but rather they prefer to use computation as a *means* and not an *end*. The means are computational methods. The end is system understanding. Hamming's frequently quoted phrase [25] is appropriate to the goals of qualitative simulation: "The purpose of computing is insight, not numbers." We want to know and understand phenomena qualitatively, and we accomplish this feat by using two translations: one translation from a qualitative problem description into a set of equations or formal propositions, and the second translation from the executed internal model to terms that we understand. This output will often be in the form of descriptive statistics, graphics, or natural language. The purpose of qualitative studies in computer simulation are to make *explicit* the mapping between qualitative variable and mathematical model; we are promoting the idea that all simulation systems should contain qualitative features so that they provide a better man–machine interface. It is unfortunate that the mechanisms by which we can translate from natural language to mathematics are often overlooked; mathematical methods are clearly defined, yet we are sometimes at a loss as to when and how they should be used.

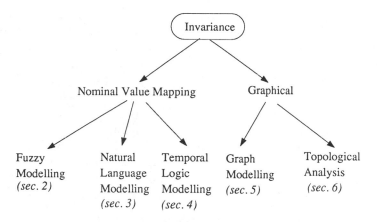

FIGURE 1.1. Themes for qualitative simulation.

Methods in qualitative simulation can be defined as methods that stress textual and pictorial understanding of systems. We view qualitative simulation, not as a specific theory, but rather as a general approach to systems and simulation that emphasizes an effective man–machine interface capable of allowing the analyst to use qualitative terminology directly in the simulation tool(s). We do not see a singular theory existing for qualitative simulation since we are advocating several related methods that will help simulationists to better understand global system behavior and specify partial knowledge in their models. Qualitative methods in simulation will be based on established subjects such as fuzzy set theory, probability theory, the qualitative theory of ordinary differential equations (ODE), and theories in temporal logic just as "quantitative simulation" relies on ODEs, PDEs, simulation, system theory, probability theory, and queuing theory, among others. Figure 1.1 depicts an overall taxonomy for qualitative simulation modeling the key concept is *invariance* that is partitioned into *nominal value* and *graphical* modeling. Example models of the leaves of Figure 1.1 are discussed in each of the following sections.

2. Fuzzy Modeling

The typical simulation model is defined in a clear and concise manner. For instance, to define a continuous model we first set up initial and boundary conditions in terms of real valued variables and then we use numerical integration methods to study system behavior as evidenced by the changing nature of the state variables. But, in some cases, we may know only the interval in which a variable may take its value, say, "[2.0, 10.0]." We are, in essence, partially specifying system inputs, if we use a method for "coarsening" variables [62, 63]. Other methods for variable coarsening include using fuzzy sets and numbers [32, 33], interval arithmetic [5] (which is subsumed by fuzzy set theory, at least if we are concerned with only system theory and simulation modelling), random variables, and the use of nominal versus ordinal or ratio variables. Cellier et al. [14, 15], based on Klir's GSPS methodology [34], produce a method of model induction from a set of integer values each of which represents a nominal value such as "too low," "too high," or "normal" that can be assumed by a nominal variable "altitude."

We have developed a method for fuzzy simulation that can involve either (1) fuzzy arithmetic rules, or (2) deterministic sampling from an n-order fuzzy number that represents a fuzzy model component such as state or initial condition. The algorithm for fuzzy simulation using the correlated method is as follows:

1. Assume a fuzzy simulation component such as a parameter ($\mathbf{p}$) in a discrete event simulation. The mean inter-arrival time into a single-server queue is an example of such a parameter. The component will be defined as a fuzzy number $\mathbf{f} = (a, b, c)$ where $\mathbf{f}$ is a triangular fuzzy number. A component of a fuzzy number is identified by brackets (i.e., $\mathbf{f}[2] = b$ when $\mathbf{f} = (a, b, c)$).

2. For $j \in \{1, 2, 3\}$:
   a. Let $\mathbf{p}[j] = \mathbf{f}[j]$.
   b. SIMULATE.
   c. $\forall i$, obtain $x_i(t_e)[j]$.

t_e is the end time for the simulation, and x_i are the state variables of interest. We will use just one state variable called x that represents the total number of entities in a system. Consider a single-server queue representing a grocery checkout line as shown in Figure 1.2. We require an answer to the following two questions:

1. What is the level of *customer satisfaction* when there is a *short* inter-arrival time between successive customers, and the cashier is *slow*?
2. What is the level of *customer satisfaction* when there is a *short* inter-arrival time between successive customers, and the cashier is *fast*?

Fuzzy simulation can help us to answer these questions if we consider mean inter-arrival time, mean service time, and customer satisfaction as linguistic (fuzzy) variables. The values, in terms of triangular fuzzy numbers, of these variables are defined in Figures 1.3 to 1.5. This system was simulated for the two conditions specified in the previous two questions. Customer satisfaction

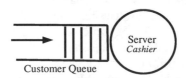

FIGURE 1.2. Grocery checkout model.

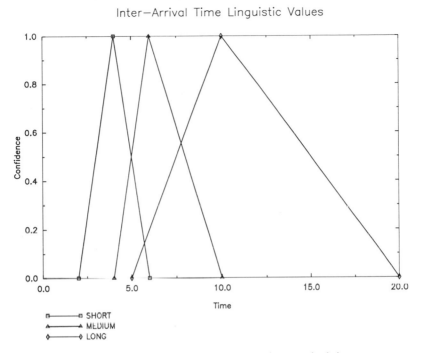

FIGURE 1.3. Linguistic values for mean inter-arrival time.

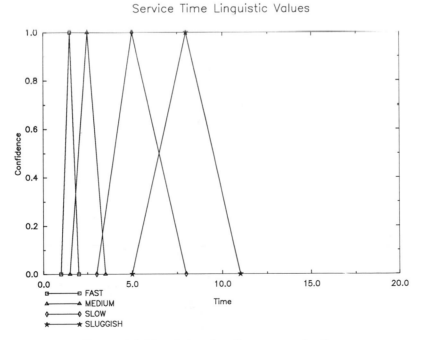

FIGURE 1.4. Linguistic values for mean service time.

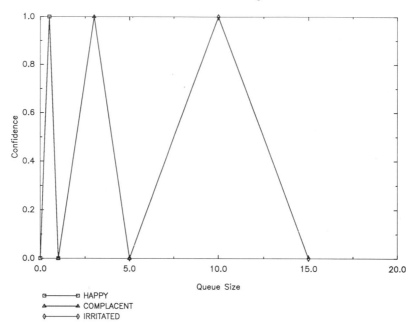

FIGURE 1.5. Linguistic values for customer satisfaction.

is defined as a function of the number of people waiting in line to be served. The simulation provides, therefore, a time variant description of customer satisfaction over time. Figure 1.6a displays the quantitative plot of system size over time for the first case. By mapping from these data to the fuzzy linguistic values for customer satisfaction, we obtain a more qualitative plot as shown in Figure 1.6b. We infer from Figure 1.6b that when the inter-arrival time is short and the service time is slow customers are fairly complacent for the beginning of the simulation; however, the steady-state solution is one where customers are irritated. However, when the server is *fast* (referring to the second question posed before), we see that customers remain happy (see Figures 1.7a and b).

Figures 1.6a and 1.7a are obtained directly from a standard discrete event simulation written in *SimPack* (a set of C-based simulation tools written by the author), except that there are three trajectories caused by using triangular fuzzy numbers in the simulation. The fuzzy numbers are mapped directly to linguistic values using a distance metric. The relationship between linguistic value and fuzzy value is specified in three vocabulary files; one file per fuzzy variable (mean inter-arrival time, mean service time, and customer satisfaction). The mapping is shown in Table 1.1. There are three fuzzy variables depicted, and means are denoted with μ.

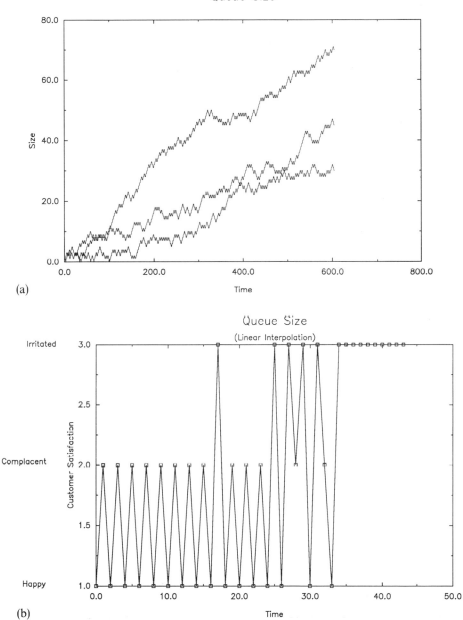

(a)

(b)

FIGURE 1.6. Simulation for *inter − arrivaltime = short* and *servicetime = slow*. (a) System size versus time (with slow service). (b) Customer satisfaction versus time (with slow service).

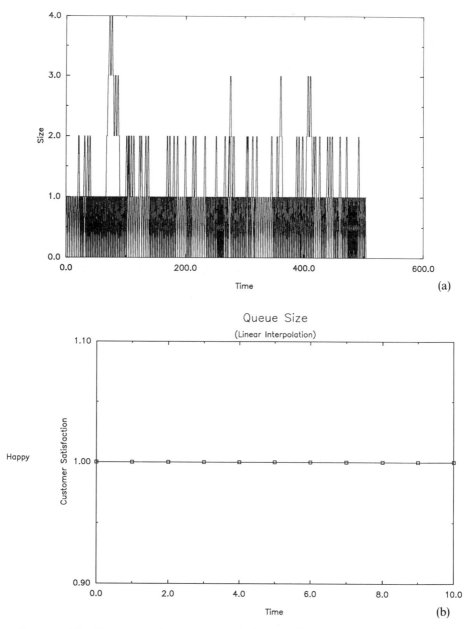

FIGURE 1.7. Simulation for *inter − arrivaltime = short* and *servicetime = fast*. (a) System size versus time (with fast service). (b) Customer satisfaction versus time (with fast service).

TABLE 1.1. Fuzzy linguistic mapping.

Variable	Value	Ordinal	Fuzzy number
μ(inter-arrival)	Short	1	(2, 4, 6)
μ(inter-arrival)	Medium	2	(4, 6, 10)
μ(inter-arrival)	Long	3	(5, 10, 20)
μ(service)	Fast	1	(1, 1.5, 2)
μ(service)	Medium	2	(1.5, 2.5, 3.5)
μ(service)	Slow	3	(3, 4, 8)
μ(service)	Sluggish	4	(5, 8, 11)
Satisfaction-level	Happy	1	(0, 0.5, 1)
Satisfaction-level	Complacent	2	(1, 3, 5)
Satisfaction-level	Irritated	3	(5, 10, 15)

The fuzzy variables μ(inter-arrival) and μ(service) take on values in terms of *minutes*, whereas the satisfaction level is a function of the numbers of entities, so its units are *entities*.

3. Natural Language Modeling

There are many information sources connected with system behavior that are encoded in natural language, such as English, French, or German. For this reason, it is important that we study the use of natural language in simulation [9, 19, 20, 27]. By using such methods we are able to (1) learn more about the way an author thinks about the process that he or she is describing, (2) determine if the author's thinking (which is reflected in his or her writing) is logically correct and complete in terms of system description, and (3) learn more about processes from textbooks. We can see the natural language models have an important role to play in future methods for computer-aided instruction (CAI) about dynamical systems. Blalock [11] suggests informal methods for building theories from more primitive knowledge sources (such as natural language text). As we discussed before, most simulation studies are done as a result of modeling concerns expressed in natural language form. We, of course, wish to express our models as sound mathematical models, but we also want to explore the qualitative–quantitative interface since it is the qualitative forms that we will use to aid us in understanding the nature of the dynamical system. There are many problems associated with natural language and simulation. Let us overview a few of them by studying the following piece of text:

The population of beetles is starting to grow larger and larger every day. The growth appeared to be slow at first, and then very fast until, finally, it leveled off at 250 beetles plus or minus 20.

Normally, it is useful to take such a paragraph and proceed to develop a causal graph (by hand). Consider the system dynamics graphs and their associated text in [48]. The example scenario text pieces used by Roberts et al. tend to be very lengthy, which is less of a problem for human comprehension than it is for computational methods. Large quantities of text can cause extremely difficult lexical problems for computational linguistics. We developed an automatic method [9] for eliciting equations or causal graphs automatically from text that tends to succeed on small paragraphs. Suppose, since the above example is a small paragraph, we choose to have it automatically analyzed by a Natural Language Processing System → Equation System. Now, consider some of the considerations and problems with analyzing this paragraph:

—Noun phrases are often represented as state variables, so "population of beetles" is represented by X.
—What does "grow larger and larger" mean? After processing this phrase, we must assume some type of growth. With prior knowledge, we can assume that this growth is exponential.
—The phrase "every day" provides us with an observation period.
—The phrase "slow at first" is consistent with our assumption of exponential growth.
—The phrase "levels off" suggests that we need an extra term that limits the growth.
—At this point, we can assume a logistic equation: $dN/dt = N(c_1 - c_2 N)$. We would obtain this equation as a "template" derived from a database of models or an expert system that suggests models based on data such as: "if $GROWTH-TYPE = limited$ and $GROWTH = exponential$ then $MODEL = logistic$."
—The amount of 250 provides us with the parameter value for the expression c_1/c_2.
—What do we do with the variance "plus or minus 20?" We might suggest that 250 is the mean of a normal distribution.

As one can see, there are many decisions that have to be made during the course of developing models from natural language. We should emphasize that natural language text presumes that *much background knowledge is known*. The text being analyzed does not, unfortunately, contain everything one needs to develop the equational models. In addition, there will be variables and constants such as c_2 (above) that are simply not mentioned at all. The analyst would have to be asked for a value for c_2, or the knowledge base would have to contain statistical information on typical values for c_2 for various domains. The automatic processing of natural language, in general, is very difficult, but it relates to qualitative simulation in that we often think in linguistic terms. At the very least, natural language is important to simulation on the *word level*; that is, we want to know what words mean in terms of quantity and formalisms. Words such as *turbulence, stability,* and *observability* invoke pictures and thoughts in our minds, but we need to map them to formal structures if we are to gain a true scientific system understanding. Research in system theory and science has suggested many tests for qualities such as stability (Routh–Hurwitz Test, Lyapunov Functions), but in qualitative simulation research, we wish to make the "quality mapped to quantity" mapping explicit and part of the set of system tools. In this way, system tools allow analysts to continue to think in qualitative terms (both input and output to/from a simulation model); the qualitative system aspect is not ignored or de-emphasized; it is, instead, made explicit. In current research, we are determining effective methods for taking simulation output and determining translation methods to natural language [20].

4. Temporal Logic Modeling

Language is closely related to formal logic, since logic is a natural mechanism that serves as the method by which lexical information is stored, retrieved, and processed via inference. First-order logic may, at first, seem an appropriate vehicle for qualitative simulation modeling and analysis. In this sense, we can view a proof as a kind of simulation in reverse. Consider the following first-order expressions representing logistic growth (let p = population size, g = population growth, and t = current time):

$$t(t_1) \wedge p(small, t1) \wedge g(slow, t1) \quad \supset t(t_2) \wedge (t_2 > t_1) \wedge p(medium, t2) \wedge g(fast, t2)$$

$$t(t_3) \wedge (t_3 > t_2) \quad \wedge p(medium, t3) \supset t(t_4) \wedge (t_4 > t_3) \wedge p(steady, t4) \wedge g(slow, t4)$$

Even though, traditionally, simulation is strictly a forward-chaining operation (i.e., time always moves forward). We can see how simulation can be seen, more generally, as a set of state trajectories [63] upon which one can operate bi-directionally, and that it is possible to ask a question such as "Does the beetle growth level off?" and to have this question answered by proof that involves the states associated with well-formed formulas in logic. For instance, we could set as a goal "? $- p(steady, T) \wedge g(X, T) \wedge t(T)$" (in the Prolog language) and have the system provide an answer in terms of previously occurring states and time constraints. If the proof cannot be performed due to incomplete information, then various expert system techniques may be employed, such as (1) querying the user for missing information or (2) using constraints to fill in empty frame slots.

Temporal logic [6, 39] has more potential as a qualitative simulation method, as compared with traditional logic, since it incorporates time implicitly within its framework; one does not explicitly encode time variables. Let us consider our logistic growth example once more and create a program in temporal logic. We use Tempura [24, 39] for our example. Consider:

$$definegrow(\ ) =$$

$$\exists N, N' \qquad : \quad \{(N = 1) \wedge$$

$$(N' \leftarrow N) \wedge$$

$$N \leftarrow N + N(100 - N)/50 \wedge$$

$$\square\ output(N) \wedge$$

$$\bigcirc\ halt(N = N')\}.$$

In Tempura, the symbol □ specifies the formula that follows is to be considered true for the entire time interval—*always* true. ◇ means *sometimes* true (at least one time during the time interval), and ○ means true for the *next state* within the interval. This program creates an "interval" with a sequence of integers that represents logistic growth (Tempura does not currently work with real data types). The program halts when it finds two successively identical values, corresponding to a weak integer definition of dynamic stability. In this way, we can ask the temporal logic program "Does the beetle growth stabilize?" or "Does the population ever reach 110?"

Why would someone use temporal logic versus a more traditional simulation modeling method? Programs in temporal logic enable the analyst to *prove* that a set of events has occurred, whereas traditional simulation methods normally consider proof as value checking and visual analysis of the simulation data. Validation in simulation usually does not involve logical proof, but rather statistical analysis and closeness of fit to observed data. On the negative side, temporal logic programs will not be able to provide precise answers about most kinds of dynamical system behavior; systems based on differential equations (for continuous systems) and queuing models (for discrete event systems) are more appropriate when numerical accuracy is a model choice criterion. Also, reasoning about real or complex-valued expressions can be difficult when one considers the state space search that can be required in logic. The cost incurred by using logical methods dictates that we use regular computer simulation, first, for most of our analysis, and use logical methods to prove key theorems about dynamical behavior. We should note, though, that most theorem proving will involve system structure and not system behavior, for instance, proof that a system stabilizes using the appropriate Lyapunov function [16]. On the positive side, though, temporal logic-based simulation models provide a "proof of correctness," which has been shown to be useful especially in digital logic verification [38]. We might, ostensibly, be able to ask questions of the simulation such as "Will state variable X ever reach the value 100.2 regardless of initial conditions?" The traditional method would be to use a Monte Carlo or perturbation approach to answer this question. Temporal logic has its greatest potential as a tool for verification of computer simulation models, although it can be clearly used to also directly model systems.

5. Graph Modeling

The use of directed graphs in simulation modeling is, perhaps, the most commonly used method for qualitative system specification. Graphs [26, 46, 47] provide a buffer between the analyst and the set of difference or differential equations that are used to model the system. Figure 1.8 displays a taxonomy for qualitative graph models based on continuous systems.

Stochastic graph methods are found in the econometric and social sciences literature primarily, although they can be widely used whenever linear systems

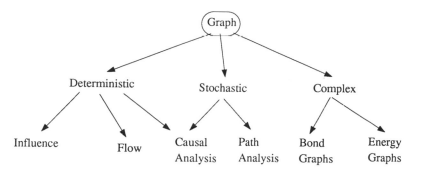

FIGURE 1.8. Graph taxonomy.

identification for illstructured and highly complex systems is needed. Problems involving the social sciences, for instance, are inherently hard problems in that it is often difficult to simply determine which variables are independent and which are dependent, let alone problems associated with determining order and degree. Other problems include identifying causal direction [55] when provided with data and correlation coefficients; the coefficient may demonstrate spurious correlation [51, 52] that can present problems when considering partial correlations as a direct method for causality assignment. Problems occur because, without extra knowledge, it is not possible to identify a causal relation between $X \to Z$ and spurious correlations where either $X \to Y \to Z$ or ($Y \to X$ and $Y \to Z$). The end result of causal assignment is often to provide a graph labeled with correlation coefficients. In this manner, one may create (or identify) a model based on only data sets. The coefficient arc labels provide us with a confidence factor that indicates the strength of the relationship between any two variables. The structure of causal graphs provides us with reasons for their possible utility, namely, that causal graphs are useful when one has data sets for variables whose relationships are completely unknown. This kind of situation is common in the social sciences, but in the physical sciences, we usually have more structural knowledge and may therefore define our relationships according to theories and laws that have empirical justification. There have been several efforts to produce programs that allow a user to partially or completely construct a set of causal graphs, such as TETRAD [23, 30].

In stochastic causal graphs, we have a graph full of arcs where arc labels reflect correlation between variables. In deterministic graphs, arc labels will usually take the form of either numeric weights or signs $(-, 0, +)$. Let us consider the graph $X \to Y \to Z$ for purposes of illustration. This can be interpreted as X causes Y, which causes Z. But what does this mean in terms of algebraic or differential equations? The first guess might be (1) and (2):

$$Y = c_1 X, \tag{1}$$

$$Z = c_2 Y. \tag{2}$$

X, Y, and Z are variables, and c_1 and c_2 are constant coefficients. Although this is fundamentally appealing, the equation does not contain time as a parameter. So, for purposes of studying time-dependent system behavior, we resort to using a difference or differential equation format. The difference is usually minor, and we have seen both when studying the literature on flow graphs for systems and simulation. If we ignore dt by setting it to 1 and use Euler's method for integration, then $dY/dt = X$ and $Y_{t+1} = Y_t + X_t$ may be considered identical. We point out, though, that difference equations of the first order can result in oscillatory behavior, whereas differential quations must be of the second order to result in oscillations. Therefore, one should be careful when switching from difference to differential equations, and vice versa. For purposes of consistency, we use the differential equation form. Note that, even though differential equations involve time-dependent variables, it is customary to specify variables as X instead of $X(t)$. It is assumed, implicitly, that all variables are actually functions of time; coefficients, though, are assumed not to be time dependent.

Our first step is to separate deterministic graphs into two types: *flow graphs* versus *influence graphs*. In practice, simulation graphs are usually one type or the other; sometimes, both capabilities exist. A flow graph is one where one can imagine a fluid flow through compartments each of which represent levels (or state variables). The key idea here is that if we have the graph $X \rightarrow Y \rightarrow Z$ then fluid can flow from the source X to Y and then on to Z; there is no replacement for fluid in X once it has passed on to Y. One can see that fluid flow modeling can represent situations where feedback is implicitly assumed; that is, the amount in X increases the amount in Y, and this increase "feeds back" to X in the form of a decrease in X. An influence graph, on the other hand, is a graph where the amount in X "influences" the amount in Y without there being any flow of some quantity. Flows are easy to visualize; what about influences? Let X be the GNP (gross national product) of the United States, and let Y be the GNP of Great Britain. There may be many potential relationships in either direction, but we might say, for instance, that the greater the GNP of the United States, the greater the GNP of Britain if one has data to support such a hypothesis. When we increase the GNP of Britain, we do not necessarily do this at the expense of (i.e., while decreasing) the U.S. GNP. Therefore, this relationship is one of influence rather than of flow. One might argue, on more philosophical grounds, that there always exists some kind of flow and that we use influence diagrams when the flow is either negligible or difficult to specify. Influence graphs often define causality (or directed action) "at a distance."

The equations for the influence connotation of $X \rightarrow Y \rightarrow Z$ (3) and (4):

$$dY/dt = c_2 X, \tag{3}$$

$$dZ/dt = c_3 Y. \tag{4}$$

Contrast these equations with the flow connotation equations (5) to (7):

$$dX/dt = -c_1 X, \tag{5}$$

$$dY/dt = c_2 X - c_3 Y, \tag{6}$$

$$dZ/dt = c_4 Y. \tag{7}$$

The flow equations, which are the result of having a graph node with at least one in-arc and one out-arc, involve an extra term that involves the feedback resulting in an exponential decay of the quantity. Most graph methods involve being able to blur the distinction between flow and influence methods by allowing the analyst to insert optional feedback loops wherever desired. Although, some graph methods are strongly oriented in terms of flow, an example being the kinetic graphs used in chemistry to describe the time-dependent conversion of a substance to various other forms (or phases) [13], the notion of "influence" does not fit the domain of chemical reactions. In loop modeling [43], compartmental modeling [31], and system dynamics [21, 44, 45], one has the option of inserting loops wherever appropriate. It is worth noting that in the system dynamics methodology the equations are often broken down so that, say, dY/dt is shown as being dependent on Y *indirectly* via a rate variable. For instance, we would introduce a new graph as shown in Figure 1.9. The equations for Figure 1.9 are (8) to (12):

$$dX/dt = -k_1 Q_X \tag{8}$$

$$dY/dt = k_2 Q_X - k_3 Q_Y \tag{9}$$

$$dZ/dt - k_4 Q_Y \tag{10}$$

$$Q_X = c_1 X \tag{11}$$

$$Q_Y = c_2 Y \tag{12}$$

In Figure 1.9, the boxes represent state (or level) variables, the valve icons represent rates, and the two curved arrows represent negative feedback. We see that these equations are the same as equations (5) to (7) once we remove the indirection via the flow rates and relabel coefficients. The equation set prompted by systems dynamics considerations is of the general form of the mass balance equations that can be defined in the form "change = growth − decay + interaction"   or,   equivalently,   "netflow = inflow − outflow + reaction." Any of the independent terms may be optionally deleted

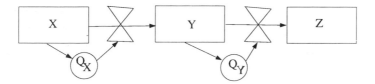

FIGURE 1.9. System dynamics graph with feedback loops.

for more compact equations (only if these terms are considered "negligible"). The term *interaction* can be deleted when specifically considering system dynamics models, since the interactions are usually embedded within the causal structures within the model.

If we reflect on the concept of mapping in qualitative methods, we see that even though equations (5) to (7) and (8) to (12) are structurally different, their encoding in causal graph form is the same if we allow only levels (or state variables) as graph nodes. This means that the qualitative graph structure [29] has permitted us to map certain graph structures with a class of equations; the graph structure is invariant to certain types of equational transformations. Other examples of invariance are seen when viewing bond graphs [49, 53].

6. Topological Analysis

Topology is seen as being a way of system understanding by, essentially, studying the "geometry" of dynamical systems [1–4] through the vehicle of the phase-plane, arbitrary planar projection, or Poincaré map. The reason for this qualitative method of analysis is due to the inherent lack of predictive capability for highly nonlinear systems: If one cannot perform prediction effectively (due to chaotic effects), then how can one understand the system at all? By using topology, we may gain an in-depth system understanding. Even when considering linear systems that are analytically tractable, it is often enlightening to view the system from a topological perspective. In doing so, there has been significant study in what, today, can be considered a fairly stable view of the qualitative theory of differential equations [12]. That is, even though we can easily predict the effects of linear models in response to perturbations, we still find it useful to classify certain types of first- and second-order behaviors. First-order, linear behaviors are strictly exponential (with point attractors), whereas second-order behaviors tend to be more angular in nature, involving conic sections and spirals [7].

Linear systems provide us with accurate measures for specifying the quality of systems. The system eigenvalues and eigenvectors provide an excellent characterization of the quality of systems that vary over minor changes to the magnitude of these values. Once the signs of these parameters change, though, the system exhibits a new *quality*. For instance, if our system exhibits a spiral phase portrait we are unlikely to provide it with a different quality if the shape of the spiral changes. We will, however, attribute a different quality as a result of parameter modification, if the spirals change to concentric circles. The indifference to quality change can be seen as a form of invariance with respect to a topological characterization. In more general terms, we say that a system changes its "quality" when a *bifurcation* occurs while sweeping through possible values in parameter space [50].

7. Discussion and Conclusions

A natural question when viewing the array of qualitative methods is "Which method should I use to model a system?" The modeler may experiment with varying types of methodology; however, we feel that he or she must first address the fundamental question concerning the exact problem that he or she is trying to solve. If one, for example, wants to solve a problem that can be stated as "I want to know what happens to the pendulum as it swings in a frictionless environment?," one must first go beyond that original problem statement to determine the level at which an answer is sought. Does the modeler care if the answer is given in terms of degrees or in terms of quadrants, or possibly in terms of a simple direction (left or right)? We must know, then, the "level of coarseness" connected with the variables that will be used as both input and output with the model. If the modeler is concerned only with left and right, he or she can use a finite-state automaton [19]. If the modeler wants a response to the effect that "The pendulum bob is pushed, which causes the pendulum to continue swinging," then the modeler can use logic as a simulation method. Temporal logic is not often used in computer simulation simply because most modelers are not interested in the system at that high a level of detail; simulationists are usually concerned with more exact data, and therefore, they require, ultimately, an equational representation even though a qualitatively specified front end (such as a directed graph model) may be advantageous. Different modeling methods provide different answers: If one is not getting the right *kind* or *level* of answer, then one should change the modeling method. This aspect of modeling is important, and for qualitative simulation, using the right model to solve the required goals is critical. Which aspect of the system is being modeled qualitatively? Is it the input, model structure itself, or the output [18, 19]? If one is "making qualitative" simulation input and output while retaining a quantitative model, then the simulation will be more robust for analysts who work well in qualitative terms. One must be extremely careful, though, when, using a *qualitative model structure* such as a structure based on logic. For instance, if one wants information at the level of "X causes Y or Z" then temporal logic may be all that is needed. However, at the level of "X stabilizes at 10.2 after 20 seconds," a more quantitative model language will be necessary. There are many adages of the type "you cannot squeeze blood from a stone," and these can be seen as appropriate metaphors also when considering model selection.

We have overviewed different methods in qualitative modeling and encapsulated the methods under the general umbrella of invariance and nominal value mapping. In this sense, qualitative simulation modeling and analysis may retain some sort of unique identity. Our purpose is to define further the nature of qualitative simulation and to encourage further research in qualitative methods, with the caveat that one always keep in mind (1) the purpose of the simulation, that is, what precise results (and to what level of coarseness) are required; and (2) the mapping from quality to quantity and vice versa. One also wants to avoid the temptation to create spurious qualities that have little relevance, and thereby to create new words and dictionaries that are full of quality definitions with little substance.

Acknowledgments. I would like to thank the National Science Foundation for partial support of this research through Grant IRI-8909152. I would also like to thank Roger Hale at Cambridge University for diligently answering all of my questions on the Tempura language and for suggesting alternate programming mechanisms in temporal logic. Many thanks also go to Bernard Zeigler of the University of Arizona, Paul Luker at California State University at Chico, and George Richardson at SUNY Albany for good critical comments on ways in which to improve the manuscript.

References

1. Abraham, R.H., and Shaw, C.D. *Dynamics—The Geometry of Behavior* (*Volume* 1: *Periodic Behavior*). Aerial Press, Santa Cruz, Calif., 1982.
2. Abraham, R.H., and Shaw, C.D. *Dynamics—The Geometry of Behavior* (*Volume* 2: *Chaotic Behavior*). Aerial Press, Santa Cruz, Calif., 1983.
3. Abraham, R.H., and Shaw, C.D. *Dynamics—The Geometry of Behavior* (*Volume* 3: *Global Behavior*). Aerial Press, Santa Cruz, Calif., 1984.
4. Abraham, R.H., and Shaw, C.D. *Dynamics—The Geometry of Behavior* (*Volume* 4: *Bifurcation Behavior*). Aerial Press, Santa Cruz, Calif., 1988.
5. Alefeld, G., and Herzberger, J. *Introduction to Interval Computations.* Academic Press, New York, 1983.
6. Allen, J.F. Maintaining knowledge about temporal intervals. *Commun. ACM 26*, 11 (Nov. 1983), 832–843.
7. Andronov, A.A., Vitt, A.A., and Khaikin, S.E. *Theory of Oscillators.* Pergammon Press (reissued by Dover in 1987), 1966.
8. Austin, W., and Khoshnevis, B. Intelligent simulation environments for system modeling. In *Institute of Industrial Engineering Conference*, May 1988.
9. Beck, H.W., and Fishwick, P.A. Incorporating natural language descriptions into modeling and simulation. *Simulation J. 52*, 3 (Mar. 1989), 102–109.
10. Beck, H.W., La Raw Maran, Fishwick, P.A., and Li, L. Architectures for knowledge based simulation and their suitability for natural language processing. In *Advances in AI and Simulation*, Tampa, Fla, Mar. 1989, pp. 103–108.
11. Blalock, H.M. *Theory Construction: From Verbal to Mathematical Formulations.* Prentice-Hall, Englewood Cliffs, N.J., 1969.
12. Brauer, F., and Nohel, J.A. *Qualitative Theory of Ordinary Differential Equations.* W.A. Benjamin, Inc., 1969.
13. Bungay, H.R. *Computer Games and Simulation for Biochemical Engineering.* Wiley, New York, 1985.

14. Cellier, F.E. Qualitative simulation of technical systems using the general system problem solving framework. *Int. J. Gen. Syst.* 13, 4 (1987), 333–344.
15. Cellier, F.E., and Yandell, D.W. SAPS-II: A new implementation of the systems approach problem solver. *Int. J. Gen. Syst.* 13, 4 (1987), 307–322.
16. Devaney, R.L. *An Introduction to Chaotic Dynamical Systems.* 2nd ed. Addison-Wesley, Reading, Mass., 1989.
17. Fishwick, P.A. The role of process abstraction in simulation. *IEEE Trans. Syst., Man Cybern.* 18, 1 (Jan./Feb. 1988), 18–39.
18. Fishwick, P.A. A study of terminology and issues in qualitative simulation. *Simulation J. 51*, 7 (Jan. 1989), 5–9.
19. Fishwick, P.A. Qualitative methodology in simulation model engineering. *Simulation J. 52*, 3 (Mar. 1989), 95–101.
20. Fishwick, P.A. Utilizing natural language for simulation reporting, 1990. (In preparation for the 1990 SCS Eastern Simulation MultiConference.)
21. Forrester, J.W. *Urban Dynamics.* MIT Press, Cambridge, Mass., 1969.
22. Franksen, O.I., Falster, P., and Evans, F.J. Qualitative aspects of large scale systems. In *Lecture Notes in Control and Information Sciences*, Vol. 17, A.V. Balakrishnan and M. Thoma, Eds. Springer-Verlag, New York, 1979.
23. Glymour, C., Scheines, R., Spirtes, P., and Kelly, K. *Discovering Causal Structure.* Academic Press, New York, 1987.
24. Hale, R. Cambridge University (personal communication).
25. Hamming, R.W. *Numerical Methods for Scientists and Engineers.* McGraw-Hill, New York, 1962.
26. Harary, F. Structural models and graph theory. In *Computer-Assisted Analysis and Model Simplification*, H.J. Greenberg and J.S. Maybee, Eds. Academic Press, New York, 1981, pp. 31–58.
27. Heidorn, G.E. English as a very high level language for simulation programming. In Proceedings of the Symposium on Very High Level Languages, vol. 9, *SIGPLAN Not.* (ACM) (Apr. 1974), 91–100.
28. Hezemans, P., and van Geffen, L. Justified use of analogies in systems science. In *Complex and Distributed Systems: Analysis, Simulation and Control.* Elsevier North-Holland, Amsterdam, 1985, pp. 61–67. (Volume IV: IMACS Transactions on Scientific Computation-85.)
29. Franklin Institute. Special issue on physical structure in modeling. *J. Franklin Inst.* 319, 1–2 (1985).
30. Iwasaki, Y., and Simon, H.A. Causality in device behavior. *Artif. Intell.* 29, 1 (July 1986), 3–32.
31. Jacquez, J.A. *Compartmental Analysis in Biology and Medicine.* 2nd ed. University of Michigan Press, 1985.
32. Kandel, A. *Fuzzy Mathematical Techniques with Applications.* Addison-Wesley, Reading, Mass., 1986.
33. Kaufmann, A., and Gupta, M.M. *Introduction to Fuzzy Arithmetic: Theory and Applications.* Van Nostrand, 1985.
34. Klir, G.J. *Architecture of Systems Problem Solving.* Plenum Press, 1985.
35. Klir, G.J., and Folger, T.A. *Fuzzy Sets, Uncertainty and Information.* Prentice-Hall, Englewood Cliffs, N.J., 1988.
36. Kosslyn, S.M. *Ghosts in the Mind's Machine.* W.W. Norton and Company, 1983.

37. Kuipers, B. Qualitative simulation. *Artif. Intell.* 29, 3 (Sept. 1986), 289–338.
38. Moszkowski, B. A temporal logic for multilevel reasoning about hardware. *Computer* 18, 2 (Feb. 1985), 10–19.
39. Moszkowski, B. *Executing Temporal Logic Programs.* Cambridge Press, Cambridge, Mass., 1986.
40. Nguyen, H. Fuzzy methods in discrete event simulation. Master's thesis, Univ. of Florida, Gainesville, 1989.
41. Odum, H.T. *Systems Ecology: An Introduction.* Wiley, New York, 1983.
42. Odum, H.T. Simulation models of ecological economics developed with energy language methods. *Simulation J. 53,* 2 (1989), 69–75.
43. Puccia, C.J., and Levins, R. *Qualitative Modeling of Complex Systems.* Harvard University Press, 1985.
44. Richardson, G.P., and Pugh, A.L. *Introduction to System Dynamics Modeling with DYNAMO.* MIT Press, Cambridge, Mass., 1981.
45. Richmond, B., Peterson, S., and Vescuso, P. *An Academic User's Guide to STELLA.* High Performance Systems, Lyme, N.H., 1987.
46. Roberts, F.S. *Discrete Mathematical Models.* Prentice-Hall, Englewood Cliffs, N.J., 1976.
47. Roberts, F.S. Structural models and graph theory. In *Computer-Assisted Analysis and Model Simplification,* H.J. Greenberg and J.S. Maybee, Eds. Academic Press, New York, 1981, pp. 59–67.
48. Roberts, N., Andersen, D., Deal, R., Garet, M., and Shaffer, W. *Introduction to Computer Simulation: A Systems Dynamics Approach.* Addison-Wesley, Reading, Mass., 1983.
49. Rosenberg, R.C., and Karnopp, D.C. *Introduction to Physical System Dynamics.* McGraw-Hill, New York, 1983.
50. Seydel, R. *From Equilibrium to Chaos: Practical Bifurcation and Stability Analysis.* Elsevier, New York, 1988.
51. Simon, H.A. On the definition of the causal relation. *J. Philos.* 44, 16 (1952), 517–528.
52. Simon, H.A. Spurious correlation: A causal interpretation. In *Causal Models in the Social Sciences,* H.M. Blalock, Ed. Aldine, New York, 1985.
53. Thoma, J. *Bond Graphs: Introduction and Application.* Pergamon Press, 1975.
54. Weld, D.S., and DeKleer, J. *Readings in Qualitative Reasoning about Physical Systems.* Morgan Kaufmann, 1990.
55. Wright, S. Correlation and causation. *J. Agricultural Res.* 20, 7 (1921).
56. Wymore, A.W. *A Mathematical Theory of Systems Engineering: The Elements.* Krieger Publishing Co., 1977.
57. Zadeh, L.A. Fuzzy sets. *Inf. Control* 8 (1965), 338–353.
58. Zadeh, L.A. The concept of a linguistic variable and its application to approximate reasoning. *Inf. Sci.* 8 (1975), 199–249.
59. Zadeh, L.A. The concept of a linguistic variable and its application to approximate reasoning. *Inf. Sci.* 8 (1975), 301–357.
60. Zadeh, L.A. The concept of a linguistic variable and its application to approximate reasoning. *Inf. Sci.* 9 (1975), 43–80.
61. Zeigler, B.P. Towards a formal theory of modelling and simulation: Structure preserving morphisms. *J. ACM* 19, 4 (1972), 742–764.
62. Zeigler, B.P. *Theory of Modelling and Simulation.* Wiley, New York, 1976.

63. Zeigler, B.P. *Multi-Facetted Modelling and Discrete Event Simulation.* Academic Press, New York, 1984.
64. Zeigler, B.P. Multifaceted systems modeling: Structure and behavior at a multiplicity of levels. In *Individual Development and Social Change: Explanatory Analysis.* Academic Press, New York, 1985, pp. 265–293.

CHAPTER 2

Aspects of Uncertainty in Qualitative Systems Modeling

George J. Klir

Abstract

It is argued in this chapter that uncertainty is a valuable commodity in systems modeling, which can be traded for a reduction of complexity or an increase of credibility of systems models. Principles of maximum and minimum uncertainty are introduced as fundamental to problems involving ampliative reasoning and problems of systems simplification, respectively. Novel mathematical theories for dealing with uncertainty and measures of relevant types of uncertainty in these theories are overviewed. It is shown that uncertainty is a multidimensional concept, and consequently, the principles of maximum and minimum uncertainty must be formulated as multiple objective criteria optimization problems.

1. Introduction

It is undeniable that recent advances in computer technology have opened a host of new methodological possibilities, and these, in turn, have contributed to the emergence of modern systems thinking. Closely connected with these developments is a significant current trend in mathematics, a trend toward generalizations of existing mathematical concepts and theories. This trend is exemplified by the gradual change in interest and emphasis from functions to relations, from graphs to hypergraphs, from ordinary geometry (Euclidean as well as non-Euclidean) to fractal geometry, from ordinary automata to dynamic cellular automata, from classical analysis to a study of singularities (catastrophe theory), from ordinary artificial languages to developmental languages, from classical two-valued logic to multiple-valued logics, modal logics, and logics of inconsistency, from single objective to multiple objective criteria optimization, and, as most relevant to the subject of this book, from quantitative to qualitative. These generalizations enrich not only our insights but also our capabilities to model the intricacies of the real world properly.

One aspect of the current trend of generalizing in mathematics, whose role in qualitative systems modeling is the subject of this chapter, involves a transition from the traditional insistence on precision and certainty to tolerance of imprecision and uncertainty as important resources to deal with complexity. This changing attitude in mathematics (i.e., a growing tendency to accept imprecision and uncertainty as respectable and useful attributes) is exemplified by the emergence of interval analysis from precise analysis, fuzzy set theory and logic from classical set theory and logic, and various types of fuzzy measures from the classical probability measures.

The purpose of this chapter is to discuss the role of uncertainty in qualitative systems modeling. It is argued that uncertainty is a valuable commodity, which can be traded for a reduction of complexity or an increase of credibility of models in systems modeling. It is also argued that several distinct types of uncertainty coexist within some of the novel mathematical theories applicable to systems modeling (such as fuzzy set theory or the Dempster–Shafer theory of evidence), and consequently, uncertainty must be viewed and dealt with as a multidimensional quantity.

2. Systems Modeling

Perhaps the most fundamental classification of sciences is into the *sciences of the natural* and the *sciences of the artificial* [26]. The two classes of sciences involve, respectively, the following two types of problem-solving activities:

1. *systems inquiry*: the full scope of activities by which we attempt to construct systems that are adequate models of some aspect of reality; and
2. *systems design*: the full scope of activities by which we attempt to construct systems that are adequate models of desirable man-made objects.

We can see that a common feature of all disciplines of science, be they oriented to the natural or to the artificial, is *systems modeling*: the construction of systems that adequately model some aspect of natural or man-made reality. It is important at this point not to confuse the concept of a system with a part of reality (an object of the real world). In this chapter a *system* is always viewed as an abstraction that characterizes an appropriate type of relationship among some abstract entities. To qualify as a *model* of some aspect of reality, a system must be supplemented with appropriate mappings from relevant entities of the real world into the abstract entities of the system, and these mappings must be *homomorphic* with respect to the relationship involved. In many instances, these mappings cannot be defined mathematically but only in terms of appropriate physical devices (measuring instruments), and their homomorphism can be established only on pragmatic grounds (relevant reality behaves as predicted by the model).

It follows from the foregoing that every model must invariably contain three principal components: a set of abstract entities, a relationship among these entities, and a set of homomorphic mappings that gives the abstract entities a real-world interpretation. In systems inquiries, a model is developed for the purpose of understanding some phenomenon of reality, be it natural or man-made, making adequate predictions or retrodictions, learning how to control the phenomenon in any desirable way, and utilizing all of these capabilities for various ends. In systems design, a model is developed for the purpose of prescribing operations by which a conceived artificial object can be constructed in such a way that desirable objective criteria are satisfied within given constraints.

3. General Systems Problem Solver (GSPS)

Systems modeling is an activity that requires a conceptual framework within which one operates. Each framework determines the scope of systems that can be described within it and leads to some specific taxonomy of these systems. A comprehensive framework is needed to capture the full scope of systems we are currently able to envision.

Several conceptual frameworks that attempt to capture the full scope of systems currently conceived have been proposed [13, 14, 19, 29, 33]. The differences in terminology and mathematical formulation among them are considerable. Little work has been done to compare rigorously the categories of systems that emerge from these seemingly different frameworks. We can only speculate, based on rather limited evidence [10], that the differences in systems categories emerging from these broad frameworks are relatively minor and can be reconciled.

One of the broad conceptual frameworks, which is employed in this chapter, is known in the literature as the *General Systems Problem Solver* (GSPS) [14]. The kernel of the GSPS is a *hierarchy of epistemological categories of systems*, which represents the most fundamental taxonomy of systems. The following is a brief outline of the basic levels in this hierarchy to facilitate our further discussion; a thorough presentation of the hierarchy is covered in a recent book [14].

At the lowest level of the epistemological hierarchy, we define an *experimental frame* in terms of appropriate variables, their state sets (value sets), and an interpretation of these as real-world attributes. In addition, some supporting medium (such as time, space, or a population) within which the variables change their states must also be specified. Furthermore, variables may be classified as input or output variables. In qualitative modeling, at least some of the variables or supporting media involved are of nominal scales or, at most, of ordinal scales. That is, the state sets of these variables are finite, and each state represents a quality of some sort rather than quantity.

An *experimental frame* (also called a *source system*) may be viewed as a *data description language*. When actual data described in this language become available, we move to the next level in the hierarchy; systems on this level are called *data systems*.

When the variables of the experimental frame are characterized by a relationship among them, we move to a level that is still higher in the hierarchy. It is assumed on this level that the relationship among the variables is invariant with respect to the supporting medium involved. That is, it is time-invariant, space-invariant, space-time-invariant, population-invariant, etc. The relationship may involve not only variables contained in the experimental frame, but also additional variables defined in terms of the former by specific translation rules in the supporting medium (e.g., lagged variables). Systems on this level are called *behavior systems*. Some of these systems can also be characterized as *state-transition systems*.

Climbing further up the hierarchy involves two principles of integrating systems as components in larger systems. According to the first principle, several behavior systems (or, sometimes, lower level systems) that may share some variables or interact in some other way are viewed as subsystems integrated into one overall system. Overall systems of this sort are called *structure systems*. The subsystems forming a structure system are often called its *elements*.

When elements of a structure system are themselves structure systems, we call the overall system a *second order structure system*. *Higher order structure systems* are defined recursively in the same way.

According to the second integrating principle, an overall system is viewed as varying (in time, space, etc.) within a class of systems of any of the other types. The change from one system to another in the delimited class is described by a replacement procedure that is invariant with respect to the supporting medium involved (time, space, etc.). Overall systems of this type are called *metasystems*.

In principle, the replacement procedure of a metasystem may also change. Then, an invariant (changeless) higher level procedure is needed to describe the change. Systems of this sort, with two levels of replacement procedures, are called *metasystems of second order*. *Higher order metasystems* are then defined recursively in the same way.

Structure systems whose elements are metasystems are also allowed by the framework, similarly as metasystems defined in terms of structure systems.

The key feature of the epistemological hierarchy is that every system defined on some level in the hierarchy entails knowledge associated with all corresponding systems on lower levels and, at the same time, contains some knowledge that is not available in any of these lower level systems.

The number of levels in the epistemological hierarchy is potentially infinite. In praxis, however, only a small number of levels is considered. For each particular number of levels, the hierarchy is a semilattice. For five levels, for example, a part of the semilattice is expressed by the Hasse diagram in Figure 2.1. The circles represent the various epistemological categories of systems; the arrows indicate the ordering from lower to higher categories. Symbols E, D, and B denote experimental frames (source systems), data systems, and behavior systems, respectively. Symbol S, used as a prefix, stands for structure systems. For example, SB denotes structure systems whose elements are behavior systems, and SD denotes structure systems whose elements are data systems. Symbol S^2 denotes structure systems of second order. For example, S^2B denotes structure systems of structure systems whose elements are beha-

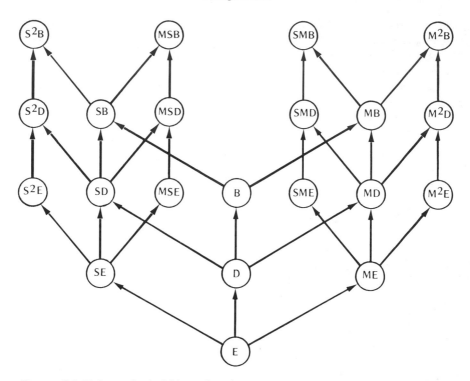

FIGURE 2.1. Epistemological hierarchy of systems categories. (Notation: E—experimental frame or source system; D—data system; B—behavior system; SE, SD, and SB—structure systems based on source, data, and behavior systems, respectively; S^2E, S^2D, and S^2B—second-order structure systems of the three types; ME, MD, and MB—metasystems based on source, data, and behavior systems, respectively; M^2E, M^2D, and M^2B—second-order metasystems of the three types; SME, SMD, and SMB—structure systems based on metasystems of the three types; MSE, MSD, and MSB—metasystems based on structure systems of the three types.

vior systems. Symbols M and M^2 denote metasystems and meta-metasystems, respectively. Combinations SM and MS denote structure systems whose elements are metasystems and metasystems whose elements are structure systems, respectively. The diagram in Figure 2.1 describes only a part of the epistemological hierarchy; it can be extended in an obvious way to combinations such as S^3B, S^2MB, SMSB, M^2SB, S^2MB, etc.

4. Uncertainty, Complexity, and Credibility of Systems Models

Possible approaches to systems modeling extend over a wide spectrum that is bounded by two extreme approaches, which are usually called a postulational approach and a discovery approach. The following is a brief characterization of these approaches in terms of the GSPS epistemological hierarchy of systems.

In the *postulational approach*, a hypothetical system is postulated within a category of systems that is epistemologically higher than the category of data systems. This postulated system is basically used for a specific type of *deductive reasoning*: Given a particular set of premises regarding conditions of the system's environment as well as initial or boundary conditions of the system itself, the system allows us to derive specific conclusions (predictions, retrodictions, etc.) at the associated level of data systems. The validity of the postulated system as a model of some specific aspect of reality depends on the degree of agreement of the derived conclusions with the relevant empirical evidence.

The *discovery approach* is data-driven. That is, models are derived by processes that discover patterns in data and utilize them for making *inductive inferences*. This approach is characterized by climbing up, from a given data system, the epistemological hierarchy of systems. The criterion of validity of models derived in this way does not involve the issue of the agreement between the empirical evidence and deductive inferences made from the model (the model was derived from given data), but rather the issue of the justification of induction.

Neither of the two extreme (and idealized) approaches is actually ever used in its pure form in praxis. In the postulational approach, the hypothetical system is not chosen arbitrarily from among an infinite number of competitors, but on the basis of "knowledge accumulated from our forebears', and our own, experience" [35]. Induction is thus involved in the postulational approach as well, but it is hidden in the general notion of "experience." In the discovery approach, we do not consider all systems that conform to the given data (their set is usually infinite), but only those satisfying also a variety of relevant extra-evidential considerations. Consequently, experience plays as important a role in the discovery approach as it does in the postulational approach.

Although aspects of both of these approaches are normally interwoven in the praxis of systems modeling, one of the approaches is usually predominant. The focus in this chapter is on a mixed approach to systems modeling in which the discovery approach is predominant. In this approach, which is usually referred to as *inductive modeling*, our background knowledge and various pragmatic considerations are employed for restricting (postulating) a class of possible models, while empirical evidence is utilized inductively for determining a particular model or, possibly, a set of admissible models from the delimited class.

The key issue in inductive modeling is the extent to which a model inferred from data and relevant extra-evidential considerations is required to account for the data. Ideally, we should require that the model represent the data completely. This is the same as requiring that the model be based on a *deterministic system* capable of reproducing the data exactly. Unfortunately, such a requirement is not realistic since it leads, in general, to excessively complex models. This fact was demonstrated by Gaines [5, 6] who showed that "the universe becomes incredibly complex and our models of it non-sensical if we assume determinism in the face of even a slight trace of acausal behavior." That is, the complexity of deterministic models inferred from data that involve any trace of acausal (nondeterministic) behavior tends to increase proportionally to the increase in data size.

The relationship between the *data size* (number of observations), the *complexity of models*, and their *predictive credibility* was studied on theoretical grounds for dichotomous deterministic models described in three alternative languages (perceptrons, Boolean formulas, and Boolean networks) by Pearl [20]. The complexity of a model with respect to a language in which the model is described is defined as the shortest description of the model in that language. The predictive credibility of a model is inversely proportional to the likelihood of finding a model of the same complexity whose predictions would conflict with the predictions of the given model. The dependence of predictive credibility of deterministic models inferred from given data on the data size and complexity of the model is determined by the language employed. Pearl showed for each of the three languages that predictive credibility increases in some fashion with the data size and decreases with model complexity.

When we combine the results obtained by Pearl [20] with those obtained by Gaines [5, 6], we may concude that no appreciable predictive credibility of deterministic models inferred from data can be obtained regardless of data size. Consequently, inductive modeling can be meaningful and practical only if it is conceptualized in terms of *nondeterministic systems* of some sort. By definition, each nondeterministic system involves some degree of predictive (or retrodictive) *uncertainty*. This degree of uncertainty, when appropriately defined, is always one of three key criteria for comparing nondeterministic models. The other key criteria are *complexity* and *credibility* of the models. In general, the more uncertainty we allow, the more we can simplify a given model or the more credible we can make it.

It clearly follows from the previous discussion that the concept of uncertainty plays a crucial role in inductive modeling. The rest of this chapter is devoted to the explanation of this role.

5. Methodological Principles of Uncertainty

In order to facilitate our discussion of the role of uncertainty in inductive modeling, it is desirable to introduce first a special connection that exists between the concepts of *uncertainty* and *information*. When our uncertainty in some situation is reduced by the outcome of an action (such as an observation, performing an experiment, receiving a message, or finding an historical record), the action may be viewed as a source of information pertaining to the situation under consideration. The amount of information obtained by the action may be measured by the reduction in uncertainty caused by the action. For example, the uncertainty in predicting the average rate of inflation in the

United States next year vanishes when the actual value is determined by aggregating relevant observations. In this case, the amount of information contained in this aggregate observation, relative to our model, is equivalent to the amount of uncertainty expressed by the model prior to the observation.

Information measured solely by the reduction of uncertainty does not involve any semantic or pragmatic aspects. Consequently, it does not fully capture the rich notion of information in human communication. This is no shortcoming, however, when the concept of uncertainty-based information is applied within given semantic and pragmatic frameworks, as is typical in systems modeling.

The capability of measuring information in terms of uncertainty is essential for dealing with two broad classes of problems that are fundamental to inductive modeling:

1. problems involving reasoning in which conclusions are not entailed in the given premises, which is usually called *ampliative reasoning*; and
2. problems of *systems simplification.*

Ampliative reasoning is indispensable for inductive modeling in a variety of ways. For example, whenever we extend the claims of a model from a description of given data into predictions (or retrodictions), from aggregated variables into disaggregated variables, from subsystems into an overall system, etc., we use ampliative reasoning. Systems simplification is, at least to some extent, opposite to ampliative reasoning in the context of inductive modeling. It involves problems such as the various ways of aggregating variables, excluding variables, breaking overall systems into subsystems, and the like. We simplify systems models either to make them more manageable and understandable or to increase their credibility.

Using common sense, we can employ the concepts of uncertainty and uncertainty-based information to formulate the following sound methodological principles for dealing with these two classes of problems.

A general *principle of ampliative reasoning* may be expressed by the following requirement: In any ampliative inference, use all, but no more than the information that is available. That is, we require that conclusions resulting from ampliative inferences maximize the relevant uncertainty within the constraints representing the premises. This principle, which may appropriately be called the *principle of maximum uncertainty*, guarantees that our ignorance be fully recognized when we try to enlarge our claims beyond the given premises and, at the same time, that all information contained in the premises be fully utilized. That is, the principle guarantees that our conclusions are maximally noncommital with regard to missing information in the premises.

A general *principle of systems simplification* may be expressed as follows: A sound simplification of a system should minimize the loss of relevant information (or increase of relevant uncertainty) while achieving the required reduction of complexity. That is, we should accept only such simplifications at any desirable level of complexity for which the loss of relevant information (or increase in relevant uncertainty) is minimal. This principle, which may be called the *principle of minimum uncertainty*, guarantees that no information is wasted in the process of simplification.

When combined, these complementary principles of maximum and minimum uncertainty form a powerful methodological tool. It is fascinating that they were recognized by the ancient Chinese philosopher Lao Tsu as early as the sixth century B.C. and expressed by two simple statements of remarkable clarity and beauty [18, sect. 71]:

Knowing ignorance is strength.
Ignoring knowledge is sickness.

6. Maximum and Minimum Entropy Principles

In order to make the principles of maximum and minimum uncertainty operational, a well-justified measure of uncertainty (and the associated information) is needed. Such a measure depends, obviously, on how uncertainty is conceptualized.

The classical mathematical apparatus for characterizing situations under uncertainty has been *probability theory*. In probability theory, uncertainty is measured by the well-known *Shannon entropy*,

$$H(p(x_i)|x_i \in X) = - \sum_{x_i \in X} p(x_i) \log_2 p(x_i), \qquad (1)$$

where $(p(x_i)|x_i \in X)$ denotes a probability distribution on a finite set X, by which we attempt to describe a situation under uncertainty. This function is firmly established as the only justifiable measure of uncertainty when uncertainty is conceptualized in terms of probability theory [15, 22, 24]. Although it is usually used in terms of appropriate conditional probabilities or in a generalized form that involves two probability distributions, these aspects are beyond the scope of this chapter.

Using the Shannon entropy as a measure of uncertainty, the maximum uncertainty principle becomes the well-established *principle of maximum entropy* [11, 12, 25]. The principle was founded, presumably, by Jaynes [11]. Its general formulation is: "Determine a probability distribution $(p(x_i)|x_i \in X)$ that maximizes the function given by eq. (1) (or an appropriate conditional variant of this function) subject to constraints $c_1, c_2, \ldots$, which express partial information about the unknown probability distribution, as well as general constraints (axioms) of probability theory" (i.e., $p(x_i)$ are nonnegative numbers that must add to 1). The most typical constraints employed in practical applications of the maximum entropy principle are mean (expected) values of one or more random variables or various marginal probability distributions of an unknown joint distribution.

As an example, consider a random variable x with possible (given) nonnegative real values $x_1, x_2, \ldots, x_n$. Assume that probabilities $p(x_i)$ are not known, but we know the mean (expected) value $E(x)$ of the variable, which is related to the unknown probabilities by the formula

$$E(x) = \sum_{i=1}^{n} x_i p(x_i).$$

(2)

Employing the maximum entropy principle, we determine the unknown probabilities $p(x_i)$, $i = 1, 2, \ldots, n$, by solving the following optimization problem: Maximize function H given by eq. (1) subject to the axiomatic constraints of probability theory and an additional constraint expressed by eq. (2), where $E(x)$ and $x_1, x_2, \ldots, x_n$ are given numbers. When solving this problem [15], we obtain

$$p(x_i) = \frac{e^{-\beta x_i}}{\sum\limits_{k=1}^{n} e^{-\beta x_k}},$$

(3)

for all $i = 1, 2, \ldots, n$, where β is a constant obtained by solving (numerically) the equation

$$\sum_{i=1}^{n} [x_i - E(x)] e^{-\beta[x_i - E(x_i)]} = 0.$$

Our only knowledge about the random variable x in this example is the knowledge of its expected value $E(x)$. It is expressed by eq. (2) as a constraint on the set of relevant probability distributions. If $E(x)$ were not known, we would be totally ignorant about x, and the maximum entropy principle would yield the uniform probability distribution (the only distribution for which the entropy reaches its absolute maximum). The entropy of the probability distribution given by eq. (3) is smaller than the entropy of the uniform distribution, but it is the largest entropy from among all the entropies of the probability distributions that conform to the given expected value $E(x)$. Hence, we utilize fully our partial knowledge while, at the same time, recognizing maximally our ignorance beyond this knowledge.

Let us turn now to the *principle of minimum entropy*. Its use in dealing with the problem of systems simplification is easy to understand. According to this principle, the appropriate form of the Shannon entropy (usually a conditional form, which represents a predictive uncertainty) is employed for ordering competing simplifications of a given probabilistic system at each relevant level of complexity. Hence, given a set of simplifications of the given system at a desirable level of complexity, we accept only those for which the entropy value is minimal. The principle is thus an arbiter by which we select admissible simplifications.

The principles of maximum and minimum entropy have been recognized and methodologically utilized with great success in various areas of science and engineering for approximately the last three decades. Perhaps the greatest skill in using these complementary principles in inductive modeling in a broad spectrum of applications has been demonstrated by Christensen [2, 3].

A significant advantage of the principles of maximum and minimum entropy (as well as their counterparts outside probability theory, discussed later in this chapter) is that they are applicable to variables of any scale. Hence, they are eminently suitable for qualitative systems modeling, as demonstrated by the methodology for qualitative systems modeling developed within the GSPS framework [14, 17].

7. Novel Mathematical Theories for Dealing with Uncertainty

In spite of the great significance and practical success of probabilistic information theory, especially the principles of maximum and minimum entropy, it has increasingly been recognized that probability theory captures only one type of uncertainty. In particular, it is ill-suited for capturing the full scope of uncertainty associated with phenomena characterized by Weaver as phenomena of *organized complexity* [28]. To model these phenomena adequately requires the use of systems that are very complex, nondeterministic, and highly holistic (resistant to decomposition). In addition, such systems usually involve uncertainty that is not of a statistical nature (the phenomena are not sufficiently random to yield meaningful statistical averages), but rather of a more general modality, often found in natural languages and human reasoning.

Since the mid-1960s, several alternative mathematical theories became available for characterizing situations under uncertainty. They are subsumed under two broad theories, a *theory of fuzzy sets* and a *theory of fuzzy measures* [15, 27, 31]. The former is a generalization of classical set theory; the latter is a generalization of probability theory.

A *fuzzy set* is a set whose boundary is not sharp. That is, the change from nonmembership to membership in a fuzzy set is gradual rather than abrupt. This gradual change is expressed by a membership grade function μ_A of the form

$$\mu_A: X \to [0, 1],$$

where A is a label of the fuzzy set defined by this function and X is the universal set under consideration; the universal set is always *crisp* (nonfuzzy). The value $\mu_A(x)$ expresses the grade of membership of element x of X in the fuzzy set A or, in other words, the degree of compatibility of x with the concept represented by the fuzzy set.

It is easy to see that the concept of a fuzzy set provides a basic mathematical framework for dealing with *vagueness* (or *fuzziness*), an important type of uncertainty, which is closely connected with natural languages and common-sense reasoning. It allows us to use and reason with vague (fuzzy) predicates (scarce, expensive, old, wealthy, and the like), vague quantifiers (many, almost all, usually, and so on), vague truth values (quite true, mostly false, more or less true, etc.), fuzzy numbers (close to 0, much greater than 1, smaller than but close to 5, etc.), and various other kinds of vague modifiers (likely, almost impossible, extremely likely, etc.).

Let X denote, again, a universal set under consideration, and let $P(X)$ denote the set of all crisp (nonfuzzy) subsets of X (i.e., the power set of X). Then, a *fuzzy measure* is defined by a function g of the form

$$g: P(X) \to [0, 1]$$

that satisfies the following requirements:

(g1) $g(\varnothing) = 0$ and $g(X) = 1$ (boundary conditions);
(g2) for all $A, B \in P(X)$, if $A \subseteq B$, then $g(A) \le g(B)$ (monotonicity); and
(g3) for every infinite sequence of subsets of X, if either $A_1 \subset A_2 \subset A_3 \subset \cdots$
    or $A_1 \supset A_2 \supset A_3 \supset \cdots$, then

$$\lim_{i \to \infty} g(A_i) = g\left(\lim_{i \to \infty} A_i\right) \quad \text{(continuity)}.$$

Function g (a fuzzy measure) assigns to each crisp subset A of X a number $g(A)$ in the unit interval $[0, 1]$ that represents the degree of available evidence or our belief that a given element of X (a priori nonlocated in any subset of X) belongs to the subset A.

In contrast to fuzzy sets, which are capable of capturing vagueness of concepts embedded in natural language, fuzzy measures capture uncertainty caused by *lack of information*. For example, by allocating specific numbers from the unit interval $[0, 1]$, in conformity with the properties (g1) to (g3), to various subsets of the state set of a system, we define a fuzzy measure on the state set by which we may express our degrees of belief (based on evidence that is fragmentary, incomplete, imprecise, unreliable, contradictory, or otherwise imperfect) that the next state of the system will belong to these various subsets.

When requirements (g1) to (g3) are augmented with some additional requirements, various special types of fuzzy measures are obtained. Names of some important special types of fuzzy measures, whose theories are well developed, are given in Figure 2.2. This figure also illustrates the inclusion relationship among these types of measures. Thus, for example, probability measures are a subset of both belief and plausibility measures, whereas possibility measures are a subset of plausibility measures that does not overlap with probability measures. Let us briefly overview properties of these various measures named in Figure 2.2; thorough coverage can be found in [15].

Belief and plausibility measures are dual: Given a belief measure Bel, the dual, plausibility measure, $P1$ is defined by the equation

$$P1(A) = 1 - \text{Bel}(\bar{A}) \tag{4}$$

for all $A \in P(X)$, where $\bar{A}$ denotes the complement of A. In addition to the requirements (g1) to (g3) of fuzzy measures, belief and plausibility measures satisfy the following subadditivity requirements:

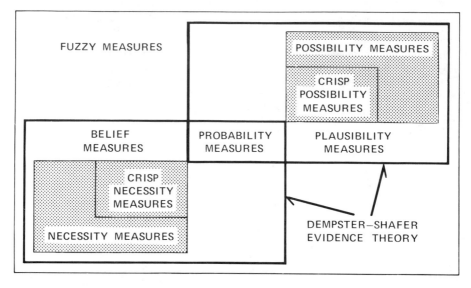

FIGURE 2.2. Types of fuzzy measures that are considered in this chapter.

$$\mathrm{Bel}(A \cup B) \geq \mathrm{Bel}(A) + \mathrm{Bel}(B) - \mathrm{Bel}(A \cap B), \qquad (5)$$

$$P1(A \cap B) \leq P1(A) + P1(B) - P1(A \cup B) \qquad (6)$$

for all $A, B \in P(X)$. When the inequalities (5) and (6) are replaced with equalities, we obtain the well-known additivity properties of probability measures. Hence, probability measures are more restrictive than belief and plausibility measures.

Every pair of belief and plausibility measures, related to each other by eq. (4), is fully characterized by a function

$$m: P(X) \to [0, 1]$$

such that

$$m(\varnothing) = 0 \quad \text{and} \quad \sum_{A \subseteq X} m(A) = 1.$$

This function is called a *basic assignment*; $m(A)$ represents the degree of belief (based on incomplete information) that a specific element of X belongs to the set A, but not to any particular subset of A. Every set $A \in P(X)$ for which $m(A) \neq 0$ is called a *focal element*. The pair (F, m), where F denotes the set of all focal elements of m, is called a *body of evidence*.

Given a basic assignment m, the associated belief and plausibility measures are determined for all $A \in P(X)$ by the equations

$$\mathrm{Bel}(A) = \sum_{B \subseteq A} m(B), \qquad (7)$$

$$P1(A) = \sum_{B \cap A \neq \varnothing} m(B). \qquad (8)$$

These equations and the definition of the basic assignment form the core of a theory referred to as the *Dempster–Shafer theory* of evidence. This theory is best described in [23].

Bel(A) takes into account not only the degree of evidence or belief that the element in question belongs to the set A alone, as described by $m(A)$, but also the additional evidence or belief focusing on subsets of A. $P1(A)$ represents not only the total evidence or belief that the element in question belongs to set A or to any of its subsets, but also the additional (plausible) evidence or belief associated with sets that overlap with A. Hence,

$$m(A) \leq \text{Bel}(A) \leq P1(A)$$

for all $A \in P(X)$.

Total ignorance is expressed in terms of the basic assignment by $m(X) = 1$ and $m(A) = 0$ for all $A \neq X$. That is, we know that the element is in the universal set X, but we have no evidence regarding its location in any subset of X. From eq. (7), this can also be expressed by $\text{Bel}(X) = 1$ and $\text{Bel}(A) = 0$ for all $A \neq X$. Alternatively, from eq. (8), we obtain $P1(\varnothing) = 0$ and $P1(A) = 1$ for all $A \neq \varnothing$ as an expression of total ignorance.

A belief measure (or a plausibility measure) becomes a *probability measure* when all focal elements are singletons. In this case, $\text{Bel}(A) = P1(A)$ for all $A \in P(X)$ as follows immediately from eqs. (7) and (8).

Special plausibility measures whose focal elements are nested (ordered by set inclusion) are called *possibility measures* [4]. A possibility measure is uniquely determined by a *possibility distribution function*

$$r: X \to [0, 1]$$

via the formula

$$\pi(A) = \sup_{x \in A} r(x) \tag{9}$$

for all $A \subset P(X)$, where sup denotes the supremum (the least upper bound) of $r(x)$ in A. Dual to possibility measures are *necessity measures*, which are a special type of belief measures. Given a possibility measure π, the dual, necessity measure η is determined for all $A \in P(X)$ by the equation

$$\eta(A) = 1 - \pi(\bar{A}). \tag{10}$$

Possibility theory can be formulated not only in terms of plausibility theory, but also in terms of fuzzy sets. It was introduced in this latter context by Zadeh [32]. Given a fuzzy set A with membership grade function μ_A, Zadeh defines a possibility distribution function r_A associated with A as numerically equal to μ_A, that is,

$$r_A(x) = \mu_A(x) \tag{11}$$

for all $x \in X$; then, he defines the corresponding possibility measure π_A by the equation

$$\pi_A(B) - \sup_{x \in B} r_A(x) \tag{12}$$

for all $B \in P(X)$. In this interpretation of possibility theory, focal elements correspond to sets

$$A_\alpha = \{x \in X | \mu_A(x) \geq \alpha\},$$

each defined for a particular value α in $[0, 1]$ such that $\mu_A(x) = \alpha$ for some $x \in X$. Sets A_α are called α-Cuts of the fuzzy set A.

A possibility measure is called a *crisp possibility measure* when it is defined in terms of a crisp set. If interpreted as a plausibility measure, a crisp possibility measure consists of only one focal element.

As observed by Yager [30], the Dempster–Shafer theory can be fuzzified. In its fuzzified form, the basic assignment is a function

$$\tilde{m}: \tilde{P}(X) \to [0, 1],$$

where $\tilde{P}(X)$ denotes the set of all fuzzy subsets of X. This function must satisfy the same requirements for the extended domain $\tilde{P}(X)$, as function m does for the domain $P(X)$. Plausibility $\tilde{P}1$ and belief $\tilde{Bel}$ based on $\tilde{m}$ are expressed by the formulas

$$\tilde{P}1(A) = \sum_{B \in F} \tilde{m}(B) \left[\max_{x \in X} \min(\mu_A(x), \mu_B(x)) \right], \tag{13}$$

$$\tilde{Bel}(A) = \sum_{B \in F} \tilde{m}(B) \left[1 - \max_{x \in X} \min(1 - \mu_A(x), \mu_B(x)) \right], \tag{14}$$

where $\mu_A(x)$ and $\mu_B(x)$ are degrees of membership of element x in fuzzy sets A and B, respectively, and F is the set of all focal elements (fuzzy sets) associated with $\tilde{m}$.

To illustrate the basic concepts introduced in this section, let me use examples of three bodies of evidence in the Dempster–Shafer theory. In these examples, which are specified in Table 2.1, $X = \{a, b, c, d\}$, and subsets of X are defined by their characteristic functions.

We can see that the focal elements of m_2 are singletons, and hence, m_2 represents a probability measure. As a consequence, $Bel_2(A) = P1_2(A)$ for all $A \in P(X)$.

Focal elements of m_3 form a family of nested subsets of X,

$$\{a\} \subset \{a, c\} \subset \{a, b, c\} \subset \{a, b, c, d\} = X,$$

which implies that m_3 represents a possibility measure. The possibility distribution function, r_3, is determined as follows:

$$r_3(a) = P1_3(\{a\}) = m_3(\{a\}) + m_3(\{a, c\}) + m_3(\{a, b, c\}) + m_3(X) = 1,$$

$$r_3(c) = P1_3(\{c\}) = \qquad\qquad m_3(\{a, c\}) + m_3(\{a, b, c\}) + m_3(X) = 0.8,$$

$$r_3(b) = P1_3(\{b\}) = \qquad\qquad\qquad\qquad m_3(\{a, b, c\}) + m_3(X) = 0.5,$$

$$r_3(d) = P1_3(\{d\}) = \qquad\qquad\qquad\qquad\qquad\qquad m_3(X) = 0.1.$$

Values of $P1_3(A)$ can be calculated by eq. (8). For example,

TABLE 2.1. Examples of three bodies of evidence in the Dempster–Shafer theory.

a	b	c	d	m_1	Bel_1	Pl_1	m_2	Bel_2	Pl_2	m_3	Bel_3	Pl_3
0	0	0	0	0	0	0	0	0	0	0	0	0
0	0	0	1	.2	.2	.4	0	0	0	0	0	.1
0	0	1	0	0	0	.5	.4	.4	.4	0	0	.8
0	0	1	1	0	.2	.9	0	.4	.4	0	0	.8
0	1	0	0	0	0	.6	.5	.5	.5	0	0	.5
0	1	0	1	0	.2	.8	0	.5	.5	0	0	.5
0	1	1	0	.3	.3	.7	0	.9	.9	0	0	.8
0	1	1	1	0	.5	.9	0	.9	.9	0	0	.8
1	0	0	0	.1	.1	.5	.1	.1	.1	.2	.2	1
1	0	0	1	0	.3	.7	0	.1	.1	0	.2	1
1	0	1	0	.1	.2	.8	0	.5	.5	.3	.5	1
1	0	1	1	0	.4	1	0	.5	.5	0	.5	1
1	1	0	0	0	1	.8	0	.6	.6	0	.2	1
1	1	0	1	.2	.5	1	0	.6	.6	0	.2	1
1	1	1	0	.1	.6	.8	0	1	1	.4	.9	1
1	1	1	1	0	1	1	0	1	1	.1	1	1

$$P1_3(\{b,d\}) = m_3(\{a,b,c\}) + m_3(X) = 0.8.$$

Alternatively, $P1_3(A) = \pi_3(A)$ can be calculated by eq. (9). For example,

$$P1_3(\{b,d\}) = \pi_3(\{b,d\}) = \max[r_3(b), r_3(d)] = 0.5.$$

Values of $Bel_3(A)$ can be calculated by eq. (7). For example,

$$Bel_3(\{a,c\}) = m_3(\{a\}) + m_3(\{a,c\}) = 0.5.$$

Alternatively, $Bel_3(A) = \eta_3(A)$ can be calculated by eq. (10) from $\pi_3(A) = P1_3(A)$. For example,

$$Bel_3(\{a,c\}) = \eta_3(\{a,c\}) = 1 - \pi_3(\{b,d\}) = 1 - 0.5 = 0.5.$$

Focal elements of m_1 are neither singletons nor nested subsets, and consequently, m_1 represents general belief and plausibility measures. To calculate $Bel_1(A)$ or $P1_1(A)$, we have to use eq. (7) or eq. (8), respectively. Once one of the measures is determined, we can use eq. (4) to calculate the other one. For example,

$$Bel_1(\{a,c,d\}) = m_1(\{d\}) + m_1(\{a\}) + m_1(\{a,c\}) = 0.2 + 0.1 + 0.1 = 0.4,$$

$$P1_1(\{b\}) = 1 - Bel_1(\{a,c,d\}) = 1 = 0.4 = 0.6.$$

8. Uncertainty Is Multidimensional: New Insights and Results

For centuries, *probability theory* has been viewed as the sole mathematical apparatus capable of characterizing situations under uncertainty. When Zadeh introduced the *theory of fuzzy sets* [31], this view was challenged. It later became obvious that probability theory and fuzzy set theory characterized two very different types of uncertainty: ambiguity and vagueness, respectively. *Ambiguity* is associated with one-to-many situations, that is, situations with two or more alternatives such that the choice among them is left unspecified. *Vagueness*, on the other hand, is associated with the difficulty of making sharp or precise distinctions in the world.

The question of how to measure the amount of vagueness or fuzziness was raised shortly after fuzzy set theory was initiated in 1965. Various measures of vagueness, more often called *measures of fuzziness*, have been proposed [15]. Of all these proposals, it seems that the most natural way of expressing the degree of fuzziness of a fuzzy set is to define it in terms of the lack of distinction between the set and its complement. Indeed it is precisely this feature that distinguishes fuzzy sets from crisp sets. The less a set differs from its complement, the fuzzier it is. Using this approach, the measure of fuzziness depends on the operator employed for fuzzy complementation and the distance function we choose to express the distinction between the set and its complement.

Let f_c denote a measure of fuzziness based on the complementation operator c and the Hamming distance. Then, assuming a finite universal set X, we have

$$f_c(A) = |X| - \sum_{x \in X} |\mu_A(x) - c(\mu_A(x))|, \tag{15}$$

where $|X|$ denotes the cardinality of the universal set X [8].

Fuzziness is not the only type of uncertainty associated with fuzzy sets. Indeed, fuzzy sets are not only more or less fuzzy, they are also more or less specific. For example, the fuzzy set of real numbers that are close to zero is less specific (less informative) than the set of real numbers that are very close to zero. The uncertainty is in this case caused by the lack of specificity, and consequently, it is reasonable to give it the name *nonspecificity*.

The first *measure of nonspecificity*, which is restricted to crisp sets, was introduced by Hartley more than 60 years ago [7], even though he referred to it as a measure of information. Given a finite crisp set A of possible alternatives, its nonspecificity (and the associated information) $I(A)$ is defined by Hartley as

$$I(A) = \log_2 |A|. \tag{16}$$

Hartley showed that this simple measure was the only meaningful measure (except for a multiplication constant) of uncertainty-based information associated with crisp sets. Later, its uniqueness was proved axiomatically by Rényi [22]. $I(A)$ expresses the number of simple propositions whose truth values must be determined in order to characterize one element of the set A.

A natural generalization of the Hartley measure for fuzzy sets and the associated possibility measures was discovered by Higashi and Klir [9]. For any normalized fuzzy set A (when $\max \mu_A(x) = 1$), it has the form

$$U(A) = \int_0^1 \log_2 |A_\alpha| \, d\alpha, \tag{17}$$

where $|A_\alpha|$ denotes the cardinality of the α-Cut A_α of the fuzzy set A. The uniqueness of this possibilistic measure of nonspecificity was proved by Klir and Mariano [16]. For fuzzy sets that are not normalized and max $\mu_A(x) = a$, $U(A)$ given by eq. (17) must be divided by a. Observe that $U(A)$ given by eq. (17) is a weighted average of the Hartley information of the α-cuts A_α, where the weights are increments of possibility degrees between successive α-cuts.

When possibility theory is interpreted as plausibility theory restricted to nested bodies of evidence (F, m), the α-cuts become the focal elements (elements of F). It follows from this interpretation that the increments in possibility degrees between successive focal elements in the nested structure are equal to the values $m(A)$ for all $A \in F$ [15]. Then, the measure of nonspecificity is expressed by a function V that, for any given body of evidence (F, m), assumes the form

$$V(m) = \sum_{A \in F} m(A) \log_2 |A|. \tag{18}$$

Clearly, when m corresponds to a possibility distribution represented by a fuzzy set A, then $V(m) = U(A)$. Furthermore, it is now well established that function V defined by eq. (18) is applicable as a measure of nonspecificity to any arbitrary body of evidence, not only those that are nested. Its uniqueness in this general setting was proved by Ramer [21].

Since focal elements of probability measures are singletons, $V(m) = 0$ for every probability measure. That is, the measure of nonspecificity does not discriminate among probability measures: All probability measures are fully specific. What, then, is actually measured by the Shannon entropy? When generalized from the narrow framework of probability theory into the broader framework of the Dempster–Shafer theory, Shannon entropy bifurcates into the following two forms [15]:

$$E(m) = - \sum_{A \in F} m(A) \log_2 Pl(A), \tag{19}$$

$$C(m) = - \sum_{A \in F} m(A) \log_2 \text{Bel}(A). \tag{20}$$

Function E is usually called a *measure of dissonance* and C is called a *measure of confusion*. Since both E and C collapse to the Shannon entropy when m represents a probability measure, they are often referred to as *entropy-like measures* of uncertainty. Let us determine what these functions actually measure.

From the general property of basic assignments (satisfied for every $A \in P(X)$), we obtain

$$\sum_{B \cap A \neq \emptyset} m(B) + \sum_{B \cap A = \emptyset} m(B) = 1.$$

Using this equation and eq. (8), $E(m)$ given by eq. (19) can be expressed as

$$E(m) = - \sum_{A \in F} m(A) \log_2 \left[1 - \sum_{B \cap A \neq \emptyset} m(B) \right]. \tag{21}$$

The term

$$K = \sum_{B \cap A \neq \varnothing} m(B)$$

in this expression for $E(m)$ clearly represents the total conflict between the belief in A and other beliefs within a given body of evidence. It is obtained simply by adding the basic assignment values of all focal elements that are disjoint with A, and consequently, the beliefs allocated to them are in conflict with the belief focusing on A. The value of K ranges from 0 to 1. The function

$$-\log_2[1 - K],$$

which is employed in eq. (21), is monotonic increasing with K; it extends the range from $[0, 1]$ to $(0, \infty)$. The choice of the logarithmic function is based on the same motivation as the choice of the logarithmic function in the Shannon entropy. Now, we can readily see that $E(m)$ defines the mean (expected) value of the conflict in beliefs associated with a given body of evidence (F, m); the name "measure of dissonance" is thus quite appropriate. This observation reinforces the previous argument that the Shannon entropy measures the degree of conflict (dissonance) among beliefs expressed by a probability distribution.

Let us now analyze the meaning of function C given by eq. (20). From eq. (7) and the general property of basic assignments (satisfied for every $A \in P(X)$),

$$\sum_{B \subseteq A} m(B) + \sum_{B \nsubseteq A} m(B) = 1,$$

we get

$$C(m) = -\sum_{A \in F} m(A) \log_2 \left[1 - \sum_{B \nsubseteq A} m(B) \right]. \tag{22}$$

The term

$$L = \sum_{B \nsubseteq A} m(B)$$

in this expression of $C(m)$ stands for the sum of all focal elements that either do not overlap with set A or overlap with it only partially. Since beliefs in these focal elements B are in actual or potential conflict with the belief in A (since $B \nsubseteq A$ by definition), L represents the total real and potential conflict with the belief in A. The reasons for using

$$-\log_2[1 - L]$$

instead of L in eq. (22) are the same as already discussed in the context of function E. The conclusion is that $C(m)$ defines the mean (expected) value of not only the real conflict (as function E does), but also of the potential conflict associated with a given body of evidence. This multitude of partially or totally conflicting focal elements is a source of confusion, hence, the name "measure of confusion."

To illustrate the three types of uncertainty that coexist in the Dempster–Shafer theory, let me show how their values are calculated for the body of evidence characterized by m_1 in Table 2.1:

$$V(m_1) = m_1(\{d\})\log_2 1 + m_1(\{b,c\})\log_2 2 + m_1(\{a\})\log_2 1$$
$$+ m_1(\{a,c\})\log_2 2 + m_1(\{a,b,d\})\log_2 3$$
$$+ m_1(\{a,b,c\})\log_2 3 = 0.876;$$

$$E(m_1) = -m_1(\{d\})\log_2 Pl_1(\{d\}) - m_1(\{b,c\})\log_2 Pl_1(\{b,c\})$$
$$-m_1(\{a\})\log_2 Pl_1(\{a\}) - m_1(\{a,c\})\log_2 Pl_1(\{a,c\})$$
$$-m_1(\{a,b,d\})\log_2 Pl_1(\{a,b,d\}) - m_1(\{a,b,c\})\log_2 Pl_1(\{a,b,c\})$$
$$= 0.413.$$

$$C(m_1) = -m_1(\{d\})\log_2 \text{Bel}_1(\{d\}) - m_1(\{b,c\})\log_2 \text{Bel}_1(\{b,c\})$$
$$-m_1(\{a\})\log_2 \text{Bel}_1(\{a\}) - m_1(\{a,c\})\log_2 \text{Bel}_1(\{a,c\})$$
$$-m_1(\{a,b,d\})\log_2 \text{Bel}_1(\{a,b,d\}) - m_1(\{a,b,c\})\log_2 \text{Bel}_1(\{a,b,c\})$$
$$= 1.824.$$

Since focal elements of possibility measures are nested, the plausibility of each focal element must be 1 (by eq. (8)) and, consequently, $E(m) = 0$ for every possibility measure. That is, possibility measures (and the dual necessity measures) are free of dissonance. In fact, they are called *consonant measures* in the Dempster–Shafer theory.

We can now see from this brief exposition of recent advances in the conceptualization and measurement of uncertainty that uncertainty and the associated uncertainty-based information are multidimensional concepts. Depending on the mathematical framework employed, uncertainty is manifested by one or more of the following four types we now recognize: *fuzziness* (vagueness), *nonspecificity* (lack of informativeness), *dissonance* (pure conflict), and *confusion* (pure and potential conflict). The multidimensionality of uncertainty was obscured when uncertainty was investigated solely in terms of classical set theory and probability theory, in each of which uncertainty is manifested only by one dimension: by nonspecificity in classical set theory (expressed by the Hartley measure) and by dissonance in probability theory (expressed by the Shannon entropy). Although we understand now that the Hartley measure and Shannon entropy quantify different types of uncertainty, this fact was obscured by the prevailing view of experts in probabilistic information theory that the Hartley measure is solely a special case of the Shannon entropy, emerging from the uniform probability distribution. This view was ill-conceived since the Hartley measure is totally independent of any probabilistic assumptions, and as we now understand, it measures a different type of uncertainty than the Shannon entropy.

The following is a summary of the applicability of the individual measures of the four types of uncertainty in the various mathematical theories capable of conceptualizing uncertainty:

1. *classical (crisp) set theory*—nonspecificity (Hartley measure), expressed by eq. (16);
2. *probability theory*—dissonance (Shannon entropy), expressed by eq. (1);
3. *fuzzy set theory*—fuzziness, exemplified by eq. (15), and nonspecificity, expressed by eq. (17);
4. *possibility theory*—nonspecificity, expressed by either eq. (17) or eq. (18), depending on the interpretation employed;
5. *Dempster–Shafer theory of evidence*—nonspecificity, dissonance, and confusion, given by eqs. (18), (19), and (20), respectively;
6. *fuzzified Dempster–Shafer theory*—nonspecificity, dissonance, and confusion, expressed by eqs. (18), (19), and (20), respectively, and fuzziness, F_c, expressed by the weighted sum of the degrees of fuzziness of focal elements, that is,

$$F_c(m) = \sum_{A \in F} m(A) f_c(A), \tag{23}$$

where $f_c(A)$ is given by eq. (15).

It is clear from the foregoing that the one-dimensional probabilistic information theory will have to be extended into a multidimensional information theory, far better equipped to capture the semantic richness of the concepts of uncertainty and uncertainty-based information. Such a research program involves many challenging philosophical, mathematical, and computational issues. For example, the maximum and minimum uncertainty principles will lead either to various multiple objective criteria optimization problems or to optimization problems in which objective functions would express meaningful aggregates of relevant types of uncertainty. Considering the Dempster–Shafer theory as an example, the uncertainty principles would be expressed either in terms of three objective functions, $V(m)$, $E(m)$, and $C(m)$, or, alternatively, in terms of a single objective function, an appropriate aggregate of these functions; for instance, we may take their sum,

$$S(m) = V(m) + E(m) + C(m).$$

In this latter case, for example, the principle of maximum uncertainty for a problem defined within a finite universal set X would be formulated as follows: Determine a basic assignment $m(A)$, for all $A \subseteq X$, that maximizes the function

$$S(m) = \sum_{A \subseteq X} m(A) \log_2 \frac{|A|}{P1(A) \cdot \text{Bel}(A)} \tag{24}$$

subject to the given constraints c_1, c_2, ..., which represent the available information relevant to the matter of concern, as well as the general constraints of the Dempster–Shafer theory.

9. An Example

Let us illustrate the use of the principle of maximum uncertainty in the Dempster–Shafer theory by the following simple example of multiple sensor target identification [1]. Since the purpose is to illustrate a general principle, the example is discussed first in general terms, and then, some numerical instances of the results are examined. Let X denote a set of possible types of hostile targets (various types of bombers, fighters, missiles, etc.), and let A and B denote particular subsets of X that can be identified by two sensors in the incoming population of targets with some degrees of belief, say, a and b, respectively. Assume that $A \cap B \neq \varnothing$. Knowing that a and b are the total degrees of belief, what degree of belief should be allocated to the set $A \cap B$? To answer this question requires a reasoning that is ampliative and that, in turn, requires a relevant principle of maximum uncertainty.

Conceptualizing the problem is terms of the Dempster–Shafer theory, we may employ the principle as an optimization problem with either three objective functions (V, E, and C, given by eqs. (18), (19), and (20), respectively) or with a single aggregate of these objective functions (e.g., their sum S, given by eq. (24)). Regardless of the optimization alternative chosen, the constraints of the optimization problem are expressed in this example by the equations and inequalities

$$m(X) + m(A) + m(B) + m(A \cap B) = 1,$$

$$m(A) + m(A \cap B) = a,$$

$$m(B) + m(A \cap B) = b,$$

$$m(X), m(A), m(B), m(A \cap B) \geq 0,$$

where $a, b \in [0, 1]$ are given numbers (total beliefs focusing on A, B, respectively) and $m(X), m(A), m(B), m(A \cap B)$ are unknown values of the basic assignment. The equations are consistent, independent, and underdetermined, with one degree of freedom. Selecting, for example, $m(A \cap B)$ as the free variable, we readily obtain

$$m(A) = a - m(A \cap B)$$

$$m(B) = b - m(A \cap B) \tag{25}$$

$$m(X) = 1 - a - b + m(A \cap B).$$

Since all the unknowns must be nonnegative, the first two equations set the upper bound of $m(A \cap B)$, whereas the third equation specifies its lower bound; we obtain

$$\max(0, a + b - 1) \leq m(A \cap B) \leq \min(a, b). \tag{26}$$

Let $R = [\max(a + b - 1), \min(a, b)]$ denote the range of values of $m(A \cap B)$ that satisfy the given constraints.

Using eqs. (25), the objective functions can be expressed solely in terms of the free variable $m(A \cap B)$. After a simple rearrangement of terms, we obtain

$$V(m) = m(A \cap B) \log_2(K_1) + K_2,$$

$$E(m) = 0,$$

$$C(m) = -m(A \cap B) \log_2 m(A \cap B) + m(A \cap B) \log_2(a \cdot b) + K_3,$$

where

$$K_1 = \frac{|X| \cdot |A \cap B|}{|A| \cdot |B|},$$

$$K_2 = (1 - a - b) \log_2 |X| + a \log_2 |A| + b \log_2 |B|,$$

$$K_3 = -a \log_2 a - b \log_2 b.$$

Let M_V, M_E, and M_C denote the values or sets of values of $m(A \cap B)$ for which functions V, E, and C, respectively, reach their maxima. Then, we can determine by simple considerations that

$$M_V = \begin{cases} \max(0, a + b - 1) & \text{when } K_1 < 1 \\ \min(a, b) & \text{when } K_1 > 1 \\ R & \text{when } K_1 = 1, \end{cases}$$

$$M_E = R,$$

$$M_C = \begin{cases} \max(0, a + b - 1) & \text{when } ab/e < \max(0, a + b - 1) \\ \min(a, b) & \text{when } ab/e > \min(a, b) \\ ab/e & \text{when } ab/e \in R, \end{cases}$$

where e is the base of natural logarithms ($e = 2.7$).

Let R_a denote the set of admissible (nondominated or noninferior) solutions of our optimization problem. There are nine possible combinations of M_V and M_C, each of which determines R_a. These combinations are specified in Table 2.2. We can see that there are actually only six different types of R_a, three of which are represented by unique numbers and the remaining three by intervals of real numbers.

When employing the total uncertainty $S(m)$, given by eq. (24), as the objective function in our example, we obtain

$$S(m) = m(A \cap B) [\log_2 K_1 - \log_2 m(A \cap B) + \log_2 ab] + K_2 + K_3$$

TABLE 2.2. Admissible solutions in the example discussed.

R_a	$K_1 < 1$	$K_1 > 1$	$K_1 = 1$
$ab/e < \max(a + b - 1)$	$\max(0, a + b - 1)$	R	$\max(0, a + b - 1)$
$ab/e > \min(a, b)$	R	$\min(a, b)$	$\min(a, b)$
$ab/e \in R$	$[\max(0, a + b - 1), ab/e]$	$[ab/e, \min(a, b)]$	ab/e

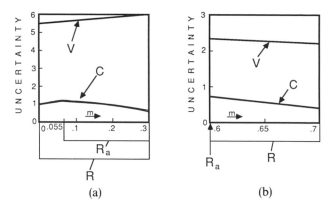

FIGURE 2.3. Example of the use of the maximum uncertainty principle in the Dempster–Shafer theory.

We can readily determine the maximum or set of maxima, M_S, of this objective function within the restricted domain R:

$$M_S = \begin{cases} \max(0, a + b - 1) & \text{when } K_1 ab/e < \max(0, a + b - 1) \\ \min(a, b) & \text{when } K_1 ab/e > \min(a, b) \\ K_1 ab/e & \text{when } K_1 ab/e \in R. \end{cases}$$

Let us examine now three numerical instances of this example.

1. Let $|X| = 150, |A| = 40, |B| = 50, |A \cap B| = 20, a = 0.5$, and $b = 0.3$. Then, $R = [0, 0.3]$, $K_1 = 1.5$, $ab/e = 0.055$, $M_V = 0.3$, $R_a = [0.055, 0.3]$, and $M_S - 0.083$ (Figure 2.3a). That is, the solution is interval-valued when we view the problem as a multiple-objective criteria optimization problem: $m(A \cap B) \in [0.055, 0.3]$. Depending on the selected value of $m(A \cap B)$, using possibly some additional objective criteria, the values of $m(A)$, $m(B)$, and $m(X)$ are determined by eqs. (25). When we use the total uncertainty $S(m)$ as the only objective function, we obtain

$$m(A \cap B) = 0.083, \qquad \text{Bel}(A \cap B) = 0.083, \qquad P1(A \cap B) = 1,$$

$$m(A) = 0.417, \qquad \text{Bel}(A) = 0.5, \qquad P1(A) = 1,$$

$$m(B) = 0.217, \qquad \text{Bel}(B) = .3, \qquad P1(B) = 1,$$

$$m(X) = 0.283, \qquad \text{Bel}(X) = 1, \qquad P1(X) = 1.$$

2. Let $|X| = 20$, $|A| = 8$, $|B| = 9$, $|A \cap B| = 3$, $a = 0.7$, and $b = 0.9$. Then, $R = [0.6, 0.7]$, $K_1 = 0.833$, $ab/e = 0.232$, $M_V = 0.6$, $R_a = 0.6$, and $M_S = 0.6$. In this case, the solution is unique, $m(A \cap B) = 0.6$, independent of the approach employed (Figure 2.3b). We obtain

$$m(A \cap B) = 0.6, \qquad \text{Bel}(A \cap B) = 0.6, \qquad P1(A \cap B) = 1,$$

$$m(A) = 0.1, \qquad \text{Bel}(A) = 0.7, \qquad P1(A) = 1,$$

$$m(B) = 0.3, \qquad \text{Bel}(B) = 0.9, \qquad \text{P1}(B) = 1,$$
$$m(X) = 0, \qquad \text{Bel}(X) = 1, \qquad \text{P1}(X) = 1.$$

3. Let $|X| = 80$, $|A| = 40$, $|B| = 50$, $|A \cap B| = 20$, $a = 0.5$, and $b = 0.6$. Then, $R = [0.1, 0.5]$, $K_1 = 0.8$, $ab/e = 0.11$, $M_V = 0.1$, $R_a = [0.1, 0.11]$, and $M_S = 0.1$. That is, $m(A \cap B) \in [0.1, 0.11]$ for the multiple-objective criteria approach, and $m(A \cap B) = 0.1$ for the single-objective criteria approach.

10. Conclusions

The relationship among complexity, credibility, and uncertainty of systems models, which is of utmost importance to systems modeling, is not well understood as yet. We only know that uncertainty is a valuable commodity in the modeling business, which can be traded for a reduction of complexity or an increase of credibility of models. That is, although uncertainty is an undesirable feature of systems models when considered alone, it becomes very valuable when considered in connection with complexity and credibility of systems models.

One of the advantages of inductive modeling is that uncertainty enters into the model naturally, in the modeling process itself. It becomes an integral part of the model from its very beginning, handled by the sound principles of maximum and minimum uncertainty. Since well-justified measures of the various types of uncertainty are now available for several mathematical frameworks in which uncertainty can be conceptualized, these principles can be made operational at a scale previously unsuspected. It is undeniable that major mathematical research must yet be undertaken to actually make these principles operational in the novel mathematical frameworks, where uncertainties of several types coexist. The issues to be researched are fairly well determined since the foundations of uncertainty have been laid out in all these frameworks.

A turning point in our understanding of the concept of uncertainty was reached when it became clear that more than one type of uncertainty must be recognized within the Dempster–Shafer theory, and even within the restricted domain of possibility theory. This new insight into the concept of uncertainty was obtained by examining uncertainty within mathematical frameworks more general than the two classical theories employed for characterizing uncertainty (classical set theory and probability theory).

References

1. Bogler, P. Shafer–Dempster reasoning with applications to multitarget identification systems. *IEEE Trans. Syst., Man, Cybern. SMC-17*, 6 (1987), 968–977.
2. Christensen, R. *Entropy Minimax Sourcebook* (4 volumes). Entropy Limited, Lincoln, Mass., 1980–1981.

3. Christensen, R. Entropy minimax multivariate statistical modeling. *Intern. J. Gen. Syst. 11*, 3 (1985–1986), 231–277 (I: Theory); *12*, 3, 227–305 (II: Applications).

4. Dubois, D., and Prade, H. *Possibility Theory*. Plenum Press, New York, 1980.

5. Gaines, B.R. On the complexity of causal models. *IEEE Trans. Syst., Man, Cybern. SMC-6* (1976), 56–59.

6. Gaines, B.R. System identification, approximation and complexity. *Intern. J. of Gen. Syst. 3*, 3 (1977), 145–174.

7. Hartley, R.V.L. Transmission of information. *The Bell Syst. Tech. J. 7*, (1928), 535–563.

8. Higashi, M., and Klir, G.J. On measures of fuzziness and fuzzy complements. *Intern. J. Gen. Syst. 8*, 3 (1982), 169–180.

9. Higashi, M., and Klir, G.J. Measures of uncertainty and information based on possibility distributions. *Intern. J. Gen. Syst. 9*, 1 (1983), 43–58.

10. Islam, S. Toward integration of two system theories by Mesarovic and Wymore. *Intern. J. Gen. Syst. 1*, 1 (1974), 35–40.

11. Jaynes, E.T. *Papers on Probability, Statistics and Statistical Physics* (edited by R.D. Rosenkrantz). D. Reidel, Boston, 1983.

12. Kapur, J.N. Twenty-five years of maximum entropy principle. *J. Math. Phys. Sci. 17*, 2 (1983), 103–156.

13. Klir, G.J. *An Approach to General Systems Theory*. Van Nostrand Reinhold, New York, 1969.

14. Klir, G.J. *Architecture of Systems Problem Solving*. Plenum Press, New York, 1985.

15. Klir, G.J., and Folger, T.A. *Fuzzy Sets, Uncertainty, and Information*. Prentice-Hall, Englewood Cliffs, N.J., 1988.

16. Klir, G.J., and Mariano, M. On the uniqueness of possibilistic measure of uncertainty and information. *Fuzzy Sets Syst. 24*, 2 (1987), 197–219.

17. Klir, G.J., and Way, E.C. Reconstructability analysis: Aims, results, open problems. *Syst. Res. 2*, 2 (1985), 141–163.

18. Lao Tsu. *Tao Te Ching*. Vintage Books, New York, 1972.

19. Mesarovic, M.D., and Takahara, Y. *General Systems Theory: Mathematical Foundations*. Academic Press, New York, 1975.

20. Pearl, J. On the connection between the complexity and credibility of inferred models. *Intern. J. Gen. Syst. 4*, 4 (1978), 255–264.

21. Ramer, A. Uniqueness of information measure in the theory of evidence. *Fuzzy Sets Syst. 24*, 2 (1987), 183–196.

22. Renyi, A. Introduction to information theory. In *Probability Theory*. North-Holland, Amsterdam, 1970, pp. 540–616.

23. Shafer, G. *A Mathematical Theory of Evidence*. Princeton University Press, Princeton, N.J., 1976.

24. Shannon, C.E. The mathematical theory of communication. *The Bell Syst. Tech. J. 27* (1948), 379–423, 623–656.

25. Shore, J.E., and Johnson, R.W. Axiomatic derivation of the principle of maximum entropy and the principle of minimum cross-entropy. *IEEE Trans. Inf. Theory 26* (1980), 26–37.

26. Simon, H.A. *The Sciences of the Artificial*. MIT Press, Cambridge, Mass., 1969.

27. Sugeno, M. Fuzzy measures and fuzzy integrals: A survey. In *Fuzzy Automata and Decision Processes*, M.M. Gupta, G.N. Saridis, and B.R. Gaines, Eds. Elsevier North-Holland, New York, pp. 89–102.

28. Weaver, W. Science and complexity. *Am. Sci. 36* (1948), 536–544.

29. Wymore, A.W. *A Mathematical Theory of Systems Engineering: The Elements.* Wiley, New York, 1969.
30. Yager, R.R. Toward general theory of reasoning with uncertainty: Nonspecificity and fuzziness. *Intern. J. Intell. Syst. 1*, 1 (1986), 45–67.
31. Zadeh, L.A. Fuzzy sets. *Inf. Control 8*, 3 (1965). 338–353.
32. Zadeh, L.A. Fuzzy sets as a basis for a theory of possibility. *Fuzzy Sets and Syst. 1*, 1 (1978), 3–28.
33. Zeigler, B.P. *Theory of Modelling and Simulation.* Wiley, New York, 1976.
34. Zeigler, B.P. *Multifacetted Modelling and Discrete Event Simulation.* Academic Press, New York, 1984.
35. Zeigler, B.P. Review of *Architecture of Systems Problem Solving. Int. J. Gen. Syst. 13*, 1 (1986) 83–84.

CHAPTER 3

General System Problem Solving Paradigm for Qualitative Modeling

François E. Cellier

Abstract

In this chapter qualitative modeling is applied to inductively reason about the behavior of physical systems. Inductive reasoning does not dwell on the principles of "naive physics" as the commonsense reasoning does, but rather implements a sort of pattern-recognition mechanism. The basic differences between *inductitive reasoning* and *commonsense reasoning* are explained. It is shown under which conditions either of the two approaches may be more successful than the other.

1. Introduction

What is qualitative simulation as opposed to quantitative simulation? Let me begin by putting some commonly quoted myths about qualitative simulation to the sword.

> Qualitative simulation is cheaper than quantitative simulation. If quantitative simulation, e.g. in a real-time situation, cannot produce the results fast enough, qualitative simulation may be the answer to the problem.

Algorithms used for qualitative simulation are by no means faster than those used in quantitative simulation. In qualitative simulation, there are generally plenty of alternative branches to be explored, whereas quantitative simulation usually produces one individual trajectory. Thus, quantitative simulation is normally faster than qualitative simulation if applicable. Thus, if your quantitative real-time simulation executes too slowly, do not go to qualitative simulation; go to a nearby computer store and buy yourself a faster computer.

> Qualitative simulation requires a less profound understanding of the mechanisms that we wish to simulate. Therefore, if we don't fully understand the mechanisms that we wish to simulate, quantitative simulation is out of the question, whereas qualitative simulation may still work.

Wrong again! Qualitative simulation has as stringent constraints as quantitative simulation; they are just a little different. It is a convenient user interface that relieves the user from some of the intricacies of detailed understanding of the simulation mechanisms and not the modeling methodology per se. Today's languages for quantitative simulation are very user friendly, more so than today's languages for qualitative simulation. This is due to the fact that quantitative simulation languages have been around for much longer. Thus, if you do not understand what you are doing, do not go to qualitative simulation; go to an expert who does.

There are today at least three different methodologies around that are all advocated under the name "qualitative modeling" and/or "qualitative simulation." One of them uses the so-called "naive physics" approach. Its original proponents were mostly found among the social sciences, and it is in those circles where the second of the above propositions is frequently heard (e.g., [1]). Today, this school of thought is mostly found among the artificial intelligence experts (e.g., [4, 5, 7]). Since none of those above is represented in this book directly, I shall briefly introduce the formulation of Kuipers [7], which seems the most advanced among these types of qualitative simulation mechanisms.

The second approach is usually referred to as *commonsense reasoning* (this term is sometimes also used by the "naive physicists") and originates from stochastic signal processing. Whereas the former approach dwells on incomplete knowledge about system parameters, this approach dwells on the signals (trajectories) produced by these models and takes into consideration the uncertainties in the obtained data. Many of the more recent results in this arena are derived from *fuzzy logic*. The most prominent advocate for these types of qualitative models is Zadeh [13–16]. Since these results are being discussed in the chapter by George Klir, I shall refrain from discussing these results within my chapter as well.

The third and last approach is called *inductive reasoning* and originates from general system theory. One of its foremost proponents is Klir [6]. It is this approach that will be explained in most detail in this chapter.

2. The Quantitative Approach

We are going to analyze a simple linear continuous-time single-input/single-output system of the type

$$\dot{\mathbf{x}} = \mathbf{A} \cdot \mathbf{x} + \mathbf{b} \cdot u,$$

$$y = \mathbf{c}' \cdot \mathbf{x} + d \cdot u,$$

where the system matrices $\mathbf{A}$, $\mathbf{b}$, $\mathbf{c}'$, and d are represented in controller-canonical form, namely,

$$\dot{\mathbf{x}} = \begin{pmatrix} 0 & 1 & 0 \\ 0 & 0 & 1 \\ -c & -b & -a \end{pmatrix} \cdot \mathbf{x} + \begin{pmatrix} 0 \\ 0 \\ 1 \end{pmatrix} \cdot u,$$

$$y = (1 \quad 0 \quad 0) \cdot \mathbf{x} + (0) \cdot u,$$

where a, b, and c are three unknown but positive parameters.

In quantitative simulation (and in control theory) this is called a *state-space representation* of the system. Most quantitative simulation languages (but not all) will require these equations to be written individually, that is, in the form:

$$\dot{x}_1 = x_2,$$

$$\dot{x}_2 = x_3,$$

$$\dot{x}_3 = -c \cdot x_1 - b \cdot x_2 - a \cdot x_3 + u,$$

$$y = x_1,$$

which can be represented through the *block diagram* shown in Figure 3.1. We executed several quantitative simulation runs with different values for the three parameters. The results of these simulations are presented in Figure 3.2. It becomes evident that this system exhibits at least four qualitatively different modes of operation: exponential decay, damped oscillation, undamped oscillation, and excited oscillation.

We can look at the system analytically. The characteristic polynomial of this system is

$$det(\lambda \cdot \mathbf{I}^{(n)} - \mathbf{A}) = \lambda^3 + a \cdot \lambda^2 + b \cdot \lambda + c = 0.0.$$

The roots of the characteristic polynomial are the eigenmodi of the system. We can analyze the stability of the system, for example, by setting up a Routh Hurwitz scheme:

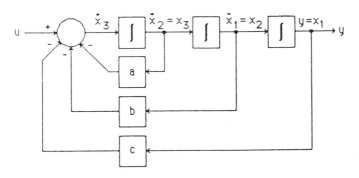

FIGURE 3.1. Block diagram for quantitative simulation.

François E. Cellier

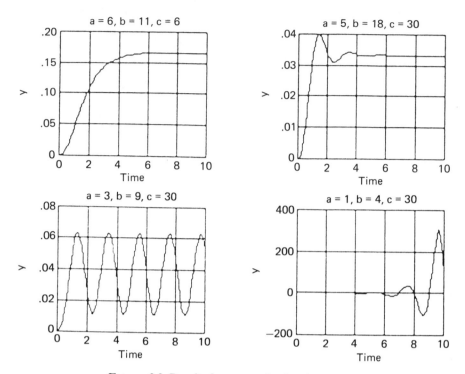

FIGURE 3.2. Results from quantitative simulation.

s^3	1	b
s^2	a	c
s^1	$\dfrac{c - ab}{a}$	
s^0	c	

If all the elements in the first column of the Routh–Hurwitz scheme are positive, the system is stable, that is, all three roots are in the left half λ-plane. Otherwise, the number of sign changes in the first column of the Routh–Hurwitz scheme determines the number of unstable poles, that is, the poles in the right half λ-plane. It can be seen that, if $c > a \cdot b$, all three poles are in the left half plane. They can all be located on the negative real axis (exponential decay), or one can be located on the negative real axis while the other two form a conjugate complex pole pair (damped oscillation). If $c = a \cdot b$, one pole is still on the negative real axis, while the two dominant poles are now on the imaginary axis itself (undamped oscillation). If $c < a \cdot b$, one pole is still on the negative real axis, while the other two poles form a conjugate complex pole pair in the right half plane (excited oscillation). These are indeed all possible cases (for positive coefficients a, b, and c), as the following analysis shows.

Consider the case of the excited oscillation with

$$\lambda_1 = -x,$$

$$\lambda_2 = y + j \cdot z,$$

$$\lambda_3 = y - j \cdot z.$$

In this case, we can write the characteristic polynomial as

$$(\lambda + x) \cdot (\lambda - y - j \cdot z) \cdot (\lambda - y + j \cdot z) = 0.0,$$

which can be rewritten as

$$\lambda^3 + (x - 2y)\lambda^2 + (y^2 + z^2 - 2xy)\lambda + x(y^2 + z^2) = 0.0,$$

which has positive coefficients iff

$$a = x - 2y > 0.0,$$

$$b = y^2 + z^2 - 2xy > 0.0,$$

$$c = x(y^2 + z^2) > 0.0,$$

whereby x, y, and z are all positive. The third condition is obviously always satisfied. The first condition can be rewritten as

$$x > 2y$$

or

$$2xy > 4y^2,$$

which we can plug into the second condition:

$$y^2 + z^2 > 2xy > 4y^2;$$

that is, in the borderline case

$$z^2 = 3y^2,$$

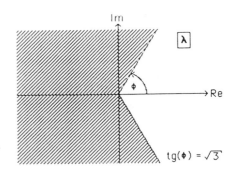

FIGURE 3.3. Domain of possible pole locations.

François E. Cellier

and therefore,

$$z = \sqrt{3} \cdot y.$$

This is shown in Figure 3.3, in which the possible pole locations for positive coefficients a, b, and c are shredded. Therefore, it was verified that this system does not exhibit any other modes of operation than the four modes shown in Figure 3.2.

3. The Naive Physics Approach

The naive physics approach has been designed to deal with exactly the type of situation that we are faced with here: a system that is structurally completely defined, but which contains a set of parameters (such as our parameters a, b, and c), the values of which are not totally determined.

Numerical mathematicians and quantitative simulationists always express their equations such that they can *integrate* signals rather than *differentiate* them (since the numerical properties of integration are much more benign than those of differentiation, the naive physicists traditionally prefer the differentiation operator, probably because naive physics evolved from the analytical physics, and not from the numerical physics).

We can easily transform our set of equations into the desired form, by solving for the x_i instead of the $\dot{x}_i$ variables

$$x_1 = -\frac{b}{c}\dot{x}_1 - \frac{a}{c}\dot{x}_2 - \frac{1}{c}\dot{x}_3 + \frac{1}{c}u,$$

$$x_2 = \dot{x}_1,$$

$$x_3 = \dot{x}_2,$$

$$y = x_1,$$

which can be represented through the block diagram shown in Figure 3.4. Kuipers [7] decomposes these equations into a set of primitive equations, for example, of the form

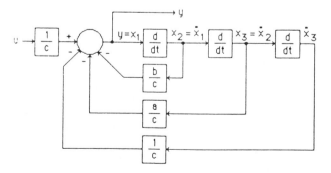

FIGURE 3.4. Block diagram using the differentiation operator.

$$H_1 = -\frac{b}{c}\dot{y},$$

$$H_2 = -\frac{a}{c}\dot{x}_2,$$

$$H_3 = -\frac{1}{c}\dot{x}_3,$$

$$H_4 = \frac{1}{c}u,$$

$$H_5 = H_1 + H_2,$$

$$H_6 = H_3 + H_4,$$

$$y = H_5 + H_6,$$

$$x_2 = \dot{y},$$

$$x_3 = \dot{x}_2.$$

At this point, we can eliminate the unknown parameters by replacing the exact first four equations by their qualitative counterparts

$$H_1 = M^-(\dot{y}),$$

$$H_2 = M^-(\dot{x}_2),$$

$$H_3 = M^-(\dot{x}_3),$$

$$H_4 = M^+(u),$$

where M^- stands for any monotonically decreasing function of the input argument and M^+ stands for any monotonically increasing function of the input argument. Using predicate logic, the nine equations can finally be represented as

$$M^-(x_2, H_1),$$

$$M^-(x_3, H_2),$$

$$M^-(\dot{x}_3, H_3),$$

$$M^+(u, H_4),$$

$$ADD(H_1, H_2, H_5),$$

$$ADD(H_3, H_4, H_6),$$

$$ADD(H_5, H_6, y),$$

$$DERIV(y, x_2),$$

$$DERIV(x_2, x_3),$$

$$DERIV(x_3, \dot{x}_3),$$

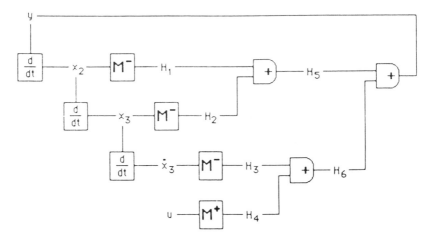

FIGURE 3.5. Kuiper's diagram.

which are ten equations (which Kuipers calls "constraints") in eleven variables (which Kuipers calls "parameters"). Kuipers [7] also uses his own form of block diagram as depicted in Figure 3.5.

4. The Constraint Propagation Approach

At this point, we are ready to perform a qualitative simulation. How this works is explained in detail in [7]. The system starts off from the initial condition (assuming that the initial condition is known) and performs one simulation step by considering all possible state transitions from the initial condition. Many (hopefully most) of these transitions will be in contradiction with one or several of the equations (constraints) and can therefore be rejected. This process of pruning is what is commonly referred to as "constraint propagation." Each state that cannot be rejected will be considered a new initial point for the next step of the simulation to be performed. If several states are possible as the outcome of one simulation step, this is considered a bifurcation point. Each branch will lead to one simulation thereafter. The simulation terminates under any of the following conditions:

1. The next system state is exactly the same as the current system state. In this case, the system has become *quiescent*.
2. The next system state is exactly the same as a previously found system state. In this case, the system has become *periodic*.
3. During the next system state, a variable becomes infinite. In this case, the system has become *divergent*.

Hopefully, there are not too many bifurcation points in the simulation since, otherwise, not much can be said about the behavior of the system.

Kuipers [7] proved that every type of behavior that is physically possible will be found by his QSIM algorithm. However, it may happen that the qualitative simulation suggests additional modes of operation that are not physically possible. This means that, without even running the example, we know for sure that QSIM will at least find four different modes of operation, namely, those that were shown in Figure 3.2.

Unfortunately, this does not tell us very much. It is almost as stating that tomorrow the weather will be the same as today, or it may change. The problem with this "simple" example is that, although it is simple from a mathematical point of view, it is not simple from a physical perspective. There are tight feedback loops in this model that create a close interaction between the various state variables, and therefore, relatively small changes in parameter values may lead to a qualitatively different pattern of overall system performance.

The "naive physics" approach works particularly well for simple physical phenomena, the basic functioning of which an untrained human observer can easily understand in qualitative terms. Feedback loops make most problems intractable for the untrained human observer and thereby defeat also the "naive physics" type of qualitative simulator.

It is this strong correlation between the types of problems that humans can analyze in qualitative terms and the types of problems that naive physics can handle that made several of the advocates of this technique proclaim that "naive physics is the way how humans go about qualitative problem solving." I personally doubt that this statement is correct and suggest that the similarity between the two types of behaviors is more of an analogy than of a homomorphism. The cause of my skepticism will be explained right away.

I have a dog who loves to play ball. I kick the ball with the side of my foot (I usually wear sandals, and a straight kick hurts my toes), and my dog runs after the ball as fast as he can. I was able to observe the following phenomenon. If I place my foot to the left of the ball, my dog will turn to the right to be able to run after the ball as soon as I hit it. He somehow *knows* that the ball will be kicked to the right. If I now change my strategy and place my foot to the right of the ball, my dog immediately swings around to be ready to run to the left. He obviously has some primitive understanding of the mechanics involved in ball kicking. However, I assure you that I never let my dog near my physics books, and thus, he had no opportunity to study Newton's laws—not even in their naive form.

I believe that my dog knows the rules of "naive physics" without knowledge of the system structure, simply as a phenomenon of *pattern recognition*. The human brain (and to some extent also the dog brain) is great at recognizing patterns that have been experienced before in a similar form. Unfortunately, our von Neumann computer architecture is very bad at reproducing this capability. It takes massive *parallel processing*, for example, in the form of a *neural network* to reproduce something faintly similar to my dog's (but not yet my own) capability of pattern recognition.

However, even if "naive physics" provides us only with an analog and not with a homomorphism to the human problem-solving approach, the technique works well when applied to the right problem. The type of problems for which the "naive physics" approach works well are characterized by the following properties:

1. The physical structure of the problem is well defined. Only some of the parameter values are incompletely known.
2. The physical structure of the problem is rather simple.
3. Subsystems are loosely coupled.
4. There are few or no feedback loops involved, and if there are feedback loops in the system, they do not dominate the system behavior.

5. An Induction-Based Approach

This time, we want to start from a completely different premise. Before, it was assumed that the structure of the system under study is known except for the numerical values of some of its parameters. This time, we want to assume that we know little to nothing about the structure of the system. The system is a "black box." All we have is a set of observations of inputs and outputs. The question now is, Can we qualitatively forecast the behavior of this system for other types on inputs for which we did not previously observe the system behavior? While the former situation could be interpreted as a *parameter estimation* problem, the latter presents itself as a *structure identification* problem.

While the goal of the previous type of qualitative simulation was to replicate the way humans reason about physical systems of which they have a basic qualitative understanding, the goal of the new type of qualitative modeling is to *learn* the behavior of an unknown system from observation. Maybe, this approach is closer to what my dog went through when he "learned" the basic properties of ball kicking.

6. Quantitative Simulation for the Purpose of Fact Gathering

Let us analyze the simple linear continuous-time single-input/multi-output system

$$\dot{\mathbf{x}} = \begin{pmatrix} 0 & 1 & 0 \\ 0 & 0 & 1 \\ -2 & -3 & -4 \end{pmatrix} \cdot \mathbf{x} + \begin{pmatrix} 0 \\ 0 \\ 1 \end{pmatrix} \cdot u,$$

$$\mathbf{y} = \begin{pmatrix} 1 & 0 & 0 \\ 0 & 1 & 0 \\ 0 & 0 & 1 \end{pmatrix} \cdot \mathbf{x} + \begin{pmatrix} 0 \\ 0 \\ 0 \end{pmatrix} \cdot u,$$

which is one particular system in the class of systems that we discussed before except for the fact that we now measure multiple outputs. The trick is that we are going to use this structure exclusively to obtain trajectory behavior using *quantitative simulation*, as if we were recording (measuring) the input/output behavior of a physical black-box system. Thereafter, we shall immediately forget all that we know about the system structure. From then on, we shall work with the recorded trajectories exclusively and see whether we can create a *qualitative model* that is able to predict the behavior of this unknown system qualitatively for an arbitrary input sequence.

We shall discretize the time axis by adequately *sampling* the three-state variables over the simulation domain. We shall then *recode* the continuous variables into a set of distinct levels using the interval mapping technique; that is, if the continuous variable is within a certain interval, it will be mapped into a discrete value. If we use, for example, five levels for a particular variable, say, a temperature reading, we can map the continuous domain of recorded temperatures into the set of integers $\{1, 2, 3, 4, 5\}$ that can be interpreted as "very cold," "cold," "moderate," "hot," and "very hot." These are what Kuipers [7] calls *landmarks*.

Selection of an adequate sampling rate and an appropriate set of landmarks is crucial to the success of the endeavor, and we shall discuss how good values for these quantities can be determined.

Thereafter, we shall discuss how we can use the recoded measurement data to come up with a qualitative model with *optimized forecasting power*.

In order to retrieve as much information from the system as possible, we decided to excite the system with a stochastic binary input signal; that is, the input is either "high" or "low," and the transitions between the two possible states are chosen at random [2].

7. The General System Problem Solving (GSPS) Framework

General System Problem Solving (GSPS) [6] is a methodological framework arising from General Systems Theory that allows the user to define and analyze types of systems problems. In this methodology, systems are defined through a hierarchically arranged set of epistemological subsystems. Forecasting and reconstruction analysis capabilities are two examples of the capabilities of the GSPS methodological tools. An on-line monitoring system can be implemented in the GSPS framework by using its inductive inference capability to imitate the human learning process.

SAPS-II [3] is software coded at the University of Arizona that implements the basic concepts of the GSPS framework. SAPS-II has been implemented as an application function library to the control systems design software CTRL-C [9]. In terms of common artificial intelligence terminology, we can say that SAPS-II employs CTRL-C as an artificial intelligence shell.

GSPS or analysis through General Systems Theory starts by defining a region in the universe where the system and the observer coexist and interact. A system in this context can be interpreted as a set of relations between some objects that belong to that region of the universe and in which the observer is interested.

Therefore, the first step to problem solving, or analysis, is the definition of the system: What is it that is of interest to us concerning the problem under study? A set of variables to represent the system has to be chosen, and this set is to be classified into *input variables* and *output variables*, which is a natural classification of the variables: Input variables depend on the environment and control the output variables.

8. The Epistemological Hierarchy

The GSPS framework is a hierarchically arranged set of epistemological subsystems. Starting at level zero, the amount of knowledge in the systems increases as we climb up the epistemological ladder. The lower level subsystems are contained in the ones that are at higher epistemological levels.

At the lowest epistemological level, we find the *source system*, which represents the system as it is recognized by the observer. The amount of information present at this level represents the basic description of the problem in which the observer is interested: which variables are relevant to the problem, what causal relationships are present among them (which are inputs and which are outputs to the system), and which are the states these variables can possibly assume along their time-history. The number of states, or levels, that each variable can potentially assume is essentially problem dependent. It should be kept as low as possible without unacceptable loss of information.

The next epistemological level in the hierarchy is represented by the *data system*. It includes the source system and, additionally, the time-history of all the variables of interest.

Yet one epistemological level higher, we find the *behavior system*, which holds, besides the knowledge inherent to both, source and data systems, a set of time-invariant relationships among the chosen variables for a given set of initial or boundary conditions. Behavior systems can be considered basic cells for yet higher epistemological levels, the so-called *structure systems*, which we shall not, however, discuss in this treatise.

The time-invariant relationships among the variables are *translation rules* mapping these variables into their common spaces. They can be used to generate new states of the variables within the time span defined in the Data Model, providing in this way an *inductive inference* capability in the methodology. Due to this characteristic, *behavior systems* are sometimes also referred to as *generative systems*.

9. The Concept of a Mask

A Data Model in the GSPS framework is an $n_{rec} \times n_{var}$ matrix, where n_{rec} is the number of recordings (data points) collected in the time span covered by the Data Model, and n_{var} is the number of variables present in the model. This is a matrix representation of the time-history of the system, and the convention is that time increases from the top to the bottom of the matrix.

A mask is a matrix representation of a translation rule for a given Data Model; hence, it is a matrix representation of a Behavior Model of the system. The dimensions of the mask are $(d + 1) \times n_{var}$, where d is the depth of the mask representing the number of sampling time units covered by the mask.

The active elements of a mask are called *sampling variables* and represent the variables that are to be considered in the translation rule associated with the time instant they occur.

Generative masks include in their structure the notion of *causality* among the variables. Elements of a generative mask are zero, negative, or positive, meaning "neutral element," "generating element," and "generated element," respectively. For example, a generative mask like

$$
\begin{array}{c}
 \\
t - 2\Delta t \\
t - \Delta t \\
t
\end{array}
\begin{pmatrix}
v_1 & v_2 & v_3 & v_4 & v_5 \\
0 & 0 & -1 & 0 & 0 \\
-2 & 0 & 0 & -3 & 0 \\
0 & -4 & 0 & 0 & +1
\end{pmatrix}
$$

corresponds to the translation rule

$$v_5(t) = f(v_3(t - 2\Delta t), v_1(t - \Delta t), v_4(t - \Delta t), v_2(t)),$$

where $v_i(\tau)$ is the state assumed by the variable v_i at time $t = \tau$. Within one set of sampling variables, for example, the inputs, the numbering sequence is immaterial. We chose to number them from the left to the right and from the top to the bottom.

10. The Sampling Interval

Note that the Behavior Model above takes samples of the Data Model at every Δtth data point to predict the state of v_5. Hence, Δt is the sampling interval t_s of the collected data set. There is not a precise way of determining the most effective sampling interval to be used, but a good rule of thumb is that the mask should cover the dynamics of the slowest mode in the model [2]. In the case of the given example, the mask has depth 2, and the sampling interval Δt should then be about half of the slowest time constant of the model. In our case, the slowest time constant was found to be approximately 3 time units. Accordingly, we select the sampling period to be 1.5 time units. Experimentation with different sampling periods verified this to be a good choice.

Notice, however, that, as outlined in [2], selection of an appropriate sampling rate is absolutely crucial to the success of our endeavor; thus, careful experimentation with this parameter is indicated under all circumstances.

11. Converting Quantitative Data into Qualitative Data

In order to be able to reason qualitatively about the behavior of our system, we need to convert the "measured" *quantitative data* (i.e., continuous variables) into *qualitative data* (i.e., variables of an enumerated type). GSPS calls this process the *recoding* of the measurement data. SAPS-II provides for various algorithms to recode *real* variables into sets of *integers*.

Due to the type of the quantitative simulation experiment, we notice that the control input u is already a binary variable and, therefore, does not require any further recoding.

The three output variables y_1, y_2, and y_3, however, are truly continuous variables, and an appropriate selection of the recoding procedure will decide over success or failure of our endeavor. The number of recoding levels to be used for each variable has, intuitively, to be odd if we want to have a "normal" range of operation and variations about it.

The choice of the appropriate number of levels (landmarks) is a somewhat problematic issue. There is always a conflict between the demands of simplicity for the purpose of a strong forecasting power, and an improved resolution for the purpose of a strong expressiveness of the model. Recoding each variable into one level only results in an infinitely "valid" model with no expressiveness whatsoever. On the other hand, recoding each variable into a high number of levels will result in a highly "expressive" model with little to no forecasting power. We decided to code each of these variables into three levels: "low," "medium," and "high."

How should the interval boundaries be chosen? It seems intuitively most appealing to request each "class" (range) to contain approximately the same number of "members" (samples). This can best be achieved by sorting each output variable separately (using the standard CTRL-C *sort*-function), thereafter split the resulting vector into three subvectors of equal size, and determine appropriate elements for the *from*-matrix used in the recoding by looking at the first and last elements of each subvector. A SAPS-II procedure implementing this algorithm was presented in [12]. However, for our simple demonstration problem, we got very good results with a much simpler algorithm, namely, by subdividing the interval between the lowest ever recorded value and the highest ever recorded value of each variable into three subintervals of equal size.

One last parameter still needs to be decided on, namely, the number of recordings that we need for our GSPS analysis. From classical statistical techniques, we know that each "class" (i.e., each possible state) should contain at least five "members" (i.e., should be recorded at least five times) [8].

Therefore, if n_{var} denotes the number of variables, and if n_{lev_i} denotes the number of levels assigned to the variable v_i after recoding, we can write down the following (optimistic) equation for the minimum necessary number of recordings (n_{rec})

$$n_{\text{rec}} = 5 \prod_{i=1}^{n_{\text{var}}} n_{\text{lev}_i};$$

that is, in our case,

$$n_{\text{rec}} = 5 * 2 * 3 * 3 * 3 = 270.$$

Thus, the number of recordings needed depends strongly on the number of levels chosen for each variable. On the other hand, if the number of available data points is given, this will decide on the maximum number of levels that each continuous variable can be recoded into. For our little demonstration problem, we got good answers with a considerably smaller number of recordings, namely, 100.

12. The Optimal Mask Analysis

Given a Data Model, any topologically compatible mask associated with it is "valid" since it denotes a representation of a relationship among the sampling variables it contains. The questions now are, "How *good* is the mask?" and "How valid is the translation rule it represents?" There are numerous possible masks that can be written for one set of variables, and it is desirable to determine among all possible masks the one that shows the least uncertainty in its generating capability, that is, the one that maximizes the forecasting power. This is exactly what the *optmask*-function of SAPS-II evaluates. The measure of uncertainty that is currently employed by this function is the Shannon entropy.

SAPS-II requests the user to specify a *mask candidate matrix* that contains the element -1 for potential generating elements (potential input), the element 0 for neutral elements (do not care variables), and $+1$ for generated elements (outputs) of the optimal mask.

In our example, the data model contains four variables, namely, the input u and the three outputs y_1, y_2, and y_3. Consequently, any valid mask must have exactly four columns, one for each variable. We want to assume the depth d of the mask to be 2, and therefore, all masks that we consider have exactly three rows.

We want to assume that concurrent states of the outputs do not affect each other, whereas the input variable may affect any of the outputs instantaneously. It seems intuitively evident that more information can be extracted from the measured trajectories if each output variable is treated independently, that is, if a separate optimal mask is generated for each of the output variables. The following set of mask candidate matrices was therefore used for the optimal mask evaluation:

$$Mcnd_1 = \begin{pmatrix} -1 & -1 & -1 & -1 \\ -1 & -1 & -1 & -1 \\ -1 & +1 & 0 & 0 \end{pmatrix},$$

$$Mcnd_2 = \begin{pmatrix} -1 & -1 & -1 & -1 \\ -1 & -1 & -1 & -1 \\ -1 & 0 & +1 & 0 \end{pmatrix},$$

$$Mcnd_3 = \begin{pmatrix} -1 & -1 & -1 & -1 \\ -1 & -1 & -1 & -1 \\ -1 & 0 & 0 & +1 \end{pmatrix}.$$

The $Mcnd_1$ matrix determines that $y_1(t)$ may be a function of up to nine different variables, namely, $u(t - 2\Delta t)$, $y_1(t - 2\Delta t)$, $y_2(t - 2\Delta t)$, $y_3(t - 2\Delta t)$, $u(t - \Delta t)$, $y_1(t - \Delta t)$, $y_2(t - \Delta t)$, $y_3(t - \Delta t)$, and finally $u(t)$. The other two mask candidate matrices can be interpreted accordingly. It is the task of the optimal mask analysis to determine which of these potential influencing variables are relevant; that is, it will identify the simplest models that allow one to forecast the behavior of the outputs in a reasonably accurate fashion from any set of given data.

The optimal mask analysis performs an exhaustive search on all masks that are structurally compatible with the mask candidate matrix. The search starts with the simplest masks, that is, with masks that contain as few nonzero elements as the mask candidate matrix permits. In our example, the simplest masks are those of *complexity two*, that is, masks that have exactly one input and one output. For each of the three mask candidate matrices, there exist exactly nine structurally compatible masks of complexity two.

Each of the possible masks is compared to the others with respect to its potential merit. The optimality of the mask is evaluated with respect to the maximization of its forecasting power. The *Shannon entropy measure* is used to determine the uncertainty associated with the forecasting of a particular output state given any feasible input state.

The Shannon entropy relative to one input is calculated from the equation

$$H_i = -\sum_{\forall o} p(o|i) \cdot \log_2(p(o|i)),$$

where $p(o|i)$ is the conditional probability of a certain output state o to occur, given that the input state i has already occurred. The term *probability* is meant in a statistical rather than in a probabilistic sense. It denotes the quotient of the observed frequency of a particular state divided by the highest possible frequency of that state.

The overall entropy of a mask is then calculated as the sum

$$H_m = \sum_{\forall i} p_i H_i,$$

where p_i is the probability of that input to occur. The highest possible entropy

H_{max} is obtained when all probabilities are equal, and a zero entropy is encountered for relationships that are totally deterministic.

A normalized overall *entropy reduction* H_r is then defined as

$$H_r = 1.0 - \frac{H_m}{H_{max}}.$$

H_r is obviously a real number in the range between 0.0 and 1.0, where higher values usually indicate an *improved forecasting power*. The *optimal mask* among a set of mask candidates is defined as the one with the highest entropy reduction.

The algorithm then proceeds to higher levels of complexity. In our example, there exist exactly 36 masks of complexity three (i.e., masks with two inputs and one output) for each of the three mask candidate matrices. These can be compared with each other for the determination of the optimal mask of complexity three. Thereafter, we can proceed to even higher degrees of complexity. In our example, the highest possible degree of complexity is 10, and there exists exactly one mask of complexity 10 for each of the three mask candidate matrices.

Masks at different complexity levels are somewhat more difficult to compare to each other. Obviously, with increasing complexity, the masks tend to give the impression of a more and more deterministic behavior. Since, with increasing mask complexity, the number of possible input states (the *possible input state set*) grows larger and larger, chances are that more and more input states in the data model are observed exactly once, which makes them look completely deterministic, whereas many other possible input states are never observed at all, a fact that does not show up in the entropy reduction measure. In the case of the ultimately complex mask, that is, a mask of depth $n_{rec} - 1$ and complexity $n_{rec} \times n_{var}$, the *observed input state set* consists of exactly one sample, whereas the *possible input state set* is extremely large. Thus, the entropy reduction measure will have a value of 1.0, and yet, the forecasting power of this mask is negligibly small.

For this reason, Uyttenhove proposed [10] the following complexity weighting factor C_m

$$C_m = \frac{n_{var} \cdot d_{act} \cdot n_{compl}}{d_{max}},$$

where n_{var} is the number of variables in the source model, d_{act} is the actual depth of the mask plus one, n_{compl} is the number of nonzero entries in the mask, and d_{max} is the maximum possible depth the mask could have (the depth of the chosen mask candidate) plus one.

For example, the complexity weighting factor of the mask

$$mask = \begin{pmatrix} 0 & 0 & 0 & 0 \\ -1 & 0 & -2 & 0 \\ -3 & 0 & 0 & 1 \end{pmatrix}$$

can be evaluated to

$$C_m = \frac{4 \times 2 \times 4}{3} = 10.667.$$

Finally, the *mask quality measure Q* is defined as

$$Q = \frac{H_r}{C_m},$$

and that is how masks of different complexity are being compared to each other. Clearly, the above formula is strictly heuristic, and we are currently experimenting with improved formulae. We now believe that what should be punished is not the complexity of a mask, but its inability to make the *observed input state set* decently represent the *possible input state set*. We therefore experiment with the following *completeness weighting factor F_c*

$$F_c = \frac{n_1 + 2 \cdot n_2 + 3 \cdot n_3 + 4 \cdot n_4 + 5 \cdot n_5}{5 \cdot n_{poss}},$$

where n_1 is the number of input states that have been observed exactly once, n_2 is the number of input states that have been observed exactly twice, n_3 is the number of input states that have been observed exactly thrice, n_4 is the number of input states that have been observed exactly four times, n_5 is the number of input states that have been observed five times or more, and n_{poss} is the possible input state set. This formula is based on the statistical rule that, in a subinterval or class analysis, each class member should be observed at least five times [8].

Using the completeness weighting factor, we redefine the *mask quality measure* as

$$Q = F_c \cdot H_r.$$

If every possible input state is observed at least five times, F_c assumes a value of 1.0.

We applied this algorithm to our example problem. By repeating the optimal mask analysis several times using different random number streams for the input, it was determined that the set of optimal masks for this problem is

$$Mask_1 = \begin{pmatrix} 0 & 0 & 0 & 0 \\ -1 & 0 & 0 & -2 \\ 0 & +1 & 0 & 0 \end{pmatrix},$$

$$Mask_2 = \begin{pmatrix} 0 & 0 & 0 & 0 \\ -1 & -2 & 0 & 0 \\ -3 & 0 & +1 & 0 \end{pmatrix},$$

$$Mask_3 = \begin{pmatrix} 0 & 0 & 0 & 0 \\ -1 & 0 & 0 & 0 \\ -2 & 0 & 0 & +1 \end{pmatrix};$$

that is,

$$y_1(t) = f_1(u(t - \Delta t), y_3(t - \Delta t)),$$
$$y_2(t) = f_2(u(t - \Delta t), y_1(t - \Delta t), u(t)),$$
$$y_3(t) = f_3(u(t - \Delta t), u(t)).$$

The details of the experiments performed to verify the validity of these optimal masks are described in [2].

13. Qualitative Inference Through Inductive Reasoning

These optimal masks can now be used to generate state-transition matrices that show the dependence of the generated elements (outputs) on the generating elements (inputs). Notice that the meaning of the words *input* and *output* is now different from before. In earlier paragraphs, these words referred to the one "input" and the three "outputs" of the physical model. Now, we talk about the "inputs" and the "outputs" of the Behavior Models. For example, the second Behavior Model has three "inputs," namely, $u(t - \Delta t)$, $y_1(t - \Delta t)$, and $u(t)$, and one "output," namely, $y_2(t)$.

Using these state-transition matrices, we can forecast the system behavior by simply looping through state transitions for any physical input sequence.

We performed the following experiment: We actually simulated the quantiative model over 200 communication intervals, that is, over a duration of 300 time units. We recoded the three continuous output variables over the entire time span. However, we thereafter used only the first 150 time units for the generation of the optimal masks. Now, we used the optimal masks found on the basis of the first 150 time units to qualitatively predict (forecast) the behavior of the system over the next 15 time units (corresponding to 10 steps) using the same input sequence as for the quantitative simulation. The following matrices compare the "measured" (i.e., quantitatively simulated) time-history to the "predicted" (i.e., qualitatively simulated) time-history:

$$
Meas = \begin{bmatrix}
1 & 2 & 1 & 1 \\
1 & 2 & 1 & 1 \\
0 & 2 & 0 & 0 \\
1 & 1 & 0 & 2 \\
0 & 1 & 1 & 0 \\
1 & 1 & 1 & 2 \\
1 & 1 & 2 & 1 \\
0 & 2 & 1 & 0 \\
1 & 1 & 0 & 2 \\
1 & 1 & 2 & 1 \\
1 & 2 & 2 & 1
\end{bmatrix},
\quad
Pred = \begin{bmatrix}
1 & 2 & 1 & 1 \\
1 & 2 & 1 & 1 \\
0 & 2 & 0 & 0 \\
1 & 1 & 0 & 2 \\
0 & 1 & 1 & 0 \\
1 & 1 & 1 & 2 \\
1 & 1 & 2 & 1 \\
0 & 2 & 1 & 0 \\
1 & 1 & 0 & 2 \\
1 & 1 & 2 & 1 \\
1 & 2 & 2 & 1
\end{bmatrix}.
$$

These two matrices contain excerpts of the data model. As before, the four columns represent the input u and the three outputs y_1, y_2, and y_3. The rows are recordings of these variables at various instances of time: $t = [150, 151.5, 153, \ldots, 173.5, 175]$. The *Meas* matrix contains the (recoded) data found during the quantitative simulation, while the *Pred* matrix contains the forecast outputs using qualitative simulation given the same past history and the same input data stream as in the quantitative case.

As can be seen, there was not a single forecasting error in this sequence. We repeated the experiment for other input sequences and found that, on the average, the forecasting would exhibit about two incorrect entries per 10 time steps, that is, the probability of correct forecasting of a value was roughly 28 out of 30, or 93%. The details of these experiments can be found in [2].

These results encouraged us to try our methodology on a much more involved system, namely, a B747 airplane in high-altitude horizontal flight. The results of that analysis were presented in [11] and [12].

14. Discussion of Results

Similar to the discussion of the "naive physics" approach, we want to analyze the conditions that must be satisfied for the "inductive reasoning" approach to be successful. Here are our findings:

1. Contrary to the naive physics approach, inductive reasoning can operate on systems, the structure of which is not completely known.
2. Inductive reasoning therefore works well in application areas, such as biomedical or social systems, where the physical laws have not been well established.
3. Contrary to the naive physics approach, with inductive reasoning, it is difficult to improve the results by incorporating more a priori knowledge of the system structure. This is one of the major drawbacks of the sheer generality of the technique.
4. Similar to the naive physics approach, also inductive reasoning mimics the way how humans (and dogs) think about the behavior of physical systems. However, while the naive physics approach tries to utilize preconceived knowledge about basic principles of operation of a physical system, inductive reasoning mimics the process of learning by observation.
5. Inductive reasoning works well for quite complex systems.
6. Feedback loops do not pose any difficulty. On the contrary, the more tightly coupled a system is, the better will be the results that we expect from the inductive reasoning process.

15. Conclusions

In this chapter we have discussed several quite different approaches to qualitative modeling and simulation. In particular, the approaches of "naive physics" and of "inductive reasoning" were discussed in more detail. It was found that all of these techniques have their particular virtues and shortcomings. The techniques presented in this chapter are not really in competition with each other. On the contrary, they complement each other rather well. It would seem worthwhile to study properties of neural networks as an alternative to the inductive reasoning approach to qualitative modeling. To our knowledge, this has not yet been tried.

References

1. Blalock, J.M., Jr. *Causal Inferences in Nonexperimental Research.* The University of North Carolina Press, Chapel Hill, N.C., 1964.
2. Cellier, F.E. Qualitative simulation of technical systems using the general system problem solving framework. *Int. J. Gen. Syst.* 13, 4 (1987), 333–344.
3. Cellier, F.E., and Yandell, D.W. SAPS-II: A new implementation of the systems approach problem solver. *Int. J. Gen. Syst.* 13, 4 (1987), 307–322.
4. Forbus, K.D. Qualitative process theory. *Artif. Intell.* 24 (1984), 85–168.
5. de Kleer, J., and Brown, J.S. A qualitative physics based on confluences. *Artif. Intell.* 24 (1984), 7–83.
6. Klir, G.J. *Architecture of Systems Problem Solving* Plenum Press, New York, 1985.
7. Kuipers, B.J. Qualitative simulation. *Artif. Intell.* 29 (1986), 289–338.
8. Law, A.M., and Kelton, W.D. *Simulation Modeling and Analysis.* McGraw Hill, New York, 1982.
9. Systems Control Technology. *CTRL-C, A Language for the Computer-Aided Design of Multivariable Control Systems, User's Guide.* Systems Control Technology, Palo Alto, Calif., 1984.
10. Uyttenhove, H.J. SAPS—System Approach Problem Solver. Ph.D. dissertation (G.J. Klir, Adv.), SUNY Binghampton, 1979.
11. Vesanterä, P.J. Qualitative Flight Simulation: A Tool for Global Decision Making. M.S. thesis, Dept. of Electrical and Computer Engineering, Univ. of Arizona, Tucson, Ariz., 1988.
12. Vesanterä, P.J., and Cellier, F.E. Building intelligence into an autopilot—Using qualitative simulation to support global decision making. *Simulation* 52, 3 (1989), 111–121.
13. Zadeh, L.A. Syllogistic reasoning in fuzzy logic and its application to usuality and reasoning with dispositions. *IEEE Trans. Syst., Man, Cybern.* SMC-15, 6 (1985), 754–763.
14. Zadeh, L.A. Test-score semantics as a basis for a computational approach to the representation of meaning. *Literary Linguistic Comput.* 1, 1 (1986), 24–35.
15. Zadeh, L.A. A simple view of the Dempster–Shafer theory of evidence and its implication for the rule of combination. *The AI Mag.* (Summer 1986), 85–90.
16. Zadeh, L.A. A computational theory of disposition. *Int. J. Intell. Syst.* 2 (1987), 39–63.

CHAPTER 4

A Qualitative Approach to Causal Modeling

Richard Scheines, Peter Spirtes, and Clark Glymour

Abstract

Linear causal models are often constructed to explain statistical data in domains in which experiments cannot be performed. We can distinguish two types of causal models. A *quantitative* linear causal model can be represented by a set of simultaneous linear equations, distributional assumptions about the independent variables, and a graph that represents the causal connections between variables. A *qualitative* causal model contains only the graph that represents the causal connections between variables. Great progress has been made in recent years in finding the correct quantitative causal model, given sample covariance matrices and the *correct* qualitative causal model. However, relatively little work has been done on finding the correct qualitative causal model from statistical data and background knowledge. Recently, several programs (including LISREL VI and EQS) have added a feature that uses numerical algorithms on an initially specified *quantitative* model to search for better qualitative and quantitative models. In contrast, we have developed a program, TETRAD II, that searches for and evaluates alternative *qualitative causal models* with fast graph algorithms that entirely bypass parameter estimation. We discuss the two approaches to model search and compare their reliability with a simulation study of 360 data sets generated from nine different linear causal models. We also discuss how our methods can be used to do more than search for modifications of an initial model. We show how TETRAD II can construct initial models from just covariance data and background knowledge.

1. Introduction

In many domains it is not possible to perform experiments, either because of practical or ethical considerations. Astrophysicists cannot perform experiments on the formation of galaxies or on the birth of the universe for obvious

The research reported in this paper was supported by the Office of Naval Research under Contract N00014-89-J-1964.

practical reasons. Social scientists cannot subject randomly chosen groups of children to a life of poverty for obvious ethical reasons. Nonetheless, as astrophysics shows, it is still possible to do science without experiments.

When experiments cannot be performed, statistical data can often be obtained. The problem that we address here is how the causal structure of linear models can be inferred from such data. Our examples are all taken from the social sciences, but our techniques are applicable in any domain where the structures of linear causal models are to be inferred from nonexperimental or quasi-experimental data.

The class of linear models that we consider here are called *linear causal models* or *structural equation models*. This class includes as special cases regression models, path analytic models, and factor analytic models. Although their linearity assumptions are rarely exactly satisfied in actual research, the computational tractability of this class of models makes them very useful for modeling a wide variety of processes. Such models are used in psychology, sociology, epidemiology, political science, biology, engineering, and educational research. A *quantitative linear causal model* is a set of jointly distributed random variables over some probability space, a set of linear equations among the random variables, the joint distribution of the independent variables, and the causal connections between the variables. The causal connections are typically represented by putting the equations into a canonical form in which an effect is expressed as a linear function of its *direct* causes. They may also be represented by a graph in which there is an edge from A to B if and only if A is an immediate cause of B. The graph alone specifies a *qualitative linear causal model*. The graph encodes the *causal structure* of the full quantitative model; that is, it encodes both the causal relations and assumptions of statistical independence implicit in the full quantitative model. The graph does *not* encode the particular numerical values of the linear coefficients, the variances of the independent variables, or the joint distribution family (e.g., multinormal).

Recently, maximum likelihood techniques for estimating the variance of multinormally distributed variables and the coefficients of the linear equations of a quantitative causal model have been implemented in such programs as LISREL and EQS. The input to these models is a sample size, a covariance matrix, initial estimates of the variances of the independent variables, initial estimates of the linear coefficients, and a qualitative causal model.[1] The accuracy of the parameter estimates depends crucially on the accuracy of the qualitative model. Different initial qualitative causal models can lead to very different estimates of both the signs and the magnitudes of the linear coefficients. For this reason, techniques such as regression and factor analysis that in effect impose stringent a priori restrictions on what qualitative causal models can be considered are often very misleading.

---

[1] This initial qualitative model is specified by fixing the linear coefficient for A in the equation for B at zero iff A is not a direct cause of B. The coefficients of the linear equations not fixed at zero are called free parameters.

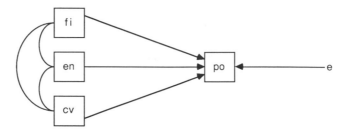

FIGURE 4.1. Timberlake and William's Regression Model.

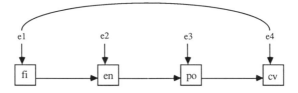

FIGURE 4.2. Our alternative.

For example, Figures 4.1 and 4.2 depict two different causal structures among the same set of variables. Both of these models were constructed to examine the influence of foreign capital investment on the level of political repression in third-world countries. They involve four measured variables: the level of foreign capital investment received (*fi*), the level of economic development as measured by the log of the energy consumed per capita (*en*), an index of the *lack* of civil liberties (*cv*), and an index of the level of political repression (*po*). The first model (Figure 4.1), is a regression model in which *e* is an error term and curves connecting pairs of independent variables represent unexplained correlations.

Estimating the regression coefficients and other free parameters in Figure 4.1, M. Timberlake and K. Williams find that the connection between *fi* to *po* is positive and significantly different than zero; thus, they conclude that foreign capital investment causes higher levels of political repression in peripheral countries [20].

By using techniques based on the principles we describe below, we can construct a series of alternative causal structures, one of which is shown in Figure 4.2. When this causal structure is estimated, the effect of foreign investment on economic development is positive and significant; thus, it asserts that more foreign money causes more economic development. The effect of economic development on political repression is *negative* and significant; thus, economic development inhibits political repression. In this model, therefore, more foreign investment causes *less* political repression. With the same variables, the same data, but a different causal structure, we arrive at a conclusion completely opposed to the one Timberlake and Williams endorse.

Given this, it is unfortunate that less attention is given to the problem of constructing qualitative causal models than to constructing quantitative causal models out of qualitative causal models, that is, to parameter estimation. Researchers typically construct qualitative causal models by using background knowledge, preliminary data analysis, previously relevant work, and anything else that helps to arrive at a candidate for testing. The model's free parameters are then estimated, and the resulting quantitative model is subjected to a statistical test. Because there are typically astronomical numbers of alternative qualitative structures, many of which do about equally well on the usual statistical tests, this process is often of dubious reliability. We cannot avoid the worry that somewhere in those trillions of models lie a few that are better on statistical grounds *and* that are as plausible as the selected model.

Recently two computer programs, LISREL and EQS, have introduced numerical techniques for improving the qualitative model part of an initial user-specified quantitative model. In contrast, the TETRAD II program improves an initial user-specified *qualitative causal model* without ever constructing quantitative causal models.[2] This enables the program to avoid many liabilities of numerical estimation techniques.

In this chapter we briefly describe these two alternative approaches to finding qualitative causal models and their merits, and present the results of a systematic Monte Carlo study that compares the reliability of algorithms based on the two approaches.

2. Quantitative Causal Models: The Received View

A causal model applies to a specified population of arbitrary units, usually limited in scope. The population may be made up of countries, counties, people on welfare, children under the age of 10, steelworkers, rivers, bridges, or any other objects worthy of study. We measure the value of certain properties of each unit (e.g., a person's score on an SAT test) for as many units in the population as is feasible, and we usually express these data in terms of their statistical properties (e.g., means, variances, and covariances). Since we cannot measure each unit in a population, we use sample data to estimate the population values of these statistics. A causal model is used, in part, to explain the variances of the measured variables and the covariances between pairs of measured variables.

2.1. Structural Equation Models

A quantitative causal model, as it is traditionally conceived (see [1]–[3], [5], [6], [12], and [13], consists of two parts: a system of linear equations among

---

[2] TETRAD is distributed by Academic Press [9]. TETRAD II is currently under development and will be available soon.

$$v = a\,T + e_1$$
$$w = b\,T + f\,v + g\,y + e_2$$
$$x = c\,T + e_3$$
$$y = d\,T + e_4$$
$$z = e\,T + e_5$$

FIGURE 4.3. Structural equations.

a set of jointly distributed random variables, and a set of statistical assumptions. The linear equations are expressed in a canonical form called "structural equations" in which one variable is set equal to a linear combination of all of its *direct* causes. For example, the set of structural equations shown in Figure 4.3 might be given to depict the relations between T, v, w, x, y, and z. In this example, the variables v to z are measured for each unit in the population, but T is a "latent construct" that is not directly measurable. All variables are usually expressed as deviations from their means and can be standardized by dividing by their respective standard deviations. The linear coefficients a, b, c, d, e, f, and g are constants unknown before the data are collected. Each structural equation includes a unique unmeasured random variable e_i, called the *disturbance term*. It is usually assumed that all variables are from a population that is jointly multinormal and that no variance is zero.

Given these assumptions, the model can be parameterized by a vector θ that includes the nonzero linear coefficients and the variance/covariance matrix for the exogenous variables. A variable is *exogenous* just in case it is a cause and not an effect. All disturbance terms are exogenous.

A full, or estimated, model—that is, one with particular values for every element in θ—can be used to calculate a predicted covariance matrix. In maximum likelihood estimations procedures, the discrepancy between the predicted covariance matrix and the observed covariance matrix is measured with the fitting function

$$F = \log|\Sigma| + tr(S\,\Sigma^{-1}) - \log|S| - t,$$

where S is the sample covariance matrix, Σ is the predicted covariance matrix, t is the total number of measured variables, and if A is a square matrix, then $|A|$ is the determinant of A and $tr(A)$ is the trace of A. The parameters that minimize the fitting function F also maximize the likelihood of the covariance matrix.

2.1.1. Causal Structure

Quantitative causal models contain an implicit causal structure that serves to fix the structural equations. Since equations are symmetric but causality is not, structural equation models impose an additional set of statistical assumptions that induce the desired asymmetry. The right side of each structural equation is just a sum in which each term is by convention a direct cause of the left side of the equation, or the effect (see Figure 4.3). The asymmetry is induced by assuming that, for each x consisting of a nondisturbance term from the right-hand side of the equation and for each equation's disturbance term y, x and y are statistically independent.[3]

2.2. Parameter Estimation

LISREL VI [13] is the most recent version in a series of computer programs that, among other things, calculate maximum likelihood estimates of the free parameters in θ. LISREL VI requires initial values for the free parameters in θ, giving it θ^1. It then carries out an iterative procedure that generates successively new vectors θ^i, such that $F_{\theta i} > F_{\theta i+1}$, until convergence is obtained. The method gives standard errors for each parameter estimate, provided that the parameter is identifiable.

Parameter estimation has a variety of well-known problems:

—Perfectly plausible causal structures might not be *identifiable*; that is, some or all of the parameters cannot be estimated uniquely.
—Some of the estimation techniques assume that all the variables in a model are jointly distributed multinormally. Small deviations from this assumption can create serious problems.
—The numerical techniques employed to perform the estimation essentially maximize a likelihood function. There is no guarantee that the maximum returned is a global maximum and not a local one.
—The researcher must supply starting values for the free parameters, and these can affect the outcome of the estimation procedure.
—The computational demands of the iterative numerical procedures involved in parameter estimation are severe.

2.3. Model Evaluation

Having estimated the parameters in a causal model M, we can assess its quality with a χ^2 goodness of fit test. The goodness-of-fit measure $G = (N - 1) * F_{min}$, where N is the sample size and F_{min} is the minimum value of F obtained by the estimation procedure. G is distributed asymptotically as χ^2 with degrees of freedom $= \frac{1}{2}k(k + 1) - t$, where k is the number of observed variables and t is the number of parameters in θ. Knowing this we can calculate the probability of observing a G as large or larger than we did, given that M describes the population from which the data were randomly sampled.

The χ^2 test can be used as a classical statistical hypothesis test. The null hypothesis is that M describes the population; we reject it if the p value is below some critical level, usually .05. This is problematic for a number of reasons. If the sample size is too small, the test is too weak; that is, false models will not be rejected. If the sample size is too large, the test is too strong; that is, approximately true models will be rejected. In large samples, the test will

---

[3] For a more detailed discussion of causal asymmetry in structural equation models, see [18].

reject a model if the data are not perfectly multinormal, are not perfectly linear, etc. Real data are never perfectly multinormal and are never generated by a purely linear process. Furthermore, accepting a model that passes the test does not take into account the fact that alternatives might exist that fare even better on the same test and that are as plausible as M.

2.4. Search Strategies

The LISREL and EQS programs have recently added the capacity to search automatically for a class of alternatives to an initial model.

One could express the structural equations of a model M that has k variables as a $k \times k$ matrix in which the ith row was the structural equation for the variable v_i. The coefficient for a direct cause v_j of v_i is placed in the cell that has i as row and j as column. In this representation all exogenous variables have a row of zeros. In a previous section, we parameterized a family of models by a vector that included only the nonzero linear coefficients. One could parameterize the family by including the entire matrix along with the specification that some parameters, especially all the zeros, are fixed. One could then characterize alternative families of models, or alternative causal structures, by specifying which fixed parameters are to be freed, by specifying which free parameters are to be fixed, or by some combination of the two. In fact, LISREL VI does exactly the former in its search for alternative quantitative causal models.

The input to the LISREL VI search procedure is a starting model specifying the values of the fixed parameters, starting values for the free parameters, a sample covariance matrix, a list of those parameters that are not to be freed under any circumstance, and a significance level. The search is guided by "modification indexes,"[4] which are defined and described as follows:

> For each fixed and constrained parameter the modification index is defined as $(N/2)$ times the ratio between the squared first-order derivative and the second-order derivative. It can be shown that this index equals the expected decrease in χ^2 if a single constraint is relaxed and all estimated parameters are held fixed at their estimated value. ([13], p. I. 42)

LISREL VI calculates the modification indexes for all of the fixed parameters[5] in the starting model. The fixed parameter with the largest modification index is freed, and the model is reestimated. If the difference in the chi-squares of the starting model and the elaborated model is significant, the parameter is freed, the elaborated model is now the starting model, and the process is repeated. When freeing the fixed parameter with the highest modification index does not result in a model with a chi-square significantly different from the starting model, the parameter is not freed and the search ends.

---

[4] LISREL outputs a number of other measures that could be used to suggest modifications to a starting model, but these are not used in the automatic search. See [4].

[5] As long as they are not in the list of parameters not to be freed.

3. The Qualitative Approach to Causal Models

The qualitative approach to causal models is based on representing the causal model as a directed graph. In such a graph, there is a directed arrow from A to B iff A is a direct cause of B. The causal graph alone implies constraints on the population covariance matrix. TETRAD II, which is a program that embodies the qualitative approach, evaluates models by estimating how well the constraints implied by the qualitative causal model match the constraints that actually hold in the population.

3.1. The Directed Graph Representation

A directed graph G is just a set of vertices V and a binary relation E imposed on V. This relation may be represented by a set of ordered pairs. In the pictures we use to represent directed graphs, an arrow (a directed edge) identifies the two members of an ordered pair and specifies their order. For example, suppose the following set of ordered pairs represents our directed graph:

$$\{\langle T, v\rangle, \langle T, w\rangle, \langle T, x\rangle, \langle T, y\rangle, \langle T, z\rangle, \langle v, w\rangle, \langle y, w\rangle\}.$$

The picture that corresponds to this set is shown in Figure 4.4.

In the equation representation of quantitative causal models, each dependent variable is a linear function of its immediate causes. Since there is an edge from A to B iff A is an immediate cause of B, we can label the edge from A to B by the coefficient of A in the linear equation for B. The label of a path or trek is simply the product of the labels of edges in the path or trek. The label of an empty path is by convention set to 1.

Using these conventions, we can simply read the structural equations in a quantitative causal model from a labeled directed graph. Figure 4.5 illustrates this point.

We will now define several important graph-theoretic concepts that will allow us to use the directed graph of causal relations alone to determine important statistical features of a causal model.

A *path from x to y* is a sequence of vertices $\langle x, v_1, \ldots, v_n, y\rangle$ beginning with

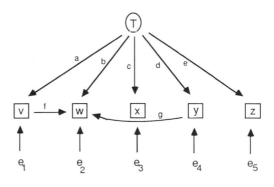

FIGURE 4.4. Ordered pairs as a directed graph.

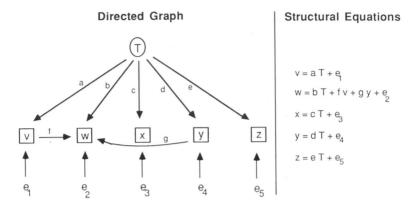

FIGURE 4.5. Structural equations from a directed graph.

x and ending with y such that each adjacent pair of vertices in the sequence is in E. A path with just one vertex in it is called an *empty path*. The length of a path is just one less than the number of vertices in the sequence. For example, in Figure 4.5; the path of length 2 from T to w is $\langle T, v, w \rangle$.

Interpreting a path in causal language is straightforward. If there is a path from x to y of length 1, then x is a direct cause of y. If there is a path of length greater than 1 from x to y, then x is an indirect cause of y. We could also say that if there is a path of length greater than 1 from x to y, then there is a path of causal influence from x to y.

We assume that the sources of covariance between variables A and B are causal chains from A to B, causal chains from B to A, or causal chains from some third variable C to A and B. These sources of covariance are represented by treks. A *trek* between two distinct variables x and y is a pair of acyclic paths from a common source w to x and y, respectively, that intersect only in w. w is called the *source of the trek*. For example, in Figure 4.5, the trek between v and x is $\langle\!\langle T, v \rangle, \langle T, x \rangle\!\rangle$. There are two treks between v and w. They are $\langle\!\langle T, v \rangle, \langle T, w \rangle\!\rangle$ and $\langle\!\langle v \rangle, \langle v, w \rangle\!\rangle$. Note that the trek $\langle\!\langle v \rangle, \langle v, w \rangle\!\rangle$ corresponds to a causal chain directly from v to w. We assume that if no treks connect x and y then the covariance of x with y is zero.

The covariance between any two variables x and y can be expressed in terms of the treks between the variables. Let T_{xy} be the set of all treks between x and y, $S(t)$ be the source of trek t, $L(t)$ be the product of labels of all edges in t, γ_{xy} be the covariance between x and y, and σ_x^2 be the variance of x. Then,[6]

$$\gamma_{xy} = \sum_{t \in T_{ij}} L(t)\sigma^2_{S(t)}.$$

For example, γ_{vw} equals $ab\sigma_T^2 + f\sigma_v^2$.

---

[6] This theorem in a different notation is proved in [11].

3.2. Constraints Implied by the Directed Graph

One fact that is crucial to the operation of TETRAD II is that the qualitative causal model alone can imply constraints on the population covariance matrix.

The first kind of constraint that we examine is called a vanishing tetrad difference. For any four distinct variables, there are three possible vanishing tetrad differences, any two of which are independent. For x, y, z, and w they are

$$\gamma_{wx}\gamma_{yz} - \gamma_{wy}\gamma_{xz} = 0,$$

$$\gamma_{wy}\gamma_{xz} - \gamma_{wz}\gamma_{xy} = 0,$$

$$\gamma_{wx}\gamma_{yz} - \gamma_{wz}\gamma_{xy} = 0.$$

The model in Figure 4.5 implies the following four equations:

$$\gamma_{vw} = ab\sigma_T^2 + dag\sigma_T^2 + fa^2\sigma_T^2 + f\sigma_{e1}^2,$$

$$\gamma_{xy} = cd\sigma_T^2,$$

$$\gamma_{wy} = bd\sigma_T^2 + daf\sigma_T^2 + gd^2\sigma_T^2 + g\sigma_{e4}^2,$$

$$\gamma_{vx} = ac\sigma_T^2.$$

Thus, the tetrad difference $\gamma_{vw}\gamma_{xy} - \gamma_{wy}\gamma_{vx} = fcd\sigma_T^2\sigma_{e1}^2 - acg\sigma_T^2\sigma_{e4}^2$.

This tetrad difference might or might not be equal to zero, depending on the values of the model's free parameters. For example, if $f = d = \sigma_{e1}^2 = a = g = \sigma_{e4}^2 = 1$, then the difference will be equal to zero. On the other hand, if $f = d = \sigma_{e1}^2 = g = \sigma_{e4}^2 = 1$, but $a = \frac{1}{2}$, then the difference will not be equal to zero. (We assume that all variances are not equal to zero.)

Now consider the tetrad difference $\gamma_{vx}\gamma_{yz} - \gamma_{vy}\gamma_{xz}$:

$$\gamma_{vx} = ac\sigma_T^2,$$

$$\gamma_{yz} = de\sigma_T^2,$$

$$\gamma_{vy} = ad\sigma_T^2,$$

$$\gamma_{xz} = ce\sigma_T^2.$$

In this case,

$$\gamma_{vx}\gamma_{yz} - \gamma_{vy}\gamma_{xz} = (ac)(de)\sigma_T^4 - (ad)(ce)\sigma_T^4 = 0$$

regardless of the values of a, c, d, e, or σ_T^4. When a tetrad difference is constrained to vanish for all values of the linear coefficients and for all variances of the independent variables in model M, we say that the constraint is *strongly implied by M*.

The set of tetrad differences that are strongly implied to vanish is geometrically determined by the unlabeled causal directed graph, that is, by the qualitative causal model. The following theorem states that the set of tetrad differences that are strongly implied to vanish by a model is determined by the intersections of the treks in the model. Let $i(t_{ij})$ be the (possibly empty) path from the source of trek t_{ij} to i, and similarly for $j(t_{ij})$.

THEOREM. $\gamma_{ij}\gamma_{kl} - \gamma_{il}\gamma_{jk} = 0$ is strongly implied by model M iff for every t_{ij} in T_{ij} and every t_{kl} in T_{kl}

—$i(t_{ij}) \cap k(t_{kl})$ or
—$j(t_{ij}) \cap l(t_{kl})$,

and for every t_{il} in T_{il} and every t_{jk} in T_{jk}

—$i(t_{il}) \cap k(t_{jk})$ or
—$j(t_{jk}) \cap l(t_{il})$.

A similar geometrical condition allows us to determine when a partial correlation constraint $\rho_{ij.k} = 0$ is strongly implied by a model M. The algorithm for calculating the set of partial correlations strongly implied by a model and the proof of its correctness for any graph is presented in [9, chap. 10]. The same chapter presents a slightly different algorithm than the one presented here for calculating the set of vanishing tetrad differences strongly implied by an acyclic model and proves its correctness.

3.3. Determining Empirical Constraints

Wishart [22] discovered a formula for the sampling variance of tetrad differences. Using this sampling variance and the assumption that the sampling distribution of tetrad differences is normal, we can calculate the probability of drawing a sample of size n that has a tetrad difference as large or larger than the observed tetrad difference, under the hypothesis that the tetrad difference is zero in the population.[7] If the probability is greater than a user-determined cutoff, the vanishing tetrad difference is judged to hold in the population.

Similarly, the well-known z transformation allows us to test statistically the hypothesis that a partial correlations is zero in the population.

3.4. Evaluating Different Qualitative Models

We base our evaluation of qualitative models on three principles.

Falsification Principle: Other things being equal, prefer a model that does not strongly imply constraints that are judged not to hold in the population to one that does.

Explanatory Principle: Other things being equal, prefer a model that does strongly imply constraints that are judged to hold in the population to one that does not.

Simplicity Principle: Other things being equal, prefer simpler models to more complex models.

Note that a model that does not strongly imply a vanishing tetrad difference judged to hold in the population for all values of its labels may imply that

---

[7] We know that the sampling distribution of tetrad differences is not normal, but the approximation is reasonable in large sample sizes.

vanishing tetrad difference for particular values of its labels. We believe, however, that implying any pattern in the data for all values of the labels is superior to implying it only for particular values. The history of science shows that a standard criterion for comparing theories is their explanatory power, and also shows that explanation by theoretical structure is superior to explanation by particular values of free parameters (see [7] to [9] and [18]).

We refer to the scoring function used by TETRAD II as the T-score. The principles described in the previous section are implemented in the T-score, which depends on two parameters, the significance level and the weight (explained below). For each possible vanishing tetrad difference, t, we calculate the probability of obtaining a tetrad difference as large or larger than the one actually observed, under the assumption that the difference is zero in the population and that the tetrad differences are normally distributed: We call this the associated probability of t and denote it by $p(t)$. For a given significance level, if $p(t)$ is larger than the significance level, we say that the vanishing tetrad difference holds in the population; otherwise, we say that the vanishing tetrad difference does not hold in the population. Let $Implied_H$ be the set of vanishing tetrads implied by a given model M that hold in the population, let $Implied_{\sim H}$ be the set of vanishing tetrads implied by M that do not hold in the population, let T be the score of model M for a given significance level, and let $weight$ be a parameter (whose significance is explained below). Then we define

$$T = \sum_{t \in Implied_H} p(t) - \sum_{t \in Implied_{\sim H}} (weight * (1 - p(t))). \tag{1}$$

The first term implements the Explanatory Principle; it gives credit for explaining vanishing residuals that hold in the population. The second term implements the Falsification Principle; it penalizes a model for predicting vanishing residuals that do not hold in the population. The Simplicity Principle is implemented by preferring, among models with identical T-scores, those that have more degrees of freedom.

The weight decides conflicts between the Explanatory Principle and the Falsification Principle. It determines the relative importance of explanation versus residual reduction. The lower the weight, the more important explanation is relative to residual reduction. Since a submodel explains at least as many vanishing tetrad residuals as any model containing it, lowering the weight tends to favor models with fewer edges.

3.5. Qualitative Search Strategies

We now turn to the task of *searching* for good models.[8]

TETRAD II takes as input a sample size, a covariance matrix, and an initial qualitative model. It outputs a set of qualitative models that are elaborations

---

[8] The search strategy described here is a slight improvement on that actually used in the Monte Carlo simulation tests described below.

of the initial causal model and that better explain certain properties of the covariance matrix.

One search strategy is obvious. Test every possible causal arrangement, and pick the set of models that do the best on these two principles. This strategy is hopeless for even simple models, however. If we consider *all* of the possibilities, then for each pair of variables A and B, there are four possible kinds of connection: A can have an effect on B but not B on A; B can have an effect on A but not A on B; A and B can each have an effect on the other, or, finally, A and B can each have no direct effect on the other. The number of distinct possible causal arrangements of n variables is therefore 4 raised to the power of the number of pairs of variables. Thus, with only six variables, there are 4^{15} different possible directed graphs or causal models. When we have it in our power to experiment, we are able to arrange circumstances so as to exclude most of these possibilities. But without experimental control, the problem of determining the correct causal structure is far more difficult. If there are twelve variables in the data set, with no restrictions imposed, there are 4^{66} alternative causal models, only one of which can be true. If the researcher knows that there are no cyclic paths in the true model, the number of alternatives is still astronomical: 521,939,651,343,829,405,020,504,063 (see [10]). If the researcher is lucky enough to be able to order the variables totally and knows that later variables cannot cause earlier variables, the number of alternatives is reduced to 2^{66}.

A better way to search a large space is to find some treelike search that takes advantage of the inheritance properties of the class of objects under study. For example, suppose we are trying to insert a name into its proper place in an already alphabetized list. We could simply start at the beginning and keep trying until we hit the right spot. In that case we would expect to try half the cards, on average. Alternatively, we could start at the middle card and ask if the card to be inserted is closer to the end or the beginning of the list than is the middle card. If it is closer to the beginning, we can eliminate every card after the middle one, because our goal card will be closer to the beginning than all of them as well. Thus, one comparison effectively cuts our search in half. With this kind of search, we can expect to perform only 2 log(number of cards) on average.

Linear causal models represented as directed graphs have just such an inheritance property.

THEOREM. *If G is a subgraph of G', then the set of tetrad equations among variables of G that are also implied by G' is a subset of those implied by G.*[9]

In other words, by adding edges, and hence treks, to a graph, we may defeat the implication of tetrad equations, but we may never cause more tetrad equations to be implied by the model that results.

This theorem enables us to define a useful quantity called *T-maxscore* in

---

[9] This is proved in [9, chap. 10].

the following way:

$$T\text{-}maxscore = \sum_{t \in Implied_H} p(t). \tag{2}$$

T-maxscore(M) is the maximum *T*-score that any elaboration of *M* could possibly receive. The *T*-score of an elaboration of *M'* of *M* equals *T-maxscore(M)* just when *M'* implies all of the vanishing tetrad differences that *M* does that are judged to hold in the population, but implies no vanishing tetrad differences that are not judged to hold in the population.

We illustrate the search that TETRAD II uses in a very simple case. Suppose that we are looking for the best elaboration of a model *M* and that there are only four possible edges, *e*1, *e*2, *e*3, and *e*4 that could be added to *M*. The top half of Figure 4.6 illustrates a full search in which no candidates could be eliminated. Each node corresponds to the model that is obtained by adding its edge to its parent. We generate the first level of nodes (2, 10, 14, and 16) by considering all elaborations of node 1, the initial model, and then ordering these nodes left to right by their *T*-maxscore. We then explore the subtree that represents all elaborations of the most promising, or leftmost, node. The numbers on the nodes correspond to the order in which we explore their subtrees. Notice that in the level of nodes that are elaborations of node 2 (3, 7, and 9) edge *e*4 is ordered ahead of edge *e*3, whereas the reverse is true on level 1. This illustrates the interactive effect edge additions often exhibit.

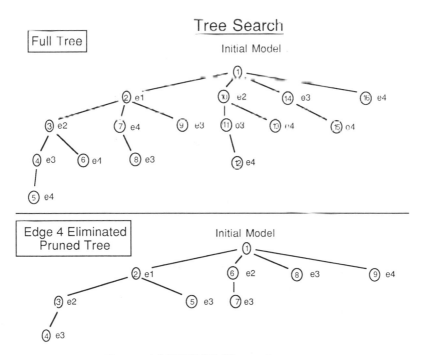

FIGURE 4.6. TETRAD II's search strategy.

Whereas the model that results from adding edge 3 to the initial model is superior to the one that adds edge 4, once edge 1 is added to the initial model the order reverses.

If we assume that

—M is a submodel of the true model,

—the T-scores and T-maxscores are calculated from the population covariances (instead of the sample covariances that we are actually given), and

—every vanishing tetrad difference that holds in the population holds because of the causal structure of the true model, and not because of the particular parameter values of the true model,

then many models can be safely eliminated from consideration without ever actually generating them. The bottom half of Figure 4.6 illustrates this point. If, on level 1, T-$Maxscore(e4)$ is less than T-$maxscore$(Initial Model M) we can eliminate all nodes in which $e4$ occurs without ever visiting them. This is because under the given assumptions any vanishing tetrad difference that holds in the population is strongly implied by the true model and, hence, also strongly implied by M. T-$maxscore(e4)$ can be less than the T-$maxscore(M)$ only if $M + e4$ fails to imply some vanishing tetrad difference X that holds in the population. By the previous theorem, no model that contains $M + e4$ implies X, which is implied by the true model. Hence, all of the nodes that represent models that contain $M + e4$ can be safely eliminated from consideration without ever generating them. The tree that results has 9 nodes instead of 16.

Of course, we must calculate T-maxscore and T-score on the basis of a sample covariance matrix, not a population covariance matrix, and we do not know that every vanishing tetrad difference that is judged to hold in the population actually does hold in the population or that it holds in the population because of the causal structure of the true model. Hence, in actual practice we allow the T-maxscore of a model to decrease slightly from its parents T-maxscore before we cut off the search. However, as the sample sizes increase, the probability approaches 1 that the sample covariance matrix is very close to the population covariance matrix.

In some cases, the search described here is too slow to be practical.[10] In those cases, either more background knowledge must be added to eliminate some branches of search, or further risks must be taken in eliminating unlikely, but possibly correct models.

4. Simulation Studies

The essential questions about any search procedure concern its reliability in the circumstances in which it is meant to be applied. The documents describing the TETRAD II and LISREL programs provide any number of applications

---

[10] This was not the case with any of the models described in our Monte Carlo simulation tests, provided that we constrained the search by allowing it to ignore all cyclic models.

of their respective procedures to empirical data sets. Unfortunately, such applications are of little use in judging the *reliability* of the procedures. The reason is obvious: In empirical cases we do not know what the true model is, so we cannot judge whether the procedures have found it. We can judge whether the procedures turn up something that is not absurd, and we can judge whether the procedures find models that pass statistical tests, but neither of these features is of central importance. What is of central importance is whether or not the automated model revision procedures find the truth. Empirical tests can sometimes be obtained of models produced by the automatic searches, and they may provide some evidence of the reliability of the procedures. In general, however, such tests have rarely been obtained, and they cannot be relied on since one does not know whether the initial model given to the program is empirically correct. It is possible to do mathematical analyses of the power of a discovery procedure to distinguish or identify alternative structures in the limit, as the sample size grows without bound. Some results of this kind pertinent to TETRAD's methods are implicit in [9], and we have subsequently proved a number of other limiting properties of the TETRAD's procedures. Limit results do not, however, address the behavior of automated discovery procedures on samples of realistic sizes, and it is that which ought most to concern empirical researchers.

The best solution available is to apply Monte Carlo methods to assess the reliability of model respecification procedures. Using a random number generator, data for a specified sample size can be generated from a known structural equation model. Part of the model used to generate the data is then given to the procedures, and we see with what reliability the procedures can recover information about the missing parts of the models used to generate the data. In this way, the reliability of the procedures can be tested in nearly ideal circumstances: The true structural equation model is known, the sampling is random, and distribution assumptions are satisfied to a good approximation. The manuals documenting the LISREL programs contain no tests of their model respecification procedures on simulated data. Three such tests are reported in *Discovering Causal Structure*.

4.1. Selection of Generating Models

The nine causal structures we studied are illustrated in Figures 4.8 to 4.10. (For simplicity of depiction, we have omitted uncorrelated error terms in the figures, but such terms were included in the linear models.) The heavier directed or undirected lines in each figure represent relationships that were included in the model used to generate simulated data, but were omitted from the models given as starting points to the two programs; that is, they represent the dependencies that the programs were to attempt to recover. The starting models are shown in Figure 4.7.

The models studied include a model with five measured variables and one latent factor, seven models each with eight measured variables and two latent variables, and one model with three latent variables and eight measured variables.

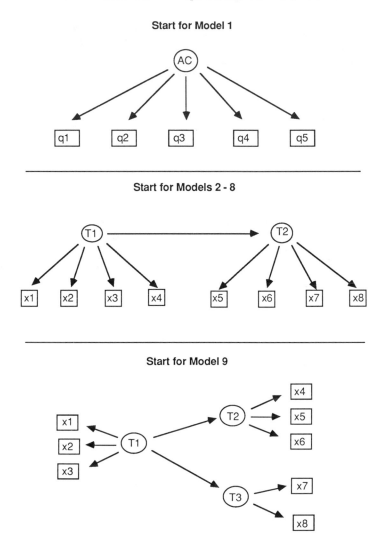

FIGURE 4.7. The starting models.

One-factor models commonly arise in psychometric and personality studies (see [14]); two-latent factor models are common in longitudinal studies in which the same measures are taken at different times (see [16]), and also arise in psychometric studies; the triangular arrangement of latent variables is a typical geometry (see [21]).

4.2. Selection of Coefficients

The linear coefficients for these models were chosen randomly from two equiprobable intervals of uniform density, one between .5 and 2.5 and the

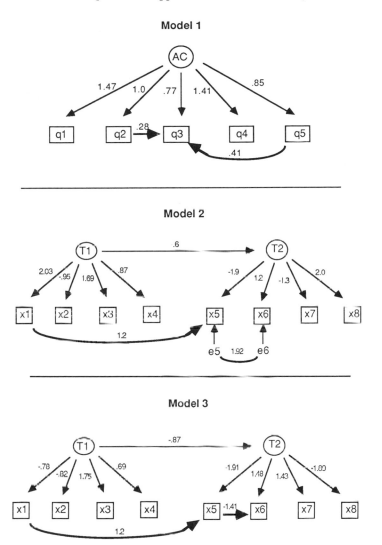

FIGURE 4.8. True Models 1 to 3.

other between -2.5 and $-.5$. We avoided the range between $-.5$ and $.5$ because parameters close to zero are insignificant and, contrary to the model's supposition, correspond to the nonexistence of edges. Given the scale of our intervals, we were practically assured that no parameter would be insignificant in the population model. It is important to choose parameters randomly, because as we have argued extensively, explanation by particular choices of parameters is inferior to explanation by causal structure. In some cases, however, the model that generates the data will happen to imply constraints in virtue of the coefficients and not in virtue of the causal structure. The

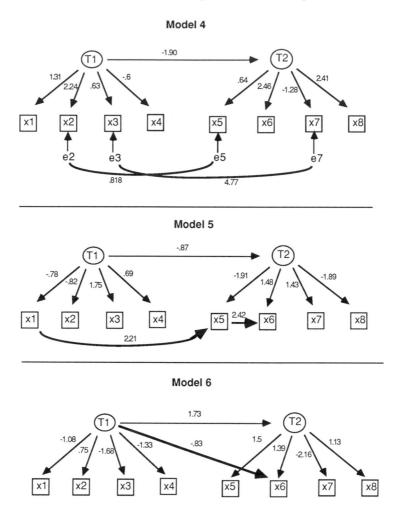

FIGURE 4.9. True Models 4 to 6.

relevant question is how *often* does nature deceive us in this way. Were we to choose parameters nonrandomly, we would have implicitly chosen an answer to this question already.

We purposely chose approximately half of our parameters to be negative. In many cases in social research, the signs of the causal connections are not known; in some they are the focus of the inquiry. As we discussed earlier, parameter estimation is sensitive to the starting values one assigns.

Our technique, since it is focused on the causal structure and not the numerical properties of a model, is utterly immune from this problem. Whether parameters are negative or positive has no effect on whether or not a model implies vanishing tetrad differences. In an auxiliary study, we gave

Model 7

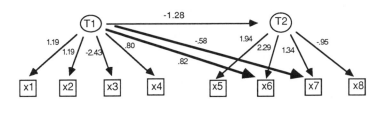

Model 8

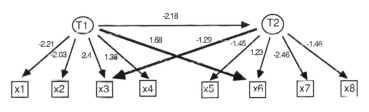

Model 9

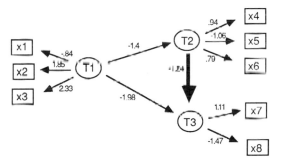

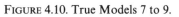

FIGURE 4.10. True Models 7 to 9.

LISREL the correct starting values for a series of runs and then starting values that were all positive. In approximately one third of the latter cases, LISREL's iterative estimation procedure could not converge from the incorrect starting values. LISREL almost always converged when it started with a submodel that had the correct parameter values. TETRAD II does not require any starting values, so its behavior was unaffected by negative coefficients.

4.3. Selection of Starting Models

Only three starting models were used in the nine cases (see Figure 4.7). The starting models are, in causal modeling terms, pure factor models or pure multiple indicator models. In graph theoretic terms, they are *trees*. In every empirical case we have read in which sample data are used to elaborate an initial latent variable model, the initial model is of this kind.

4.4. Generation of Data

For each of nine cases, 20 data sets with $n = 200$ and 20 data sets with $n = 2,000$ were obtained by first generating values for each of the exogenous variables[11] (including error variables) with a random-number generator giving a standard normal distribution,[12] then calculating the value of each of these variables' immediate effects, and continuing to propagate values through the system until all variables had values for a single case. This process was repeated for the n cases in a single data set. Finally, variances and covariances were calculated from the raw data, and these were input to the programs.

4.5. Implementation

The LISREL VI runs in the primary study were performed with the personal computer version of the program, run on a Compaq 386 computer. This machine is many times faster than IBM AT machines. All TETRAD II runs were performed on Sun 3/50 workstations. TETRAD II, when given the same problem on a Sun 3/50 workstation and a Compaq 386, took about the same amount of time to run.

4.6. Results

For each data set and initial model, TETRAD II produces a set of alternative elaborations that are tied for the highest *T*-score. In some cases, that set

---

[11] An exogenous variable is "outside" the system; that is, it is a cause but not an effect.

[12] First, a number was pseudorandomly selected from a uniform distribution by calling the "random" system call on the UNIX operating system. Then this number was input to a function that turned it into a pseudorandom sample from a standard normal distribution.

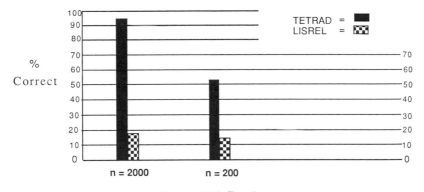

FIGURE 4.11 Results.

consists of a single model; typically, it consists of two or three alternatives. LISREL VI produces as output a single elaboration of the initial model. The information provided by each program is scored "correct" when the output contains the true model.[13]

For large sample sizes, TETRAD II was able to identify the correct elaboration in 95% of the cases, whereas LISREL VI was able to do so 18.8% of the time (Figure 4.11). For small sample sizes, TETRAD II corrected the misspecification 52.2% of the time, whereas LISREL VI corrected the misspecification 15% of the time. For either sample size, were we to have randomly chosen one of TETRAD II's suggestions, we would have chosen the correct model more often than LISREL VI.

Some of the comparatively poor performance of LISREL VI can be traced to its search strategy. When several alternative models have the same or virtually the same (e.g., differing by round-off error) modification indexes, LISREL VI picks one of them by no principle we can find documented.[14] All of the other alternatives are discarded, and the program proceeds to look for further modifications to the one selected best alternative. This *beam search* strategy produces many errors for obvious reasons. The TETRAD II performance would be better approximated by LISREL VI if, when several models with virtually identical maximal scores are found, their searches were to branch and the program were to report all of the alternatives found. A branching search is computationally costly however and would, of course, require at least an order of magnitude more time.

---

[13] We have devised an elaborate classification for cases in which the programs were not correct; for example, LISREL's model was in TETRAD II's set of best suggestions, but we neglect to go into it here. See [19].

[14] The PC and mainframe versions of LISREL VI will in some cases make different choices given the same data and initial model.

5. Constructing Models from Scratch

In the class of cases we tested, TETRAD II's search reliably identifies a set of models that contains the correct elaboration of an initial causal structure. In our simulation studies, unlike empirical research, the initial causal structure input to TETRAD is invariably a submodel of the causal model that generated the data. Since the program will not remove edges from the model it is given, its overall success depends crucially on being given an initial model that satisfies this condition. Because of this we, encourage empirical researchers to perform the widest possible search for plausible initial models. The combinatorics of this search problem are prohibitive, however (see Section 3.5).

To help empirical researchers perform a more systematic and thorough search for plausible causal models, we have used many of the same principles we describe above in order to program TETRAD II to search for initial models that it can then elaborate.

The strategy we implement is currently limited to producing initial models that are among a class called *multiple factor models*. A "factor" in such a model is a theoretical construct that is the cause of or is caused by several "indicators," which are simply measured variables. All the measured variables are causally adjacent to at least one factor in such models, although there can be additional causal structure. We show a one factor model in Figure 4.12. The theoretical factor AC is interpreted as a person's disposition toward authority, and it is taken to cause the way that person answers the five interview questions represented by q1 to q5.[15]

We currently consider only models in this class because they alone imply tetrad constraints, but no partial correlation constraints, among the measured variables. Thus, by examining the data we can determine if the initial models should be of this class. If so, we use a divide-and-conquer strategy to identify a set of simple factor models, each of which can be elaborated by TETRAD

---

[15] This factor model occurs in a study described in [9], [14], and [17].

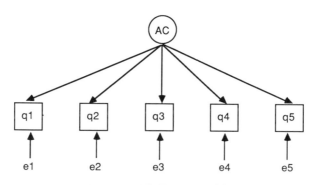

FIGURE 4.12. Factor model.

II. In both of two initial Monte Carlo simulation tests, the program identified a set of initial structures that included the correct one, and then found a set of elaborations of these initial models that included the model that generated the data.

We tested the program's ability to search for initial models on an empirical case as well. Consider data from a longitudinal study of the performances of 799 schoolgirls on the Scholastic Aptitude Test. The same cohort of students took the test in the fifth, seventh, ninth, and eleventh grades (see [15]).

We judged, from the sample data, that one tetrad equation holds in the population but that no partial correlations vanish. Thus, according to our simple heuristic, an adequate linear model for this data will include a latent variable. If, for example, we instead attempt to model the data by supposing that each measurement is a direct cause of the succeeding measurement (e.g., Figure 4.13), then the model implies the correct tetrad equation, and no other vanishing tetrad differences; but it also implies several vanishing partial correlations, for example, that q5 and q11 vanish when partialed on q9.

To locate factor models that would not imply any vanishing partial correlations, we set TETRAD II's initial model builder loose, and it returned 12 different multiple factor models. We then eliminated a number of initial models on substantive grounds. Finally, we input into the elaborator the initial models that we thought most plausible, as well as a set of substantive constraints upon the search. (E.g., no variable could cause another variable that was measured earlier.) In this way we not only found the model suggested in Joreskog [15] (see Figure 4.14), we also found several alternative plausible models that perform as well on standard statistical tests.

We are currently improving the interface to allow easier and more flexible entry of domain knowledge to constrain the searches performed by the elaborator and the initial model builder, we are also improving the initial model builder in order to extract more information from the statistical data.

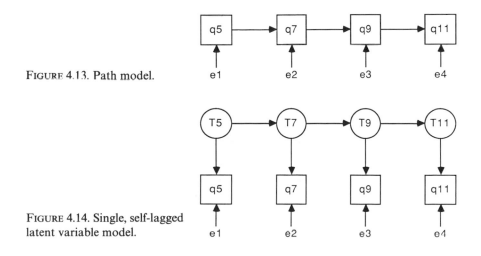

FIGURE 4.13. Path model.

FIGURE 4.14. Single, self-lagged latent variable model.

6. Conclusion

TETRAD II is a program that searches for qualitative causal models without ever constructing a quantitative causal model by estimating parameters. The fundamental concept underlying TETRAD II's evaluation of qualitative models is that explanation of covariance matrix constraints judged to hold in the population that hold for all values of the free parameters of a model are superior to explanations that hold only for particular values. Put in another way, explanations based on qualitative features of a causal model (the causal structure) are superior to explanations based on quantitative features of a causal model (the actual magnitudes of the free parameters). In the quantitative approach taken by LISREL and EQS, this distinction is not made.

The advantages of the qualitative approach to model evaluation taken by TETRAD II are that

—it does not require any initial parameter estimates,
—it never fails to converge and never converges to local maxima, and
—preliminary tests indicate that it is robust over nonnormal distributions.

The advantages of the quantitative approach to model evaluation taken by LISREL and EQS are that

—it provides estimates of parameter sizes as well as evaluations of causal structures; and
—since it uses more information about the covariance matrix than does does TETRAD II, there are instances in which TETRAD II considers a model quite promising even though LISREL can correctly detect that it is quite unlikely to be true.

Overall, the advantages of the quantitative approach to model evaluation are significant enough that, if evaluating a few models that approximately fit the assumptions made by LISREL were the only task facing a researcher, the quantitative approach should be used. However, if the task is to *search* through a large number of models or to implicitly evaluate a large number of models, there are several key advantages to the qualitative approach to model search:

—Evaluation of models is very fast.
—Most of the computational work that goes into evaluating a model M can also be used for evaluating any elaborations of M.
—The properties that elaborations of model M inherit from M allow many branches of search to be cut off without any explicit evaluation.
—Monte Carlo simulation tests indicate that the techniques used by TETRAD II for evaluating the promise of a branch of search are more reliable than the techniques used by LISREL and EQS.

All of these features of the qualitative search allow TETRAD II to explore many more promising models than either LISREL and EQS. This, in turn, contributes to the greater reliability of TETRAD II.

References

1. Bagozzi, R.P. *Causal Models In Marketing.* Wiley, New York, 1980.
2. Bentler, P. *Theory and Implementation of EQS: A Structural Equations Program.* BMDP Statistical Software, Inc., Los Angeles, Calif. 1985.
3. Blalock, H.M., Ed. *Causal Models in the Social Sciences.* Aldine Publishing Co., New York, 1971.
4. Costner, H., and Herting, J. Respecification in multiple indicator models. In *Causal Models in the Social Sciences: 2nd Edition*, H. Blalock, Ed. Aldine Publishing Co., New York, 1985, pp. 321–393.
5. Duncan, O. *Introduction to Structural Equation Models.* Academic Press, New York, 1975.
6. Fox, J. *Linear Statistical Models and Related Methods.* Wiley, New York, 1984.
7. Glymour, C. Social science and social physics. *Behav. Sci. 28* (1983).
8. Glymour, C. Explanation and realism. In *Realism.* J. Leplin, University of California Press, 1985.
9. Glymour, C., Scheines, R., Spirtes, P., and Kelly, K. *Discovering Causal Structure.* Academic Press, San Diego, Calif. 1987.
10. Harary, F., and Palmer, E. *Graphical Enumeration.* Academic Press, New York, 1973.
11. Heise, D. *Causal Analysis.* Wiley, New York, 1975.
12. James, L., Mulaik, S., and Brett, J. *Causal Analysis. Assumptions, Models and Data* Sage Publications, Beverley Hills, Calif., 1982.
13. Joreskog, K., and Sorbom, D. *LISREL VI User's Guide.* 3rd ed. Scientific Software, Inc., Mooresville, Indiana, 1984.
14. Kohn, M. *Class and Conformity.* Dorsey Press, Homewood, Ill., 1969.
15. Magidson, J., Ed. *Advances In Factor Analysis and Structural Equation Models.* Abt Books, Cambridge, Mass., 1979.
16. McPherson, J.M., Welch, S., and Clark, C. The stability and reliability of political efficacy: Using path analysis to test alternative models. *Am. Political Sci. Rev. 71* (1977), 509–521.
17. Miller, J., Slomczynski, K., and Schoenberg, R. Assessing comparability of measurement in cross-national research: Authoritarian-Conservatism in different sociocultural setting. *Soc. Psychol. Qu. 44* (1981), 178–191.
18. Scheines, R. Causal models in social science. Ph.D. thesis, Dept. of History and Philosophy of Science, Univ. of Pittsburgh, 1987.
19. Spirtes, P., Scheines, R., and Glymour, C. Simulation studies of the reliability of computer aided specification using the TETRAD, EQS, and LISREL programs. *Sociological Meth. Res.* To be published.
20. Timberlake, M., and Williams, K.R. Dependence, political exclusion, and government repression: Some cross-national evidence. *Am. Sociological Rev. 49* (1984), 141–146.
21. Wheaton, B., Muthen, B., Alwin, D., and Summers, G. Assessing reliability and stability in panel models. In *Sociological Methodology 1977*, D. Heise, Ed. Jossey-Bass, San Francisco, Calif., 1977, pp. 84–136.
22. Wishart, J. Sampling errors in the theory of two factors. *British J. Psychol. 19* (1928–1929), 180–187.

CHAPTER 5

Causal Ordering Analysis

Yumi Iwasaki

Abstract

For a long time, the formal treatment of the foundations of science avoided notions of causation and spoke only of functional relations among variables. Nevertheless, even when a formal description of a phenomenon is given in terms of acausal, mathematical relations, statements of the form, "*A* causes *B*" are exceedingly common in informal descriptions. There is little doubt that the notion of causality plays an important role in human understanding of real-world phenomena. If a computer program that reasons about behavior is to be able to give intuitive, causal explanations to humans, it is necessary for it to understand the notion of causality and to be able to reason causally.

Knowledge of causal dependency relations among variables is also essential in a number of practical problems, such as diagnosis, design, and prediction. When one is given a model represented as a set of equations and is told that one of the variables has an abnormal value, it is not a trivial task to determine what other variables can be responsible for the abnormality, what additional variables should be affected, and what observations are only spuriously correlated. The difficulty grows quickly as the number of variables and equations involved in the model increases. It is the purpose of this chapter to describe a computational mechanism to infer such causal relations in a model stated in an acausal language of mathematical equations.

1. Introduction

A set of simultaneous equations is often used to describe the behavior of a physical system in terms of functional relations. For example, let s be a binary variable indicating the position of the power switch on an iron that is plugged into a house circuit (1 if ON, O otherwise), and i a binary variable indicating whether or not a current is flowing in the circuit. The functional relations

This research was sponsored by the Defense Advanced Research Projects Agency (DOD), ARPA Order No. 4976, under Contract F33615-87-C-1499.

between s and i can be expressed as

$$s = i.$$

Now, if l is a binary variable indicating whether the pilot lamp on the iron is lit (1 if LIT, O otherwise), the relation between l and i can be expressed as

$$l = i.$$

Although the functional relations expressed in these two equations are identical in form, we would not treat them symmetrically if we were to express them in a causal language. We would ordinarily say "the position of the switch (on or off) causes the current to flow or halt," but not "the pilot light being on or off causes the current to flow or to stop." While the equations are wholly symmetric and could be commuted without changing their mathematical content, the causal statements are asymmetric and could not be commuted without a change in their meaning. To say, "the current's flowing or interruption causes the switch to be on or off" would mean something quite different from "the position of the switch causes the current to flow or halt." Nevertheless, it is true mathematically that the value of the variable l, if known, determines the value of the variable i, and the value of the variable i determines the value of s.

Hence, we see that the causal relation is directed, whereas the functional relation is not.[1] If we wished to express the causal relation that is implicit in the two equations given above, we would need to use an asymmetric notation such as

$$s \rightarrow i \rightarrow l.$$

It is our belief that the notion of causality is context-dependent in the sense that the direction of causal relations is determined not only from the knowledge of the model of the system itself but also from its surrounding circumstances. For example, consider the ideal gas law

$$PV = nRT.$$

By itself, this equation simply expresses a functional relation between the quantities. However, if we know in one situation that the volume is held constant while the pressure is manipulated by some external means, we will give the law the causal interpretation: "A change in the pressure will cause a change in the temperature." However, in another situation where the temperature is the directly manipulated variable, we will give the same law a different causal interpretation: "A change in the temperature will cause a change in the pressure."

There have been many artificial intelligence programs built that perform causal reasoning [1, 2, 7, 9]. However, most of them do not infer causal relations, but they reason with prespecified causal knowledge in the knowl-

---

[1] This same asymmetry of the causal relation shows that it cannot be interpreted as truth-functional.

edge base given in the form of specific causal interpretations.[2] If we have a means to take into account knowledge about the circumstances surrounding a model in order to infer causal relations, the information in the knowledge base can be stated in a more general form of acausal functional relations. Such knowledge has much broader range of applicability than specific causal knowledge because it can be interpreted to produce different causal interpretations depending on the situation.

The remainder of this chapter presents a computational approach, based on the theory of *causal ordering*, for determining causal relations in a mathematical model [3, 4, 10]. The foundations of our formulation have already been laid in a substantial literature that grew, some thirty years ago, out of concerns with the causal relation in the field of econometrics.[3] Our approach is based on the formal (syntactic) definition of the causal relation employed in that literature. In Section 2 we present the formal definition of causal ordering in an equilibrium model of a system. In Section 3 we present the definition in a dynamic model. In Section 4 we extend these definitions to a model consisting of a mixture of dynamic and equilibrium equations and discuss the relationship of such mixed models to dynamic models as abstraction of the latter. Section 6 summarizes the ideas in this chapter.

2. Causal Ordering in an Equilibrium System

The theory of causal ordering provides a technique for inferring the causal relations among variables in a set of functional relations. Causal ordering is an asymmetric relation among the variables in a self-contained structure, which seems to reflect people's intuitive notion of causal dependency relations among variables in a system. Establishing a causal ordering involves finding subsets of variables whose values can be computed independently of the remaining variables, and using those values to reduce the structure to a smaller set of equations containing only the remaining variables. The approach offers a computational mechanism for defining causal dependency relations in a set of equations.

Causal ordering was initially defined by Simon for a self-contained, equilibrium structure of equations [10]. First, let us define an equilibrium structure:

Definition 1. A *self-contained equilibrium structure* is a system of n equilibrium equations in n variables that possesses the following special properties:[4]

---

[2] One notable exception is the ENVISION program by de Kleer and Brown [6].

[3] The formal basis for the concepts of causality we will explicate here is developed by Simon [10], (reprinted as Chapters 2.1 and 2.2 in [11]). See also Chapters 2.3 and 2.4 in the latter volume.

[4] This definition of a self-contained structure is slightly more general than the initial definition given by Simon. In addition to the properties included here, the initial definition required the equations to be linear. However, we removed this condition because it plays no role in determining causal ordering.

1. That in any subset of k equations taken from the structure at least k different variables appear with nonzero coefficients in one or more of the equations of the subset.
2. That in any subset of k equations in which $m \geq k$ variables appear with nonzero coefficients, if the values of any $(m - k)$ variables are chosen arbitrarily, then the equations can be solved for unique values of the remaining k variables.

Condition (1) above ensures that no part of the structure is overdetermined. Condition (2) ensures that the equations are not mutually dependent, because if they are the equations cannot be solved for unique values of the variables.

The idea of causal ordering in a self-contained equilibrium structure can be described roughly as follows: Given a self-contained equilibrium structure, S, if there is a proper subset, s, of S that is also self-contained and that does not contain a proper self-contained subset, s is called a minimal complete subset. Let S_0 be the union of all such minimal complete subsets of S; then, S_0 is called the set of minimal complete subsets of zero order. Since S_0 is self-contained, the values of all the variables in S_0 can, in general, be obtained by solving the equations in S_0. By substituting these values for all the occurrences of these variables in the equations of the set $(S - S_0)$, one obtains a new self-contained structure, which is called the *derived structure of first order*. Let S_1 be the set of minimal complete subsets of this derived structure. It is called the set of complete subsets of first order. Repeat the above procedure until the derived structure of the highest order contains no proper subset that is self-contained. For each equation e_i in S, the variable that was eliminated from the structure last is said to be *directly causally dependent* on all the other variables in the equation.

Let us illustrate the above procedure with an example.

Example 2.1. Causal ordering in an evaporator. An evaporator is the component of a refrigerator in which the refrigerant evaporates, absorbing heat from the air in the refrigerator chamber. Figure 5.1 shows an evaporator. Liquid refrigerant flows through an expansion valve from the receiver into the evaporator. When it goes through the valve, it starts to vaporize because of the sudden pressure drop, which causes the refrigerant's boiling temperature to fall below its current temperature. At first, vaporization takes place without any heat flowing from the chamber into the refrigerant, because thermal

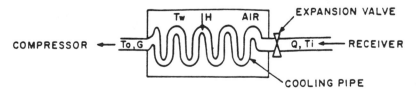

FIGURE 5.1. Evaporator.

energy in the liquid supplies the requisite latent heat to convert it into vapor, resulting in a sharp decrease in the temperature of the liquid refrigerant.

The refrigerant temperature continues to drop sharply until it becomes equal to the temperature, T_w, of the air within the refrigerator. It continues to decrease, but more slowly, because T_w's now being higher than the refrigerant temperature causes heat to start flowing into the refrigerant from the air in the refrigerator chamber. Eventually, the refrigerant temperature falls to the condensing temperature at the ambient pressure and stabilizes, but the refrigerant continues to boil, the latent heat now being entirely supplied by the heat absorbed through the cooling-pipe wall from the refrigerator chamber.

The refrigerant that passes through the expansion valve is in liquid phase. The refrigerant that leaves the chamber is at the condensing temperature and is vapor, liquid, or a mixture of both. In terms of equations, the process just described can be symbolized thus:

Variables

Q	Refrigerant flow rate (mass/second)
T_i, T_o	Temperatures of incoming and outgoing refrigerant
G	Ratio of vapor to the total mass of outgoing refrigerant
H	Heat gained by the refrigerant
P	Pressure of refrigerant within the cooling-pipe
T_c	Condensing temperature of the refrigerant
T_w	Temperature of air in refrigerator chamber

Constants

s	Specific heat of the refrigerant in liquid phase
l	Latent heat of the refrigerant
k	Heat conduction coefficient of the cooling pipe wall

Equations

$$H = k\,(T_w - T_c) \tag{1}$$

The rate of heat transfer between the air in the chamber and the refrigerant is proportional to the temperature difference.

$$H = GQl - (T_i - T_o)Qs \tag{2}$$

Conservation of energy. The energy in the outgoing fluid ($GQl + T_oQs$) is the sum of the heat absorbed (H) and the energy of the incoming fluid (T_iQs).

$$T_c = f_2(P) \tag{3}$$

The condensing temperature is a monotonically increasing function, f_2, of the pressure.

$$T_o = T_c \tag{4}$$

The output temperature of the refrigerant is equal to the condensing temperature.

Equations (1) to (4) do not comprise a self-contained structure, because there are only four equations in eight variables. We will add four more equations, in order to make it self-contained.

$$T_i = c_1 \tag{5}$$

$$Q = c_2 \tag{6}$$

$$P = c_3 \tag{7}$$

$$T_w = c_4 \tag{8}$$

These equations represent the assumptions that the variables, T_i, Q, P, and T_w, are determined solely by factors that lie outside the system under consideration. We will have more to say about these assumptions later in Section 2.1.1.

The whole structure with the addition of the new equations is shown in Table 5.1. The rows represent equations, and the columns, variables. A 1 appears in the jth column of the ith row of the table if and only if the jth variable appears in the ith equation with a nonzero coefficient.

Each one of eqs. (5) to (8) above, involving only a single variable, is a minimal complete subset. Together, they constitute the minimal complete subsets of zero order. By substituting the values, c_1 through c_4 for I_w, Q, T_i, and P in equations (1) to (4), the derived structure of the first order, shown in Table 5.2, is obtained. The only minimal complete subset of the derived structure is the singleton set $\{3\}$, which is the complete subset of first order. By repeating the above procedure, the derived structures of second and third order are obtained, which are shown in Tables 5.3 and 5.4.

Figure 5.2 shows the causal structure as a directed graph that is produced by this process. In the graph, there is an edge from variable v_i to v_j if and only if v_j is directly causally dependent on variable v_i according to Definition 1. For instance, in eq. (2), since G was eliminated from the structure after all the other variables in the equation, G is directly causally dependent on H, Q, T_i, and T_o.

TABLE 5.1. Self-contained structure of equations for the evaporator.

Equation	H	G	Q	T_i	T_o	T_w	T_c	P
(1)	1					1	1	
(2)	1	1	1	1	1			
(3)							1	1
(4)					1		1	
(5)				1				
(6)			1					
(7)								1
(8)						1		

Minimal complete subsets of zero order: $\{5\}$, $\{6\}$, $\{7\}$, $\{8\}$
Variables in the minimal complete subsets: T_i, Q, P, T_w

Yumi Iwasaki

TABLE 5.2. Derived structure of first
order for the evaporator.

Equation	H	G	T_o	T_c
(1)	1			1
(2)	1	1	1	
(3)				1
(4)			1	1

Complete subsets of first order: {3}
Variables in the complete subsets: T_c

TABLE 5.3. Derived structure
of second order for the
evaporator.

Equation	H	G	T_o
(1)	1		
(2)	1	1	1
(4)			1

Minimal complete subsets of second
order: {1}, {4}
Variables in the minimal complete
subset: H, T_o

TABLE 5.4. Derived structure of
third order for the evaporator.

Equation	G
(2)	1

Minimal complete subsets: {2}
Variables in the minimal complete
subset: G

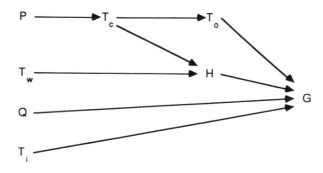

FIGURE 5.2. Causal ordering in the evaporator.

The causal structure shown in **Figure 5.2** can be interpreted in English as follows:

> The condensing temperature depends on the pressure (eq. (3)), and the output temperature depends on the condensing temperature (Equation (4)). The amount of heat absorbed is determined by the condensing temperature and the temperature of the air in the refrigerator. The percentage of vapor in the outgoing refrigerant depends on the condensing temperature, heat absorbed, flow rate, and input temperature (eq. (2)). The pressure inside the evaporator, the flow rate of the refrigerant, the input temperature, and the temperature in the chamber are determined exogenously, that is, independently of the operation of the evaporator itself.

2.1. Modeling

The procedure presented above for determining causal dependency relations in a set of equations is a purely syntactic one. In order for this syntactic procedure to produce a causal structure that actually reflects our intuitive understanding of the causal relations in a real situation, each equation in a model must come from understanding of a conceptually distinct mechanism in the situation. Since this is crucial to the causal ordering theory, let us discuss this point further in this section.

Equations comprising a model come from the understanding of mechanisms. The term *mechanism* is used here in a general sense to refer to distinct conceptual parts in terms of whose functions the working of the whole system is to be explained. Mechanisms include such things as laws describing physical processes and local components operating according to such laws.

Each equation in a structure should stand for one such mechanism, through which variables influence other variables. Individual mechanisms refer to conceptually distinct parts of the total system, though these parts may or may not be physically separate. For each mechanism there must be an equation in the structure. Describing a system in terms of the mechanisms that determine the values of its individual variables is fundamental to causal analysis. Equations describing such mechanisms are called *structural equations* in economic literature, a term we use throughout this chapter. The requirement that the model must be comprised of structural equations is fundamental to causal ordering analysis.

In the example of the evaporator presented in the previous section, eqs. (1) to (4) are structural equations, because each represents a specific mechanism for determining the value of a particular variable. Equation (1) corresponds to the law governing heat conduction and determines the rate of heat flow into the evaporator. Equation (2) conserves the total energy by determining what fraction of the refrigerant is vaporized. Equation (3) determines the condensing temperature of the refrigerant, which is a function of its pressure. Equation (4) determines the outgoing temperature, which is the same as the internal (condensing) temperature, corresponding to the function of the local component, the cooling pipe, which is constructed so that the incoming refrigerant evaporates and its temperature reaches the condensing temperature as it flows through the evaporator.

If we combine the eqs. (1) and (2), representing physical laws governing heat conduction and conservation of energy in this case, we obtain the following equation:

$$k(T_w - T_c) = GQl - (T_i - T_o)Qs. \tag{9}$$

Equation (9) is mathematically equivalent to eqs. (1) and (2), simply eliminating the variable H between them, but it is not a structural equation because it merges and confuses two distinct mechanisms. However, if our understanding of thermodynamics were such that conduction of heat and conservation of energy were considered to be inseparable phenomena governed by one physical law, eq. (9) would be a structural equation.

Another example of a nonstructural equation is an equation representing a purely incidental mathematical relation without any underlying causal mechanism. For instance, consider an electrical circuit with two resistors in series. If resistance r_1 of one resistor is equal to 0.1 ohm and resistance r_2 of the other happens to be 0.2 ohm, the equation

$$r_1 = 2r_2$$

describes the situation correctly. However, unless there is some special mechanism that somehow controls the resistance of one resistor depending on the other, and unless this control mechanism is considered to be part of the system being modeled, the above equation is not a structural equation.

The idea of the correspondence between structural equations on one hand and components or laws on the other is this: If a component is replaced or begins to operate in a defective fashion, or if the situation is altered so that its behavior is now governed by a different law, then the corresponding structural equation must be altered to reflect the change in mechanism. Specific equations are localized to individual mechanisms, whereas they are not if we combine structural equations algebraically; for combination destroys the one-to-one correspondence between equations and mechanisms, though it does not alter the solution of the entire system of equations.

This characterization of structural equations does not tell us how we know that an equation is structural, instead of representing some mélange of mechanisms. There is no simple formal answer to this question,[5] but a number of heuristic principles may be applied to find practical answers. For example, a subsystem may be regarded as a component if it occupies a local region and its parts are highly connected (by known varieties of interaction) in comparison with their weak connections to other parts of the system. If we are describing a social system, we would assume that parts are unconnected if

---

[5] This question is further discussed by Simon [10], who points out the close relation between the concept of identifiability of equations and structural equations.

there are no means of communication between them. If the system is a bridge truss, we would assume that nodes are directly connected only if they have a physical member connecting them. In other physical and chemical systems, electrical and magnetic force fields would determine interconnectedness and, hence, the boundaries of subsystems.

2.1.1. Exogenous Variables

An equation by itself expresses only a symmetric functional relation among variables and does not give us direct grounds for treating such a relation as an asymmetric, causal relation. The asymmetry must be introduced by making assumptions about which variables can be considered *exogenous*. Treating a variable as exogenous means excluding from the system under study any mechanism that controls the value of that variable. In the model of the evaporator in Example 2.1, variables T_i, Q, P, and T_w are exogenous variables. We will sometimes call equations, such as eqs. (5) to (8), that represent assumptions about exogeneity of variables *exogenous variable equations*. The result of causal ordering analysis depends very much on the choice of exogenous variables as well as on the choice of equations.

We may know (or believe) that a variable is exogenous to the subsystem we are studying if we have a scientific theory of its determination that does not include the subsystem. The temperature of the atmosphere will be an exogenous variable of this kind if the subsystem under study is a cooling tower of a power plant. We may know that a variable is exogenous because we can manipulate and control it experimentally. Hence, it may be easier to establish asymmetry in experimental rather than in observational science. We may know that a variable is exogenous because its value is established at an earlier time than the values of the subsystem variables in which we are interested. Thus, in systems of differential (or difference) equations, there is an asymmetric relation between the derivatives, which fix values for the next time interval, and the variables in the equations that determine the derivatives. (Section 3 discusses causal ordering in a system of differential equations.) We may know or believe that a variable is exogenous because it operates in a system involving much larger energies than the subsystem of interest with which it is interacting. For example, part of our belief that the temperature of the atmosphere is exogenous to a cooling tower rests on the argument that the energies involved in the weather system is orders of magnitude larger than those in a power plant.

This list of criteria for exogeneity can make no claim to completeness. It shows clearly how the formulation of structural equations to describe a subsystem is bound both by existing scientific theories and beliefs and by the means that are available for exercising control over particular variables. Establishing the structural equations for a system is as much an empirical as a formal matter and certainly is not a syntactical exercise. Nevertheless, once a structural description of a system has been agreed on, it has interesting formal consequences, including a formal attribution of causal relations among variables that appears to agree well with our intuitive notion of causality.

2.2. Minimal Complete Subsets of Several Variables

In the example of the evaporator, each of the variables is the sole member of a unique minimal complete subset of some order. This is a special case; in general, we may expect some of the minimal complete subsets to contain more than one variable each. When a minimal complete subset contains multiple variables, the variables stand in no unique causal ordering, but instead there is feedback among them. In this section we present an example involving a feedback loop. Although the evaporator in Example 2.1 does not involve any feedback, feedback is present as a control element in many devices and offers an interesting problem for causal analysis.

Consider the following example of a device involving feedback. The device is a pressure regulator, shown in Figure 5.3.[6]

Example 2.2. Causal ordering in a pressure regulator. A pressure regulator is a valve with a pressure sensor that is connected to an automatic control mechanism to adjust the valve opening. In the figure fluid flows from left to right, and the pressure sensor is simply a diaphragm. When the output pressure rises, the diaphragm is pushed down, pushing down the spring and reducing the valve opening.

------

[6] This is the same device analyzed by de Kleer and Brown [6]. Here, we simplified their notation and description of the regulator slightly without omitting any essential elements.

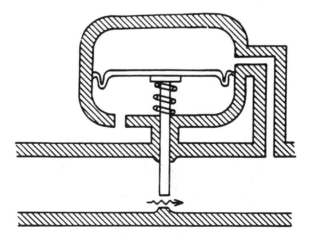

FIGURE 5.3. Pressure regulator.

Variables

X_s Size of the valve opening
P_{in} Inlet pressure
P_{out} Outlet pressure
Q Flow rate

Equations

$$X_s = c_1 - c_2 P_{out} \tag{10}$$

This equation describes the behavior of the pressure sensor controlling the valve opening. The pressure sensor senses the pressure at the outlet of the valve and adjusts the opening of the valve, increasing it when the pressure drops and decreasing it when the pressure rises.

$$P_{out} = c_3 Q \tag{11}$$

The pressure at the outlet is proportional to the flow through the valve.

$$Q = c_4(P_{in} - P_{out})X_s \tag{12}$$

The flow through the valve increases with the pressure drop from inlet to outlet and with the opening of the valve.

$$P_{in} = c_5 \tag{13}$$

The inlet pressure is exogenous.

Table 5.5 shows the self-contained structure comprised of eqs. (10) to (13). The minimal complete subset is the set containing eq. (13), involving P_{in}. Reducing the structure by eliminating P_{in} from the rest of the equations, we obtain the derived structure of first order shown in Table 5.6. The derived structure contains no proper subset that is self-contained

The causal structure of the entire system is shown in Figure 5.4. As the figure shows, there is no particular ordering among variables X_s, P_{out}, and Q, but together they are causally dependent on P_{in}.

TABLE 5.5. Self-contained structure of equations for the pressure regulator.

Equation	X_s	P_{in}	P_{out}	Q
(10)	1		1	
(11)			1	1
(12)	1	1	1	1
(13)		1		

Minimal complete subsets of zero order:
{13}
Variables in the minimal complete subsets:
P_{in}

TABLE 5.6. Derived structure of
first order for the pressure
regulator.

Equation	X_s	P_{out}	Q
(10)	1	1	
(11)	1	1	1
(12)	1	1	1

Minimal complete subsets of zero
order: $\{10, 11, 12\}$
Variables in the minimal complete
subsets: X_s, P_{out}, Q

$$P_{in} \longrightarrow (X_s, P_{out}, Q)$$

FIGURE 5.4. Causal ordering in the
pressure regulator.

When feedback is present, the causal ordering analysis applied to an equilibrium model does not reveal the direction of causality around the feedback loop. To discover the direction of causality within a feedback loop, we must use a more detailed model of the behavior of the system; in particular, we need to analyze a model of the dynamic behavior of the system. We turn to the topic of causal ordering in dynamic models in the following section.

3. Causal Ordering in a Dynamic Structure

While the causal ordering introduced in Section 3 provides a means to determine causal dependency relations in a model describing an equilibrium state, the word *behavior* usually implies changes over time. In this section we introduce causal ordering in such a dynamic system. In particular, we consider causal relations in a system of first-order differential equations. A system involving higher order differential equations can be converted into a system of first-order equations by introducing new variables to stand for derivatives.

The following is the definition of a self-contained dynamic structure [13]:

Definition 2. A *self-contained dynamic structure*[7] is a set of n first-order differential equations involving n variables such that

1. in any subset of k functions of the structure the first derivative of at least k different variables appear; and
2. in any subset of k functions in which r ($r \geq k$) first derivatives appear, if the values of any $(r - k)$ first derivatives are chosen arbitrarily, then the remaining k are determined uniquely as functions of the n variables.

---

[7] Again, this definition is slightly more general than initially proposed by Simon in [10], as it does not require equations to be linear.

The above definition of self-containment for a dynamic structure is analogous to that for an equilibrium structure. As in the case of an equilibrium structure, condition (1) above ensures that no part of the structure is overdetermined, while condition (2) ensures that the structure is not underconstrained.

Given a self-contained dynamic structure, one can perform elementary row operations to the equations to solve them for the n derivatives. This operation produces an equivalent system of equations in *canonical form*,

$$\frac{dx_i}{dt} = f_i(x_1, x_2, \ldots, x_n) \quad \text{for } i = 1 \cdots n,$$

where the expression on the right-hand side does not contain any derivatives. A self-contained dynamic structure in n variables, $x_1, \ldots, x_n$, in canonical form consists of n equations in canonical form such that the derivative of each variable appears on the left-hand side of one and only one of the n equations.

We interpret the equations of a structure in this form to be *mechanisms* of the system. Therefore, the ith equation, the only one containing the derivative of x_i, is regarded as the mechanism determining the time path of x_i. Furthermore, variable x_i, whose derivative appear in the ith equation, is said to be directly causally dependent on the variables that appear with a nonzero coefficient in the equation.

Example 3.1. Dynamic model of the pressure regulator. Consider, again, the pressure regulator described in Example 2.2. Here, we present a model of its dynamic behavior. In constructing the following dynamic model, it is assumed that when variables X_s, P_{out}, and Q are disturbed from equilibrium, the speeds at which they return to equilibrium are proportional to their displacement from the equilibrium values.

$$\frac{dX_s}{dt} = c_6(c_1 - c_2 P_{out} - X_s) \tag{14}$$

$$\frac{dP_{out}}{dt} = c_7(P_{out} - c_3 Q) \tag{15}$$

$$\frac{dQ}{dt} = c_8[c_4(P_{in} - P_{out})X_s - Q] \tag{16}$$

$$\frac{dP_{in}}{dt} = c_9 \tag{17}$$

Figure 5.5 shows the causal structure in this dynamic model. The arrows in broken lines indicate causal links. The arrows marked i indicate integration links. An integration link connects the derivative of a variable to the variable itself. The causal structure of Figure 5.5 can be interpreted in English as follows:

> The rate at which the flow rate through the valve changes depends on the current values of the input pressure, the valve opening, the output

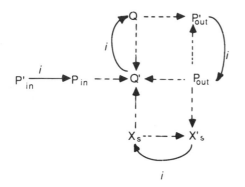

FIGURE 5.5. Causal ordering in the dynamic model of pressure regulator.

pressure, and the flow rate itself. The rate at which the regulator valve opens or closes depends on the current values of the opening and the output pressure. The rate of change in the output pressure depends on the values of the flow rate and the output pressure itself.

In the equilibrium structure of the pressure regulator in Example 2.2, it was found that variables X_s, P_{out}, and Q formed a minimal complete subset, and therefore, there was no causal ordering among them. In contrast, the dynamic causal structure shows internal causal loops,

$$\frac{dQ}{dt} \xrightarrow{i} Q \to \frac{dP_{out}}{dt} \xrightarrow{i} P_{out} \to \frac{dQ}{dt}$$

and

$$\frac{dQ}{dt} \xrightarrow{i} Q \to \frac{dP_{out}}{dt} \xrightarrow{i} P_{out} \to \frac{dX_s}{dt} \xrightarrow{i} X_s \to \frac{dQ}{dt}$$

within the minimal complete subset.

4. Causal Ordering in a Mixed Structure

When the behavior of a system is described in terms of equations, the description often consists of a mixture of dynamic and equilibrium equations rather than consisting entirely of dynamic equations. The concepts of self-contained structures and of causal ordering were extended to apply to such mixed systems [3]. First, we define self-containment for mixed systems. Causal ordering in a mixed system is a natural extension of those for equilibrium and dynamic structures.

Before defining self-containment for mixed structures, we must introduce some notations. Let M be a system of n equations in n variables such that some of the equations are equilibrium equations and others are first-order differential equations. We define $Dynamic(M)$ to be the subset of M consisting of all the differential equations in M, and $Static(M)$ to be the set consisting of all the equilibrium equations in M plus one constant equation for every variable v whose derivative appears in $Dynamic(M)$. A constant equation of variable, v, is an equation of the form

$$v = c,$$

where c is a constant.

The intuitive meaning of the set $Static(M)$ may be understood as follows: The set of equilibrium equations in a mixed set represents mechanisms that restore equilibrium so quickly that they can be considered to hold in zero units of time within some time frame (e.g., days if the time frame is centuries). On the other hand, the dynamic equations represent slower mechanisms that require nonzero units of time to affect appreciably the variables whose derivatives appear in them. Therefore, in a very short period of time—shorter than is required for variables whose derivatives appear in the differential equations to be affected by other variables—those variables can be considered unchanging. Thus, set $Static(M)$ represents a snapshot picture (i.e., a very short-term equilibrium description) of the dynamic behavior of mixed structure M.

Definition 3. The set M of n equations in n variables is a self-contained mixed structure iff

1. one or more of the n equations are first-order differential equations and the rest are equilibrium equations;
2. in any subset of size k of $Dynamic(M)$ the first derivatives of at least k different variables appear;
3. in any subset of size k of $Dynamic(M)$ in which r $(r \geq k)$ first derivatives appear, if the values of any $(r - k)$ first derivatives are chosen arbitrarily, then the remaining k are determined uniquely as functions of the n variables;
4. the first derivatives of exactly d different variables appear in $Dynamic(M)$, where d is the size of the set $Dynamic(M)$; and
5. $Static(M)$ is a self-contained static structure.

Conditions (2) to (4) in the above definition ensure that the dynamic part of the model is neither overconstrained nor underconstrained. Condition (5) ensures that its short-term, snapshot picture is also self-contained.

Given a self-contained mixed structure, as defined above, the causal ordering among its variables and derivatives follows the definitions of causal ordering in dynamic and static structures. In other words, the causal ordering in a mixed structure can be determined as follows:

1. The ordering among the variables and derivatives in $Dynamic(M)$ is analogous to the definition of causal ordering in a dynamics structure. First, put the differential equations in canonical form. Then, for each equation, the derivative on its left-hand side is said to be directly causally dependent on each of the variables on the right-hand side.
2. The ordering among variables in $Static(M)$ is given by the definition of causal ordering in a static structure.

Example 4.1. *A mixed model of the pressure regulator.* Consider the pressure regulator in Example 2.2, again. Let M be the mixed structure of the pressure regulator constructed by replacing eqs. (15) to (17) by their corresponding equilibrium equations (11) to (13). M consists of the following four equations:

$$\frac{dX_s}{dt} = c_6(c_1 - c_2 P_{out} - X_s) \tag{14}$$

$$P_{out} = c_3 Q \tag{11}$$

$$Q = c_4(P_{in} - P_{out})X_s \tag{12}$$

$$P_{in} = c_5 \tag{13}$$

The reason eqs. (11) to (13) were replaced by equilibrium ones is that the relations they represent are restored to equilibrium very quickly when disturbed out of equilibrium, whereas the relation represented by eq. (10) is restored relatively slowly. Therefore, in an analysis of a medium temporal grain-size, it is reasonable to regard the former equilibrium relations to always hold while regarding the latter as taking time to return to equilibrium.

M satisfies conditions (1) to (4) of the definition of a self-contained mixed structure. *Dynamic*(M) consists of eq. (14). *Static*(M) consists of eqs. (11) to (13) and the following constant equation of X_s:

$$X_s = c_{10} \tag{18}$$

The equilibrium structure *Static*(M), shown in Table 5.7, is self-contained. Each one of eqs. (13) and (18) forms a minimal complete subset of zero order. Removing these equations and variables from *Static*(M) produces the derived structure of first order consisting of two equations, both of which involve two variables, Q and P_{out}. Therefore, the derived structure cannot be reduced any further. The resulting causal ordering in M is shown in Figure 5.6. Causal links in *Dynamic*(M) are indicated by arrows in broken lines. Solid arrows indicate causal links in *Static*(M).

TABLE 5.7. Self-contained structure of *Static*(M).

Equation	X_s	Q	P_{out}	P_{in}
(18)	1			
(11)		1	1	
(12)	1	1	1	1
(13)				1

Minimal complete subsets of zero order: $\{18\}, \{13\}$
Variables in the minimal complete subsets: X_s, P_{in}

FIGURE 5.6. Causal ordering in the mixed model of the
pressure regulator.

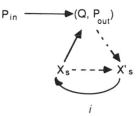

5. A Mixed Structure as an Approximation to a Dynamic Structure

The mixed model in Example 4.1 was created from the dynamic model based on the assumption that when the variables on the right-hand side of eqs. (15) and (16) are disturbed the mechanisms represented by these equations respond very quickly to restore relative equilibrium. This suggests that one can create a mixed structure as an approximation of a dynamic structure. When a mechanism in a dynamic structure restores relative equilibrium much more quickly than other mechanisms, one may wish to regard it instantaneous. Alternatively, when a mechanism acts so much more slowly than other mechanisms in the system that its effect on the variable it controls is negligible over the time period of interest, the variable may be considered constant. In these cases, the description of the system's dynamic behavior may be simplified by representing the fast-acting mechanism by an equilibrium equation or the slow mechanism by a constant equation. This section discusses generating a mixed structure from a dynamic structure as an approximation to the latter through these two techniques.

5.1. Equilibration

We use the term *equilibrating* to refer to the operation of replacing a dynamic equation by its corresponding equilibrium equation. In a model where differential equations are in canonical form, equilibration is accomplished by replacing the left-hand side of a differential equation by 0.

There is a whole range of mixed structures between the completely dynamic structure and the equilibrium structure, depending on the temporal grain size selected for the model. However, substituting an arbitrary subset of a dynamic self-contained structure with the corresponding static equations will not necessarily produce a self-contained mixed structure.

Let us call a variable *self-regulating* if its derivative is a function of the variable itself, and *non-self-regulating* otherwise. It has been proved that equilibrating any number of self-regulating equations in a self-contained dynamic or mixed structure will always produce a self-contained mixed structure (or a self-contained equilibrium structure if no more dynamic equations are left). However, equilibrating a non-self-regulating equations may produce an overconstrained structure. The following theorem states this fact [3]:

THEOREM 1. *Equilibrating any number of self-regulating equations in a self-contained dynamic or mixed structure always produces a self-contained mixed structure (or a self-contained equilibrium structure if all the dynamic equations in the original structure have been equilibrated).*

5.2. Exogenization

In contrast to variables that adjust to changes in other variables very quickly to restore relative equilibrium, some variables respond so slowly to changes in other variables that they can be regarded as almost independent of other variables. The equation corresponding to such a variable can be replaced by an exogenous variable equation. We call this operation of replacing a dynamic equation by an exogenous variable equation *exogenizing*.

Conceptually, exogenizing is the opposite of equilibrating. Exogenizing a variable amounts to deleting from the system under consideration the mechanism that determines the value of the variable by placing the mechanism outside the scope of the system. It is reasonable to do so only when the feedback to the variable from those inside the system is negligible. Exogenizing a variable in a self-contained structure always produces a self-contained structure. The following theorem states this fact [3]. The proof follows directly from the definition of self-containment of a mixed structure.

THEOREM 2. *Exogenizing an equation in a self-contained dynamic or mixed structure always produces a self-contained structure.*

5.3. Mixed Structures and Nearly Decomposable Systems

The two operators introduced in this section, equilibration and exogenization, can be used to generate more abstract models from a dynamic model when assumptions about significant differences in relative adjustment speeds of mechanisms can be made, as discussed in Sections 5.1 and 5.2. Making such assumptions amounts to classifying the variables into three categories:

1. Variables whose rates of change are influenced only very little by other variables. These are candidate variables for exogenization.
2. Variables that adjust so quickly that they are always close to relative equilibrium with other variables. These are candidates for equilibration.
3. All other variables.

This idea of classification of variables depending on their relative adjustment speeds is also the basis for the theory of aggregation of nearly decomposable dynamic systems described by Simon and Ando [12]. Nearly decomposable systems are those consisting of subsystems of variables such that the variables within a subsystem interact strongly while the interactions among subsystems are much weaker. Simon and Ando showed that when a given dynamic system was nearly decomposable, and if one was only interested in the middle- to long-term dynamics of the system, then one could aggregate the subsystems, assuming them to be always in steady-state relative equilibrium, and consider only the movements of the aggregated systems. Their work provides theoretical justification for generation of mixed structures as an abstraction of completely dynamic structures using the techniques discussed here.

6. Summary

In this chapter we have described the method of causal ordering, a computational technique for inferring the causal dependency relations in an equation model. We first presented the method as applied to an equilibrium model of behavior and subsequently extended the method to dynamic and mixed models.

The method requires the model to be self-contained. Also, the equations in the model must come from an understanding of conceptually distinct mechanisms in the situation being modeled. Some of the equations may be exogenous variable equations, representing the assumptions that certain variables are controlled by external forces. When applied to a model that satisfies these requirements, the method of causal ordering reveals the asymmetric relations among its variables that reflect intuitive concepts of causality. The method can be applied to qualitative as well as quantitative models.

Mixed models can be created from dynamic models as abstractions of the latter based on assumptions about relative adjustment speeds of mechanisms in the dynamic model. We introduced two abstraction operators, equilibration and exogenization, for generating a more temporally coarse model from a finer model. This concept of mixed models as temporal abstractions of dynamic models is closely related to aggregation of nearly decomposable dynamic systems.

The causal ordering in a model produced by the method can be used for various tasks requiring reasoning about behavior such as diagnosis, prediction, and design modification. The method of causal ordering analysis presented in this chapter has been implemented as part of a computer program named CAOS for reasoning about the behavior of a system. The program consists of a collection of modules for generation of equation models, causal analysis of models, dynamic stability analysis, and qualitative prediction of the effects of external disturbances [3]. The method has also been used for several different purposes including diagnosis [8] and generation of if–then rules for parametric design [5].

Acknowledgment. The author would like to thank Herb Simon for providing guidance in this research.

References

1. Davis, R. Diagnostic reasoning based on structure and behavior. *Artif. Intell. 24* (1984).
2. Forbus, D.K. Qualitative process theory. *Artif. Intell. 24* (1984).
3. Iwasaki, Y. Model-based reasoning of device behavior with causal ordering. Ph.D. thesis, Dept. of Computer Science, Carnegie Mellon Univ. Pittsburgh, Pa., 1988.
4. Iwasaki, Y., and Simon, H.A. Causality in device behavior. *Artif. Intell. 29* (1986).
5. Keller, R., Manago, C., Iwasaki, Y., and Tanaka, K. Compiling special purpose rules from general purpose device models. Tech. Rep. KSL-89-50, Knowledge Systems Laboratory, Dept. of Computer Science, Stanford Univ., 1989.
6. de Kleer, J., and Brown, J.S. Qualitative physics based on confluences. *Artif. Intell. 24* (1984).
7. Kuipers, B. Qualitative simulation as causal explanation. *IEEE Trans. Syst., Man Cybern.* (1987).
8. Lambert, H., Eshelman, L., and Iwasaki, Y. Using qualitative physics to guide the acquisition of diagnostic knowledge. In *Proceedings of the 3rd International Conference on Applications of Artificial Intelligence in Engineering.* 1988.
9. Patil, R., Szolovits, R., and Schwartz, W. Causal understanding of patient illness in medical diagnosis. In *Proceedings of the 7th International Joint Conference on Artificial Intelligence.* 1981, pp. 893–899.
10. Simon, H.A. On the definition of the causal relation. *J. Philos. 49* (1952), 517–528.
11. Simon, H.A. *Models of Discovery.* D. Reidel Publishing Company, 1977.
12. Simon, H.A., and Ando, A. Aggregation of variables in dynamic systems. *Eonometrica 29* (1961).
13. Simon, H.A., and Rescher, N. Causes and counterfactual. *Philos. Sci. 33* (1966), 323–340.

CHAPTER 6

Qualitative Modeling in Ecology: Loop Analysis, Signed Digraphs, and Time Averaging

Charles J. Puccia and Richard Levins

Abstract

Nature can be overwhelming both in the complexity of interactions and in their measurements. Models reduce complexity through simplification of the interactions, and qualitative models reduce the number of measurements. Qualitative models in ecology have taken the form of signed-digraphs or loop models. These assume that ecological systems are at or near equilibrium. For biotic systems far from equilibrium, the method of time averaging has been developed.

A loop model is a pictorial representation of a community matrix that represents the interactions among organisms and also with abiotic variables. The analysis uses standard dynamical systems methods translated into signed-digraph terms. Hence, the Routh–Hurwitz criterion for stability becomes a combination of feedback loops based on links and paths. Likewise, the direction of changes in species' equilibrium numbers—whether they increase, decrease, or remain unchanged—as the parameter values in their rates of growth are altered, are determined by a formula using the paths and feedbacks.

Qualitative models in ecology are used for explanations. Often logical arguments can lead to opposite conclusions. These are not resolved by quantification of parameters, or from the observations of correlations among the species. Autonomous, independent variables can be obtained in ecological systems through their position in the network, through dynamic separation, and through spatial scale. How this can happen is explained through the use of loop analysis.

Ecological systems do not have to be in equilibrium or near equilibrium. Systems that are subject to high perturbation or in which parameters are temporal and change on a rate commensurate with the species growth rates are conditions that can lead to sustained bounded motion. In these systems, the time-averaging method must be applied.

Ecological systems are bounded; they are not infinite, nor can species become negative. Hence, an expected value operator analagous to that used in statistics can be defined as

$$E_t[x(t)] = \frac{1}{t} \int_0^1 x(s)\,ds.$$

Since $x(s)$ can be any function, then for a derivative of a bounded variable as t goes to the limit,

$$E\left[\frac{dx}{dt}\right] = \lim_{t\to\infty} \frac{[x(t) - x(0)]}{t},$$

with the following consequence:

$$E\left[\frac{dx}{dt}\right] = 0.$$

With the definition of a time average and because the average of a derivative of a bounded function is zero, it is possible to determine the conditions of sustained bounded motion. From the environmental perspective, it is often the mass of information that we cannot handle that requires reduction of the problem. One use of time averaging is to elucidate what are the likely points of entry of a pollution source.

Qualitative modeling in ecology is not only a methodology for the analysis of systems without parametric quantification, it is also the development of a new scientific approach to the study of the natural world.

1. Introduction

The demands of a modern technological society have outpaced traditional quantitative analysis for ecological systems. These demands are in understanding problems of complex interactions. Ecological interactions are often difficult to measure in any practical way, or the measurement itself alters the value. In the long run, the real ecological questions are not exact values of parameters or variables at some future date but the direction of change, resilience and stability of ecological systems. For example, in modern society, where an ever-increasing diversity of chemicals is appearing, the challenge to ecological models is to understand what effect an increased mortality rate in crop pests will have on the periodicity of outbreaks or the stability of the ecological community, which includes the natural predators of the pest.

In ecology, qualitative modeling operates as a sequence of three different levels of generality: Local equilibrium, moving equilibrium, and sustained bounded motion. The first three sections of this chapter discuss the local and moving equilibrium domains of qualitative modeling; the remaining sections are devoted to time averaging, as used to study systems far from equilibrium. Models are qualitative when only the signs of interactions among variables are known, not their magnitude, regardless of whether the variable levels are themselves quantifiable.

Qualitative modeling, as described in the following section, is first a binary choice between loop analysis (signed digraphs) and matrix analysis. If most variables are connected to each other, then the graph structure does not yield any real information. In that case, the statistical distribution of coefficients in the matrix is the important property of the system. As the matrix becomes increasingly sparse, relatively low connectivity in the system, even with many variables interconnected but the percentage of interconnections small, more information is loaded into the digraph structure, and there is less concern in the quantitative structure of the coefficients.

In ecological systems of low connectivity or low number of interactions [2], there is a choice of working at the level of local equilibrium, moving equilibrium, or time averaging. The procedure has been to start with models with the strongest tools and to examine the results to discover which carry over into the next level of generality. There is also a scientific strategy associated with qualitative modeling. Again, there are two choices: Start with the biological knowledge to build a loop model, or construct the generalized equations; or obtain the data, and find a signed digraph consistent with it. The actual scientific process of qualitative analysis goes back and forth between the two choices. This is different from a quantitative analysis, such as in simulation, which may appear like the same kind of iteration, but is not. In the simulation approach, a discrepancy between predictions and observations leads to improving estimation of parameters; in the qualitative approach, the model is changed. Each level of qualitative analysis, from the loop analysis to the time-averaging approach, presents a set of many models for any given system. The test of the utility of an approach is that it gives understanding, explains the observed behavior, and predicts the future. But the approach is not a hypothesis in a narrow sense, so the failure of any model does not discard it. Rather, it is a metahypothesis about research that proves its usefulness when it leads to answers. Therefore, qualitative models provide us with answers both about ecological systems and other systems as well as about research approaches.

2. Fundamental Definitions and Equations

Classical dynamical systems theory begins with a set of ordinary differential equations:

$$\frac{dx_i}{dt} = f_i(x_1, x_2, \ldots, x_n; c_1, c_2, \ldots, c_m) \qquad (i = 1, n). \qquad (1)$$

In an ecological context, the xs are species abundances, nutrient levels, or some nonbiological resource like substrate space. The cs are parameters that govern the growth rates such as birth rates, mortality rates, feeding rates, etc. The parameters depend on the environment and the biology of the organisms. When all the derivatives are zero, $\frac{dx_i}{dt} = 0$ for all i, the values of the x_i are the equilibrium values. There may be more than one equilibrium point of the system. In the neighborhood of any equilibrium point, the system matrix becomes

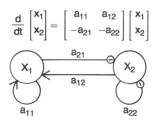

$$\frac{d}{dt}\begin{bmatrix} x_1 \\ x_2 \end{bmatrix} = \begin{bmatrix} a_{11} & a_{12} \\ -a_{21} & -a_{22} \end{bmatrix}\begin{bmatrix} x_1 \\ x_2 \end{bmatrix}$$

FIGURE 6.1. Signed digraph for predator–prey model.

$$\mathbf{A} = a_{ij} = \frac{\partial f_i}{\partial x_j}\bigg|_{x^*} \qquad (2)$$

from the vector-matrix equation $\dot{x} = Ax$.

A signed digraph is formed from the systems matrix, $\mathbf{A}$. The variables x_i form the n vertices, with the line connecting them determined by the elements of the matrix. (A detailed description is given in [3].) The diagonal elements form links starting and ending on the same variable. The sign of the element determines the link, positive indicated by an arrow and negative with a small circle enclosing a dash, as in Figure 6.1.

Predation is the consumption of one species by another, as in Figure 6.1. The predator (x_1) has a negative effect on the prey (x_2); the prey, a positive effect on the predator. Competitive species have negative effects on each other. Mutualists effect each other positively. The sign is independent of the magnitude of the links. Self-effects arise from density-dependent growth rates, immigration, and emigration. Negative self-loops or self-damping are caused by density-dependent growth rates and immigration or an external source of the variable, as in the case of nutrients. Positive self-effects or self-enhancing are generally a result of emigration or loss from the community. An example of self-effect is the input of a nutrient N into a lake that depends on runoff I, while removal is through consumption by algae G in the lake:

$$\frac{dN}{dt} = I - GN. \qquad (3)$$

So,

$$a_{NN} = \frac{\partial}{\partial N}\left(\frac{dN}{dt}\right)_{N^*,G^*} = -G^*$$

at the equilibrium level $N^*G^* = I$.

Every ecological system has at its "lowest" level variables that are not self-reproducing but depend on input from outside. Generally these are nutrients, water, and sunlight. When these variables are not explicitly included in a model, then their self-damping is transferred to the next variables that interact with them and that are represented in the model.

The characteristic equation of eq. 1 is given by

$$p(\lambda) = |\mathbf{A} - \lambda\mathbf{I}| = 0, \qquad (4)$$

where $\mathbf{A}$ is the system matrix of eq. (2) and $\mathbf{I}$ is the n-dimensional identity matrix. The roots or eigenvalues, λ, of the characteristic equation may be real or complex. Negative real roots indicate that the system returns to equilibrium after perturbation. Positive real roots produce unstable systems: When perturbed the system moves away from the equilibrium. A complex eigenvalue determines stability by the real part and the frequency of oscillation by the imaginary part. A zero real part of the eigenvalue is neutral stability, while an unstable equilibrium can appear if there are multiple zeros.

It is not necessary to solve the polynomial characteristic equation to determine whether the real parts of the eigenvalues are negative. Rather, the application of the Routh–Hurwitz criterion to the system matrix $\mathbf{A}$ is sufficient. The criterion can be developed in terms of the signed digraph.

The determinant of order n for the $\mathbf{A}$ matrix is

$$D_n = \sum (-1)^{n+m} L(m, n), \tag{5a}$$

where $L(m, n)$ is the product of the elements a_{ij} of the $\mathbf{A}$ matrix around m disjunct loops. The zero-order determinant is $D_0 = 1$. For the signed digraph or loop model, feedback is introduced. Thus, feedback at level n is given by

$$F_n = \sum (-1)^{m+1} L(m, n). \tag{5b}$$

This is, again, the summation of all products of disjunct loops in the graph. If all the loops in a product are negative, then the whole product contributes a negative component. The characteristic polynomial in terms of feedback levels is

$$p(\lambda) = -\sum_{k=0}^{n} \lambda^n F_{n-k}. \tag{6}$$

The real part of the eigenvalues will be negative provided the following two criteria are met:

Criterion 1

$$F_i < 0 \quad \text{for all } i. \tag{7a}$$

Criterion 2

$$\begin{vmatrix} F_1 F_3 F_5, \ldots, F_{2n-2} \\ F_0 F_2 F_4, \ldots, F_{2n-2} \\ 0, F_1 F_3, \ldots, F_{2n-3} \\ \ldots\ldots\ldots\ldots\ldots \\ \ldots\ldots\ldots\ldots\ldots \\ \ldots\ldots\ldots\ldots\ldots \\ 0\ 0\ 0, \ldots, F_{2n} \end{vmatrix} > 0. \tag{7b}$$

As a consequence of (7a), $F_0 \equiv -1$. The second criterion of (7b) for systems of three variables is given by

$$F_1 F_2 + F_3 > 0 \tag{8a}$$

and for five variables by

$$F_1 F_2 + F_3^2 - F_1^2 F_4 - F_1 F_5 > 0. \tag{8b}$$

Equations (8a) and (8b) also apply to systems of four and six variables, by the Liénard–Chipart theorem [1]. Expansion for higher order systems is daunting.

Feedback at level one is the sum of the diagonal terms, or self-effect terms in the loop model. This corresponds to the sum of the eigenvalues, or

$$F_1 = \sum \lambda_i = \sum a_{ii}. \tag{9}$$

Then the average eigenvalue $\bar{\lambda}$ is

$$\bar{\lambda} = \frac{1}{n} \sum \lambda_i = \frac{1}{n} \sum a_{ii} = \bar{a}_{ii} \tag{10}$$

or the average of the self-effect terms. Consequently, changes in the magnitudes of the links between variables only redistribute the eigenvalues around the same mean. The squared deviation or variance of the eigenvalues follows, as

$$var(\lambda) = \frac{1}{n} \sum \lambda_i^2 - \bar{\lambda}^2 \tag{11}$$

where

$$\sum \lambda_i^2 = \sum a_{ii}^2 + 2 \sum_{i \neq j} a_{ij} a_{ji}. \tag{12}$$

Substituting (12) and (10) into (11) and the fact that there are $(n)(n-1)/2$ terms like a_{ij} and $i \neq j$, then

$$var(\lambda) = \frac{1}{n} \sum a_{ii}^2 - \left(\frac{1}{n} \sum a_{ii}\right)^2 + (n-1)\overline{a_{ij} a_{ji}} \tag{13a}$$

or

$$var(\lambda) = var(a_{ii}) + (n-1)\overline{a_{ij} a_{ji}}. \tag{13b}$$

The variance of the eigenvalues becomes negative only when the sum of the eigenvalues is complex. The first term on the right-hand side of eq. (13b) must be positive for real coefficients of any ecological system. Only the arithmetic average of the loops of length two, $a_{ij} a_{ji}$, can be negative. Hence, strong competition in a community can provide both stability and oscillatory behavior. The oscillation is diminished or eliminated by strong self-effects. As the a_{ij} begin to dominate, they effectively "decouple" the variables. Strongly decoupled variables can be variables that change at very different rates. A spread in the a_{ii} or self-terms when the variables are uncoupled remains as though independent when in the whole system.

3. Systems of Moving Equilibria

A system may be at equilibrium, or parameters of the system may be changing. Parameters that change slowly compared to variables permit a system to be in moving equilibrium; the variable levels track the equilibrium. The partial derivative of the system equations with respect to any system parameter can be solved as the variables approach equilibrium, in principle, for the new equilibrium values of the variables. From eq. (1),

$$\frac{\partial f_i}{\partial c_h} + \sum \frac{\partial f_i}{\partial x_j} \frac{\partial x_j^*}{\partial c_h} = 0. \tag{14}$$

The $\dfrac{\partial f_i}{\partial x_j}$ are the coefficients a_{ij} in the system matrix given by eq. (2). The unknown quantity is the change in the equilibrium level of variable x_i as parameter c_h changes, $\dfrac{\partial x_j^*}{\partial c_h}$. This new set of linear equations is

$$\sum_j a_{ij} \frac{\partial x_j^*}{\partial c_h} = -\frac{\partial f_i}{\partial c_h} \qquad (i = 1, \dots, n) \tag{15}$$

with the solution

$$\frac{\partial x_j^*}{\partial c_h} = \frac{\det \begin{vmatrix} a_{11}, \dots, a_{1j-1} \dfrac{\partial f_1}{\partial c_h} a_{1j+1}, \dots, a_{1n} \\ a_{21}, \dots, a_{2j-1} \dfrac{\partial f_2}{\partial c_h} a_{2j+1}, \dots, a_{2n} \\ \dots\dots\dots\dots\dots\dots\dots\dots \\ \dots\dots\dots\dots\dots\dots\dots\dots \\ \dots\dots\dots\dots\dots\dots\dots\dots \\ a_{n1}, \dots, a_{nj-1} \dfrac{\partial f_n}{\partial c_h} a_{nj+1}, \dots, a_{nn} \end{vmatrix}}{|\mathbf{A}|}. \tag{16}$$

The solution in terms of the loop model notation is

$$\frac{\partial x_i}{\partial c_h} = \frac{\sum_{j=1}^{n} \left(\dfrac{\partial f_j}{\partial c_h} \right) p_{ij}^{(k)} F_{n-k}^{(comp)}}{F_n}, \tag{17}$$

where c_h is the hth parameter that is changing; $\partial f_j / \partial c_h$ is the effect of the c_h parameter on the growth rate of the jth variable; $p_{ij}^{(k)}$ is the path *from* the jth *to* the ith variable and includes a total of k variables; and $F_{n-k}^{(comp)}$ is the feedback, as defined in eq. (5b), of the complementary subsystem, that is, the subsystem formed by those variables *not* on the path $p_{ij}^{(k)}$.

PATHS

path = (a)(-b)(c) = -abc

path = (a)(-c)(-d) = +acd
path ≠ (a)(-c)(-d)(b)
(X_2 entered twice)

LOOPS

Case: One disjunct loop

Loop of length 1: L(1,1)
$L(1,1) = -a_{11}$

Loop of length 4: L(1,4)
$L(1,4) = +(a_{21}a_{32}a_{43}a_{14})$

Case: Two disjunct loops

Total loop length 3: L(2,3)
$L(2,3) = (-1)(-a_{11})(-a_{23}a_{32})$
$= -a_{11}a_{23}a_{32}$

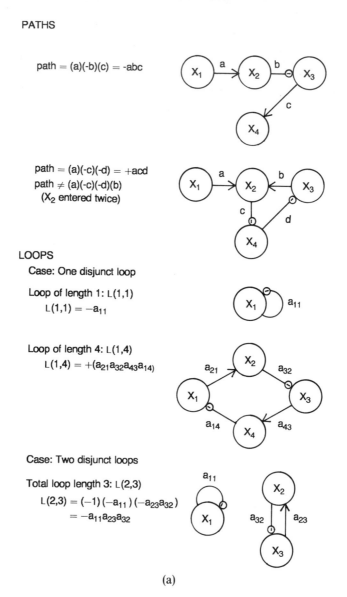

(a)

FIGURE 6.2a. Loop terminology: Paths and loops.

Figure 6.2 illustrates the meaning of the loop terminology and gives example calculations to determine stability and the direction of change in equilibrium values with a changing parameter in a system.

Equation (4) may be applied for each changing parameter that affects the growth rate of each variable. The result may be tabulated to give a table

FEEDBACK

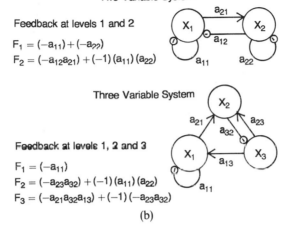

One Variable System

Feedback at level 1

$F_1 = -a_{11}$

Two Variable System

Feedback at levels 1 and 2

$F_1 = (-a_{11}) + (-a_{22})$
$F_2 = (-a_{12}a_{21}) + (-1)(a_{11})(a_{22})$

Three Variable System

Feedback at levels 1, 2 and 3

$F_1 = (-a_{11})$
$F_2 = (-a_{23}a_{32}) + (-1)(a_{11})(a_{22})$
$F_3 = (-a_{21}a_{32}a_{13}) + (-1)(-a_{23}a_{32})$

(b)

FIGURE 6.2b. Loop terminology: Feedback.

COMPLEMENTARY SUBSYSTEMS

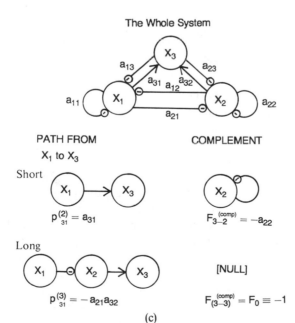

The Whole System

PATH FROM
X_1 to X_3

COMPLEMENT

Short

$p_{31}^{(2)} = a_{31}$

$F_{3-2}^{(comp)} = -a_{22}$

Long

$p_{31}^{(3)} = -a_{21}a_{32}$

[NULL]

$F_{(3-3)}^{(comp)} = F_0 \equiv -1$

(c)

FIGURE 6.2c. Loop terminology: Complementary subsystems.

CHANGE IN EQUILIBRIUM ABUNDANCE

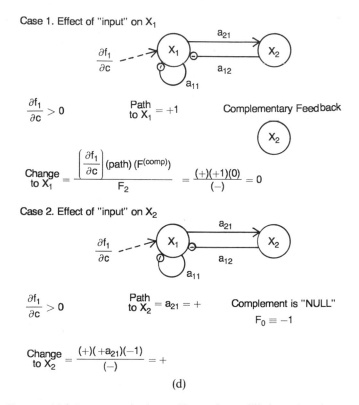

Case 1. Effect of "input" on X_1

$$\frac{\partial f_1}{\partial c} > 0 \qquad \frac{\text{Path}}{\text{to } X_1} = +1 \qquad \text{Complementary Feedback}$$

$$\text{Change} \atop \text{to } X_1 = \frac{\left(\frac{\partial f_1}{\partial c}\right)(\text{path})(F^{(\text{comp})})}{F_2} = \frac{(+)(+1)(0)}{(-)} = 0$$

Case 2. Effect of "input" on X_2

$$\frac{\partial f_1}{\partial c} > 0 \qquad \frac{\text{Path}}{\text{to } X_2} = a_{21} = + \qquad \text{Complement is "NULL"}$$
$$F_0 \equiv -1$$

$$\text{Change} \atop \text{to } X_2 = \frac{(+)(+a_{21})(-1)}{(-)} = +$$

(d)

FIGURE 6.2d. Loop terminology: Change in equilibrium abundance.

of predictions, which indicates the direction of change in equilibrium for a changing parameter that affects one variable, loosely referred to as a "parameter input" or "input."

Relations among variables are determined from the table of predictions. For example, in a predator-prey population model an increase in the feeding rate of the predator will affect the predator's growth rate. The predator equilibrium abundance increases while the prey abundance decreases. A change in another parameter of the predator's growth rate function, such as the natural mortality rate increasing with a subsequent decline in the growth rate function, will cause the predator population numbers to be reduced while the prey population will increase. A parameter change resulting in either increase or decrease in the predator growth rate always changes the equilibrium abundances of the predator and prey in opposite directions. If the variation in a parameter in the predator-prey system affects the prey growth rate, only the equilibrium

TWO CORRELATION TABLES
FROM A TABLE OF PREDICTIONS

Positive Input to	Change in Equilibrium Abundance			
	X_1	X_2	X_3	X_4
X_1	+	-	-	-
X_2	+	-	-	+
X_3	-	+	-	+
X_4	+	-	0	+

CORRELATION TABLE
FOR INPUT TO X_1

	X_2	X_3	X_4
X_1	-	-	-
X_2		+	+
X_3			+

CORRELATION TABLE
FOR INPUT TO X_4

	X_2	X_3	X_4
X_1	-	0	+
X_2		0	-
X_3			-

FIGURE 6.3. Two correlation tables from a table of predictions.

level of the predator changes. The prey abundance is fixed. There is no correlation between predator and prey. Figure 6.3 illustrates correlation tables produced from a table of predictions. Each correlation table in Figure 6.3 corresponds to an input row, x_1 and x_4 in this example.

4. Partial Autonomy in Ecological Systems

In ecological systems there is no real autonomy of variables in the sense that variables are independent of all other variables. There can be the appearance of autonomy or partial autonomy because of indirect linkage of variables. The longer the path between variables, the more likely it is at first to consider the variables partially autonomous. But this is only a trivial interpretation of autonomy.

Consider the model of Figure 6.4. Predator 1, $P1$ is a generalist and will consume either herbivore, $H1$ or $H2$. Predator 2, $P2$ is a specialist on herbivore 2, $H2$. Both herbivore populations are regulated by the consumption of plants and are self-damped.

Predator 2 is called a satellite of $H2$. A satellite is a subsystem of zero feedback having a single linkage pair to only one variable—the one to which it is a satellite. Any other linkages are single and emanate from the satellite to the system and have no other links from the system directed to it.

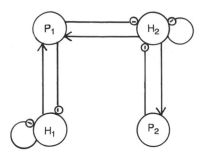

FIGURE 6.4. Model with two predator and two prey species.

TABLE 6.1. Effect of parameter changes on the two-predator/two-prey model.

Positive input	Change in equilibrium abundance			
	P1	P2	H1	H2
P1	+	−	−	0
P2	−	+	+	−
H1	+	−	+	0
H2	0	+	0	−

The effect of parameter changes that act as positive inputs to only one variable at a time can be observed from Table 6.1.

Inputs to either $P1$ or $H1$ have no effect on $H2$. Likewise, an input to $H2$ has no effect on $P1$ or $H1$. Even though $H2$ is causally connected to both predator 1 and herbivore 1, the behavior is as if they are autonomous. Autonomy in this case is a dynamic property of the system rather than a lack of connection—structural separation. Autonomy is not achieved by cutting connections, but rather by homeostasis. This is a result of the "satellite" variables, which may be present in ecological systems.

Another type of autonomy is dynamic autonomy. Variables are dynamically coupled both by their interaction and by their changing at the same rates. Variables that change at rates that differ greatly from the objects of interest become temporary parameters. Again, using a predator–prey example, the metabolism of the predator is almost always much faster than the rate of consumption of prey. Or, in another example, plant growth is not on the same time scale as geological changes in climate. Hence, variables become semi-autonomous because they are separated by their rate of change.

Autonomy can be produced by spatial scale as can be illustrated with this verbal description of the intertidal ecology. Tide pools form in the intertidal zone. They are inhabited by sessile invertebrates such as mussels and limpets, and slow moving animals, including various gastropods, and swifter organisms like crabs and small fish; of course, there are various algae. In any tide pool, growth of the sessile forms will be affected by, among other things, the exposure of the pool to waves, the height above mean low water, and the frequency of storms. From the point of view of the entire rocky coastline, the populations are all interacting. Selected tide pools contain populations of organisms autonomous from other pools, but over a longer time scale, the populations are part of the larger geographic area. Spatial scale may produce autonomy that is intermittent. Moreover, a shift in scale and the concomitant change in autonomy can also change stability.

For example, in a simple model of benthic communities that may be enclosed in an estuary, some species are moving to local extinction. But, from the point of view of several estuaries or the entire bay, the overall system can be stable. Even though the community experiences losses of some species, immigration from other areas causes reintroduction of those species. Hence, the suite of organisms survives, while at any specific site at any time, individual populations may disappear.

5. Conclusions on Loop Models

The exposition given is of a sketch of loop models or signed digraphs and the analysis near equilibrium. The models presented are not intended to represent actual ecological systems, but rather to demonstrate the kinds of arguments that may be developed. The strength of the method lies in the ability to use a vast amount of biological and ecological knowledge where only partial measurements of parameters have been made. Future developments will have to be in the area of elucidating uncertainty or ambiguity in models' predictions, either because of multiple paths or subsystems with both positive and negative feedbacks. The trajectory or return pattern of systems when perturbed from equilibrium requires an eigenvector analysis and interpretation of the patterns, which have only begun. Developments will also be needed to include the effects of time lags, both on stability and predicting change. The sensitivity of eigenvalues to the changes at the various feedback levels can be described in more detail for a better understanding of the relation of link interactions among variables and the overall behavior of the system: We know that low-order feedbacks play a major role when an eigenvalue is relatively large, while conversely, it is the higher order feedbacks that are important for eigenvalues that become vanishingly small. Finally, there may be short-term scientific and practical questions that require an amalgamation of qualitative and quantitative methods, and this interface between approaches has not been explored.

6. Time Averaging and Sustained Bounded Motion

Time averaging is a simple and powerful tool for the qualitative analysis of partially specified systems that are not at equilibrium and is therefore an extension of the graphical methods developed in Puccia and Levins [3]. It can be applied to test for local stability of differential equations, to identify the point of entry of a forcing function in a multivariate system, differentiate among alternative models, and to find invariant relationships in processes that may be chaotic. The objects of interest are systems of variables having sustained bounded motion (SBM); that is, all the variables are bounded, and if x is a variable in that system, then the variance of x over time is greater than zero. It is most useful with differential equations, including those with time delays, but can also be used with some modification for difference equations. The property SBM was defined in order to avoid having to differentiate among periodic, almost periodic, and chaotic flows.

The method of time averaging uses orthogonal measures of a process, which are analogs of the statistical moments, although they do not presume any randomness.

6.1. Definitions and Elementary Operations

Define the expected value of a function by

$$E_t\{x(t)\} = (1/t) \int_0^t x(s)\,ds, \tag{18}$$

the variance by

$$Var_t\{x(t)\} = (1/t) \int_0^t [x(s) - E\{x\}]^2\,ds, \tag{19}$$

and the covariance by

$$Cov_t\{x, y\} = (1/t) \int_0^t [x(s) - E\{x\}][y(s) - E(y)]\,ds. \tag{20}$$

Other moments can be defined analogously. If a variable is bounded, then we can pass to the limit and obtain

$$E(x) = \lim_{t\to\infty} E_t\{x\}. \tag{21}$$

When this procedure is applied to the derivative of a function,

$$E(dx/dt) = \lim_{t\to\infty} [x(t) - x(0)]/t. \tag{22}$$

Since $x(t) - x(0) \le Max(x) - Min(x)$, it follows that if $x(t)$ is a bounded variable then

$$E\{dx/dt\} = 0. \tag{23}$$

This definition can be made less restrictive. In random processes it is often the case that $x(t) = O(\sqrt{t})$. In which case, (23) still holds.

If $f(x)$ is a bounded function of x for $Min(x) \le x \le Max(x)$, then $f(x)\,dx/dt$ is the derivative of some bounded function $\int f(x)\,dx$, and therefore,

$$E\{f(x)\,dx/dt\} = 0. \tag{24}$$

This allows us to multiply a differential equation by $f(x)$ before taking expectations. In particular, we find that

$$E\{x\,dx/dt\} = 0. \tag{25}$$

This is surprising, since population biologists have been concerned with whether population growth is density-dependent or not and have sought to resolve this question by determining if the rate of increase is negatively correlated with population size. Our result shows that it is not correlated and that this has no bearing on density dependence.

Since

$$d(xy)/dt = y\,dx/dt + x\,dy/dt, \tag{26}$$

$$E\{x\,dy/dt\} = -E(y\,dx/dt). \tag{27}$$

We can also multiply the equations by the derivative. If

$$dx/dt = f(x) - g(y), \tag{28}$$

then

$$(dx/dt)^2 = f(x)\,dx/dt + g(y)\,dx/dt. \tag{29}$$

The left side has a positive value if there is sustained motion, and $E\{f(x)\,dx/dt\} = 0$ so that $E\{g(y)\,dx/dt\} > 0$ and therefore $E\{x\,\partial g(y)/\partial y\,dy/dt\} < 0$.

6.2. Excluding Sustained Bounded Motion

Sustained bounded motion requires that the variance of each variable in the system be positive. Therefore, we can exclude SBM by showing that the variance is zero.

First consider the trivial example of the familiar logistic equation for population growth:

$$dx/dt = rx(K - x). \tag{30}$$

Taking expected values, we have

$$rE(x)[E(K - x)] - r\,Var(x) = 0. \tag{31}$$

Now divide (30) by x before taking expectations. This is valid only if x is bounded away from zero. Then

$$E\{r(K - x)\} = 0. \tag{32}$$

Therefore, $Var(x) = 0$, and SBM is excluded: This equation has only equilibrium solutions at $x = 0$ or $x = K$.

The same technique can be applied to systems of equations. For example, suppose that we have a pair of interacting species

$$dx/dt = x[K_1 + a_{11}x + a_{12}y], \tag{33}$$

$$dy/dt = y[K_2 + a_{21}x + a_{22}y]. \tag{34}$$

Then taking expected values we have

$$E(x)E\{K1 + a11X + a12y\} + a11\,Var(x) + a12\,Cov(x, y) = 0 \qquad (35)$$

and

$$E(y)E\{K2 + a21x + a22y\} + a21\,Cov(x, y) + a22\,Var(y) = 0. \qquad (36)$$

If we restrict the range of x and y so that they are both bounded away from zero, we can divide (33) by x and (34) by y before taking expectations and obtain

$$E\{K_1 + a_{11}x + a_{12}y\} = 0 \qquad (37)$$

and

$$E\{K_2 + a_{21}x + a_{22}y\} = 0, \qquad (38)$$

so that

$$Cov(x, y) = -(a_{11}/a_{12})\,Var(x) \qquad (39)$$

and

$$Cov(x, y) = (a_{22}/a_{21})\,Var(y). \qquad (40)$$

Therefore, we conclude that if a_{11}/a_{12} and a_{22}/a_{11} have opposite signs then there can be no SBM and the nontrivial system reaches a globally stable equilibrium. This method can be extended to more complex networks of interacting species in constant environments (with constant parameters) provided that the graph has a tree structure. Then for n species there are n equations and $n - 1$ covariances (n vertices and $n - 1$ edges). Any $n - 1$ of these equations can be solved for the covariances in terms of the unknown but nonnegative variances. But depending on the coefficients, these solutions may be shown to be compatible only for zero variances and covariances.

A second example is the time delay equation

$$x'(t) + px(t) + qx(t - s) = 0, \qquad (41)$$

where s is a constant and the prime denotes d/dt.

Taking expected values and applying (6), we have

$$pE\{x(t)\} = -qE\{x(t - s)\}. \qquad (42)$$

But for a bounded variable we can show that

$$E\{x(t)\} = E\{x(t - s)\}, \qquad (43)$$

so that if $p \neq -q$ then $E\{x\} = 0$.

Now multiply the equation by $x(t)$ and take expectations. $E\{x(t)x'(t)\}$ is the derivative of the bounded function $x^2(t)/2$ and has an expected value of zero so that we have

$$p\,Var\{x\} = -q\,Cov\{x(t), X(t - s)\}. \qquad (44)$$

Since $x(t)$ and $x(t - s)$ have the same variance while the correlation coefficient is between -1 and 1,

$$Var(x) \geq Cov\{x(t), x(t - s)\}. \tag{45}$$

Since

$$(p/q) \, Var(x) \geq Cov\{x(t), x(t - s)\}. \tag{46}$$

If $(p/q)^2 > 1$, then $Var(x) = 0$. Thus, sustained bounded motion is only possible when $p^2 < q^2$.

The same argument would hold if $p = q(x)$ is any function of $x(t)$ whose variance is greater than or equal to the variance of x. For example, $p(x)$ can be any monotonic function of x for which $\partial p(x)/\partial x > q$.

Finally, consider a second-order differential equation of the form

$$x'' + f(x)x' + g(x) = 0. \tag{47}$$

Since both x'' and $f(x)x'$ are derivatives of bounded functions and therefore have zero expectation, it follows that $E[g(x)] = 0$. Therefore, either $x(t)$ is arbitrarily close to a root of $g(x) = 0$ for $t > t_1$ or $x(t)$ crosses a root of $g(x) = 0$ infinitely often. Finally, it follows that if $g(x) = 0$ has no real roots then $x(y)$ cannot be bounded.

Now multiply (47) by x' before averaging:

$$xx' + f(x)x'^2 + g(x)x' = 0. \tag{48}$$

The first and last terms are derivatives of bounded functions and thus have zero expectation. Therefore,

$$E\{f(x)x'^2\} = 0. \tag{49}$$

This requires any of the following: $x' = 0$ identically, $x(t) = 0$ is arbitrarily close to a root of $f(x) = 0$ for $t > t_2$, and $x(t)$ crosses some root of $f(X) = 0$ infinitely often. If $f(x)$ and $g(x)$ have no real roots in common, then either $x(t)$ is unbounded or $x(t)$ oscillates on a trajectory that crosses roots of both $f(x)$ and $g(x)$. This gives a minimum range for the oscillation.

6.3. The Locus of a Forcing Function

The dynamics of population interactions are complicated by the variability of the environment. Sometimes we are inundated by a mass of environmental measurements without being able to decide which are relevant or how they influence an ecosystem. But the pattern of covariances sometimes allows us to identify which variable in the system is the point of entry of the environmental forcing function.

Most ecological community models take as variables only population numbers. But there are many resources that are not themselves populations but rather the products of organisms such as detritus, pollen or sap, or leaf litter. The model that follows considers a non-self-reproducing resource of this kind.

Consider a plant resource R, perhaps the soluble photosynthate available to an herbivore H that has two predator species X and Y. Y has density-dependent self-inhibition, but X does not, so that

$$dR/dt = a - R(pH + c) \tag{50}$$

$$dH/dt = H(pR - m_0 - q_1 X - q_2 Y) \tag{51}$$

$$dX/dt = X(q_1 H - m_1) \tag{52}$$

$$dY/dt = Y(q_2 H - m_2 - Y). \tag{53}$$

The parameter a measures the rate at which photosynthate becomes available, p is its uptake by the herbivore, c the rate of removal by other processes such as incorporation into the harvestable yield, the m_i are density-independent mortalities, and the qs are predation rates. Unnecessary constants have been omitted for convenience.

The analysis always begins with an autonomous equation. Suppose first that environmental variation enters the system through a variable $a(t)$. Then we begin at equation (53) and find that

$$E\{Y\}E\{q_2 H - m_2 - Y\} + q_2 Cov(H, Y) - Var(Y) = 0. \tag{54}$$

Dividing equation (53) by Y before averaging, we get

$$E\{q_2 H - m_2 - Y\} = 0, \tag{55}$$

so that

$$Cov(H, Y) = Var(Y)/q_2 > 0. \tag{56}$$

A similar procedure gives

$$Cov(H, X) = 0. \tag{57}$$

Then from (51) the same procedure gives

$$p\,Cov(R, H) = q_2 Cov(H, Y) > 0. \tag{58}$$

If variation enters through a time-dependent m_1, we first find that, as before, $Cov(H, Y) > 0$. But

$$q_1 Cov(H, X) = Cov(X, m_1), \tag{59}$$

which is not very informative. Therefore, we examine eq. (50):

$$a = E\{R\}E\{pH + c\} + p\,Cov(R, H), \tag{60}$$

or

$$a/E\{R\} = E\{pH + c\} + p\,Cov(R, H)/E\{R\}. \tag{61}$$

Dividing by R before averaging, we have

$$aE\{1/R\} = E\{pH + c\}. \tag{62}$$

But, for a variable, positive R, $E\{1/R\} > 1/E\{R\}$. Therefore,

$$Cov(R, H) < 0, \tag{63}$$

TABLE 6.2.

Source of variation	$Cov(R,H)$	$Cov(H,X)$	$Cov(H,Y)$
R	+	0	+
H	−	0	+
X	−	−	+
Y	−	0	−

and from (51)

$$p\,Cov(R,H) = q_1\,Cov(H,X) + q_2\,Cov(H,Y) \tag{64}$$

so that $Cov(H,X) < 0$.

If the forcing function is $m_2(t)$, then $Cov(H,X) = 0$ and $Cov(R,H) < 0$. Therefore, $Cov(H,Y) < 0$. And, if m_0 is the major environmental variable, then $Cov(R,H) < 0$, $Cov(H,X) = 0$, and $Cov(H,Y) > 0$. The results are summarized in Table 6.2.

The average level of the herbivore population is determined completely by eq. (52). That is, no matter which predator consumes more H, the one without self-damping controls the average level. Any efforts to enhance the viability or abundance of Y can alter its relative share of the prey but not the average prey abundance. This calls attention to the unexpected fallacy in assigning a "dominant" role to the major predator. Since consumption depends on the co-occurrence of the predator and prey, the share of X is $pE\{H\}E\{X\} + p\,Cov(H,X)$ and of Y is $qE\{H\}E\{Y\} + q\,Cov(H,Y)$. We see from Table 6.2 that the predator that is more sensitive to the environment has a negative covariance with its prey and therefore a smaller share of the prey, but it is the self-damping that determines which predator controls the average prey level.

Therefore, it is useful to note the sources of self-damping. In addition to any direct-density dependence, migration contributes to self-damping. Suppose that

$$dY/dt = Y(q_2 H - m_2) + M, \tag{65}$$

where M is an immigration rate. This can be rewritten as

$$dY/dt = Y(q_2 H - m_2 + M/Y). \tag{66}$$

Then we would find

$$q_2\,Cov(H,Y) = M\,Cov(Y,1/Y) > 0. \tag{67}$$

Thus, highly mobile predators tend to be positively correlated with their prey abundance even without active searching.

In agricultural pest control, we sometimes focus on reducing herbivore levels. But what is really of interest is increasing the yield. This depends on R rather than on H. The average level of R can be found from (50) in two ways. Taking average values and solving for $E\{R\}$ gives

$$E\{R\} = [E\{a\} - p\, Cov(R, H)]/(pE\{H\} + c). \tag{68}$$

Therefore, the average R is reduced by the average H and by the covariance. A negative covariance increase R, while positive covariance reduces R. Therefore, a predator that is more sensitive to the environment, by generating a negative $Cov(R, H)$, increases yield even if it does not affect the average herbivore level. We could also divide (58) by $pH + c$ before averaging. Then,

$$E\{R\} = E\{a/(pH + c)\}. \tag{69}$$

If a is constant, then R increases with the variance of H, once again favoring an environmentally sensitive predator.

6.4. An Autonomous Oscillation

In models of resource/consumer interaction, it is usual to assume that the rate of growth of the consumer population is a function of present resource level. This is a reasonable assumption if food is used immediately. But, if it is stored, the reproductive rate will depend on past resources, and it is therefore sometimes convenient to introduce a new intervening variable between resource and consumer population that measures the physiological state (perhaps body weight) of the consumer. One example is the R, s, X system given by

$$dR/dt = a - R(pX + c) \tag{70}$$

$$ds/dt = pR - ms \tag{71}$$

$$dX/dt = rX(s - s_0). \tag{72}$$

If m is sufficiently large compared to r, then reproduction is approximately in equilibrium with resource, and without parameter variation, the variables reach equilibrium at $s = s_0$, $R = ms_0/p$, $X = a/ms_0 - c/p$. But, for a sufficiently high r, the equilibrium is unstable, and we have a periodic solution in which $E(s) = s_0$, $E(R) = ms_0/p$. $E(X)$ depends on the covariances.

From equation (71) we find immediately that $Cov(R, s) > 0$. By averaging (72), dividing by X, and averaging again, we can show that $Cov(X, s) = 0$. The covariance of R and X can be shown to be negative by the method given in Section 6.3 for constant a, but also by another procedure that does not require a to be constant. Consider

$$d(Xs)/dt = X\, ds/dt + s\, dX/dt, \tag{73}$$

$$s\, dX/dt = rX(s - s_0)(s - s_0 + s_0). \tag{74}$$

Its expected value is positive, since $X > 0$ and $(s - s_0)^2 \geq 0$. Therefore,

$$E\{X\, ds/dt\} < 0. \tag{75}$$

But

$$X\, ds/dt = E\{X\}E\{pR - ms\} + p\, Cov(R, X) - m\, Cov(X, s). \tag{76}$$

The first term on the right is zero, since $E\{pR - ms\} = 0$. The last term has already been shown to be zero, so that

$$Cov(R, X) < 0. \tag{77}$$

This holds, even if $a(t)$ is an arbitrary time-dependent function, as long as it is bounded.

We can also find relative magnitudes of some variances. Multiplying (71) by ds/dt gives

$$(ds/dt)^2 = pR \, ds/dt - ms \, ds/dt. \tag{78}$$

The left side is positive, and the second term on the right has zero expected value, so that

$$E\{pR \, ds/dt\} > 0. \tag{79}$$

But

$$R \, ds/dt = pR^2 - mRs, \tag{80}$$

which has average values, and

$$p \, Var(R) = m \, Cov(R, s). \tag{81}$$

From (71) we find that

$$Cov(R, s) = m \, Var(s)/p. \tag{82}$$

Therefore,

$$p \, Var(R) - m^2 \, Var(s)/p > 0 \tag{83}$$

or

$$p^2 \, Var(R) > m^2 \, Var(s). \tag{84}$$

Similar procedures can be extended further. Since $E\{R \, ds/st\} > 0$, $E\{s \, dR/dt\} < 0$. This allows us to use eq. (70) to find higher order statistics such as $E\{RsX\}$.

6.5. A Demographic Example

Individuals pass through a sequence of developmental stages or size classes that may differ in easily identified ways and in biological important behaviors. This leads us to study systems of equations of the form

$$dX_{k+1}/dt = a_k X_k - b_k X_{k+1} \tag{85}$$

for $k > 1$ and

$$dX_0/dt = \sum m_k X_k, \tag{86}$$

where a_k is the rate of development or growth from stage k to stage $k + 1$, b_{k+1} is $a_{k+1} +$ mortality during stage $k + 1$, and m_k is the fecundity of X_k. If the parameters are constant, then

$$E\{X_k\}/E\{X_{k+1}\} = b_{k+1}/a_k. \tag{87}$$

Dividing (85) and averaging, we get

$$E\{X_k/X_{k+1}\} = b_{k+1}/a_k. \tag{88}$$

Thus, for constant parameters, the average of the ratio is the ratio of the averages. But, if either of the parameters varies due to external factors or is a function of any of the X_k, then this will not be so. The value of k for which the ratio of the averages differs most from the average ratio is the locus of autonomous regulation or environmental impact.

The ratio of variables is also important in another context. Consider a plant/herbivore pair in which

$$dP/dt = rP(K - P - qH) \tag{89}$$

and

$$dH/dt = sH(qP - m). \tag{90}$$

Natural selection in the plant for resistance to the herbivore depends on the herbivore load on a plant. If the herbivores are effective in finding their hosts, this will depend on the average ratio H/P, whereas evolution for herbivore effectiveness depends on plant density alone. The ratio H/P is minimum when H and P have a positive correlation, and increases inversely as their correlation and directly with the variance of P. If K is constant and m variable, the correlation is negative, while if m is constant, the correlation is zero, and if H were itself density dependent, the correlation would be positive. Thus, variation entering the system through the plant's environment favors the selection of resistant plants compared to a system driven from the herbivore's environmental sensitivity, or conversely a self-damped, environmentally sensitive herbivore is less likely to be thwarted by the evolution of plant resistance. Since we have shown that self-damping is increased by migration, we also conclude that herbivores with high mobility are more likely to be ahead of their host plants in the coevolution of resistance and the overcoming of resistance.

6.6. A Note on Discrete Models

It is more difficult to work with discrete models since equation (24) no longer holds. However, it can be replaced by inequalities. Consider the equation

$$X_{t+1} = X_t + f(X_t). \tag{91}$$

Instead of the derivative, we have the discrete change

$$D_t(X) = X_{t+1} - X_t. \tag{92}$$

In the limit

$$E\{X_{t+1} - X_t\} = 0, \tag{93}$$

so that

$$E\{f(X_t)\} = 0. \tag{94}$$

Now consider

$$D_t(X^2) = X_{t+1}^2 - X_t^2, \tag{95}$$

so that

$$D_t(X^2) = 2X_t D_t(X) + D_t(X)^2. \tag{96}$$

The left-hand side has an average value of zero. Whereas in a differential equation the second term on the right vanishes, here it is positive, so that

$$E\{XD(X)\} < 0. \tag{97}$$

Similarly,

$$D_t(\log X) = D(X)/X - D^2(X)/2X^2 + \cdots < D(X)/X. \tag{98}$$

Therefore,

$$E\{D/X\} > 0. \tag{99}$$

We can apply this result to the discrete analog of the logistic

$$D_t(X) = (r - 1)X_t - eX_t^2 \tag{100}$$

to show that

$$E\{X\} < (r - 1)/r. \tag{101}$$

In fact,

$$E\{X\} = (r - 1)/r - Var(X)/E\{X\}. \tag{102}$$

The ratio of successive terms is

$$X_{t+1}/X_t = r - 1 - rX_t. \tag{103}$$

The product of the ratios around any periodic orbit is 1. Therefore,

$$\Pi(r - 1 - rX) = 1 \tag{104}$$

for all orbits. And in holds approximately for any trajectory in the limit.

6.7. A Case of Coexistence

A familiar ecological rule derived from Gause's work in the 1930s states that two species cannot occupy the same niche. Despite difficulties that arise in defining sameness, it has proved useful as a guide to posing questions. For example, when can two species coexist on the same resource? Suppose that

$$dX/dt = Xf(R) \tag{105}$$

and

$$dY/dt = Yg(R) \tag{106}$$

for resource R. At equilibrium,

$$f(R) = 0 \tag{107}$$

and

$$g(R) = 0. \tag{108}$$

But there is no reason to expect any of the roots of f and g to coincide. The exclusion principle therefore follows from there being two equations in one unknown. But if we allow for nonequilibrium coexistence, the situation changes. Suppose, for example, that

$$dX/dt = X(pR - m_1) \tag{109}$$

and

$$dY/dt = Y(qR^2 - m_2). \tag{110}$$

Divide (109) by X and (110) by Y, and take averages. Then

$$pE\{R\} = m_1 \tag{111}$$

and

$$qE\{R\}^2 + q\,Var(R) = m_2. \tag{112}$$

Now there are two equations with two unknowns, and we find

$$E\{R\} = m_1/p \tag{113}$$

and

$$Var(R) = [m_2 - q(m_1/p)^2]/q, \tag{114}$$

provided this is positive. The third equation for R, not shown here, will determine whether there is enough variation in the system to allow that variance in R. The result is that a necessary condition for coexistence of two species on a single resource without any density dependence in the consumers is that there be a nonlinearity so that higher statistical moments such as the variance enter, and a source of variation so that these are not zero. When these conditions are met, it is as if the mean and the variance of R function like different resources.

6.8. Conclusions

The examples presented here were selected for ease of exposition, but the method of time averaging is robust enough to extend to a wider range of models. For instance, if

$$dX/dt = f(X)[g(X) - Y], \tag{115}$$

where $f(X)$ is strictly positive and $g(X)$ is a monotonically increasing function of X, then $Cov(X, g(X))$ is positive, and therefore, $Cov(X, Y)$ is positive. It is not necessary to take expected values to the limit of t. If t is small, we may prefer to use

$$E\{dX/dt\} = (X(t) - X(0))/t \tag{116}$$

and make the corresponding adjustments in the results.

There are a number of issues that are awaiting further investigation. Since we are able to work with the variances of X and dX/dt, it is tempting to use the ratio $Var(dx/dt)/Var(X)$ as a measure of the frequency of an oscillation. For simple cases such as sinusoidal or step function Xs, it satisfies our intuition, but still has to be generalized. Another direction examines the dependence on initial conditions $\partial(dx/dt)/\partial X_0$. Let

$$X(t + dt) = X(t) + dt\, f(X). \tag{117}$$

Then

$$\partial X(t + dt)/\partial X_0 = 1 + dt\, \partial f(X)/\partial X\, \partial X(t)/\partial X_0. \tag{118}$$

Then, iterating this process,

$$\partial X(t + dt)/\partial X_0 = \Pi[1 + dt\, \partial f(X)/\partial X], \tag{119}$$

and as $dt \to 0$, this becomes $1 + \int \partial f/\partial X\, dt$.

If the process approaches a stable equilibrium, then

$$\partial X/\partial X_0 = 0 \tag{120}$$

and

$$E\{\partial f(X)/\partial X\} < 0. \tag{121}$$

For points around an attracting limit cycle, we suspect that

$$\partial X/\partial X_0 - 1 \tag{122}$$

and

$$E\{\partial f(X)/\partial X\} = 0. \tag{123}$$

But, if points arbitrarily close together can give divergent outcomes, then $\partial X/\partial X_0$ becomes infinite, so that

$$E\{\partial f(X)/\partial X\} > 0. \tag{124}$$

References

1. Gantmacher, S.R. *The Theory of Matrices*. Vol. 2. Chelsea Publishing Co., New York, 1960.
2. Pimm, S.L. *Food Webs*. Chapman and Hall, New York, 1982.
3. Puccia, C.J., and Levins, R. *Qualitative Modeling of Complex Systems*. Harvard University Press, Cambridge, Mass., 1985.

CHAPTER 7

System Dynamics: Simulation for Policy Analysis from a Feedback Perspective

George P. Richardson

Abstract

System dynamics is a computer-aided approach to policy analysis and design. With origins in servomechanisms engineering and management, the approach uses a perspective based on information feedback and circular causality to understand the dynamics of complex social systems.

The loop concept underlying feedback and circular causality is not sufficient by itself, however. The explanatory power and insightfulness of feedback understandings also rest on the notions of active system structure and loop dominance, concepts that arise only in nonlinear systems. Computer simulation is the tool that makes it possible to trace the dynamic implications of nonlinear systems. The system dynamicist's feedback perspective is strengthened further by approaching complex problems from a particular conceptual distance, one that blurs discrete events and decisions into continuous patterns of behavior. This continuous view, expressed in stocks, flows, and information links, focuses not on discrete decisions but on the policy structure underlying decisions.

This chapter describes the system dynamics approach and provides an entry into the literature in the field. It explores the wide range of diagramming tools used to conceptualize and explain the stock-and-flow feedback structure responsible for observed behavior. It discusses several simulation environments that are increasing our conceptual and technical modeling abilities and points to principles of systems that facilitate the formulation of insightful models.

An example of policy analysis in school finance is sketched. The insights dervied from that study are linked to a growing list of generic simulation-based policy insights in complex systems.

The background of the field of system dynamics and its current directions are contained in an extensive bibliography.

1. Introduction

System dynamics is a computer-aided approach to policy analysis and design. It applies to *dynamic* problems—problems that involve change over time—arising in complex social, managerial, economic, or ecological systems—literally any dynamic systems characterized by interdependence, mutual inter-action, information feedback, and circular causality.

The field developed from the work of Jay W. Forrester (1958). His seminal book *Industrial Dynamics* [14] is still a significant statement of philosophy and methodology in the field. Within ten years of its publication, the span of applications grew from corporate and industrial problems to include the management of research and development, urban stagnation and decay [1, 17], commodity cycles, and the dynamics of growth in a finite world. It is now applied in economics, public policy, environmental studies, defense, theory-building in social science, and others, as well as in management. The name *industrial dynamics* no longer does justice to the breadth of the field, so it has become generalized to *system dynamics*.[1]

The system dynamics approach involves

—defining problems dynamically, in terms of graphs over time;
—striving for an endogenous, behavioral view of the significant dynamics of a system, a focus inward on the characteristics of a system that themselves generate or exacerbate the perceived problem;
  thinking of all concepts in the real system as continuous quantities inter-connected in loops of information feedback and circular causality;
—identifying independent stocks or accumulations (levels) in the system and their inflows and outflows (rates);
—formulating a behavioral model capable of reproducing, by itself, the dy-namic problem of concern—the model is usually a computer simulation model expressed in nonlinear equations, but is occasionally left unquanti-fied as a diagram capturing the stock-and-flow/causal feedback structure of the system;
—deriving understandings and applicable policy insights from the resulting model;
—implementing changes resulting from model-based understandings and insights.

This is a skeletal list. The field is broad, and there are practitioners world wide who would add to or alter these emphases. Mathematically, the basic structure of a formal system dynamics computer simulation model is easily, if not very helpfully, described as a system of coupled, nonlinear, first-order differential (or integral) equations,

$$\frac{d}{dt}\mathbf{x}(t) = \mathbf{f}(\mathbf{x}, \mathbf{p}),$$

where $\mathbf{x}$ is a vector of levels (stocks or state variables), $\mathbf{p}$ is a set of parameters,

---

[1] The modern name suggests links to other systems methodologies, but the links are weak and misleading. System dynamics emerges out of servomechanisms engineer-ing, not general systems theory or cybernetics [38, 39].

and **f** is a nonlinear vector-valued function.[2] Some practitioners in the field work on the mathematics of such structures, including the theory and mechanics of computer simulation (e.g., [35]), analysis and simplification of dynamic systems (e.g., [22]), policy optimization (e.g., [24, 26, 61]), dynamical systems theory (e.g., [3, 31]), and complex nonlinear dynamics and deterministic chaos.[3]

Although recognizing these important mathematical directions within the field and not wanting to slight them, here we shall limit our focus to the core of the field that studies perceived problems in complex systems and presses toward qualitative understandings and policy insights. This chapter begins with a broad view of some of the characteristics of the system dynamics approach, discussing in turn feedback thinking, loop dominance in dynamic feedback systems, and the system dynamicist's endogenous point of view. The discussion then focuses on some of the details, including the concept of levels and rates, continuity, diagrams for conceptualization and communication, and existing simulation languages for system dynamics modeling. At the end of the chapter, we drop back from the details to consider broader modeling heuristics and principles of systems, a policy analysis example, generic simulation-based policy insights, and directions for further reading.

2. Feedback Thinking

Conceptually, the feedback concept is at the heart of the system dynamics approach. Diagrams of loops of information feedback and circular causality are tools for conceptualizing the structure of a complex system and for communicating model-based insights. Intuitively, a feedback loops exists when information resulting from some action travels through a system and eventually returns in some form to its point of origin, potentially influencing future action. If the tendency in the loop is to reinforce the initial action, the loop is called a *positive* feedback loop; if the tendency is to oppose the initial action, the loop is called a *negative* feedback loop. The sign of the loop is called its *polarity*. Negative loops can be variously characterized as goal-seeking, equilibrating, or stabilizing processes. They can sometimes generate oscillations, as a pendulum seeking its equilibrium goal gathers momentum and overshoots it. Positive loops are sources of growth or accelerating collapse; they are disequilibrating and destabilizing. Combined, positive and negative circular causal feedback loops can generate all manner of dynamic patterns.

The loop concept is familiar to readers of this volume. It finds expression in a number of qualitative approaches presented here. Its attractiveness as a

---

[2] Such a system has been variously called a *state-determined system* in the engineering literature, an *absolute system* [4], an *equifinal system* [57], and a *dynamical system* [32].

[3] See *System Dynamics Review 4*, 1–2 (1988), a special issue on chaos.

basis for modern qualitative technologies is no accident, for feedback thought has been present implicitly or explicitly for hundreds of years in the social sciences [38, 39, 55]. We have the vicious circle originating in classical logic, the invisible hand of Adam Smith, Malthus's correct observation of population growth as a self-reinforcing process, Keynes's consumption multiplier, the investment accelerator of Hicks and Samuelson, compound interest or inflation, the biological concepts of proprioception and homeostasis [7], Gregory Bateson's schismogenesis (the generation and maintenance of a split between cultures in contact) [5, 6], Festinger's cognitive dissonance, the bandwagon effect, Myrdal's principle of cumulative causation, Venn's idea of a suicidal prophecy, Merton's related notion of a self-fulfilling prophecy, and so on. Each of these ideas can be concisely and insightfully represented as one or more loops of causal influences with positive or negative polarities. Great social scientists are feedback thinkers; great social theories are feedback thoughts.

3. Loop Dominance

The loop concept underlying feedback and circular causality by itself is not enough, however. The explanatory power and insightfulness of feedback understandings also rest on the notions of active structure and loop dominance.

We know that social systems change over time. What focuses concern in one period is overshadowed by other concerns at other times and conditions. There are discernible patterns in newspaper headlines and legislative efforts as pressures shift from national affairs to international affairs, defense, or the balance of payments. Goals and negative feedback structures that dominate governmental efforts in times of persistent inflation change and evolve as the main economic problems are perceived to shift to, say, persistently high unemployment. No static view of the structure of a dynamic social system is likely to be perceived to be powerful. A crucial requirement for a powerful feedback view of a dynamic system is the ability of a mental or formal model to change the strengths of influences as conditions change, that is to say, the ability to shift *active* or *dominant structure*.

An overly simplified example can make the concept clear. Consider the life cycle of a finite resource, such as global petroleum. Figure 7.1 shows two highly aggregated feedback loops that can describe the dynamics of the life cycle. As oil is discovered and production begins, economies find uses for the resource and demand for it increases. Furthermore, accumulating experience with discovery, recovery, and production leads to more sophisticated and efficient technologies, further accelerating the rate at which the resource can be produced. The feedback loop on the right side of Figure 7.1 is a positive loop. In this highly simplified view, the self-reinforcing tendencies this loop represents are responsible for the growth of the use of the resource. Oil production would

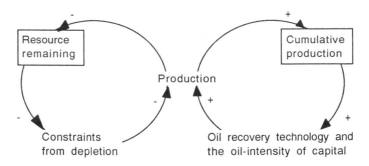

FIGURE 7.1. Positive and negative feedback loops in the life cycle of a finite resource such as petroleum.

increase, and its rate of increase would also increase; a graph of oil production and cumulative oil production would curve upward, looking like exponential growth.

The left side of Figure 7.1 is a negative loop representing the effects of the depletion of this finite resource. In the early stages of the petroleum life cycle, this loop is not influential. It might not even be perceived to exist. Whatever minor effects it might have are completely overshadowed by the growth-producing self-reinforcing processes aggregated in the right-side loop. However, under the assumption that the resource is finite, this negative loop must eventually become the dominant factor in our ability to produce and consume petroleum. Eventually, as the resource becomes scarce, the difficulties and costs of discovery and production will slow production and pull supply below the growing demand. Toward the end of the life cycle, the price of the resource will have risen well beyond the price of substitute energy sources, and substitution will increasingly occur.

The graph of production will rise, peak, and eventually enter a persistent though noisy decline. Cumulative production over time will show a more-or-less S-shaped pattern. The upward curving period of exponential growth changes to a still-increasing but downward-curving pattern that eventually comes into equilibrium by the end of the life cycle. The pattern of cumulative production shifts from accelerating, limitless growth to a decelerating approach to a limit. The change in the pattern is insightfully seen as a *shift in dominance* from self-reinforcing positive loop processes to constraining, equilibrating, negative loop processes.

The qualitative notion of a shift in loop dominance can be made rigorous in such a simple system, and an important modeling understanding emerges. Consider the Verhulst equation (the logistic equation) for population growth: $dP/dt = aP - bP^2$. Verhulst intended the term aP to represent the self-reinforcing growth tendencies of the population, while the term bP^2 is to represent the constraints on growth that would come from human interaction (assumed proportional to $P*P$). Thus, the system can be viewed as a pair of feedback loops, as shown in Figure 7.2.

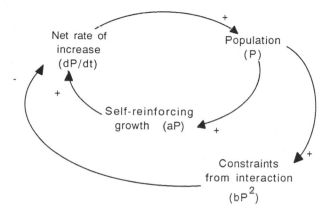

FIGURE 7.2. Feedback loops in the Verhulst (logistic) equation.

The dominant polarity of this system can be defined as the sign of dP'/dP, where $P' = dP/dt$. Intuitively, we trace the aggregate effect in this system of a small increase dP in population. If the effect is positive and so self-reinforcing, the positive polarity dominates; if it is negative, the negative polarity dominates.

Since $P' = dP/dt = aP - bP^2$, we compute $dP'/dP = a - 2bP$, which is positive for $P < a/(2b)$ and negative for $P > a/(2b)$. Noting that population growth halts when P reaches a/b, we conclude that the positive loop dominates until the population size reaches half its maximum and from there on the negative loop dominates. Thus, the classic logistic growth pattern can be seen as the consequence of a shift in loop dominance from a positive feedback loop to a negative feedback loop.

Two things about this example are critically important and generalizable to a feedback view of dynamic systems. First, the shift in loop dominance comes as a consequence of the *nonlinearity* of the Verhulst equation. If the equation were $dP/dt = aP - bP$, no such shift in loop dominance would occur. If $a > b$, the positive loop would always dominate, and the system would show limitless exponential growth; if $a < b$, the negative loop would always dominate, and the system would exhibit exponential decline to the goal of zero. Furthermore, if the system were $dP/dt = aP - bP^3$ or $aP - bP \ln P$ (the Gompertz curve), it would show qualitatively the same behavior as the classic logistic equation, for in either of these equations the negative, nonlinear constraint term can start small and then overtake the positive, self-reinforcing growth term. Thus, *nonlinear* models have the property that they can exhibit shifts in loop dominance. Linear models cannot.

From a feedback perspective, the ability of nonlinearities to generate shifts in loop dominance is the fundamental reason for advocating nonlinear models of social system behavior. Real systems are perceived to change their active or dominant structure over time. Only nonlinear models can do that, so the best mathematical models of dynamic social systems must be nonlinear. In

BETHANY
COLLEGE
LIBRARY

fact, without the concept of shifting loop dominance—without nonlinearities in formal models of complex systems—the feedback concept is justifiably perceived to be a weak tool incapable of capturing important dynamics in real systems.

4. The Endogenous Point of View

A second but even more powerful insight is that a shift in loop dominance in these nonlinear models comes about *endogenously*. The shift from positive loop to negative loop in the Verhulst equation is not engineered from outside the system; it happens *internally* as the system plays itself out over time. The system changes its own dominant structure as it evolves. Yet we could easily imagine an exogenous intervention—a random blip, a switch, even the re-writing of an equation part way through—that could produce fundamental changes in structure and dynamics. We really must qualify the strong conclusion previously reached: Nonlinearities in a formal dynamic model are essential if one wishes to obtain changes in active structure *endogenously*.

The concept of endogenous change is fundamental to the system dynamics approach. Practitioners strive for an *endogenous point of view*. The goal is to derive the essential dynamic characteristics of a system from the inner workings of the system itself. It is an inward-looking perspective. Look for sources of urban decay within the structure and policies of the city itself; look for sources of cyclical customer orders in the inventory and production policies of the company itself. The goal is to view problems as consequences of a complex system of interacting subsystems, not as the unavoidable result of exogenous disturbances.

The endogenous point of view is variously expressed. Forrester [15, 17] signaled it when he outlined his general hierarchical theory of system structure:

Closed boundary
   Feedback loops
     Levels
     Rates
       Goal
       Observed condition
       Discrepancy
       Desired action

The *closed boundary* in this hierarchy is not "closed" in the general system theory sense [57]. A system dynamics model—of a company, an urban area, a school district—interchanges material (orders, people, money) with its environment, so it is not closed in the general system theory sense. Forrester intended the word here to mean *causally* closed:

> The boundary encloses the system of interest. It states that the modes of
> behavior under study are created by the interaction of the system compo-

nents within the boundary. The boundary implies that no influences from outside of the boundary are necessary for generating the particular behavior being investigated. [15, 16, p. 84]

The modeler's goal is to assemble a formal structure that can, *by itself*, without exogenous explanations, reproduce the essential characteristics of a dynamic problem.[4]

The importance of the endogenous point of view must not be under-estimated. It dictates aspects of model formulation: exogenous disturbances are seen at most as *triggers* of system behavior (like displacing a pendulum); the *causes* are contained within the structure of the system itself (like the interaction of a pendulum's position and momentum that produces oscillations). Corrective responses are also not modeled as functions of time, but are dependent on conditions within the system. Time by itself is not seen as a cause.

But, more importantly, theory building and policy analysis are significantly affected by this endogenous perspective. Taking an endogenous view changes the focus of policymakers from trying to anticipate a whimsical environment to trying to understand the inner workings of the system that create or amplify perceived problems. It exposes the natural *compensating* tendencies in social systems that conspire to defeat many policy initiatives.

It is seen as an essential foundation of good theory. Exogenous explanations of system behavior are simply not as interesting. They can even be misleading: There are no exogenous events that cause the turnaround in the swing of a pendulum, and perhaps none in the peak or trough of the business cycle.

Finally, the endogenous point of view is an empowering perspective that focuses attention on aspects of the system over which people may hope to have some control. If the cause of urban decay is seen as not enough federal funding, then restoring urban health lies outside the control of urban actors. But, if urban decay is seen to have components that are internal to the city, then local policymakers can strive to improve matters no matter what the federal government decides to do. The effort to find endogenous sources of dynamic problems is essential if endogenous solutions are to be found.

The endogenous point of view is the feedback view pressed to an extreme. In fact, the feedback view can be seen as a *consequence* of the effort to capture dynamics within a closed causal boundary. Without causal loops, all variables must trace the sources of their variation ultimately outside a system. Without loops we are forced to an exogenous view of the causes of system behavior. Assuming instead that the causes of all significant behavior in the system are contained within some closed causal boundary forces causal influences to feed back upon themselves, forming causal loops. Feedback loops enable the endogenous point of view and give it structure.

This endogenous point of view has come to be summarized in a shorthand

---

[4] There is some debate about the practicality of creating endogenous models of real policy problems. Fundamentally, the debate concerns the appropriate model boundary for a given policy analysis.

tenet: *Behavior is a consequence of structure.* Behavior here means dynamic behavior, phrased in terms of graphs over time. Structure refers to feedback structure: a circular causal complexity composed of stocks (levels), flows (rates), and information links. The phrase is, at the same time, a grand conjecture, an article of faith, and a proposition repeatedly verified in the practice of building and simulating models of social systems.

5. Levels and Rates

Stocks and the flows that affect them are essential components of system structure. A map of causal influences and feedback loops is not enough to determine the dynamic behavior of a system. Stocks—accumulations—are the memory of a dynamic system and are the sources of disequilibrium. An inventory, for example, exists to decouple the flow of the production from the flow of shipments. If shipments exceed production, inventory absorbs the inequity by declining. A population similarly absorbs inequity between births per year and deaths per year. And changes in such levels generate other changes. A rising population would produce more births per year, for example, which would in turn push population still higher, ceteris paribus. A declining inventory would eventually generate pressures to slow shipments or increase production. Stocks, or *levels* in the system dynamicist's intuitive terminology, and the rates that affect them are the sources of dynamic behavior.[5]

Levels also persist through time. If time were to stop, it is the levels, the conceptual and physical stocks in the system, that would still exist and be in some sense measurable. We could tell the size of inventories and the work force, for example, but we could not know the rate of production.

6. Continuity and Conceptual Distance

The importance of levels and rates appears most clearly when one takes a *continuous* view of structure and dynamics. Although a discrete view, focusing on separate events and decisions, is entirely compatible with an endogenous feedback perspective, the system dynamics approach emphasizes a continuous view. System dynamics models are continuous representations of system structure and dynamics.[6]

---

[5] In engineering terminology, levels are the *state* variables; rates are the components of the derivatives or rates of change of the system states.

[6] To be excruciatingly precise, a system dynamics model simulated on a digital computer is a discrete approximation of a continuous system. For computation purposes, model TIME is segmented into short chunks of length *DT*, and the model is stepped discretely through TIME. However, this discreteness is an unavoidable accident of digital simulation; it has nothing to do with the intent or perspective of the modeler. A system dynamics model is most properly seen as a continuous system composed of differential equations (really integral equations), not a discrete system made up of difference equations.

The continuous view has several advantages and one or two disadvantages. Its major disadvantage is that it is hard to achieve. In daily, lifelong experience, we see discrete events and make discrete decisions. Forrester [14] argued, however, that a continuous view helps to focus us on what is most important in dynamic social systems. He cautioned us to be "on guard against unnecessarily cluttering our formulation with the detail of discrete events that only obscure the momentum and continuity" of social systems [14].[7] The continuous view strives to look beyond events to see the dynamic patterns underlying them. Model not the appearance of a discrete new housing unit, but focus instead on the rise and fall of aggregate numbers of housing units. Moreover, the continuous view focuses not on discrete decisions but on the *policy structure* underlying decisions: not why this particular apartment building was constructed but what persistent pressures exist in the urban system that produce decisions that change housing availability in the city. Events and decisions are seen as surface phenomena that ride on an underlying tide of system structure and behavior. It is that underlying tide of policy structure and continuous behavior that is the system dynamicist's focus.

There is thus a *distancing* inherent in the system dynamics approach, not so close as to be confused by discrete decisions and myriad operational details, but not so far away as to miss the critical elements of policy structure and behavior. Events are deliberately blurred into dynamic behavior. Decisions are deliberately blurred into perceived policy structures. Insights into the connections between system structure and behavior come from this particular distance of perspective.[8]

7. Modeling Tools: Diagrams

Diagrams are essential for conceptualizing system structure and communicating model-based insights about feedback structure and dynamic behavior. We will mention four kinds that prove useful in various stages of a policy simulation study.

The kind of diagram that contains the greatest amount of information about system structure is exemplified in Figure 7.3; it is perhaps best referred to as a *stock-and-flow/feedback diagram*. Each symbol in such a detailed diagram refers to a unique equation in the formal model the diagram represents. Types of equations are distinguished: levels are rectangles and auxiliaries (algebraic computations or relationships expressed graphically) are circles: constants are marked with a line; rates are shown with a symbol representing a valve that controls a flow. The arrows also convey information: Conserved flows, shown as solid or double arrows, are distinguished from information links, which are identified with dotted arrows. There is such a lack of ambiguity in such

---

[7] See also [10, p. 64], [33], and [34, p. 21].
[8] For further comments on conceptual distance, see [11, p. 377], [14, p. 96], and [39, p. 508].

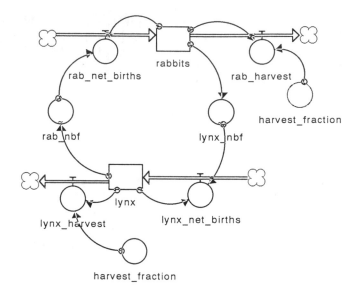

rabbits

rab_net_births   rab_harvest

                                                    harvest_fraction

rab_nbf   lynx_nbf

                              lynx

lynx_harvest   lynx_net_births

                    harvest_fraction

FIGURE 7.3. Stock-and-flow/feedback structure diagram of a simple predator–prey system.

diagrams that one can come close to recreating a model's equations (without parameters) from well-drawn stock-and-flow/feedback structure diagrams. Their very detail and precision, however, limits the audiences to which they communicate well.

A much simpler diagram at the same structural level is a picture of a feedback system consisting simply of words and arrows, so-called *causal-loop diagrams* or *influence diagrams* (Figure 7.2, or Figures 7.1 and 7.7 without the rectangles, would be examples). Frequently, causal-loop diagrams are suggested as the first step in model conceptualization [20, 42, 47]. Their greatest strength—simplicity—is also their greatest weakness. They omit the critical distinction between material flows and information links and consequently obscure the accumulations in a system. Furthermore, they make it easy to draw a picture of systemic interactions that focuses on sequences of events. The arrows can come to mean sequence ("and then ..."), not causal influence. An event orientation severely inhibits formulating a quantitative model of a complex system, particularly one striving to capture the fundamental structure and pressures present in the system that persist through time.[9]

The troubles simple influence diagrams and causal loops can cause in the

---

[9] The flexibility of the technique of *cognitive mapping* frequently results in word-and-arrow diagrams that mix causal structure with sequences of events; see, for example, some of the cognitive maps in [13]. For the kinds of translations event-oriented diagrams require, see [42].

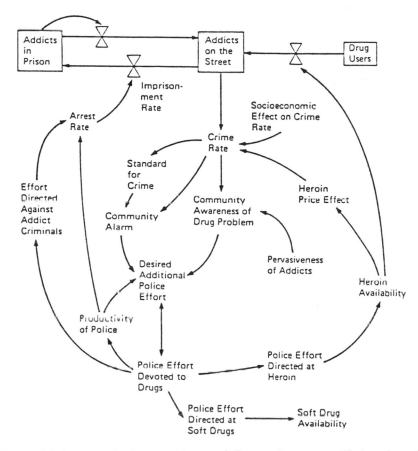

FIGURE 7.4. An example of a causal-loop or influence diagram modified to show the distinctions between accumulations (levels) and other variables and between information links and material flows [25, p. 27]. (See, also, [62, Figs. 1 and 7] for other approaches.)

conceptualization stages of a simulation study have prompted most practitioners to find ways to modify them to show levels and rates. Figures 7.4 and 7.7 show examples. Suffice it to say, experience suggests that simple word-and-arrow diagrams are best reserved for communicating system structure and insights toward the *end* of a study, not as a step in model conceptualization or formulation. In the formulation phase, there appears to be no substitute for trying to identify important accumulations and the rates that change them.

A powerful extension of influence diagrams with explicit rates and levels is Morecroft's notion of policy structure diagrams [29, 30]. Figure 7.5 shows an example.

These diagrams focus on the important levels and rates in a portion or *sector* of a complex system, along with an aggregated view of important information

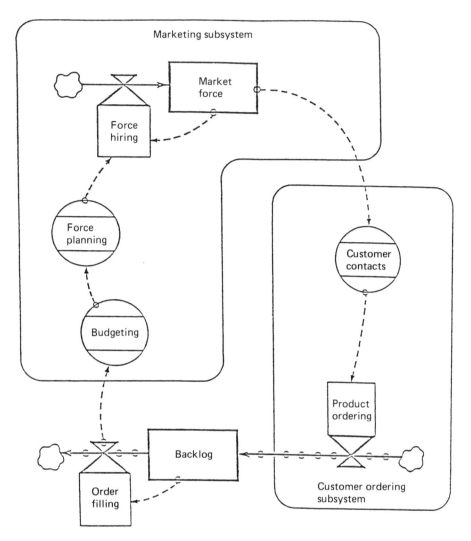

FIGURE 7.5. A policy structure diagram [29]. The diagram presents a view of part of Forrester's market growth model [15].

connections among those levels and rates. They highlight the key policy areas in the sector and show the information streams that combine to produce decisions under those policies. Some of the information streams would be deliberate components of policy, while others would be unavoidable pressures on policy decisions from various parts of the system. The advantages of policy structure diagrams are an appropriate level of detail for clients; explicit representation on stocks and flows, which helps to sensitize clients to the importance of accumulations in the dynamics of the system; and a focus on policy, which matches the client's locus of concern. Their main disadvantage

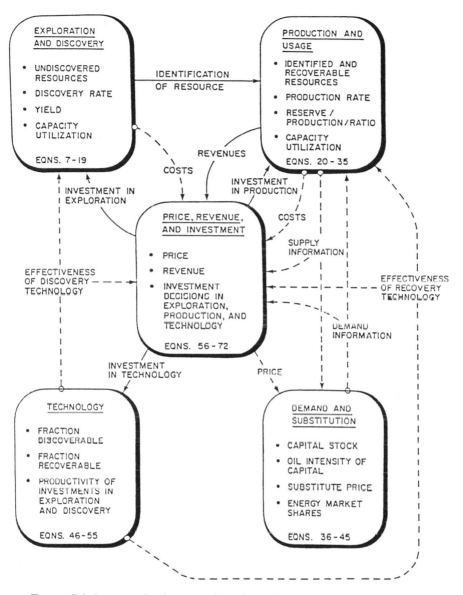

FIGURE 7.6. An example of an overview of model and sector boundaries [54].

is their tendency to obscure the existence and the character of feedback loops in the system. Their use in the system dynamics literature is limited. Nonetheless, for system conceptualization and for communication about model structure, policy structure diagrams have considerable promise.

A fourth kind of diagram useful for both conceptualization and communication is an *overview of model and sector boundaries*. Figure 7.6 shows an example. Such diagrams strive to capture the organization of a simulation model, to show a summary of what is included and what is excluded, and to show the main interconnections among the identifiable sectors in the system. Such a diagram is really a visual outline of the system and the model formulated to represent it for policy analysis. Formulated and presented at the outset of a study, an overview of model and sector boundaries helps to orient and join (if different) the modeler and the client. Throughout a study, such diagrams provide quick introductions and summaries of the scope of the study.

Rarely, however, can a study of policy alternatives in a complex social system stop at the level of diagrams.[10] Our means of making reliable deductions about the dynamic implications of a complex stock-and-flow/feedback structure is computer simulation.

8. Modeling Tools: Simulation Environments

As could be expected, there have been and continue to be dramatic developments in the software available to support system dynamics modeling. Many languages have the capabilities to represent and simulate dynamic systems; even general-purpose languages like BASIC or Pascal suffice. But special-purpose languages make the modeling task far easier. The original simulation language in the field was called SIMPLE, a cute acronym standing for Simulating Industrial Management Problems with Lots of Equations. It was followed quickly by DYNAMO [36, 42], for DYNAmic MOdels, which is still the language of choice for a majority of practitioners in the field. DYNAMO relieves the modeler from thoughts about *programming*. To a remarkable extent, it leaves one free to concentrate on the real system. The order of equations in a model, for example, can be arranged to suit the tastes and understandings of the modeler and the audience or clients. The equations can be arranged to tell a sensible story; DYNAMO handles the task of putting them in a computable order a machine can execute.

DYNAMO provides timescripts J, K, and L, analogous to subscripts, that make clear what is being computed when. K is "now," the time of the current computation; J is the previous moment, the time of the previous computation; and L is the time of the next computation. A level equation for population, for example, might look like

$$L \quad POP.K = POP.J + DT*(BIRTHS.JK - DEATHS.JK)$$

Here,

---

[10] An example of system dynamics studies that did is [62]. The potential for flawed conclusions from causal-loop diagrams without simulation is shown by [58], for example, who rests some of his analysis on the false claim that an even number of negative loops in a system creates a "deviation amplifying system" (see, e.g., [58, p. 133]).

POP.K   represents population at time *K* (current population);

POP.J   represents population at the previous computation;

DT   represents the length of simulated time between times *J* and *K*; and

BIRTHS.JK   represents the number of births per year that occurred in the time interval from time *J* to *K*.

DEATHS.JK represents the number of deaths per year that occurred from *J* to *K*. The *L* tells DYNAMO to expect a level equation in more or less this form. The language has extensive error-checking capabilities that can signal the user when unusual formats (errors usually) are encountered. The form of this level equation shows that the variable *POP* accumulates *BIRTHS* and *DEATHS* over time.[11]

Rearranging slightly, we see that the level equation is equivalent to the statement that

$$\frac{\Delta POP}{\Delta T} = \frac{POP.K - POP.J}{DT} = BIRTHS.JK - DEATHS.JK,$$

that is, that the net rate of change of population is births per year minus deaths per year, as we would require.

The computation interval *DT* in such equations is a fiction. The modeler's intent, in this case, is to capture population growth as a continuous process. To simulate a continuous process, we break simulated *TIME* into discrete chunks and *step* the model through time, one discrete *DT* at a time. The modeler chooses *DT* small enough so that it has no discernible effect on model behavior. Calculus and derivatives and integrals are lurking in the not-so-distant background here, but simulation relieves the practitioner from concentrating on them. In fact, simulation makes possible the creation and use of models that can not be solved in closed form. Simulation expands the range of problems we can model, the complexity of models we formulate, and the number of people who can build and understand them.

Several other languages, including NDTRAN[12] and DYSMAP [8], have been developed that have the look and feel of DYNAMO with various other capabilities. All of these have recently been migrated to IBM-compatible personal computers.[13] For further information about these simulation

---

[11] It also tells advanced simulation modelers that DYNAMO's default integration scheme is Euler integration. In social systems, modeling that conceptually simple approach is computationally accurate enough for almost all purposes [35]. Most simulation languages, including DYNAMO, provide more accurate integration options (e.g., Runge-Kutta) that a knowledgeable user can invoke.

[12] W. Davisson and J. Uhran, University of Notre Dame, Notre Dame, Indiana.

[13] Professional DYNAMO and Professional DYNAMO Plus, Pugh-Roberts Associates, Cambridge, MA. 02139; DYSMAP2, University of Salford, M5 4WT Salford, England.

environments, the reader should consult the references in the notes. However, it is worth repeating a frequently heard but vital warning: Even the most detailed knowledge of a simulation language is little assurance of readiness to formulate and analyze insightful simulation models of social system dynamics. Knowledge of vocabulary and syntax are only meager first steps toward writing that is worth reading. Like a writer, a modeler must have something to say, born of intimate knowledge of the subject and great skill in translating that understanding into a form that a machine can simulate and people can learn from.

A recent breakthrough in simulation software that extends modeling capabilities still further is STELLA™ on the Macintosh [43, 44]. In this simulation environment, the modeler concentrates on *drawing* in a structured way the stock-and-flow feedback structure of the system on the computer screen, and the software writes the model equations in the background. Figure 7.3 is an example of a STELLA diagram. Each icon in the figure represents an equation in the system that must be carefully thought about, but the modeler concentrates most on the interconnected structure. STELLA (an acronym that stands for Structural Thinking, Experiential Learning Laboratory with Animation) is a major step toward making quantitative dynamic modeling qualitative. The manual with the language is really an excellent state-of-the-art text in modeling.

9. Modeling Heuristics and Principles of Systems

Forrester [16] distilled a number of mathematical formalisms and system insights into a set of *principles of systems*. Quite literally, they are an enlightened collection of biases about good modeling practice. Some examples follow:

1. A feedback loop consists of two distinctly different types of variables: the levels (states) and the rates (actions). Except for constants, these two are sufficient to represent a feedback loop. Both are necessary.
2. Levels integrate (or accumulate) the results of action in a system. ...
3. Levels are changed only by the rates ....
4. Levels and rates are not distinguished by units of measure.[14] ... The identification must recognize the difference between a variable created by integration and one that is a policy statement in the system.
5. Rates [are] not instantaneously measurable. ... No rate can, in principle, control another rate without an intervening level variable.
6. Level variables and rate variables [in a feedback loop] must alternate. ...
7. Levels completely describe the system condition.

---

[14] "People per year" could be the units of a rate (births or deaths) or an *average rate* over a period of time, which would be a level since an average involves an accumulation. Velocity could be a level in a model of pendulum dynamics.

8. Levels exist in conservative subsystems; they can be changed only by moving the contents between levels (or to or from a source or sink).
9. Information is not a conservative flow; information is not depleted by its use.[15]
10. Decisions (rates) are based only on available information.

... and so on.

In Forrester [16] there are more than 30 such principles. Some constitute a verbal description, in largely nonmathematical terms, of the engineer's and mathematician's notion of a *state-determined* system. Others, such as (5) and (6) above, reflect qualitative wisdom about social systems, often stemming from an endogenous point of view or a particular conceptual distance. Still others, such as (10), are explicit biases about what may and may not be assumed in a formal model of a social system. Some scholars have chosen explicitly or implicitly to ignore some of these principles.[16] That is a possible but perilous course. Far better is to understand deeply the principle and its rationale, to be always alert for errors related to it, and to know under what conditions it may be violated. It takes a good acrobat to be a clown.

There are some circumstances, for example, when one rate can instantaneously influence another (see (5) above). An example occurs in the dynamics of financial systems, where the rate of flow of payments into assets is also the rate at which the stock of payments due are reduced. But the principle that information about one rate cannot instantaneously be used to govern another rate is an extremely good one; information almost always takes time to be collected and transmitted from one part of a system to another. It is almost always an error to formulate one rate as an instantaneous function of another rate. What we usually know in social systems is not the current value of a rate (such as GNP or highway accidents) but a recent *average* rate, and an average is actually a level, as it involves a sum — an accumulation.

Many of Forrester's principles have found their way into the simulation languages system dynamicists use. DYNAMO and DYSMAP, for example, will respond with a warning if a level equation is written to say the level is changed by something that does not look like a rate. STELLA will simply not let the modeler draw a causal link directly to a level—the link evaporates. Both languages will refuse to accept a feedback loop that does not contain at

---

[15] The distinction between information and material (conserved) flows is a critical insight of the information age. An information link from, say, the rabbit population to the lynx growth rate in Figure 7.3 does not subtract from the rabbit population, but the material flow of the "rabbit harvest" does. Unlike material, information is not a conserved quantity: Using it does not deplete it.

[16] See, for example, [4, p. 54] and [9, p. 21]; both stumble because they use a difference equation representation, which allows them to violate the principle of at least one accumulation in every feedback loop. Hanneman [23], advocating DYNAMO simulation in sociology, explicitly rejects what he calls the "conceptual baggage" of system dynamics. In the process he leaves behind some powerful modeling heuristics that would have improved his sociological model building.

least one level [in violation of (1), (7), and implicitly, (10)]. Such a loop implies that information travels instantaneously around the loop, creating a simultaneity that is both philosophically and computationally troublesome. There are no such simultaneous loops in continuous systems, so there are none in system dynamics models.

Others have added to Forrester's list, often identifying generalizations repeatedly seen in past work. Model a *problem*, not a *system*. Have a clear purpose for the effort (a model without a purpose is like a ship without a sail, a boat without a rudder, a hammer without a nail ...). Distinguish desired quantities from obtainable quantities, and perceived quantities from actual ones. And so on.

Although these principles and heuristics, and the modeling guidelines built into the languages we use, are enormously helpful, they are still not enough to guarantee that people who know the languages will build good models. In spite of people's attempts to embed expert knowledge in simulation languages and to formulate wise modeling heuristics, modeling is still an art.

10. Policy Analysis Based on System Dynamics Simulation

The goal of a system dynamics policy study is understanding: understanding the interactions in a complex system that are conspiring to create a problem, and understanding the structure and dynamic implications of policy changes intended to improve the system's behavior.

It is useful to distinguish two kinds of policy insights that can come from simulation studies. Some insights are system specific, applying to a particular company, government, or ecosystem during a particular period. As an example, consider the following simulation-based analysis of state aid to local school districts.

The problem the study addressed dealt with inequities in per-pupil expenditures among rich and poor school districts. Like many other states, Connecticut had pursued a particular funding policy known as a Guaranteed Wealth or Guaranteed Tax Base formula. In theory the formula would bring all school districts up to the same level of wealth, so that if they taxed themselves the same, there would be the same amount of money available to fund school systems across the state. The court-mandated goal of equal expenditures per pupil among rich and poor school districts in a state would be achieved.

Figure 7.7 shows an overview of the theory of local district planning captured in the simulation model in this study. The darker loops in the upper part of the figure show a simplified view of the the process a local district follows to set staffing levels. Presuming there are sufficient funds, staffing levels are set to achieve a desired staff-per-pupil ratio. This goal for staff-per-pupil is presumed to be strongly influenced by the district's traditional staff-per-pupil ratio, as both the literature and anecdotal evidence suggest. The traditional staff-per-pupil ratio leads to a desired staff level that functions as an "anchor" (see [49] and [56]) in the policy process that finally results in a decision about planned tax rates and planned staff. Given a tight budgetary

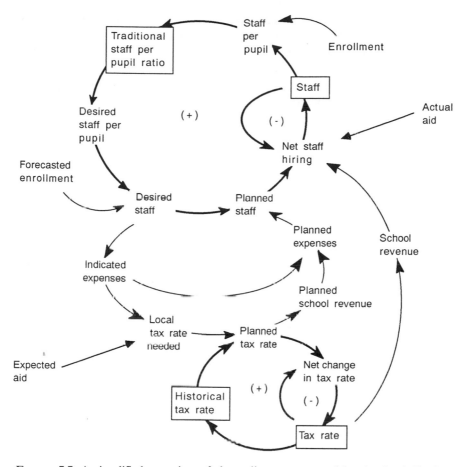

FIGURE 7.7. A simplified overview of the policy structures of local school district planning, captured in a simulation model of state aid to education. The rectangles identify levels (states) in the system.

year, the planned staff might be adjusted somewhat below this anchor, the desired staff level. Or, given unexpected revenues or other sources of slack in a town's budget, the planned staff level could rise above the traditionally desired level of staff.

When goals are anchored on historical or traditional achievements, it follows that the goals themselves may slowly change over time. If pressures combine to drag down staff-per-pupil ratios, and the lowered levels of staffing continue over a long period of time, then lower staff-per-pupil ratios can become the new standard, the new goal in the staffing policy process. Goals based on traditional achievements can slide.[17] They can gradually drift up, as

---

[17] The feedback structure underlying the phenomenon of adaptive or sliding goals was first described in [15].

well as slide down, if unexpected revenues or other positive pressures combine to produce increases in staffing levels that are then sustained over a sufficiently long period of time to change the way people think about standards.

On the tax side of this policy picture, an analogous sliding goals structure is responsible for the potential of local districts to become *addicted* to state aid. Tax planning comes to be based on, or anchored on, a traditional tax rate structure. A sustained period of state aid results in a historical or traditional tax rate structure in a local district that is lower than would be required without the aid. The school and tax traditions in the local district in effect are addicted to the continuation of state aid.

The structure shown in Figure 7.7 and captured in the simulation model provides an explanation of why the state's Guaranteed Wealth formula failed. A local district, planning and budgeting as shown in the diagram, would initially set staffing goals based on recent levels of staffing within its locale. Expected state aid would be incorporated into the planning process. The local district can respond to anticipated aid to education by putting more of its local money into other pressing demands. Untargeted aid-to-education that can be anticipated and planned for can indirectly be used to fill potholes in neighborhood streets. The implication is that local goals can frustrate state goals in the way local districts use general, anticipated grants. The study concluded that general, anticipated grants, GAGs, will not work.

The direct opposite of GAGs, the study suggested, are TUGs—*targeted, unanticipated grants*. The structure of local budgeting behavior in the simulation model and its resulting behavior suggest that states should try TUGing local districts to achieve the aims of state aid-to-education. The extent to which aid can be targeted to fulfill the purposes intended by state policy, the more likely that aid will not be used for other purposes. Still, there is the potential that, if the aid can be anticipated in the local budget and tax planning process, relief of the need for school revenues in may translate into tax savings or increased expenditures elsewhere. The greatest potential, then, according to this reasoning, would come from *unanticipated* grants—state aid-to-education that local districts do not know is coming or cannot rely on fully. The study pushed these simulation-based feedback insights further to discuss the potential of SLUGs (short-lived unanticipated grants) and concluded that TUGing and SLUGing in state aid-to-education may work, where other approaches have not.

11. Generic Simulation-Based Policy Insights

Other simulation-based policy insights have a more generic character and apply to a wide range of systems in a wide variety of circumstances. Two interesting collections in the system dynamics literature of these more general policy insights about complex dynamic feedback systems are contained in [17] and [27]. In both collections the sliding goals structure shown in the school finance study above was identified. In addition, we have

—*insensitivity*: complex systems are remarkably insensitive to changes in many system parameters;
—*compensating feedback*: complex systems counteract and compensate for externally applied corrective efforts;
—*policy resistance*: complex systems resist most policy changes;
—*leverage points*: complex systems contain influential pressure points, often in unexpected places, from which forces will radiate to alter system balance;
—*worse-before-better and better-before-worse behavior*: complex systems often react to a policy change in the long run in a way opposite to how they react in the short run;
—*drift to low performance*: complex social systems tend toward a condition of poor performance;
—*addiction*: action in complex social systems may appear to make the system better and create the apparent need for the continuation of the action, while actually over the long term it is making matters worse; and
—*shifting the burden to the intervener (official addiction)*: action improving the behavior of a complex social system may lead to the atrophy of endogenous mechanisms striving for the same goals.

The reader should consult [17] and [27] for further discussion of these generic simulation-based insights about complex dynamic feedback systems.

Suffice it to say here, deriving deep insights about system structure and behavior is one of the tantalizing goals of dynamic feedback simulation. Success requires technical and conceptual skills and very good simulation models, of course, but also a drive to strive for lessons that go beyond the limits of the particular. The best system dynamics work ultimately leaves the equations behind and pushes toward qualitative and conceptual statements of the implications of computer simulations. The goal is understanding.

12. Directions for Further Reading

This brief overview of system dynamics as a qualitative modeling methodology has, of necessity, selected a small number of topics for discussion and ignored many others. Several additional topic areas particularly deserve the attention of interested readers:

—Good sources of classic applications and examples include [18] and [46].
—The modeling stages of problem definition and system conceptualization are particularly difficult. Andersen and Richardson [2] surveyed the state of the art. The best sources of advice since then are [37], [42], [44], [47], [60], and [62]. Wolstenholme and Coyle (1983). Focusing exclusively on urban dynamics, [1] also manages to be an excellent general introduction to system dynamics modeling.
—Model evaluation (validation) in system dynamics differs considerably from

other quantitative methodologies in the range and depth of its qualitative criteria. The emphasis is on building confidence in the suitability of the model for its intended purposes and its consistency with observed reality. Forrester and Senge [19] detail 17 rigorous tests for building confidence in system dynamics models, which deserve careful study (see also [42, pp. 310–320]).

—Implementation of model-based policy insights should be an early concern in a simulation-based study of policy options. Roberts [45] and Weil [59] describe why implementation is difficult and how to improve its chance of success. Stenberg [48] discusses the problem in the context of public policy.

—Finally, current directions in the field reveal a diversity of interests. Traditional policy simulation studies remain a central focus, but increasingly, practitioners are turning to the potential of simulation games for communicating insights about dynamic feedback systems [28, 53]. Computerized case studies appear to hold considerable promise in that regard [21]. Efforts are under way to provide greater computer support in the search for model-based understanding and optimal policies in exceedingly complex systems [24, 61]. Complex nonlinear dynamics and chaos are naturally of interest (e.g., [31] and *System Dynamics Review 4*, 1–2 (1988)—special issue on chaos). Sterman [49, 50] has shown that policies people actually follow in some limited contexts produce deterministic chaos when simulated. The even greater significance of that research line [51, 52] may be in the extensions it provides to our understandings of patterned weaknesses in human dynamic decision-making complicated by feedback effects.

References

1. Alfeld, L.E., and Graham, A.K. MIT Press, Cambridge, Mass., 1976.
2. Andersen, D.F., and Richardson, G.P. Toward a pedagogy of system dynamics. *TIMS Studies Manage. Sci. 14* (System Dynamics) (1980), 91–106.
3. Aracil, J. Qualitative analysis and bifurcations in system dynamics models. *IEEE Trans. Syst., Man, Cybern. SMC-14*, 4 (1984), 688–696.
4. Ashby, W.R. *Introduction to Cybernetics*. Wiley, New York, 1956.
5. Bateson, G. Culture contact and schismogenesis. *Man 35* (1935), 178–183. (Reprinted in Bateson, G., *Steps to an Ecology of Mind*, Ballantine Books, New York, 1972.)
6. Bateson, G. *Naven*. Cambridge University Press. Cambridge, Mass., 1936. (2nd ed., Stanford University Press, Stanford, Calif., 1958.)
7. Cannon, W.B. *The Wisdom of the Body*. W.W. Norton, New York, 1932.
8. Cavana, R.Y., and Coyle, R.G. *DYSMAP User Manual*. System Dynamics Research Group, Univ. of Bradford, England, 1982.
9. Culbertson, J.M. *Macroeconomic Theory and Stabilization Policy*. McGraw-Hill, New York, 1968.
10. Dewey, J. The reflex arc concept in psychology. *Psychol. Rev. 3* (1896), 357–370.
11. Easton, D. *A Systems Analysis of Political Life*. Prentice-Hall, Englewood Cliffs, N.J., 1965.

12. Easton, D. Simplification and understanding of models. *Sys. Dynamics Rev.* 5, 1 (Winter 1989), 51–68.
13. Eden, C., Jones, S., and Sims, D. *Messing About in Problems.* Pergamon Press, Oxford, 1983.
14. Forrester, J.W. *Industrial Dynamics.* MIT Press, Cambridge, Mass., 1961.
15. Forrester, J.W. Market growth as influenced by capital investment. *Industrial Manage. Rev.* (now the *Sloan Manage. Rev.*) 9, 2 (Winter 1968), 83–106.
16. Forrester, J.W. *Principles of Systems.* MIT Press, Cambridge, Mass., 1968.
17. Forrester, J.W. *Urban Dynamics.* MIT Press, Cambridge, Mass., 1969.
18. Forrester, J.W. *Collected Papers of Jay W. Forrester.* MIT Press, Cambridge, Mass., 1975.
19. Forrester, J.W., and Senge, P.M. Tests for building confidence in system dynamics models. *TMS Stud. Manage. Sci.* 14 (System Dynamics) (1980), 209–228.
20. Goodman, M.R. *Study Notes in System Dynamics.* MIT Press, Cambridge, Mass., 1974.
21. Graham, A.K. Generic models as a basis for computer-based case studies. In *Proceedings of the 1988 International System Dynamics Conference* (San Diego, Calif.). 1988.
22. Graham, A.K., and Pugh, A.L., III. Behavior analysis software for large Dynamo models. In *Proceedings of the 1983 International System Dynamics Conference* (Chestnut Hill, Mass.). 1983.
23. Hanneman, R. *Computer-Assisted Theory Building: Modeling Dynamic Social Systems.* Sage Publications, Newbury Park, Calif., 1989.
24. Keloharju, R. *Relativity Dynamics.* The Helsinki School of Economics, Helsinki, 1983.
25. Levin, G., Hirsch, G.B., and Roberts, E.B. *The Persistent Poppy: A Computer Aided Search for Heroin Policy.* Ballinger, Cambridge, Mass., 1975.
26. Macedo, J. A reference approach for policy optimization in system dynamics models. *Syst. Dynamics Rev.* 5 2 (Summer 1989).
27. Meadows D.H. Whole earth models and systems. *Coevolution Q.* (Summer 1981), 98–108.
28. Meadows, D.L. *Strategem I.* Resource Policy Center, Dartmouth College, Hanover, N.H., 1988.
29. Morecroft, J.D.W. A critical review of diagramming tools for system dynamics. *Dynamica* 8, 2 (Summer 1982), 20–29.
30. Morecroft, J.D.W. Rationality in the analysis of behavioral simulation models. *Manage. Sci.* 31, 7 (July 1985), 900–916.
31. Mosekilde, E., Aracil, J., and Allen, P.M. Instabilities and chaos in nonlinear dynamic systems. *Syst. Dynamics Rev.* 4, 1–2 (1988), 14–55.
32. Nicholis, G., and Prigogine, I. *Self-Organization in Nonequilibrium Systems: From Dissipative Structures to Order Through Fluctuations.* Wiley, New York, 1977.
33. Phillips, A.W. Stabilization policy in a closed economy. *Econ. J.* (June 1954), 290–305.
34. Powers, W.T. *Behavior: The Control of Perception.* Aldine, Chicago, 1973.
35. Pugh, A.L. Integration method: Euler or other for system dynamics. *TIMS Stud. Manage. Sci.* 14 (System Dynamics) (1980), 179–188.
36. Pugh, A.L. *DYNAMO User's Manual.* 6th ed. MIT Press, Cambridge, Mass., 1983.
37. Randers, J. Guidelines for model conceptualization. In *Elements of the System*

Dynamics Method: Proceedigs of the 1976 International System Dynamics Conference, J. Randers, Ed. (Geilo, Norway). MIT Press, Cambridge, Mass., 1980.

38. Richardson, G.P. The evolution of the feedback concept in American social science, with implications for system dynamics. Plenary paper. In *Proceedings of the 1983 International System Dynamics Conference* (Chestnut Hill, Mass.). 1983.

39. Richardson, G.P. The evolution of the feedback concept in American social science. Ph.D. dissertation, Sloan School of Management, MIT Press, Cambridge, Mass., 1985.

40. Richardson, G.P. Problems with causal-loop diagrams. *Syst. Dynamics Rev. 3*, 2 (Summer 1986), 158–170.

41. Richardson, G.P. *Feedback Thought in Social Science.* To be published.

42. Richardson, G.P., and Pugh, A.L., III. *Introduction to System Dynamics Modeling with DYNAMO.* MIT Press, Cambridge, Mass., 1981.

43. Richmond, B., Peterson, S., and Vescuso, P. *STELLA^{TM} for Business.* High Performance Systems, Inc., Lyme, N.H., 1985.

44. Richmond, B., Peterson, S., and Vescuso, P. *An Academic User's Guide to STELLA^{TM}.* High Performance Systems, Inc., Lyme, N.H., 1987.

45. Roberts, E.B. Strategies for effective implementation of complex corporate models. *Interfaces 8*, 1 (1977), Part I.

46. Roberts, E.B., Ed. *Managerial Applications of System Dynamics.* MIT Press, Cambridge, Mass., 1978.

47. Roberts, N., Andersen, D.F., Deal, R., Garet, M., and Shaffer, W. *Introduction to Computer Simulation: A System Dynamics Modelling Approach.* Addison-Wesley, Reading, Mass., 1983.

48. Stenberg, L. A modeling procedure for public policy. In *Elements of the System Dynamics Method: Proceedings of the 1976 International System Dynamics Conference*, J. Randers, Ed. (Geilo, Norway). MIT Press, Cambridge, Mass., 1980.

49. Sterman, J.D. 1987. Testing behavioral simulation models by direct experiment. *Manage. Sci. 33*, 12 (1987), 1572–1592.

50. Sterman, J.D. Deterministic chaos in models of human behavior: Methodological issues and experimental results. *Syst. Dynamics Rev. 4* 1–2 (1988), 148–178.

51. Sterman, J.D. Misperceptions of feedback in dynamic decision making. *Organ. Behav. Human Dec. Proc. 43* (June 1989).

52. Sterman, J.D. Modeling managerial behavior: Misperceptions of feedback in a dynamic decision making experiment. *Manage. Sci. 35*, 3 (Mar. 1989).

53. Sterman, J.D., and Meadows, D.L. Strategem-2: A microcomputer simulation game of the Kondratiev cycle. *Sim. Games 16* (1985), 174–202.

54. Sterman, J.D., and Richardson, G.P. An experiment to evaluate methods of estimating fossil fuel resources. *J. Forecasting 4* (1985), 197–226.

55. Stinchcomb, A.L. *Constructing Social Theories.* Harcourt, Brace and World, New York, 1968.

56. Tversky, A., and Kahneman, D. Judgement under uncertainty: Heuristics and biases. *Science 185* (1974), 1124–1131.

57. von Bertalanffy, L. *General Systems Theory: Foundations, Develpment, Applications.* George Braziller, New York, 1968.

58. Weick, K.E. *The Social Psychology of Organizing.* 2nd ed. Addison-Wesley, Reading, Mass., 1979.

59. Weil, H.B. The Evolution of an approach for achieving implemented results from system dynamics projects. In *Elements of the System Dynamics Method: Proceedings*

of the 1976 International System Dynamics Conference, J. Randers, Ed. (Geilo, Norway). MIT Press, Cambridge, Mass., 1980.

60. Wolstenholme, E.F. A methodology for qualitative system dynamics. In *Proceedings of the 1985 International System Dynamics Conference* (Keystone, Colo.). 1985.

61. Wolstenholme, E.F., and Al-Alusi, A.S. System dynamics and heuristic optimization in defense analysis. *Syst. Dynamics Rev. 3,* 2 (Summer 1987), 102–115.

62. Wolstenholme, E.F., and Coyle, R.G. The development of system dynamics as a methodology for system description and qualitative analysis. *J. Oper. Res. 34,* 7 (1983), 569–581.

Chapter 8

Analogy Theory for a Systems Approach to Physical and Technical Systems

Peter M.A.L. Hezemans and Leo C.M.M. van Geffen

Abstract

Research in the use of analogies in science and technology during the last two centuries reveals that, besides the striking successes of applications of these analogies, there are also dramatic failures, not to speak of sophistic misuses, in the logic reasoning.

Searching for the reasons for success and failure forces us to lose ourselves in a mechanism of analogy-thinking that is governed by logic, this resulting in the creation of a sharp division between analogy-reasoning and analogy-application.

By realistically starting from the idea that an analogy supposes, besides similarities, also differences, it is justifiable to make use of them in systems science. In order to achieve this, in this chapter some conditions are first formulated. Next examples are given that show that the use of analogies is of good service for modeling. With the help of bond-graphs, an analogy can be critically applied, such that it can be seen visually, physically, and mathematically simultaneously and in a recognizable way. The application of algebraic topology in this field makes it possible to design a dual system from a certain original system. Finally, some rigorous conclusions are drawn and recommendations are made with respect to justified use of analogies in multidisciplinary systems approaches. With respect to engineering design, some expectations are entertained.

1. Introduction

1.1. Definition

Coming from the Greek word *ana-logon*, literally "in proportion," one can define concisely the word *analog* as a concurrence of some aspects of phenomena that are otherwise essentially different. It is not infrequent that an analogy points primarily to a very large difference and secondarily to some resemblance.

1.2. Analogy-Use and Analogy-Reasoning

One can make use of analogies in a correct and justified way in order to elucidate and comprehend a complicated problem, an abstract representation, or an obscure relation between certain facts or a system, which is difficult to approach. In system science it is required that the use of an analogy can only be correct and justified if it is rigorously proved.

Analogy-reasoning is reasoning from which a correspondence between two entities in a certain aspect is implied by a similar correspondence in another connected respect. We try to prove something with analogies. The analogy proof is an argument that starts from a partial similarity between two entities, in order to conclude their complete similarity. Generalizing in this way can be taken too far. In applications, analogies have failed because the analogy was not rigorously proved. The attribution of properties to an entity by means of analogy hopefully reveals new phenomena and thereby advances knowledge, but it is always fortuitous, and as a systematic approach to the advance of knowledge, it is, in a way, an extraordinarily clumsy technique. The price of analogy is, indeed, eternal vigilance.

1.3. Critical View of the Use of Analogies

Historical examples show that analogies have been turned to good advantage in the infancy of certain sciences, but failed in later research due to their imperfections. Analogies certainly form a reliable guide to the phenomena we can expect, but they never give a definite insight into what we will discover. One hypothesizes on the basis of an analogy and tests it critically [31, 55, 85].

1.4. Criterion for Analogy-Use in Systems Science

If one wishes to use analogies critically, one must restrict oneself to entities between which analogies have been determined or proved. From here, interpretations can be made and conclusions drawn that are only valid with regard to the connected aspects.

1.5. Requirements for the Application of Analogy

Before one decides to use an analogy, three requirements have to be fulfilled:

1. mathematical analogy, which implies that two models obey identical sets of equations;
2. physical analogy, which implies that generalized components obey identical physical laws; and
3. visual analogy, which implies a visual association of shape between elements or systems.

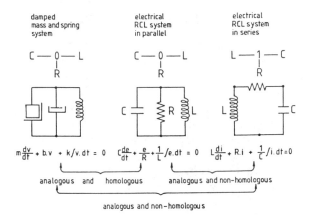

FIGURE 8.1. Distinction between analogy and homology.

1.6. Homology

Homology is defined as an abstraction of morphological resemblance between systems. By disregarding the component function, homology implies only a geometrical resemblance in system structure. The system and component functions are completely insignificant here. Analogous models that have identical mathematical functions need by no means be homologous. We can see this in Figure 8.1.

1.7. Duality

The peculiar developed relationship between analogy and homology can be explained by considering the concept of duality. Duality means ambiguity. On the one hand, one tries to formalize two different principles, conceptions, equations, or systems into one higher principle, broader conception, more universal equation, or more generalized system, respectively. On the other hand, if a system is modeled formally, one can often draw different possible conclusions about which seemingly contradictory (dual) interpretations can be made. In systems theory, duality results in a formalized system having two analogous, but nonhomologous models. In terms of the preceding example, the "series model" is a dual of the "parallel model."

2. Analogy Between Systems

In order to set up a system model quickly, a clear arrangement of thinking is required: *analogy-thinking.* It is therefore necessary to identify the analogy between systems and the analogy between treatment methodology. *Analogous systems* are systems obeying identical mathematical models, and *analogous treatment methods* are identical ways of treating systems, even if they are not analogous. *Analogy-seeing* has to take place systematically by observing the above mentioned requirements. Before deciding on an analogy between systems, one has to check if each of the three partial analogies is fulfilled:

1. analogy between variables,
2. analogy between system components, and
3. analogy between system structures.

2.1. Analogy Between Variables

Firestone [22] introduced the distinction between two types of physical variable: *across-variables* and *through-variables*. Across-variables, like velocity, voltage, pressure, temperature, and concentration (chemical potential), are expressed as differences and are measured across two spatially distinct points. The corresponding through-variables, such as force, current, fluid flow, entropy flow, and mass flow, are measurable at a single point. The product of each corresponding variable pair has the dimension of power.

The work of Trent [84] provided a more rigorous basis for Firestone's "complete" analogies, as well as algorithmic rules for their construction, by the use of the linear graph concept and its associated matrix algebra. In Table 8.1, α- and τ-variables are displayed for some physically different systems.

The question whether this "across-through" concept is "correct," can be answered only after discussing another concept: the *effort-flow* concept. Based on this comparison, conclusions can be drawn with respect to the efficient use of one of these concepts.

2.1.1. Effort-Flow Concept (ef-analogy) [41]

In this concept a variable pair that consists of two variables is used, having an association with, respectively, a "flow" and an "effort."

TABLE 8.1. Through- and across-variables for physical systems. $\sigma = \int \tau \alpha t$; $\lambda = \int \alpha \, dt$.

System	Through-variable τ	Integrated through-variable σ	Across-variable α	Integrated across-variable λ
Mechanical-translational	Force F	Translational momentum p	Velocity difference v_{21}	Displacement difference x_{21}
Mechanical-rotational	Torque T	Angular momentum h	Angular velocity difference Ω_{21}	Angular displacement difference Θ_{21}
Electrical	Current i	Charge q	Voltage difference v_{21}	Flux linkage λ_{21}
Fluid	Fluid flow Q	Volume V	Pressure difference P_{21}	Pressure-momentum Γ_{21}
Thermal	Heat flow q	Heat energy $\mathscr{H}$	Temperature difference θ_{21}	Not used in general

TABLE 8.2. *ef*-analogy.

	Effort	Flow
Hydraulical	Pressure	Flow
Mechanical	Force	Velocity

TABLE 8.3. $\alpha\tau$-analogy.

	Across	Through
Hydraulical	Pressure	Flow
Mechanical	Velocity	Force

To be more illustrative, the energetic interpretation of these two variables in a hydraulical and mechanical energy domain is given in Table 8.2.

An argument in favor of this concept is the analogy in the example between the pressure p and the force F. Besides that, it is known that a hydraulic accumulator can be considered equivalent to a mechanical spring, by which it can be concluded that both are capacities. They store potential energy. For obvious reasons (from an electrical point of view), this concept is often called *mass-inductance analogy*.

Being correct, this *ef*-analogy is not efficient methodically, as we shall see later on.

2.1.2. Across-Through Concept ($\alpha\tau$-analogy) [22]

In this concept a variable pair is used that consists of two variables, having an association with, respectively, an "across-quantity" and a "through-quantity."

As with the *ef*-concept, Table 8.3 shows the interpretation of these abstract variables in a hydraulical and a mechanical energy domain. For obvious reasons (from an electrical point of view), this concept is often called *mass-capacitance analogy*.

The question to be asked is, What variable-pairs have most "natural correspondence" to one another? At first sight one should choose the *ef*-concept, because the pressure p and the force F represent "intensities" (how strong?), while flow Q and velocity v represent "extensities" (how much?). Regarding this choice, unfortunately there exists no unanimity in professional circles. Supporters of the *ef*-concept refer to fundamental-physical arguments, while supporters of the $\alpha\tau$-analogy give preference to analogy-aspects in the systematical and methodical approach, thereby using homology-considerations (this is analogy with special attention to form and structure resemblance).

Supporters of the $\alpha\tau$-concept consistently make use of analogy between "single-point" and "two-point" measurements, which emanates from the basic idea that a system can be described only if it can be inspected and observed (by means of the two topologically describable variables!). Because of the topological nature of the $\alpha\tau$-concept, it belongs to cohomology theory, to be discussed further on.

The choice of the $\alpha\tau$-concept by the authors of this chapter comes from the pragmatic nature of systems science, which aims at uniformity in a systematical and methodical approach and consideration. In contrast with the $\alpha\tau$-concept, the *ef*-concept has to make use of two different methods (dual to each other!) in the modeling process [41].

2.2. Analogy Between System Components

In physically different energy domains, one comes across certain components with analogous functions. In Table 8.4 a functional classification is shown of analogous components with matching (generalized) function descriptions defined in terms of α- and τ-variables.

2.3. Analogy Between System Structures

If two physically different systems display identical structures, they are called *structurally analogous*. This means that they possess identical structure equations.

2.4. Definition of Analogous Systems

If all three partial analogies are fulfilled, we speak of *analogous systems*. In Figure 8.2 analogous electrical, hydraulical, and mechanical systems are drawn, together with their three partial analogies.

TABLE 8.4. Analogous components.

Generalized resistor $\tau = \alpha/R$	with R = generalized ideal resistance $1/b$ = reciprocal translational damping $\mathbf{R}$ = electrical resistance $\mathbf{R}_f$ = fluid resistance $\mathbf{R}_t$ = thermal resistance
Generalized capacitor $\tau = C \cdot d\alpha/dt$	with C = generalized ideal capacitance m = mass $\mathbf{C}$ = electrical capacitance $\mathbf{C}_f$ = fluid capacitance $\mathbf{C}_t$ = thermal capacitance
Generalized inductor $\alpha = L \cdot d\tau/dt$	with L = generalized ideal inductance $1/k$ = reciprocal translational stiffness $\mathbf{L}$ = electrical inductance $\mathbf{L}_f$ = fluid inertance

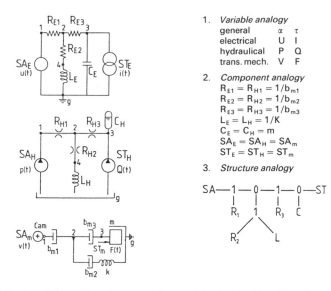

1. *Variable analogy*

general	α	τ
electrical	U	I
hydraulical	P	Q
trans. mech.	V	F

2. *Component analogy*

$R_{E1} = R_{H1} = 1/b_{m1}$
$R_{E2} = R_{H2} = 1/b_{m2}$
$R_{E3} = R_{H3} = 1/b_{m3}$
$L_E = L_H = 1/K$
$C_E = C_H = m$
$SA_E = SA_H = SA_m$
$ST_E = ST_H = ST_m$

3. *Structure analogy*

$$SA—1—0—1—0—ST$$

FIGURE 8.2. Complete analogy between electrical, hydraulical, and mechanical systems.

2.5. Analogy Between Methods of Derivation

In the systems science literature, one comes across two different methods for setting up so-called structure equations: linear graphs [13] and bond-graphs. It has to be mentioned that this chapter presupposes some knowledge of bond-graph theory. Outsiders who wish to become acquainted with $\alpha\tau$- and *ef*-bond-graphs are referred to

—$\alpha\tau$-bond-graphs: [10, 33, 34, 88];
—*ef*-bond-graphs: [41, 69, 78] and Chapter 9, "BondGraphs for Qualitative and Quantitative System Modeling" by Jean U. Thoma, in this volume.

Suppose that a bond-graph is set up with the power direction arrows pointing toward the elements, including sources, TFs, GYs, and multiports. Supposing then that the powers absorbed in and produced by the energy port are, respectively, positive and negative, a generalized method can be constructed for deducing the structure equations. Figure 8.3 illustrates this method.

Only the energy ports are numbered, not the bonds. Two groups of components are formed (Table 8.5). In the column vector on the left-hand side of the matrix structure equation, one stacks the through-variables of group ⊶ on top of the across-variables of group —⊶. In the column vector on the right-hand side, one stacks the across-variables of group ⊶ on top of the across variables of —⊶. This is done in index rank order.

Application of generalized laws of Kirchhoff ($\sum \tau_i = 0$ and $\sum \alpha_j = 0$) yields two submatrices B and C. Rearranging the above-mentioned variables in rank

FIGURE 8.3. Causal bond-graph, an abstraction of the three analogous systems of Figure 8.2.

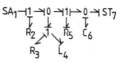

⊣ treevariable

→ cotreevariable

TABLE 8.5. Distinction between tree- and cotree-variables.

	Group	System components	Port numbers
Tree	⊣	SA_1, R_2, R_3, C_6	1, 2, 3, 6
Cotree	→	L_4, R_5, ST_7	4, 5, 7

order (first ⊣, then →) gives the complete structure equation:

$$\underline{\tau}_t = B\underline{\tau}_c \rightarrow \begin{bmatrix} \tau_1 \\ \tau_2 \\ \tau_3 \\ \tau_6 \end{bmatrix} = \begin{bmatrix} 1 & 1 & 0 \\ 1 & 1 & 0 \\ 1 & 0 & 0 \\ 0 & 1 & -1 \end{bmatrix} \begin{bmatrix} \tau_4 \\ \tau_5 \\ \tau_7 \end{bmatrix} \left.\begin{matrix} \\ \\ \\ \\ \end{matrix}\right\} \begin{bmatrix} \tau_1 \\ \tau_2 \\ \tau_3 \\ \tau_6 \end{bmatrix}$$

$$\underline{\alpha}_c = -C_t^T \underline{\alpha}_t \rightarrow \begin{bmatrix} \alpha_4 \\ \alpha_5 \\ \alpha_7 \end{bmatrix} = \begin{bmatrix} -1 & -1 & -1 & 0 \\ -1 & -1 & 0 & -1 \\ 0 & 0 & 0 & 1 \end{bmatrix} \begin{bmatrix} \alpha_1 \\ \alpha_2 \\ \alpha_3 \\ \alpha_6 \end{bmatrix} \begin{bmatrix} \alpha_4 \\ \alpha_5 \\ \alpha_7 \end{bmatrix}$$

$$= \begin{bmatrix} & & & & 1 & 1 & 0 \\ & \underline{0} & & & 1 & 1 & 0 \\ & & & & 1 & 0 & 0 \\ & & & & 0 & 1 & -1 \\ -1 & -1 & -1 & 0 & & & \\ -1 & -1 & 0 & -1 & & \underline{0} & \\ 0 & 0 & 0 & 1 & & & \end{bmatrix} \begin{bmatrix} \alpha_1 \\ \alpha_2 \\ \alpha_3 \\ \alpha_6 \\ \tau_4 \\ \tau_5 \\ \tau_7 \end{bmatrix}$$

with τ_t = tree-throughvariables, τ_c = cotree-throughvariables, α_c = cotree-acrossvariables, and α_t = tree-acrossvariables. A known network theory property is revealed: $B = C_t^T$ (T = transposed).

The relationship with linear graphs is immediately clear. Indeed, one recognizes group ⊣ as edges of the "tree" of a linear graph, and group → as the edges of the "cotree." For bond-graph theory, one can obviously reap the fruits of network theory for linear graphs, that is, network synthesis, network optimization, interpretation possibilities by means of reciprocity, passivity and symmetry theorems, and network analysis of three- and multidimensional networks. Famous works such as Gabriel Kron's "Diakoptics" [46] can then be studied with less effort.

3. Duality Between Systems

In order to determine a duality between systems, it is also necessary to identify three partial dualities:

1. duality between variables,
2. duality between system components, and
3. duality between system structures.

3.1. Duality Between Variables

Because through- and across-variables can be formalized into the higher concepts of "physical quantities" the α-variables of a certain system can dually be understood as the τ-variables of another system, and vice versa. The energy nature remains unchanged.

3.2. Duality Between System Components

It is striking that, with regard to a generalized inductor, α equals a constant times the time derivative of τ, and that for a generalized capacitor τ equals a constant times the time derivative of α. By interchanging the αs and τs, one can obtain the dual system components, such as in Table 8.6.

3.3. Duality Between System Structures

In the dual case, interchanging αs and τs leads to dual structure equations, as given in Table 8.7.

3.4. Definition of Dual Systems

If two given systems contain all three partial dualities, then they are dual to one another.

TABLE 8.6. Component duals.

Original		Dual	
Impedance	Z	Admittance	Y
Admittance	Y	Impedance	Z
Inductor	L	Capacitor	C
Capacitor	C	Inductor	L
Resistor	R	Conductor	G
Conductor	G	Resistor	R
α-source	SA	τ-source	ST
τ-source	ST	α-source	SA
Transformer	TF	Dual transformer	TF
Gyrator	GY	Dual gyrator	GY

TABLE 8.7. Structure
duals.

Original	Dual
0	1
1	0
B	$-C_t^T$
$-C_t^T$	B

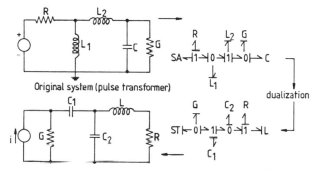

FIGURE 8.4. Dualization process.

4. Examples

4.1 *First illustrative example: Dualization process.* In this example the essence of a dualization process is briefly demonstrated with help of an electrical circuit, pictured in Figure 8.4.

Furthermore, it is possible to get the dual system component from the graphical characteristic of the original system component by constructing the corresponding dual characteristic.

4.2 *Second worked example: Thévenin versus Norton.* In Figure 8.5a and b, a Thévenin and a Norton network are shown. From electrical engineering it is known that these networks are each other's duals. This can be ascertained with help of Tables 8.6. and 8.7.

A more "abstract concept" for these networks appears to be the so-called "Kron-equivalent," portrayed in Figure 8.5c. It is exactly this equivalent that enables the incorporation of bond-graph theory and network theory, to be discussed later on, into cohomology theory.

4.3 *Third worked example: Constructing the dual from a pressure control valve.* In this example two devices are discussed that, after careful analysis,

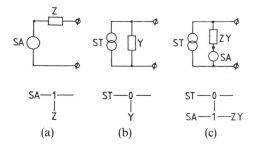

FIGURE 8.5. (a) Thévenin, (b) Norton, and (c) Kron equivalents.

appear to be each other's dual. The systems concerned are a pressure control valve and a flow control valve. By means of a systematic approach it is demonstrated that after

1. a carefully carried out analysis of the pressure control valve, resulting in a bond-graph,
2. a carefully carried out dualization process of this bond-graph, and
3. a carefully carried out synthesis of this bond-graph into a physical realization,

a flow control valve has been "designed." The analysis—respectively, synthesis—"route" stepwisely form each other's dual, while the procedure in both routes runs analogously!

Analogy theory has been successfully used here to design a dual system from a given system. Both processes are portrayed in Figures 8.6a and b. In the left part of this figure, the pressure control valve is shown. Here two "controllable" parameters can be localized, namely, the hydraulical resistance R_0 and the spring stiffness $1/L_0$. In the right part of the figure, the flow control valve is shown. Here the two "controllable" parameters are the hydraulical resistance R_d and the hydraulical inertance L_d.

Consistent handling of the duality-principle compels us to remark that "intensitivity" is the dual of "sensitivity." Now, in the case of the pressure control valve, R_0 and $1/L_0$, respectively, are the "insensitive" and the "sensitive" parameters, while in the case of the flow control valve, R_d and L_d, are the "sensitive" and the "insensitive" parameters, respectively.

In practice the adjustment parameters for the pressure control valve and the flow control valve, respectively, are $1/L_0$ and R_d. The subsequent steps in the illustrations are evident.

4.4 *Fourth worked example: Design of a controlled speed regulator.* In this example an analysis is made from a controlled frictional clutch, in order to construct a dual physical system from it. For this "original ↔ dual" transformation, in Figure 8.7, multiport representations are shown.

By reason of duality considerations, the dual system turns out to be a controlled speed regulator.

Now, how can it be constructed? From the abstract scheme of Figure 8.8,

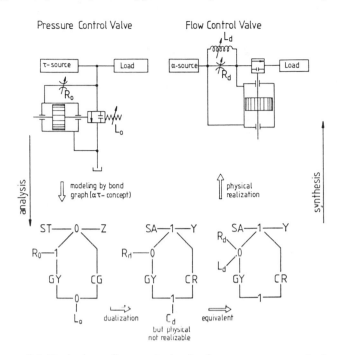

FIGURE 8.6. Designing a flow control valve from a pressure control valve.

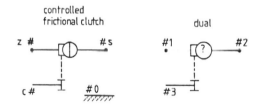

FIGURE 8.7. Controlled frictional clutch and its unknown dual.

a bond-graph is set up in Figure 8.9, which is transformed, after some pre-manipulation in Figure 8.10a, into the dual bond-graph in Figure 8.10b.

In Figure 8.9 CG is a controlled conductance and the section of the bond-graph associated with it should be read as; $\rightarrowtail$ CG $\leftarrowtail$, according to the equation for the torque due to coulomb friction:

$$T = T(N, \omega) = f.N.R. \qquad \text{where } f = \text{friction coefficient,}$$

$$N = \text{controlled normal force,}$$

$$R = \text{radius,}$$

$$\omega = \text{rotational speed,}$$

$$T = \text{torque.}$$

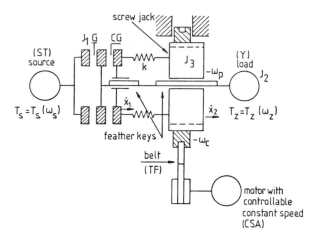

FIGURE 8.8. Controlled frictional clutch.

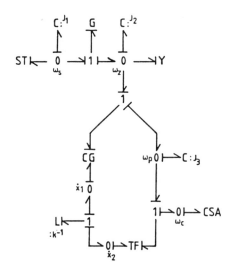

FIGURE 8.9. Bond-graph for Figure 8.8.

After reduction, the bond-graph looks like Figure 8.10a, where

$$C \dashv 0 \qquad 0 \dashv CST$$
$$\quad\; \mathrel{\llcorner\!\!\rightarrow} TF \mathrel{\lrcorner}$$

equals

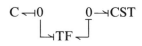

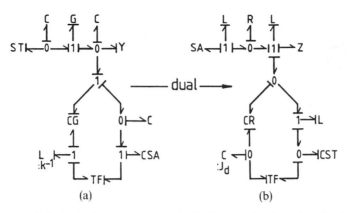

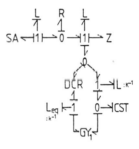

FIGURE 8.10. (a) Reduced bond-graph. (b) "Nonrealization" dual for (a).

FIGURE 8.11. "Realizable" dual for Figure 8.10a.

equals

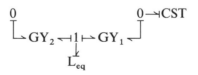

equals

$$
\begin{array}{c}
0 \qquad\qquad\qquad 0 \rightarrow\!\!\text{CST} \\
\text{L}\!\!\rightarrow\!\text{GY}_2 \dashv\!1\!\mapsto\text{GY}_1 \dashv \\
\text{L}_{eq}
\end{array}
$$

In the dual bond-graph in Figure 10b, the controlled resistance CR is the dual of CG.

By finally combining ⊢CR ⊢0⊢GY₂ ⊣ to ⊢DCR ⊣ (read as "to dual-controlled resistance") in Figure 10b, a transformation into a physical system is then constructed for the dual bond-graph in Figure 8.11. In Figure 8.12 the physical realization of Figure 8.11 is shown.

It is not the purpose of this example to claim that every dual system component can be realized physically. On the contrary, it appears that most

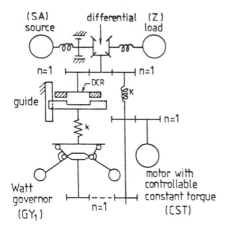

FIGURE 8.12. Centrifugal clutch: Realization of Figure 8.11.

duals are physically not realizable. From a technical point of view, a dual from Figure 8.10b is more difficult to construct than a dual from Figure 8.11.

5. Choice Between Analogy and Dualogy

A *dualog* is defined as an analog of a dual or a dual of an analog, as shown in Figure 8.13.

The message of the contribution presented here, is to give preference to analogies above dualogies. First, the process of "analogy-seeing" with analogies is essentially easier than with dualogies, as is confirmed by the structural similarities between the systems in Figure 8.14. Second, for a "nonplanar system," as portrayed in Figure 8.15, a dualog cannot always be constructed, whereas an analog always can. The adjective *nonplanar* comes from graph theory and refers to a certain property of a graph. Here, a planar graph is a graph that can be embedded (and may be deformed) in a plane in such a way that no two edges intersect geometrically except at a vertex to which they are both incident. The graph in Figure 8.16a is fundamentally nonplanar, as can be seen from Figure 8.16b. The linear graph of Figure 8.15 is, according to the definition, also nonplanar (see Figure 8.15c).

In 1932 Whitney [90] proved that from a nonplanar network one can never construct a dual. As long as a mechanical system can be represented by a planar graph, no practical difficulties arise from using analogs or dualogs because of the "planar graph theorem." When the graph is nonplanar, however, the mass $\leftrightarrow$ inductance analogy is the one that fails. The mass $\leftrightarrow$ capacitance analogy always applies because of its topological equivalence. "For pedagogical reasons, therefore, the mass $\leftrightarrow$ inductance analogy owing its existence solely to the planar graph theorem, should be discarded in favor of the mass $\leftrightarrow$ capacitance analogy which is fundamentally the correct one" [90]. According to Breedveld, this is too strong, since "the planar graph

FIGURE 8.13. Relations between duals, analogs, and dualogs.

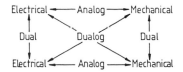

FIGURE 8.14. Problem of recognizing analog versus dualog.

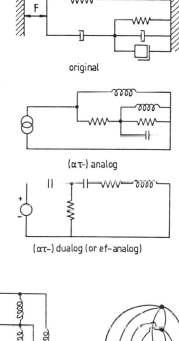

original

($\alpha\tau$-) analog

($\alpha\tau$-) dualog (or ef–analog)

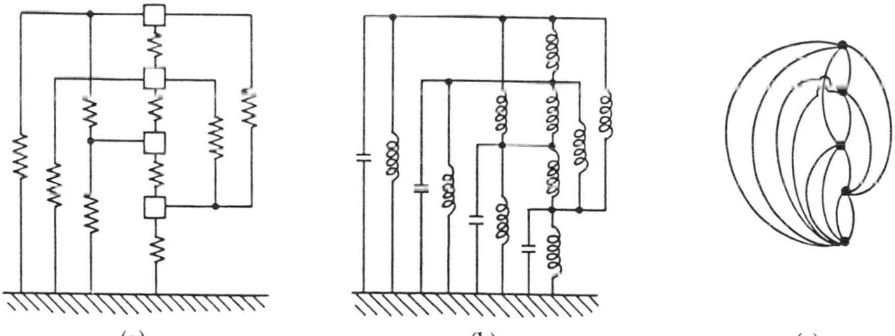

(a)   (b)   (c)

FIGURE 8.15. Mechanical system for which mass ↔ inductance analogy does not exist.

theorem states only planar graphs can be dualized. The fact however that some systems can be dualized and some not, does not provide a criterion to choose between the mass ↔ inductance or mass ↔ capacitance analogy" [13]. Indeed, no final verdict can be delivered, because the choice of analogs for mechanical systems depends on the requirements of the modeling techniques for the structure, which differ from application to application. Although it is

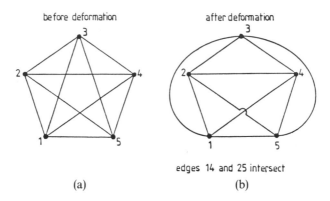

FIGURE 8.16. Definition of a nonplanar graph.

pointless to discuss the "correct" analogy, since both are equally valid when they exist, the mass ↔ capacitance (or αт- or mobility-) analogy has considerable advantages. This is specially so in the process of analogy-seeing:

1. The mass ↔ capacitance analogy is set up very easily;
2. for every possible mechanical combination (planar or nonplanar), an electric analog exists, whereas an electric dualog does not necessarily exist;
3. the topological concept allows us to construct analogs visually;
4. in the modeling process, it suffices to use only one procedure, whereas in mass ↔ inductance analogy, two procedures are necessary: one for mechanical and one for nonmechanical systems;
5. analogs of nonplanar systems are always physically interpretable (realizable), whereas duals or dualogs of nonplanar systems are not.

6. Analogy Between Physical Theories

As it appears to be possible to set up analogous systems in physically different domains, one's intuition suggests that a common analogy for physical theories must also exist, such that we may generalize electrical, hydraulical, mechanical, thermodynamical, etc., theories. This will become apparent, when we investigate how physical theories have been constructed over the last four centuries with the aid of geometry: There can hardly be a physical theory without geometry! [47, 66].

Just as Tonti [83] suggests, "in every physical theory there are basic physical quantities that are naturally referred to the most simple geometrical and chronometrical elements like points, lines, surfaces, volumes, time instants and time intervals and combinations of them," with the consequence that "in every physical theory there are basic physical laws that a physical quantity referred to a p-dimensional manifold ω like lines, surfaces, volumes, time intervals, etc. is equal to a physical quantity referred to its boundary $\partial\omega$". According to Tonti, this leads to "the possibility of doing the rational investigation of the analogies between two physical theories according to the criterion that follows: to every physical quantity of one theory there corresponds that physical quantity of the other theory that is referred to the same geometrical entry."

Tonti proved that this was true. The instigator of these ideas was Gabriel Kron, who continually emphasized that there must be an underlying justification for the proliferation of electrical and mechanical analogs used in modeling a diverse range of physical phenomena. He introduced the use of homology theory (topology) in this context as the basis of his network and systems theory. By extending Kron's and more recent works into a unified theory beginning with a topological analysis of "system invariance," this leads to systematic procedures for deriving and solving matrix and tensor models, and efficient solution algorithms and a philosophy that should contribute toward the understanding and teaching methodology in general [11]. Branin [12] presents a treatment of the network concept not only in its usual context related to linear graph theory but also in relation to cohomology theory. This theory uses complexes and simplexes, homology and cohomology sequences, chains and cochains, and boundary and coboundary operators. The physical interest in the process of constructing sequential chains arises from the fact that the structure equations of every physcial theory state that "one chain is the coboundary of another."

In conclusion, the sensible way in which to achieve a deep understanding of cohomology theory appears to us to be to demonstrate, first with a simple example of network analysis and then by a more complex example from electromagnetism, that the whole of physics is based on topology (popularly said, "physics is geometry" and, moreover, that cohomology theory appears to be nothing other than a very consistent applied analogy theory). Here we attempt to give a new perspective on the work of Kron, Roth, Branin, and Nicholson [12, 46, 58, 70].

6.1. Simple Example: System Network Analysis

Take, for example, the generalized system model of Figure 8.2 with the associated causal bond-graph of Figure 8.3. By way of a particular procedure, as described in [7], [32], and [61], this bond-graph is transformed into the linear graph of Figure 8.17, with tree and cotrees as indicated. This linear

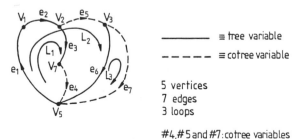

$\equiv$ tree variable

$\equiv$ cotree variable

5 vertices
7 edges
3 loops

#4, #5 and #7 : cotree variables

FIGURE 8.17. Linear graph for Figure 8.3.

graph is topologically representable only in terms of vertices ($\in$V), edges ($\in$e) and loops ($\in$L), such that the structure of it can be represented in the incidence matrices H(0, 1) and H(1, 2) below. These matrices, respectively, define the relationship between vertices and edges and between edges and loops, and thereby fully identify the system structure.

Edges

		e_1	e_2	e_3	e_6	e_4	e_5	e_7
	V_1	1	-1	0	0	0	0	0
	V_2	0	1	-1	0	0	-1	0
Vertices	V_3	0	0	0	-1	0	1	-1
	V_4	0	0	1	0	-1	0	0
	V_5	-1	0	0	1	1	0	1

Loops

		L_1	L_2	L_3
	e_1	1	1	0
	e_2	1	1	0
	e_3	1	0	0
Edges	e_6	0	1	-1
	e_4	1	0	0
	e_5	0	1	0
	e_7	0	0	1

From this follows

$$H(0,1) = \begin{bmatrix} 1 & -1 & 0 & 0 & 0 & 0 & 0 \\ 0 & 1 & -1 & 0 & 0 & -1 & 0 \\ 0 & 0 & 0 & -1 & 0 & 1 & -1 \\ 0 & 0 & 1 & 0 & -1 & 0 & 0 \\ -1 & 0 & 0 & 1 & 1 & 0 & 1 \end{bmatrix} = A^T;$$

$$H(1,2) = \begin{bmatrix} 1 & 1 & 0 \\ 1 & 1 & 0 \\ 1 & 0 & 0 \\ 0 & 1 & -1 \\ 1 & 0 & 0 \\ 0 & 1 & 0 \\ 0 & 0 & 1 \end{bmatrix} = C.$$

From this follows that

$$A^T \underline{\tau} = \underline{0}; \tag{1}$$

$$\underline{\alpha} = A\underline{\alpha}_0; \tag{2}$$

FIGURE 8.18. Topological string without impedance-link.

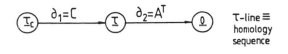

T-line ≡ homology sequence

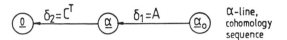

α-line, cohomology sequence

$$C^T \underline{\alpha} = \underline{0};$$ (3)

$$\underline{\tau} = C\underline{\tau}_c.$$ (4)

with $\underline{\alpha}$ = across-variables with $\underline{\alpha}^T = [\alpha_1, \alpha_2, \alpha_3, \alpha_6, \alpha_4, \alpha_5, \alpha_7]$; $\underline{\tau}$ = through-variables with $\underline{\tau}^T = [\tau_1, \tau_2, \tau_3, \tau_6, \tau_4, \tau_5, \tau_7]$; $\underline{\alpha}$ = across-potentials with respect to a reference frame; and $\underline{\tau}_c$ = cotree through-variables with $\underline{\tau}_c^T = [\tau_4, \tau_5, \tau_7]$.

We shall now construct a signal flow diagram with the aid of eqs. (1) to (4). This diagram is called a *(topological) string.* Figure 8.18 shows two bilateral signal flows, one for τ to the right and the other for α to the left.

The multiplication by juxtaposition of the two operators on each line gives

$$A^T C = \underline{0} \quad \text{for } \tau\text{-line};$$ (5)

$$C^T A = \underline{0} \quad \text{for } \alpha\text{-line}.$$ (6)

The proof of the correctness of (5) and (6) can only be given thermodynamically. Tellegen's theorem [63, 77] states the following:

$$P = \underline{\tau}^T \underline{\alpha} = 0$$ (7)

and

$$P = \underline{\alpha}^T \underline{\tau} = 0.$$ (8)

Substitution of (2) and (4) in (7) gives

$$P = (C\underline{\tau}_c)^T A\underline{\alpha}_0 = \underline{\tau}_c^T C^T A\underline{\alpha}_0 = 0,$$

from which it follows that $C^T A = \underline{0}$. In a similar way (substitution of (2) and (4) in (8)), it follows that $A^T C = \underline{0}$.

Equations (5) and (6) are the interpretations of the first law of thermodynamics.

Finally, in order to obtain the constitutive relationship between the τ- and α-sequence, we introduce the *Kron-equivalent.* The Kron-equivalent is defined as a combination of one passive element Z and two (active) sources, SA and ST. This "Kron-element" can thus be used as a passive element and/or as a source. Figure 8.19 illustrates this abstract concept and the acausal bond-graph associated with this Kron-element. For this Kron-element, the following set of element equations holds:

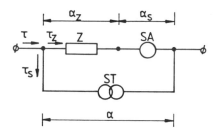

FIGURE 8.19. Visual definition of the Kron-element.

$$
\left.\begin{array}{l}
\alpha_z = Z\tau_z \\
\alpha_z = \alpha - \alpha_s \\
\tau_z = \tau - \tau_s
\end{array}\right\} \quad \text{with}
$$

Z = impedance,

α_z, τ_z = across- and through-variables of the passive elements (A, L, C),

α_s, τ_s = across- and through-variables of the source.

     It appears that the Kron-element can be interpreted as a more highly abstracted version of Thévenin and Norton equivalents (see Example 4.2).

     With the introduction of this type of generalized element, it is possible to consider every general bond-graph structure as being composed of n Kron-elements. In vector notation, the element equations now are

$$
\left.\begin{array}{l}
\underline{\alpha}_z = Z\underline{\tau}_z \\
\underline{\alpha}_z = \underline{\alpha} - \underline{\alpha}_s \\
\underline{\tau}_z = \underline{\tau} - \underline{\tau}_s
\end{array}\right\} \quad
\left.\begin{array}{l}
Z = \text{matrix impedance,} \\
\text{underscore} = \text{vector symbol.}
\end{array}\right\} \tag{9}
$$

After applying a vector link Z between the τ-sequence and the α-sequence in the string of Figure 8.18, it holds that

$$
(\underline{\alpha} - \underline{\alpha}_s) = Z(\underline{\tau} - \underline{\tau}_s). \tag{10}
$$

This process is demonstrated in Figure 8.20. Premultiplication of (10) by C^T yields

$$
C^T(\underline{\alpha} - \underline{\alpha}_s) = C^T Z(\underline{\tau} - \underline{\tau}_s). \tag{11}
$$

After substitution of (3) and (4), we get

$$
(\underline{0} - C^T\underline{\alpha}_s) = C^T Z C\underline{\tau}_c - C^T Z\underline{\tau}_s. \tag{12}
$$

The Z-string in Figure 8.21 gives a signal flow interpretation of (12).

     As far as the inversion of $C^T Z C$ ($=(C^T Z C)^{-1}$) (which always exists [51]) is concerned, premultiplication of (12) with $(C^T Z C)^{-1}$ and some additional manipulations leads to

$$
-(C^T Z C)^{-1} C^T\underline{\alpha}_s = (C^T Z C)^{-1} C^T Z\underline{\tau} - (C^T Z C)^{-1} C^T Z\underline{\tau}_s,
$$

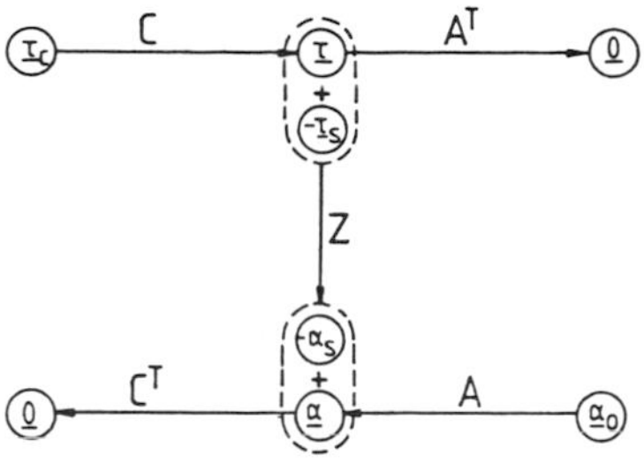

FIGURE 8.20. Z-link between the τ- and α- sequence.

FIGURE 8.21. Z-string. $\underline{\alpha}'_s = C^T\underline{\alpha}_s$.

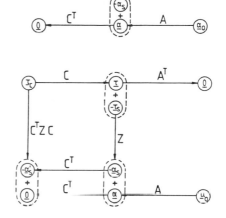

which, after substitution of (4), gives

$$-(C^TZC)^{-1}C^T\underline{\alpha}_s = \underline{\tau}_c - (C^TZC)^{-1}C^TZ\underline{\tau}_s$$

or

$$-C(C^TZC)^{-1}C^T\underline{\alpha}_s = \underline{\tau} - C(C^TZC)^{-1}C^TZ\underline{\tau}_s. \qquad (13)$$

By premultiplying the inverse of (10), $(\underline{\tau} - \underline{\tau}_s) = Y(\underline{\alpha} - \underline{\alpha}_s)$ (with Y = matrix admittance), by A^T and substituting (1) and (2), we arrive in a similar way at

$$(\underline{0} - A^T\underline{\tau}_s) = A^TYA\underline{\alpha}_0 - A^TY\underline{\alpha}_s \qquad (14)$$

and thereafter at

$$-A(A^TYA)^{-1}A^T\underline{\tau}_s = \underline{\alpha} - A(A^TYA)^{-1}A^TY\underline{\alpha}_s. \qquad (15)$$

In a similar way the corresponding Y-string for (15) is constructed and shown in Figure 8.22.

Figure 8.23 shows how Figure 8.21 and Figure 8.22 are superimposed upon one another.

Equations (13) and (15) are the "singular" answer to the "network" problem, formulated by Gabriel Kron and J. Paul Roth, which can be characterized in a generalized way as "given a network of known topology, known elements C, G, R, and/or L, and known across-and through-sources $\underline{\alpha}_s$ and $\underline{\tau}_s$, find the response across- and through-variables $\underline{\alpha}$ and $\underline{\tau}$ such that the constitutive laws and topological constraints are satisfied simultaneously" [70]. This can be translated as "given (1) a bond-graph, which determines the matrices A and

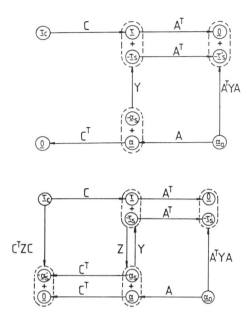

FIGURE 8.22. Y-string. $\underline{\tau}'_s = A^T \underline{\tau}_s$.

FIGURE 8.23. H-string: The combination of the Z-string and Y-string.

C, (2) the transformation matrix Z and/or its inverse Y, and (3) the arbitrary source vectors $\underline{\alpha}_s$ and $\underline{\tau}_s$, find the vectors $\underline{\alpha}$ and $\underline{\tau}$ such that (1) $\underline{\alpha} - \underline{\alpha}_s = Z(\underline{\tau} - \underline{\tau}_s)$ and/or $\underline{\tau} - \underline{\tau}_s = Y(\underline{\alpha} - \underline{\alpha}_s)$, (2) $A^T\underline{\tau} = 0$, and (3) $C^T\underline{\alpha} = 0$.

We call (C^TZC) and (A^TYA), respectively, the Roth-transformations of system impedance and system admittance, which are used by Kron as tensors [12, 14, 45, 70, 71, 74].

One recognizes (13) and (15), respectively, as the generalized "node" method and "loop" method, by which the network equations are set up (see, e.g., [9], [51], and [72]. In [51] these methods are combined in the so-called "mixed" method, of which Figure 23 is a visual representation.

There is also a third generalized method, which leads to state equations: the so-called MacFarlane method [50]. In general, one proceeds as follows: First,

$$C^T\underline{\alpha} = [C_t^T | I]\begin{bmatrix} \underline{\alpha}_t \\ \underline{\alpha}_c \end{bmatrix} = \underline{0} \qquad ([I] \equiv \text{unit matrix})$$

or

$$C_t^T\underline{\alpha}_t + \underline{\alpha}_c = \underline{0}. \tag{16}$$

Second,

$$A^T\underline{\tau} = [A_t^T | A_c^T]\begin{bmatrix} \underline{\tau}_t \\ \underline{\tau}_s \end{bmatrix} = \underline{0}$$

or

$$A_t^T\underline{\tau}_t + A_c^T\underline{\tau}_c = \underline{0}$$

or

$$\underline{\tau}_t + (A_t^T)^{-1}A_c^T\underline{\tau}_c = \underline{0}. \tag{17}$$

Premultiplication of (16) by $\underline{\tau}_c^T$ yields

$$\underline{\tau}_c^T C_t^T\underline{\alpha}_t + \underline{\tau}_c^T\underline{\alpha}_c = \underline{0}. \tag{18}$$

Premultiplication of (17) by $\underline{\alpha}_t^T$ gives

$$\underline{\alpha}_t^T\underline{\tau}_t + \underline{\alpha}_t^T(A_t^T)^{-1}A_c^T\underline{\tau}_c = \underline{0}. \tag{19}$$

Summation of (18) and (19) yields

$$-\underline{\alpha}_t^T[C_t + (A_t^T)^{-1}A_c^T]\underline{\tau}_c = \underline{\tau}_c^T\underline{\alpha}_c + \underline{\alpha}_t^T\underline{\tau}_t = \underline{\tau}_c^T\underline{\alpha}_c + \underline{\tau}_t^T\underline{\alpha}_t = \underline{\tau}^T\underline{\alpha}. \tag{20}$$

According to Tellegen's theorem, the right-hand side of eq. (20) equals zero. It can be shown that

$$(A_t^T)^{-1}A_c^T = -C_t. \tag{21}$$

This is to say that, if

$$\underline{\alpha}_c = C_t^T\underline{\alpha}_t,$$

then

$$\underline{\tau}_t = C_t\underline{\tau}_c, \tag{22}$$

which implies that

$$\begin{bmatrix} \underline{\tau}_t \\ \underline{\alpha}_c \end{bmatrix} = \begin{bmatrix} 0 & C_t \\ -C_t^T & 0 \end{bmatrix} \begin{bmatrix} \underline{\alpha}_t \\ \underline{\tau}_c \end{bmatrix}. \tag{23}$$

Substitution of the element equations of the form

$$\underline{\alpha} = Z(\underline{\tau} - \underline{\tau}_s) + \underline{\alpha}_s \quad \text{and/or} \quad \underline{\tau} = Y(\underline{\alpha} - \underline{\alpha}_s) + \underline{\tau}_s$$

with $\underline{\tau}^T = [\underline{\tau}_t^T, \underline{\tau}_c^T]$ and $\underline{\alpha}^T = [\underline{\alpha}_t^T, \underline{\alpha}_c^T]$ in (23) gives, after elimination of certain algebraic equations, the state equations of the following form:

$$\underline{\dot{x}} = A\underline{x} + B\underline{u} \quad \text{with } [\underline{x}]^T = [\underline{\alpha}_t^T, \underline{\tau}_c^T] \quad \text{and} \quad [\underline{u}]^T = [\underline{\tau}_{st}^T, \underline{\alpha}_{sc}^T], \tag{24}$$

where t = tree, c = cotree, st = tree-source, and sc = cotree-source.

6.2. Algebraic-Topological Interpretation of the Roth-Problem [12]

Given is the following system description:

1. a set of elements;
2. between these elements, certain relationships exist; and
3. certain properties are assigned to the elements and/or relations.

By interpreting Figure 8.2 and Fig. 8.17 topologically, this system description formally abstracts to a topological description that is characterized by three aspects:

1. a set V, consisting of vertices;
2. a set E, consisting of edges; and
3. a relationship between the edges and vertices.

In the Appendix, simplicial topology with its associated terminology, is presented "in a nutshell." The earlier treated example of Figure 8.2 is analyzed again, but now topologically.

Given the finite oriented two-dimensional simplicial complex K from Figure 8.2 and Figure 8.17, with

$$s_0 = 5 \quad \text{0-simplexes: } \sigma_{0;1}, \ldots, \sigma_{0;5} \quad (= V_1, V_2, V_3, V_4, V_5),$$

$$s_1 = 7 \quad \text{1-simplexes: } \sigma_{1;1}, \ldots, \sigma_{1;7} \quad (= e_1, e_2, e_3, e_4, e_5, e_6, e_7),$$

$$s_2 = 3 \quad \text{2-simplexes: } \sigma_{2;1}, \ldots, \sigma_{2;3} \quad (= L_1, L_2, L_3).$$

Application of the coboundary operator δ to the 0-simplexes yields

$$\delta_1(\sigma_{0;1}) = \sigma_{1;1} - \sigma_{1;2},$$

$$\delta_1(\sigma_{0;2}) = \sigma_{1;2} - \sigma_{1;3} - \sigma_{1;5},$$

$$\delta_1(\sigma_{0;3}) = -\sigma_{1;6} + \sigma_{1;5} - \sigma_{1;7},$$

$$\delta_1(\sigma_{0;4}) = \sigma_{1;3} - \sigma_{1;4},$$

$$\delta_1(\sigma_{0;5}) = -\sigma_{1;1} + \sigma_{1;6} + \sigma_{1;4} + \sigma_{1;7}.$$

In this way it is shown that the coboundary of the 0-simplex is a 1-cochain.
    The coboundary of the coboundary is

$$\delta_2\delta_1(\sigma_{0;1}) = \delta(\sigma_{1;1} - \sigma_{1;2}) = \delta(\sigma_{1;1}) - \delta(\sigma_{1;2})$$

$$= (\sigma_{2;1} + \sigma_{2;2}) - (\sigma_{2;1} + \sigma_{2;2}) = 0$$

$$\delta_2\delta_1(\sigma_{0;2}) = \delta(\sigma_{1;2} - \sigma_{1;3} - \sigma_{1;5}) = \delta(\sigma_{1;2}) - \delta(\sigma_{1;3}) - \delta(\sigma_{1;5})$$

$$= (\sigma_{2;1} + \sigma_{2;2}) - (\sigma_{2;1}) - (\sigma_{2;2}) = 0$$

$$\delta_2\delta_1(\sigma_{0;3}) = \delta(-\sigma_{1;6} + \sigma_{1;5} - \sigma_{1;7}) = -\delta(\sigma_{1;6}) + \delta(\sigma_{1;5}) - \delta(\sigma_{1;7})$$

$$= -(\sigma_{2;2} - \sigma_{2;3}) + (\sigma_{2;2}) - (\sigma_{2;3}) = 0$$

$$\delta_2\delta_1(\sigma_{0;4}) = \delta(\sigma_{1;3} - \sigma_{1;4}) = \delta(\sigma_{1;3}) - \delta(\sigma_{1;4})$$

$$= (\sigma_{2;1}) - (\sigma_{2;1}) = 0$$

$$\delta_2\delta_1(\sigma_{0;5}) = \delta(-\sigma_{1;1} + \sigma_{1;6} + \sigma_{1;4} + \sigma_{1;7})$$

$$= -(\sigma_{2;1} + \sigma_{2;2}) + (\sigma_{2;2} - \sigma_{2;3}) + (\sigma_{2;1}) + (\sigma_{2;3}) = 0,$$

from which we may conclude that

1. the coboundary of the coboundary is zero;
2. a 1-cochain with coboundary zero is a 1-cocycle; and
3. this 1-cocycle represents the generalized across-law of Kirchhoff, $\sum \underline{\alpha} = 0$.

Application of the boundary operator ∂ to 2-simplexes yields the following:

$$\partial_1(\sigma_{2;1}) = (\sigma_{1;1} + \sigma_{1;2} + \sigma_{1;3} + \sigma_{1;4}),$$

$$\partial_1(\sigma_{2;2}) = (\sigma_{1;1} + \sigma_{1;2} + \sigma_{1;6} + \sigma_{1;5}),$$

$$\partial_1(\sigma_{2;3}) = (-\sigma_{1;6} + \sigma_{1;7}),$$

from which we find that the boundary of the 2-simplex is a 1-chain. The boundary of the boundary is

$$\partial_2\partial_1(\sigma_{2;1}) = \partial(\sigma_{1;1} + \sigma_{1;2} + \sigma_{1;3} + \sigma_{1;4})$$

$$= (\sigma_{0;1} - \sigma_{0;5}) + (-\sigma_{0;1} + \sigma_{0;2}) + (-\sigma_{0;2} + \sigma_{0;4})$$

$$+ (-\sigma_{0;4} + \sigma_{0;5})$$

$$= 0$$

$$\partial_2\partial_1(\sigma_{2;2}) = \partial(\sigma_{1;1} + \sigma_{1;2} + \sigma_{1;6} + \sigma_{1;5})$$

$$= (\sigma_{0;1} - \sigma_{0;5}) + (-\sigma_{0;1} + \sigma_{0;2}) + (-\sigma_{0;3} + \sigma_{0;5})$$

$$+ (-\sigma_{0;2} + \sigma_{0;3})$$

$$= 0$$

$$\partial_2\partial_1(\sigma_{2;3}) = \partial(-\sigma_{1;6} + \sigma_{1;7}) = -(-\sigma_{0;3} + \sigma_{0;5}) + (-\sigma_{0;3} + \sigma_{0;5}) = 0,$$

from which the following conclusions can be drawn:

1. The boundary of the boundary is zero;
2. a 1-chain with boundary zero is a 1-cycle; and
3. this 1-cycle represents the generalized through-law of Kirchhoff, $\sum \tau = 0$.

The Appendix shows how the incidence matrices can be derived. It appears that

$$H(0, 1) = A^T \quad \text{and} \quad H(1, 2) = C$$

and also that

$$\partial_2\partial_1 = H(0, 1) \cdot H(1, 2) = A^T C = \underline{0} \quad \text{and}$$

$$\delta_2\delta_1 = H^T(1, 2) \cdot H^T(0, 1) = C^T A = \underline{0}.$$

6.3. Abstract Extension to n-Simplexes [12]

So far we have only handled simplexes of up to and including order 2. The question arising here is, of course, whether we may proceed with simplexes of higher order; in other words, are there analogous forms of $A^T C$ and $C^T A$ for n-simplexes?

Completely analogous to Figure 23, and applying the theory in the Appendix, which in principle concerns n-simplexes, for example, a 3-complex

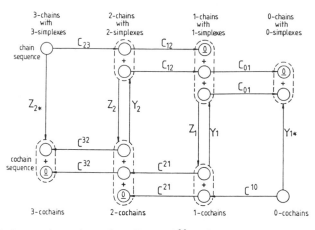

FIGURE 8.24. 3-complex string, where $Z_{2*} = C^{32}Z_2C_{23}$ and $Y_{1*} = C_{01}Y_1C^{10}$; $C^{32} = C_{23}^T$; $C^{21} = C_{12}^T$; $C^{10} = C_{01}^T$.

(containing 3-, 2-, 1-, and 0-simplexes), as illustrated in Figure 8.24, can be constructed.

In conformity with simplicial topology, the next statement for Figure 8.24 has to hold: The (co)boundary of the (co)boundary is zero.

In Figure 8.26 this means that for each $i = 1 + j$ and $k = j + 1$ it holds that

$$C_{ij}C_{jk} = \underline{0} \quad \text{and} \quad C^{kj}C^{ji} = C_{jk}^T C_{ij}^T = \underline{0}. \tag{25}$$

6.4. Poincaré Duality [12]

The Appendix roughly indicates how the concept of duality can be incorporated in homology theory. With the help of Poincaré's duality proposition, Table 8.8 can be set up in analogy with Table 8.7.

In Figure 8.25 the chain sequence is replaced by a dual cochain. For the sake of clarity, the cochain and dual cochain sequences are, respectively, cohomology and homology sequences.

In Figure 8.26 a bare skeleton of the so-called cohomology "string" is shown.

6.5. Vector Calculus [12, 74]

Before physical theories are worked into the generalized string, first it has to be checked if the known rules of vector calculus can be applied to this string. Earlier it was made clear that the across- and through-variables can be considered as vectors and that the system structure can be incorporated in the incidence matrices. Now it is clear that it has to be checked whether vector calculus includes analogous forms of

$$A^T C = \underline{0} \quad \text{and} \quad C^T A = \underline{0}.$$

TABLE 8.8. Poincaré Duals, with $0 < p \le n = 3$.

Primal 3-complex	Dual 3-complex
p-simplexes	$(3 - p)$-simplexes
p-chains	$(3 - p)$-cochains
p-cochains	$(3 - p)$-chains
C_{01}	$\underline{C}^{32} = \underline{C}^T_{23}$
C_{12}	$\underline{C}^{21} = \underline{C}^T_{12}$
C_{23}	$\underline{C}^{10} = \underline{C}^T_{01}$
C^T_{01}	$\underline{C}_{23}$
C^T_{12}	$\underline{C}_{12}$
C^T_{23}	$\underline{C}_{01}$

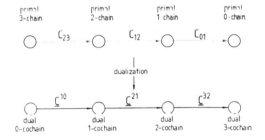

FIGURE 8.25. Dual of a chain sequence.

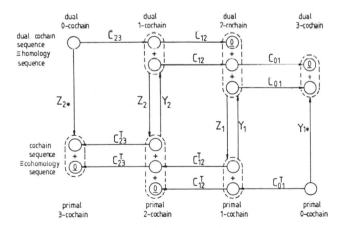

FIGURE 8.26. Cohomology string (generalized for a 3-complex).

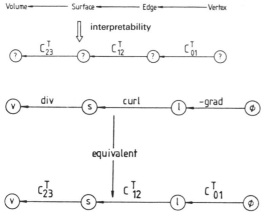

FIGURE 8.27. Interpretability of geometric transformations.

FIGURE 8.28. Integral-statements in a topological sequence.

In simplicial topology 0-, 1-, 2-, 3-, and n-simplexes identify with, respectively, vertex, edge, surface, volume, and hypervolume elements.

In Figure 8.27 the subsequent transformations of the geometric elements in rank order of dimension are briefly indicated.

The question now is how to interpret these transformations vector-algebraically. In rank order of dimension, the well-known integral-statements of vector calculus are

$$\phi(a) - \phi(b) = -\int_a^b \operatorname{grad} \underline{\phi} \cdot \mathrm{d}\underline{l} \qquad \text{(line integral)} \qquad (26)$$

$$\oint \underline{A} \cdot \mathrm{d}\underline{l} = \int_S \operatorname{curl} \underline{A} \cdot \mathrm{d}\underline{s} \qquad \text{(Stokes's theorem)} \qquad (27)$$

$$\int \underline{B} \cdot \mathrm{d}\underline{s} = \int_V \operatorname{div} \underline{B} \cdot \mathrm{d}\underline{v} \qquad \text{(Gauss's theorem)} \qquad (28)$$

If we now consider gradient, curl, and divergence as linear operators, and if they are placed in a sequence in rank order of dimension, then Figure 8.28 shows clearly how these integral-statements are to be interpreted topologically.

The known vector identities

$$\operatorname{curl} \operatorname{grad}(f) = 0 \qquad (29)$$

and

$$\operatorname{div} \operatorname{curl} \underline{H} = 0 \qquad (30)$$

confirm the correctness of the application of (25). These identities are obviously analogous interpretations of

$$A^T C = \underline{0} \quad \text{and} \quad C^T A = \underline{0}.$$

7. The Incorporation of Physical Theories in Cohomology Theory [3, 12]

The inclusion of Maxwell's equations of electromagnetism in cohomology theory is laid out here according to a logical scheme:

—first, the inclusion of the analyzed static cases of electromagnetism, for example, electrostatics and magnetostatics (which, as is known, are independent from each other), in their cohomology strings;

—next, the incorporation of the time derivatives of some particular quantities of the static cases; and

—finally, the coupling of these strings, as can be seen later in the schematized development phases in Figures 8.29 to 8.31.

7.1. Electrostatics

The quantities concerned are arranged in a certain rank order of dimension:

$$\phi = \text{field potential [V]},$$

$$\underline{E} = \text{electric field [V/m]},$$

$$\underline{h} \equiv \text{vector potential [C/m]},$$

$$\underline{D} + \underline{d} \equiv \text{dielectric displacement } [C/m^2] = [As/m^2],$$

$$\rho \equiv \text{charge density } [C/m^3] = [As/m^3].$$

Fundamental relations of electrostatics are

$$\text{div}\,\underline{d} = 0, \tag{31}$$

$$\text{div}\,\underline{D} = \rho(\underline{x}), \tag{32}$$

$$\text{curl}\,\underline{E} - \underline{0}, \tag{33}$$

$$\text{curl}\,\underline{h} = \underline{d}, \tag{34}$$

$$\underline{D} + \underline{d} = \varepsilon\underline{E}. \tag{35}$$

with $\varepsilon = $ dielectric constant or permittivity $[C/(V \cdot m)]$.

The dimensions of the quantities concerned clearly determine their position in the string.

From this string-diagram (Figure 8.29), the relations below follow:

$$\rho(\underline{x}) = -\text{div}\,\varepsilon\,\text{grad}\,\phi(\underline{x}) \tag{36}$$

$$\phi(\underline{x}) = -(\text{div}\,\varepsilon\,\text{grad})^{-1}\rho(\underline{x}) \tag{37}$$

$$\phi(\underline{x}) = -(\text{div}\,\varepsilon\,\text{grad})^{-1}\,\text{div}\,\underline{D} \tag{38}$$

$$\underline{E} = -\text{grad}\,\phi(\underline{x}) = \text{grad}\,(\text{div}\,\varepsilon\,\text{grad})^{-1}\rho(\underline{x}) \tag{39}$$

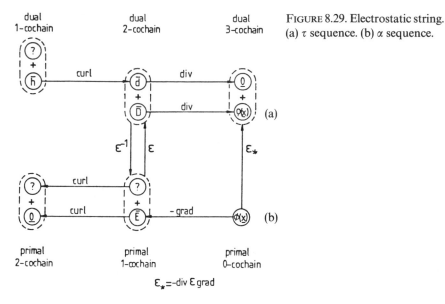

FIGURE 8.29. Electrostatic string. (a) τ sequence. (b) α sequence.

$$\text{curl}\,\varepsilon^{-1}\,\text{curl}\,\underline{h} = \text{curl}\,\varepsilon^{-1}\underline{D} \tag{40}$$

$$\underline{h} = -(\text{curl}\,\varepsilon^{-1}\,\text{curl})^{-1}\,\text{curl}\,\varepsilon^{-1}\underline{D} \tag{41}$$

$$\underline{d} = -\text{curl}(\text{curl}\,\varepsilon^{-1}\,\text{curl})^{-1}\,\text{curl}\,\varepsilon^{-1}\underline{D}, \quad \therefore \underline{d} = \underline{d}(\underline{D}) \tag{42}$$

7.2. Magnetostatics

The quantities concerned are arranged in the same way as in the previous case:

$$\underline{A} \equiv \text{vector potential } [\text{W/m}] = [\text{Vs/m}],$$

$$\underline{B} \equiv \text{inductive field } [\text{W/m}^2] = [\text{Vs/m}^2],$$

$$\underline{H} \equiv \text{magnetic field intensity } [\text{A/m}],$$

$$\underline{J} \equiv \text{current density } [\text{A/m}^2].$$

Fundamental relations of magnetostatics are

$$\text{curl}\,\underline{H} = \underline{J} \tag{43}$$

$$\text{curl}\,\underline{A} = \underline{B} \tag{44}$$

$$\text{div}\,\underline{B} = 0 \tag{45}$$

$$\underline{B} = \mu\underline{H} \tag{46}$$

with μ = permeability $[\text{W}/(\text{A}\cdot\text{m})]$

In Figure 8.30 we can see how these relations are included. From this string-diagram, the known derivatives follow:

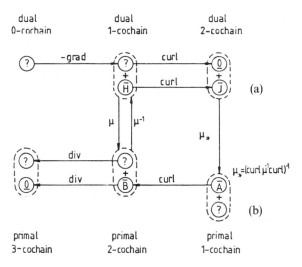

FIGURE 8.30. Magnetostatic string. (a) τ sequence. (b) α sequence.

$$\underline{J} = \text{curl}\,\mu^{-1}\,\text{curl}\,\underline{A} \tag{47}$$

$$\underline{A} = (\text{curl}\,\mu^{-1}\,\text{curl})^{-1}\underline{J} \tag{48}$$

$$\underline{B} = \text{curl}\,\underline{A} = \text{curl}(\text{curl}\,\mu^{-1}\,\text{curl})^{-1}\underline{J} \tag{49}$$

7.3. The Coupling of Electrostatic and Magnetostatic Strings

A comparison of the electrostatic and magnetostatic strings (Table 8.9) indicates that it is impossible to connect these strings "statically" to one another, since they are not dimensionally consistent. Looked at physically, this is the reason why electrostatics and magnetostatics are independent of each other.

In the dual 2-cochain $\underline{d}$ and $\underline{J}$ are dimensionally mutually incompatible: $[\underline{d}] \neq [\underline{J}]$. In the primal 1-cochain, this is also true of $\underline{E}$ and $\underline{B}$: $[\underline{E}] \neq [\underline{B}]$. Moreover, it is seen that the incompatibility arises from one dimension only, namely, that of time! This motivates us to introduce the time derivatives of ρ, $\underline{D}$, $\underline{d}$, $\underline{A}$, and $\underline{B}$.

In Figure 8.31 we can see how the electrodynamic and magnetodynamic strings can be linked to one another thanks to the time derivatives. The "coupled" strings yield the well-known equations of Maxwell, which comprise

1. Structure equations:

$$\text{curl}\,\underline{E} = -\partial \underline{B}/\partial t \qquad \text{(Faraday's law)}, \tag{50}$$

$$\text{curl}\,\underline{H} = \underline{J} + \partial \underline{D}/\partial t \qquad \text{(Ampere's law)}, \tag{51}$$

$$\text{div}\,\underline{B} = 0 \qquad \text{(Gauss' law)}, \tag{52}$$

$$\text{div}\,\underline{J} = -\partial \rho/\partial t \qquad \text{(Coulomb's law)}, \tag{53}$$

TABLE 8.9. Comparison between dimensions.

	Electrostatics	Magnetostatics
α sequence	$\begin{cases} [V] \\ [V/m] \end{cases}$	$[W/m] = [Vs/m]$ $[W/m^2] = [Vs/m^2]$
τ sequence	$\begin{cases} [C/m] = [As/m] \\ [C/m^2] = [As/m^2] \\ [C/m^3] = [As/m^3] \end{cases}$	$[A/m]$ $[A/m^2]$

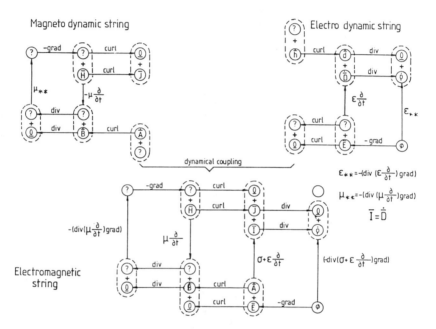

FIGURE 8.31. Electromagnetic string.

2. Constitutive laws:

$$\underline{D} = \varepsilon_0 \underline{E} + \underline{P} = (1 + \chi_e)\varepsilon_0 \underline{E} = \varepsilon\underline{E}, \qquad (54)$$

$$\underline{B} = \mu_0 \underline{H} + \mu_0 \underline{M} = (1 + \chi_m)\mu_0 \underline{H} = \mu\underline{H}, \qquad (55)$$

$$\underline{J} = \sigma\underline{E}, \qquad (56)$$

with σ = conductivity $[A/(V \cdot m)]$,

from which, for the sake of reminder, some important derivatives follow:

$$\text{curl } \underline{B} = \mu\underline{J} + \varepsilon\mu\partial\underline{E}/\partial t \qquad (57)$$

$$\dot{\rho} = \text{div}(\sigma + \varepsilon\partial/\partial t)(\underline{E} + \dot{\underline{A}}) \qquad (58)$$

$$\text{div } \underline{E} = \rho/\varepsilon \quad \text{for } \sigma = 0 \text{ and } \dot{\underline{A}} = 0 \qquad (59)$$

$$\text{div } \underline{D} = \rho \tag{60}$$

$$\phi = -[\text{div}(\sigma + \varepsilon\partial/\partial t)\text{grad}]^{-1} \text{div}[\underline{I} - (\sigma + \varepsilon\partial/dt)\underline{\dot{A}}] \tag{61}$$

$$\underline{H} = -[\text{curl}[S_1 - [\text{curl } T_2 \text{ curl}]^{-1}]\text{curl}]^{-1}\text{curl } S_1 \underline{I} \tag{62}$$

with $S_1 = (\sigma + \varepsilon\partial/\partial t)^{-1}$ and $T_2 = (\mu\partial/\partial t)^{-1}$. Moreover, we recognize some interesting "by-products":

—Application of the divergence operator to (50) gives, via

$$\text{div curl } \underline{E} = \text{div}(-\partial B/\partial t) = -\partial(\text{div } \underline{B})/\partial t = 0 \quad \text{(see (30))},$$

the expression div $\underline{B} = 0$, which confirms (52).

—Application of the divergence operator to (51) leads, via

$$\text{div curl } \underline{H} = \text{div}(\underline{J} + \partial\underline{D}/\partial t) = \text{div } \underline{J} + \text{div}(\partial\underline{D}/\partial t)$$

$$= \text{div } \underline{J} + \partial(\text{div } \underline{D})/\partial t = 0 \quad \text{and} \quad \text{div } \underline{D} = \rho \quad \text{(see (32))},$$

to the result

$$\text{div } \underline{J} + \partial\rho/\partial t = 0,$$

which confirms (53).

By carrying the latter argument further, it may be shown that eqs. (52) and (53) are consistent with (50) and (51).

From the local relations (50) to (55), we can derive a differential equation in vector notation for $\underline{E}$ and $\underline{B}$:

—By applying the curl operator to (51), combined with the substitution of (50), we obtain

$$\text{curl curl } H = \text{curl } \underline{J} + \text{curl}(\partial D/\partial t) = \text{curl } \underline{J} + \partial(\text{curl } \underline{D})/\partial t,$$

which with (55) and (54) and (50) yields

$$\text{curl curl } \underline{B} + \varepsilon\mu\partial^2\underline{B}/\partial t^2 = \mu \text{ curl } \underline{J}. \tag{63}$$

—In an analogous way, application of the curl operator to (50) gives

$$\text{curl curl } \underline{E} + \varepsilon\mu\partial^2\underline{E}/\partial t^2 = -\mu\partial\underline{J}/\partial t. \tag{64}$$

By supposing, for example, that $\underline{J}$ is a differentiable function of space and time at every point of a vacuum, we can in principle find the electric field $\underline{E}$ and the inductive field $\underline{B}$ by solving at least one of these differential equations, say, (63). By substituting the computed $\underline{B}$ field in (50) and (51), the associated $\underline{E}$ field can then be found. Equations (63) and (64) are nothing other than the electromagnetic wave equations, from which it may be shown that

$$(\varepsilon\mu)^{-1/2} = c,$$

with $c \equiv$ propagation velocity of the electromagnetic wave (= velocity of light).

The attentive reader will quickly remark that the magnetic space charge ρ_m is absent [48, 87]. This can be remedied by the use of the concept of symmetry. Figure 8.31 is actually symmetrical with respect to the central vertical axis. If we rotate this figure 180 degrees, then we have another string connection that describes a supplementary set of "magnetoelectric" field equations (sic!), wherein the magnetic space charge is fundamental rather than the electric space charge. Page and Adams have shown, not only that this possibility exists, but also that every linear combination of electric and magnetic space charges leads to a self-consistent theory of electromagnetism [62].

7.4. Implications for Extension of Cohomology Theory

To conclude, we have seen how Maxwell's laws may be incorporated, without difficulty, into cohomology theory, not losing sight of the fact that these laws describe "fields" and result in a field theory! It is logical to expect that we will produce "analog" field theories, in, among others, hydrodynamics, gravitational fields, acoustics, thermodynamics, magnetohydrodynamics, continuum mechanics, relativity theory, Schrödinger fields, meson fields, and thermoelastodynamics. They operate with "analog" Poisson, Laplace, diffusion, and Helmholtz equations (in fact, with partial differential equations of elliptic, parabolic, and hyperbolic type in tensor notation). This means that these field theories should be considered as different (read: specific) cohomology theories. It is to the honor of Tonti [83], who, on the basis of [79–82], has worked out a number of illustrative examples in different energy domains; he consistently develops physical theories from one cohomology theory.

8. Is Something Higher than Cohomology Theory Possible?

Before answering the question "Is there a higher (read: unifying) theory for the cohomology theories upon which the analogy between these last theories can be laid down 'visually, physically and mathematically'?", we must first mention recent developments in advanced physics. There are, up to the present, four sorts of forces of nature: gravitational force; electromagnetic force; strong nuclear force between the hadrons, built up with quarks; and weak nuclear force between hadrons as well as leptons (a hadron is a collective name for protons, neutrons, pions, and more exotic elementary particles, and a lepton is a collective name for, among others, electrons, muons, and neutrinos). These four forces of nature are, respectively, incorporated under the gravitational field, the electromagnetic field, and the Yang–Mills field, with and without Higgs field.

For the well-intentioned topologist, it is no longer surprising that the equations of the Yang–Mills field are analogies of those of Maxwell's theory of electromagnetic fields; in other words, they fit into the cohomology theory and so have a topological string. So, for each of these four forces of nature we have a string. Just as we have seen how the electrodynamic and magneto-dynamic strings may be linked to one another, we can also link these four strings together. So evolves a superstring theory as an answer to the last question posed. In theories such as that in [27], one even comes across "analog" forms of the Roth-transformations. Different sorts of symmetry are brought together under one "supersymmetry." One can follow up how far these analogous forms of $A^T C = \underline{0}$ and $C^T A = \underline{0}$ carry through in the super-string theory. One even comes across H-strings!

Such a superstring model, with various branchings and intertwinings, would be very appropriate for making a permanent link between physical theories in the form of their cohomology theories. It is exactly the complicated structure of the superstring model that provides so many difficulties at present that one must for now keep cohomology theories apart. The mathematical difficulties can certainly be eliminated provided very stringent conditions (i.e., supersymmetry (sic!)) are fulfilled.

Another interesting "analogy-seeing" is the analogous interpretation of the law of conservation. In the network of Figure 8.23 (as 2-complex), A^T and C^T symbolize the (dual) conservation laws of energy, namely, the first and second generalized laws of Kirchhoff, while in the 3-complex of electromagnetism of Figure 8.31, C_{01} and C_{23} represent the conservation laws of electric and magnetic charge, respectively. In the superstring model, there are about 12 laws of conservation: mass-energy, impulse, angular impulse, electron family number, muon family number, baryon family number, time inversion, space inversion, charge conjugation, combined space inversion and charge conjugation, strangeness, and isotopic spin. As the laws of conservation possess their validity everywhere and always, there are "inviolable" rules that determine the form of all interactions. A few of the conservation laws are in fact "invariance principles." Other conservation laws concern the family numbers, which may be viewed as analogies of the Euler–Poincaré formula for polyhedrons.

Totally independent from physics, simplicial topology ascertains that the conservation laws are in fact based on symmetries; in other words, conservation laws are symmetry laws. Why?

9. Symmetry and Invariance

In analogy theory, questions of symmetry and invariance have come to play an increasingly prominent part in the systematic classification of links, transformations, strings, and geometric configurations. It is interesting to note that implicitly, ideas of symmetry and invariance have governed the whole evolution of physics since Newton's days.

Qua definition, symmetry has two meanings: a geometric meaning and an algebraic meaning. In the first sense, we could reckon the following: translational symmetry as, for example, frieze decorations, rotational symmetry as column and rosette decorations, and bilateral symmetry in the form of reflections, such as "right hand versus left hand," a symmetrically drawn heart, and handwriting versus mirror writing. Combinations of the above-mentioned symmetries also exist: In art we meet with examples such as the famous images of Escher, a jewel of a cutting-art of Bohemian crystal goblet, and different tapestry-symmetries; and in nature we find, for example, the antlers of a deer, symmetrically colored wings of a butterfly, and, not to be forgotten, a pretty girl with symmetry-beauties.

In the second sense, a whole is defined symmetric if it has interchangeable parts. The vagueness of this definition implies that many kinds of symmetry can exist. They differ in the number of interchangeable parts and in the operations that exchange the parts. Algebraically, we describe these different kinds of symmetry in terms of topological properties that remain invariant under a certain mapping of any set of elements. Symmetry properties of a system are characterized in terms of groups of transformations that leave the system unchanged. If a system proves invariant under a certain group of transformations, then this symmetry feature relates to the conservation of a certain "dynamical" quantity. That is why the existence of conservation laws is directly related to the symmetry of the laws of nature, that is, to their invariance or changelessness under various symmetry operations such as rotations, translations, and reflections of the spatial and temporal coordinates.

We may safely say that all a priori statements in physics have their origin in symmetry considerations [20, 21, 30, 59, 67, 68]. As Weyl [89] has phrased it, "if conditions which uniquely determine their effect possess certain symmetries, then the effect will exhibit the same symmetry." In such a way, Sophie Lie created the foundations for the science of symmetry of differential equations. Recently, on the occasion of the 150th anniversary of the birth of James Clerk Maxwell, Fushchick and Nikitin presented their work, titled "Symmetries of Maxwell's Equations" [24]. Obviously, the symmetry applications range from the direct link between one-dimensional symmetry groups and conservation laws (Noether's theorem) to the use of linear and nonlinear group representation theory in various contexts and in higher dimensions (such as, e.g., in superstring theory with supersymmetry).

The aim of the previous contemplation about symmetry is to apply symmetry consistently in analogy-thinking, analogy-seeing, and modeling of physical and technical systems. In this way, for such systems we can obtain complete symmetry between the set of through-variables and the set of across-variables, as shown in Table 8.10.

In Table 8.10 it is shown that the relationships between these two sets are symmetrical (or complementary or dually) to each other. This duality, complementarity, or symmetrical relationship between the through-variables and across-variables is emphasized qualitatively by the mere existence of the first law of thermodynamics.

In this context analogies, dualities, and dualogies may be considered as symmetries. Moreover, consequent use of symmetry in matrix theory, just as

TABLE 8.10. Symmetries
between τ-set and α-set.

τ-set	α-set
$A^T\underline{\tau} = \underline{0}$	$C^T\underline{\alpha} = \underline{0}$
$A^TC = \underline{0}$	$C^TA = \underline{0}$
$\underline{\tau} = Y\underline{\alpha}$	$\underline{\alpha} = Z\underline{\tau}$

in network and bond-graph theory, leads to time-saving manipulations and computations.

Concerning analogy-thinking, the transition of ideas and models from one physical field to another must be based on invariances, forming analogous laws and relations [43].

We have seen that analogy-seeing, based on cohomology theory, can reduce the whole of physics to geometry. The intriguing question "What precisely is geometry?" leads us to the "Erlanger program" of Felix Klein [44]. The general idea of this program is resolved in Klein's definition, which may be rendered as follows: "A geometry is the study of those properties of a space which remain invariant when the elements of the space are subjected to the transformations of some group of transformations." This establishment has paramount scope, because, in the field of geometry, catastrophe theory [25, 91] (analyzing mathematical instabilities) and fractal theory [4–6, 52, 53, 65] (trying to understand chaos in nature) advance in the direction of physics. Thus, analogy theory can comprehend all these theories very nicely in the future.

10. Completeness and Consistency

Can this "higher" (physical) theory be consistent and complete? This question will definitely be answered negatively by virtue of Gödel's Incompleteness Theorem [26, 57]. Without proof and in a more popular way, this theorem states that

> All consistent axiomatic formulations of a theory include undecidable propositions.

When popularizing this theorem, the next analogies show striking resemblance:

— Epimenides's Paradox or the liar's paradox: "All Cretans are liars." More explicitly this statement can be written as "A liar says he lies; so he lies and he does not lie at the same time."
— Eubulides' Dilemma (approx. 400 B.C.) about the liar who says he lies, Electra who owns and does not own her brother Crestes, and so on.
— Maxwell's Demon [64].

— Ubbink's Cuckoo [18].
— Church's Undecidability Theorem [16].
— Turing's Halting Theorem [25].
— Tarski's Truth Theorem [76].

More precisely, the proof of Gödel's Incompleteness Theorem hinges on the formulation of a self-referential mathematical statement, precisely as Epimenides' Paradox is a self-referential statement of language. This means that it is impossible to accept the challenge of irrefutably proving that this theory is both consistent (free of contradictions) and complete (i.e., every true statement of the theory can be derived within the framework drawn up by this theory itself).

It is true, one can complete the (higher physical) theory concerned further on and make it more consistent (in terms of Gödel's theory: Increase the Gödel numbers); however, "completely complete" and 100% consistent, this theory shall never be. Even if the "superstring" model continues expanding, full completeness and consistency will never be reached.

Analogy theory itself can in this case subscribe to Gödel's theorem. If one theory is deduced from another theory in an analogical way (analogized), eventually the completeness and consistency will be increased, but their "full" completeness and consistency will not be reached. Analogy, namely, has, in this case, to indicate differences next to the aimed similarities. It is these very differences that are responsible for the incompleteness and inconsistency of the "analogized" theory. By incorporating physical theories in one cohomology theory, physical theories are in fact analogies of each other. In other words, with respect to each other they are incomplete and inconsistent. After all, these imperfections form no obstacle for the judgement of the acceptance, usefulness, and attractiveness of physical theories. The applicability of such a theory is, in fact, determined by pragmatic factors, such as agreement with observed facts, simplicity, and elegance, agreement with common sense (analogy-seeing and -thinking), fitness to support desirable human conduct, and, last but not least, agreement with purpose for which the theory has been developed.

11. Relationship Between Analogy Theory and Artificial Intelligence

Douglas R. Hofstadter summed up some essential abilities for intelligence:

   — to respond to situations very flexibly;
   — to take advantage of fortuitous circumstances;
   — to make sense out of ambiguous or contradictory messages;
   — to recognize the relative importance of different elements of a situations;
   — to find similarities between situations despite differences which may separate them (sic!);

— to draw distinctions between situations despite similarities which may link them (sic!);
— to synthesize new concepts by taking old concepts and putting them together in new ways;
— to come up with ideas which are novel. [38]

These abilities can, on the basis of analogy with control theory, graph theory, information theory, and mathematical logic, more or less be incorporated in an artificial intelligence (AI) model. By virtue of Gödel's theorem, this AI-model will never be complete and consistent, but from psychology and psychiatry, we know that human intelligence is not consistent and complete either. This is the similarity between artificial and human intelligence. The difference lies in their respective Gödel numbers. If Gödel's number of AI is higher or lower than the one of human intelligence, then AI is superior, respectively, inferior, to human intellect. Hopefully the previous argument, developed with help of analogy theory, can throw light upon a controversy between Hofstadter and Lucas, as can be read in Hofstadter's magisterial book *Gödel, Escher, Bach: An Eternal Golden Braid* [38]. Lucas [49] claims that human intellect can principally not be imitated by a computer program. While his argumentation is completely based on Gödel's Incompleteness Theorem, this is not only disputed by Hofstadter but also by Arbib in his book *Brains, Machines and Mathematics* [2].

12. Epilogue

It is certain that the most general theory (read: in casu the analogy theory), which includes existing phenomena and can take up new phenomena, is best and most powerful; from such a theory, simple theories can always be deducted. This is, for example, how Newtonian mechanics can be considered as a more specific "case" of Albert Einstein's relativity theory.

The fertility of cohomology theory as analogy theory does not in the last instance manifest itself clearly in the unconstrained explanation, that it provides for already known phenomena. That is the reason why it is produced at all [17, 40, 74]. Of course, when such a theory gives a natural explanation of many phenomena, particularly if these are of widely different nature, then such a theory impresses; it lays down the unity, which leads to multiplicity. But such a theory shall gain yet more in convincingness when there are phenomena that can be explained, of which nothing is yet known at the time that the theory was set up. This is the nicest aspect of analogy theory, bearing in mind, however, that the analogy-use should critically be applied.

According to Maxwell, who, in his address to the British Association, stated that analogy was "not only a legitimate product of science, but capable of generating science in its turn ...." Analogy theory is apparently "science-forming" for physical theories and "model-forming" for technical systems.

It is now shown that the Analogy theory, due to its universality, can be conceived as a "general" cohomology theory. In 1945 Eilenberg and Steenrod gave an axiomatic formulation of the homology [39 theory]. They set seven axioms on which a so-called theory should be based in order to be called real, and they, in general, derived the propositions that hold for such a theory. In that, we shall find again the stringent conditions for the justified use of analogies in systems science.

Analogy theory has indeed provided insight in the way analogies should be critically used. This, however, does not directly answer the pragmatic question, What do we want to do with analogies? The intentions of "analogy users" are very diverse, due to the wide applicability of analogy-thinking. The motives can roughly be classified as follows:

1. Analogies form a central concept, playing an important role in several different mathematical, physical, and other scientific specialized areas.
2. The transformation of new applications of the results and ideas from one area of scientific endeavor into another is stimulated by analogies.
3. Analogies have contributed largely to the influences that concepts, problems, and results of one field of inquiry have and have had on the development of another.

As a consequence of these three motivations, the following developments in the field of engineering design ("theory application" rather than "theory development") are currently observed:

— Analogical reasoning becomes more and more important from a design methodology point of view. The search for design methodologies and strategies to be used in a certain engineering field, equivalent to those already emerged in related engineering disciplines, has lead to multi-disciplinary approaches. To this, a new, higher discipline owes its existence: systems engineering.
— The power of analogical reasoning for generating new ideas, concepts, and hypotheses has been appreciated in fields of very diverse nature, and it can therefore be used intelligently by design engineers especially in the conceptual stage of design.

It is therefore necessary to supply assistance in identifying and applying analogs most effectively. This assistance could be concretized by providing design engineers with

— data banks filled with analogous attributes and cases. These databases should contain sufficient details to support the analogical reasoning process.
— Strategies for applying analogs. This, as has been stated before, should be carefully and critically done.

In this way, the engineering design field, with its synthesizing nature, could benefit a lot from the modeling concepts with a more analytical nature. Morphological analysis schemes, which are helpful in engineering design, could then be transformed into inductive "morphological synthesis tools," expressing the very essence behind the use of them.

Finally, because of the central theme of this book, *simulation*, a short implication of the previously described concepts will be given: As already stated before, every analogy can be used visually, physically, and mathematically. Due to the fact that physics can represent/explain mathematics as well as geometry, "mathematical" and "visual-topological" analogies remain as the elements of the basic description idiom for implementation in a computer program.

We have two types of computer programs at our disposal for implementing the analogy concept to be used in systems engineering:

1. network-oriented software, such as ECAP, NAP, (PC-)SPICE, μ-CAP; and
2. equation-oriented software, such as CSSL, CSMP, ACSL, PSI, TUTSIM, and MOSIS.

Two salient particularities can be observed:

1. Recently, "physical analogies," as in [56], are being used less and less.
2. Equation-oriented software with time-consuming integration methods has lower performance than network-oriented software.

From this it can be concluded that for systems simulation the future lies in network-oriented software, actually modeling the problem "topologically."

References

1. Anderson, A.R., Ed. *Minds and Machines*. Prentice-Hall, Englewood Cliffs, N.J., 1964.
2. Arbib, M.A. *Brains, Machines and Mathematics*. McGraw-Hill, New York, 1965.
3. Balasubramanian, N.V., Lynn, J.W., and Sen Gupta, O.P. *Differential Forms on Electromagnetic Networks*. Butterworths, London, 1970.
4. Barnsley, M.F. *Fractals Everywhere*. Academic Press, Boston, 1988.
5. Barnsley, M.F., and Demko, S.G. *Chaotic Dynamic and Fractals*. Academic Press, Boston, 1987.
6. Becker, K.H., and Dörfler, M. *Dynamische Systeme und Fraktale*. Vierweg, Braunschweig, 1989.
7. Bell, A., and Martens, H.R. A comparison of linear graphs and bond graphs in the modeling proces. In *JACC Proceedings*. 1974, pp. 777–794.
8. Blackett, D.W. *Elementary Topology, a Combinatorial and Algebraic Approach*. Academic Press, New York, 1967.
9. Blackwell, W.A. *Mathematical Modeling of Physical Networks*. MacMillan, New York, 1968.
10. Blundell, A. *Bond Graphs for Modeling Engineering Systems*. Wiley, Chichester (W. Sussex), 1982.
11. Bowden, K.G. An introduction to homological systems theory: Topological analysis of invariant systems zeros. *Matrix Tensor Q*. (1980), 36–52.
12. Branin, F.H. *The Algebraic-Topological Basis for Network Analogies and the Vector*

   Calculus, Symposium on Generalized Networks. Brooklyn Polytechnic Institute, Apr. 1966, pp. 453–491.
13. Breedveld, P.C. Physical systems theory in terms of bond graphs. Ph.D. thesis, Univ. of Twente, The Netherlands, 1984.
14. Bryant, P.R. The algebra and topology of electrical networks. In *Proceedings of I.E.E.,* Vol. 108c. 1961, p. 215.
15. Cairns, S.S. *Introductory Topology.* The Ronald Press Co., New York, 1961.
16. Church, A. *Introduction to Mathematic Logic.* Princeton University Press, Princeton, N.J., 1956.
17. Curtis, W.D., and Millar, F.R. *Differential Manifolds and Theoretical Physics.* Academic Press, Orlando, Fla.; Orlando, 1985.
18. De Froe. *Filosofische Oriëntering in de Natuurwetenschappen* (in Dutch). Aulabooks no 347, Het Spectrum, Utrecht, 1967.
19. Dixhoorn, J.J., and Evans, F.J. *Physical Structure in Systems Theory.* Academic Press, London, 1974.
20. Elliott, J.P., and Dawber, P.G. *Principles and Simple Applications Symmetry in Physics* (two parts). Macmillan Press, London, 1979.
21. Feynman, R. *The Character of Physical Law.* MIT Press, Cambridge, Mass., 1965.
22. Firestone, F.A. A new Analogy between mechanical and electrical systems. *J. Acoustical Soc. 4* (Jan. 1933), 249–267.
23. Franz, W. *Topologie.* Part 2: *Algebraische Topologie, Sammlung Göschen Band 1182.* Walter de Gruyter, Berlin, 1965.
24. Fushchick, W.I., and Nikitin, A.G. Symmetries of Maxwell's equations. Reidel, Dordrecht, 1987.
25. Gleick, J. *Chaos, Making a New Science.* Penguin Books, New York, 1987.
26. Gödel, K. *Über Formal Unentscheidbare Sättze der Principia Mathematica und Verwandter Systeme, I* (Part II has not appeared). Monatshefte für Mathematik und Physik, Vol. 38, (1931), pp. 173–198. This is now available in an English translation; see Gödel, K., *On Formally Undecidable Propositions of Principia Mathematica and Related Systems.* Translated by B. Meltzer, with an introduction by R.B. Braithwaite. Basic Books, Inc., Publishers, New York, 1962.
27. Green, M.B., Schwarz, J.H., and Witten, E. *Superstring Theory.* Vol. I and II. Cambridge Monographs on Mathematical Physics, Cambridge University Press, New York, 1987.
28. Harary, F. *Graph Theory and Theoretical Physics.* Academic Press, London, 1967.
29. Harary, F. *Graph Theory.* Addison-Wesley, Reading, Mass., 1972.
30. Hargittai, I., Ed. *Symmetry, Unifying Human Understanding.* Pergamon Press, New York, 1986.
31. Hesse, M.B. *Models and Analogies.* University of Notre Dame Press, Notre Dame, Indi., 1966.
32. Hezemans, P.M.A.L. *Introduction to Systemengineering* (in Dutch). Lecture Notes. Eindhoven University of Technology, Eindhoven, 1979.
33. Hezemans, P.M.A.L. *Systemengineering for the Power Transmissions* (in Dutch). Lecture Notes. Eindhoven University of Technology, Eindhoven, 1985.
34. Hezemans, P.M.A.L. *Gestructureerde Aanpak Systeemanalyse, Modelvorming en Simulation* (in Dutch). Aandrijftechniek, 1987–1988.
35. Hilton, P. *Lecture in Homological Algebra.* American Mathematical Society, Providence, R.I., 1971.

36. Hilton, P. *General Cohomology Theory and K-Theory.* Cambridge University Press, London, 1971.
37. Hilton, P.J., and Wylie, S. *Homology Theory, An Introduction to Algebraic Topology.* Cambridge University Press, London, 1960.
38. Hofstadter, D.R. *Gödel, Escher, Bach: An Eternal Golden Braid.* Basic Books, New York, 1979.
39. Hu, S.T. *Homology Theory.* Holden-Day Inc., San Francisco, 1966.
40. Jones, A, Gray, A., and Hutton, R. *Manifolds and Mechanics.* Cambridge University Press, Cambridge, London, 1987.
41. Karnopp, D., and Rosenberg, R. *Systems Dynamics, A Unified Approach.* Wiley, New York, 1971.
42. Karnopp, D., and Rosenberg, R.C. Rosenberg, *Analysis and Simulation of Multiport Systems, The Bondgraph Approach to Physical System Dynamics.* MIT Press, Cambridge, Mass., 1968.
43. Karunakaran, T., and Satsangi, P.S. On the identity between power invariance and topological invariance. *Matrix Tensor Q.* (June 1970), 124–127.
44. Klein, F. Vergleichende Betrachtungen über neuere geometrische Forschungen. *Mathemaische Annalen 43* (1893), 63–100.
45. Kron, G. *Tensor Analysis of Networks.* Wilcy, New York, 1939.
46. Kron, G. *Diakoptics.* MacDonald, London, 1963.
47. Lindsay, R.B., and Margenau, H. *Foundations of Physics.* Dover publications, New York, 1957.
48. Lorrain, P., and Corson, D.R. *Electromagnetism.* Freeman, San Francisco, 1979.
49. Lucas, J.R. Minds, machines and Gödel. *Philosophy 36* (1961), 112; reprinted in [1].
50. MacFarlane, A.G.J. *Engineering Analysis.* Harrap, London, 1964.
51. MacFarlane, A.G.J. *Dynamical System Models.* Harrap, London, 1970.
52. Mandelbrot, B.B. *Fractals: Form, Chance, and Dimension.* Freeman and Co. New York, 1977.
53. Mandelbrot, B.B. *The Fractal Geometry of Nature.* Freeman, New York, 1983.
54. Massey, W.S. *Singular Homology Theory.* Springer-Verlag, New York, 1980.
55. Maxwell, J.C. Are there real analogies in nature? In *The Life of James Clerk Maxwell*, L. Campbell and W. Garnett. Johnson Reprint Corporation, New York, 1969.
56. Murphy, G., Shippy, D.J., and Luo, H.L. *Engineering Analogies.* Iowa State University Press, Ames, Iowa, 1963.
57. Nagel, E., and Newman, J.R. *Gödel's Proof.* New York University Press, New York, 1958.
58. Nicholson, H. *Structure of Interconnected Systems.* Peter Peregrinus (IEE), 1978.
59. Nussbaum, A. *Applied Group Theory for Chemists, Physicists and Engineers.* Prentice-Hall, Englewood Cliffs, N.J., 1971.
60. Ore, O. *Graphs and Their Uses.* Random House, New York, 1963.
61. Ort, J.R., and Martens, H.R. A topological procedure for converting a bond graph to a linear graph. *J. Dynamic Syst., Measurement, Control ASME* (Sept. 1974), 307–314.
62. Page, L., and Adams, N.I. *Electrodynamics.* Van Nostrand, New York, 1940.
63. Penfield, P., Spence, R., and Duinker, S. *Tellegen's Theorem and Electrical Networks.* Research Monograph 58. MIT Press, Cambridge, Mass., 1970.
64. Pierce, J.R. *Symbols, Signals and Noise.* Harper and Brothers, New York, 1961.

65. Pietronero, L., and Tosatti, E. *Fractals in Physics*. North-Holland, Amsterdam, 1986.
66. Poincaré, H. *Science and Hypothesis*. Dover Publications, New York, 1952.
67. Rosen, J. *Symmetry Discovered: Concepts and Applications in Nature and Science*. Cambridge University Press, Cambridge Mass., 1975.
68. Rosen, J. *A Symmetry Primer for Scientists*. Wiley-Interscience, New York, 1983.
69. Rosenberg, R.C., and Karnopp, D.C. *Introduction to Physical System Dynamics*. McGraw-Hill, New York, 1983.
70. Roth, J.P. An application of algebraic topology to numerical analysis: On the existence of a solution to the network problem. In *Proceedings of the National Academy of Science*, Vol. 41. 1955, pp. 518–521.
71. Salzer, C. *Quart. Appl. Maths, Vol. II*. 1953, p. 119.
72. Seely, S. *Dynamic Systems Analysis*. Reinhold Publishing Corporation, New York 1964.
73. Shearer, J.L., Murphy, A.T., and Richardson, H.H. *Introduction to Systemdynamics*. Addison-Wesley, Reading, Mass., 1967.
74. Strang, G. A framework for equilibrium equations. *SIAM Rev. 30*, 2 (June 1988), 283–297.
75. Swamy, M.N.S., and Thulasiraman, K. *Graphs, Networks and Algorithms*. Wiley-Interscience, New York, 1981.
76. Tarski, A. *Logics, Semantics, Metamathematics, Papers from 1923 to 1938*. Oxford University Press, New York, 1956.
77. Tellegen, B.D.H. A general network theorem, with applications. *Philips Res. Reps. 7*, 4 (Aug. 1952), 259–269.
78. Thoma, J. *Introduction to Bond Graphs and Their Applications*. Pergamon Press, Oxford, 1979.
79. Tonti, E. *On the Mathematical Structure of a Large Class of Physical Theories*. Rend. Acc. Lincei, Vol. VII, 1972, pp. 48–56.
80. Tonti, E. *A Mathematical Model for Physical Theories*. Rend. Acc. Lincei, Vol. VII, 1972, First part pp. 175–181, second part pp. 350–356.
81. Tonti, E. *On the Mathematical Structure of Physical Theories*. Quaderno del Consiglio Nazionale delle Ricerche, 1975.
82. Tonti, E. *On the Formal Structure of Physical Theories*. Quad. di Gruppi di Ricerca Matematica, Instituto di Matematica del Politecnico, Milano, 1975.
83. Tonti, E. The reason for analogies between physical theories. *Appl. Math. Modelling 1* (June 1976), 37–50.
84. Trent, M.T. Isomorphisms between oriented linear graphs and lumped physical systems. *J. Acoustical Soc. Am. 27* (May 1955), 500–527.
85. Turner, J. Maxwell on the method of physical analogy. *British J. Philos. 6* (1955), 226–238.
86. Veblen, O. *Analysis Situs*. American Mathematical Society, Providence, 1931.
87. Wangsness, R.K. *Electromagnetic Fields*. Wiley, New York, 1979.
88. Wellstead, P.E. *Introduction to Physical System Modelling*. Academic Press, London, 1979.
89. Weyl, H. *Symmetry*. Princeton University Press, Princeton, N.J. 1952.
90. Whitney, E. Non-separable and planar graphs. *Trans. Am. Math. Soc. 34* (1932), 339–362.
91. Woodcock, A.E.R., and Poston, T. *A Geometrical Study of Elementary Catastrophes*. Springer-Verlag, New York, 1974.

Appendix

Simplicial Topology [8, 15, 23, 35–37, 39, 54, 86]

In simplicial topology, network figures (called complexes) are built up from a network of vertices, edges, triangles, tetrahedrons, and polyhedrons of higher dimensions; these components are determined completely by their vertices, and one can show that $n + 1$ vertices form an n-dimensional simplex (σ_n).

A 1-simplex $(\sigma_1 = \langle p_0 p_1 \rangle)$, determined by the vertices p_0 and p_1, is provided with an orientation, from p_0 to p_1 or from p_1 to p_0, and is called, accordingly, $\sigma_1 = \langle p_0 p_1 \rangle$ or $\langle p_1 p_0 \rangle = -\langle p_0 p_1 \rangle$.

A 2-simplex $(\sigma_2 = \langle p_0 p_1 p_2 \rangle$, determined by vertices p_0, p_1, and p_2, is provided with an loop orientation and is called, accordingly, $\sigma_2 = \langle p_0 p_1 p_2 \rangle = \langle p_1 p_2 p_0 \rangle = \langle p_2 p_0 p_1 \rangle$ or $-\langle p_0 p_2 p_1 \rangle = -\langle p_1 p_0 p_2 \rangle = -\langle p_2 p_1 p_0 \rangle = \langle p_0 p_1 p_2 \rangle$.

Thus, n-simplexes can be described by $\sigma_n = \langle p_0 p_1 \cdots p_n \rangle$; a 0-simplex consists of an equal number of vertices $\sigma_0 = \langle p_0 \rangle$ or $\sigma_0 = -\langle p_0 \rangle$.

A formal sum of n-simplexes $c_n = a_1 \sigma_{n1} + a_2 \sigma_{n2} + \cdots + a_k \sigma_{nk}$, where a_j are natural numbers and the σ_{nj} are n-simplexes, is an n-chain. For example, if the 1-chain consists of 1-simplexes, one has a curve; the a_js indicate how often and in what direction (depending on the sign of a_j) the 1-simplexes are being passed along.

The boundary of the 1-simplex $\sigma_1 = \langle p_0 p_1 \rangle$ is called a 0-chain, $\partial \sigma_1 = \langle p_1 \rangle - \langle p_0 \rangle$.

The boundary of the 2-simplex $\sigma_2 = \langle p_0 p_1 p_2 \rangle$ is called a 1-chain, $\partial \sigma_2 = \langle p_1 p_2 \rangle - \langle p_0 p_2 \rangle + \langle p_0 p_1 \rangle$.

The boundary of the 3-simplex $\sigma_3 = \langle p_0 p_1 p_2 p_3 \rangle$ is called a 2-chain, $\partial \sigma_3 = \langle p_1 p_2 p_3 \rangle - \langle p_0 p_2 p_1 \rangle + \langle p_0 p_1 p_3 \rangle - \langle p_0 p_1 p_2 \rangle$.

In general, if $\sigma_n = \langle p_0 p_1 \cdots p_n \rangle$ then, by definition, the boundary of σ_n is $\partial \sigma_n = \Sigma (-1)^i \langle p_0 p_1 \cdots \hat{p}_i \cdots p_n \rangle$. The accent $\hat{}$ above p_i means that the vertex p_i must be left out: $\langle p_0 p_1 \cdots \hat{p}_i \cdots p_n \rangle = \langle p_0 p_1 \cdots p_{i-1} p_{i+1} \cdots p_n \rangle$; ∂ is by definition a boundary operator. If $\sigma_n = + \langle p_0 p_1 \cdots p_n \rangle$, then $\sigma_{n-1,i} = (-1)^i \langle p_0 \cdots \hat{p}_i \cdots p_n \rangle$ such that $\partial \sigma_n = \Sigma \sigma_{n-i,i}$. For an n-chain, the boundary is defined as $\partial c_n = a_1 \partial \sigma_{n1} + a_2 \partial \sigma_{n2} + \cdots + a_k \partial \sigma_{nk}$, where $\partial \sigma_{nj}$ is the boundary of σ_{nj}.

The boundary of an n-chain, c_n, is an $(n - 1)$-chain. An n-chain with boundary zero is an n-cycle. It can be shown that the boundary of a boundary is zero, so that each boundary is a cycle. One can further prove that the n-cycles that are not boundaries of an $(n + 1)$-chain, form a group under the addition operator. The coboundary operator δ adds to every k-cochain a $(k + 1)$-cochain, while every k-coboundary is a k-cocycle. It also holds that the coboundary of a coboundary is zero. Two (co-)cycles are called homolog if they differ by one boundary. If one considers homology n-(co-)cycles as equivalent, then one gets an n-(co-)homology group of an n-Betti-group of the complex.

The simplicial homology just described is called homology theory.

Cohomology Theory

In (simplicial) cohomology theory, the building blocks are maps of simplexes into natural numbers rather than simplexes themselves. There is a close connection between the homology groups $(K_n(X))$ and the cohomology groups $(K^n(X))$ in a topological space. According to Poincaré's duality theorem for a particular class of spaces (the coherent oriented variety), the pth homology group and qth cohomology group are equal to one another if the dimension of the variety $n = p + q$.

Incidence

The incidence between an oriented n-simplex $\sigma_n \in K (n > 0)$ and the $(n-1)$-simplexes $\sigma_{n-1;i} \in K$, with $i = 1, \ldots, \alpha_{n-1}$, is described by the incidence number:

$\text{inc}(\sigma_{n-1;i}, \sigma_n) = 0$,   if $\sigma_{n-1;i}$ and σ_n are not incident,

$\qquad\qquad = 1$,   if $\sigma_{n-1;i}$ and σ_n are incident (in other words, $\sigma_{n-1;i}$ is the boundary simplex of σ_n) and coherently oriented,

$\qquad\qquad = -1$,   if $\sigma_{n-1;i}$ and σ_n are incident and not coherently oriented.

These incidence numbers are the elements of an $\alpha_{n-1} \times \alpha_n$-matrix:

$$H(n-1;n) = [\text{inc}(\sigma_{n-1;i}, \sigma_{n;j})]$$

with row index number $i = 1, \ldots, \alpha_{n-1}$ and column index number $j = 1, \ldots, \alpha_n$.

First Incidence Matrix A^T

The matrix entry a_{ij} describes the incidence between the ith vertex $V_i (i = 1, \ldots, k)$ and the jth edge $e_j (j = 1, \ldots, t)$ as follows:

$a_{ij} = +1$,   if V_i and e_j are incident and e_j is oriented toward V_i;

$a_{ij} = -1$,   if V_i and e_j are incident and e_j is oppositely oriented toward V_i;

$a_{ij} = 0$,   if V_i and e_j are not incident.

Second Incidence Matrix C

A loop orientation is assigned to every directed loop. The matrix entry c_{ij} describes the incidence between the ith loop $L_i (i = 1, \ldots, l)$ and the jth oriented edge $e_j (j = 1, \ldots, t)$ as follows:

$c_{ij} = 1$,   if L_i and e_j are incident and if the loop orientation of L_i and the direction of e_j coincide;

$c_{ij} = -1$,   if L_i and e_j are incident and if the loop orientation of L_i and the direction of e_j are opposed;

$c_{ij} = 0$,   if L_i and e_j are not incident.

CHAPTER 9

Bondgraphs for Qualitative and Quantitative Systems Modeling

Jean U. Thoma

Abstract

BG (Bondgraphs) are a systems representation that uses systematically the analogies between the engineering disciplines and prepares efficiently for simulation, even without writing equations. At the same time, they are useful for qualitative simulation since they give an idea of system behavior by inspection. After an introduction to the BG method and symbols, application to thermodynamics, chemistry, and osmosis is discussed; this is mostly qualitative since parameters are not well known. A pressure regulating valve is used as a worked example of a quantitative engineering simulation, yet this system appears in the literature on qualitative reasoning.

1. Bondgraphs in a Qualitative Context

A *Bondgraph* (*BG*) is a systems representation with letter symbols and connecting lines, "bonds," that carry both sign and programming information (causality). In lighter terms, if a sheet of paper looks as if a chicken had run over it with dirty feet, it is probably a BG. The BG technique was developed at MIT in the 1960s for the simulation of power and control systems with electric, hydraulic, and mechanical parts. Its history is associated with the names of Henry Paynter, the original genius, Dean Karnopp, and Ronald Rosenberg [4, 5], the people who condensed the original, Olympian ideas into a working technique of great power and beauty .

In particular, although BGs have been created for concrete engineering problems, they turned out to be a versatile modeling language for extended simulation requirements with concepts like entropy, chemical potential, and even osmosis. Such ideas and their consequences lead already toward qualitative simulation.

The simulation produces numerical data that are often represented as graphical plots. Yet the quantity of data is often overwhelming and masks the essential points, problems, or design issues. In other words, normal numerical simulation is like shooting birds with heavy cannon (a German metaphor),

217

or an overkill (a less sympathetic American expression). Here we are at the starting point of qualitative modeling. BGs certainly give qualitative insight without generating enormous quantities of numerical data. Expressed differently, they help to train the intuition of the user. Our contribution revolves around this central point.

A related point is common horse sense, in American parlance, or the healthy human judgment (German: *der gesunde Menschenverstand*). Only too often it is buried in too many data and details of the simulation process, whence the health of judgment deteriorates. Here we find a task for qualitative simulation in general and for Bondgraphing in particular.

Yet another method is global analysis of a problem, using known input data and general conservation principles without details of the process for approximate outputs. The method is often called "back of the envelope calculation"; it is very efficient to reveal gross programming errors. So it is related to qualitative modeling.

As pointed out by Fishwick [3], qualitative and quantitative modeling are the opposite ends of a continuous beam. This we illustrate with Figure 9.1, with the beam as a heavy line between two end points (circle for qualitative, square for quantitative). The arrows represent the following additional thoughts:

1. Qualitative models at left are related to ideas and concepts, much less to numbers as indicated by the broken arrow.
2. As one travels toward quantitative modeling, numbers become more prominent (continuous arrows), and their accuracy increases.

In fact, the importance of numerical accuracy is usually overlooked: It makes quite a difference whether engineering accuracy ($\sim 2\%$) or physics accuracy ($\sim 0.1\%$) is required, not only from the computational, but also from the conceptual point of view. Furthermore, if we want to reach calibration accuracy (better than $1.0{*}E - 0.4$), problems with definitions of some quantities arise, while other quantities are equal by definition to any accuracy. So qualitative simulation can shed light on these questions with the help of BG.

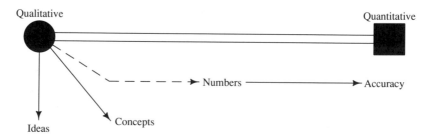

FIGURE 9.1. Qualitative and quantitative simulation at opposite sides of a beam. Ideas and concepts are mostly on the qualitative side, and numerical accuracy appears and increases with the transit to the quantitative side.

In this contribution we develop the BG technique from an engineering point of view in Section 2, go to extended, speculative simulation in Section 3, and later return to BG in a qualitative context.

2. Bondgraphs as an Interdisciplinary, Engineering-Oriented Language

2.1. Introduction

We use BG here as a tool for quantitative simulation on a model of an engineering system to ascertain that it behaves as desired. This includes checking that all variables remain within acceptable limits and varying the parameters in the design phase until performance is acceptable. The crucial point is to prepare a good model, both intuitive and suitable for programming. A set of equations is certainly suitable but counterintuitive. BGs are an intuitive model that allow a simulation to be programmed without writing equations.

BGs were defined in Section 1; here we start with an example. Figure 9.2 shows on top a simple electric circuit, in the middle a systematic BG, and a simplified one below. We note that

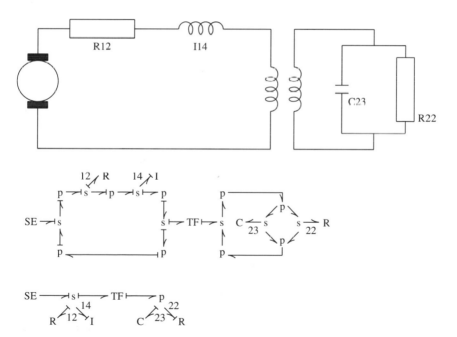

FIGURE 9.2. Electric circuit (top), systematically written BG (middle), and simplified BG (below). Simplification comes from grounding the lower bonds; it is precise, not an approximation.

220 Jean U. Thoma

— in the circuit the elements appear as a kind of picture of the real components, and in the BG, as mnemonic letters (R for resistance, C for capacitance, TF for transformer, etc.).
— Elements are connected by lines, "bonds," and by junctions, s and p (series and parallel). The lines carry marks for computation, the half arrow for positive power flux and the cross-stroke for causality, that is, the selection of dependent and independent variables. Causality is a central concept of computation.
— The systematic BG in the middle has a topological similarity with the circuit, which disappears in the simplified BG. Here we have essentially grounded the lower bonds. Hence, all voltages and power fluxes are referred to the ground.

Both circuits and SFP (Signal Flow Plans, also called block diagrams) are system representations in the sense of our definition in Section 1. In fact, BGs are a kind of crossbreeding that reproduces the best features of the parents, as in cattle raising.

In a circuit, each line carries two variables, voltage and current, in the electrical case; their product is the power flux. No direction of cause to effect, that is, no causality is represented. In the connections of a SFP, we find only one variable that originates from a block and acts on another. Thus, there is a definite causality, as indicated by the (full) arrow. BGs, on the other hand, are written like a circuit without causalities; they are added later, according to certain rules for optimum computability.

BGs are really a network of lumped elements. Writing a BG is also called doing a reticulation, especially in conceptual and qualitative analysis (*rete = net* in Italian). So this term is used often in chemical reactions and biology and will be used below.

Distributed parameter systems like beams or fluid pipes can be handled by BGs, by dividing the fluid pipe into segments, giving to each a capacitance, resistance, and inductance ("salami method"). More sophisticated is to solve the PDE (Partial Differential Equation) with suitable boundary conditions to obtain a series of particular solutions. Then each solution (or mode) is represented by C-, R-, and I-elements with couplings [4]. For a comparison of both methods, see [11].

2.2. Analogies, Efforts, and Flows with Power

The dynamic variables of engineering systems can be divided into voltage-like and current-like variables, called *effort* and *flow*. Examples of efforts are voltage, hydraulic pressure, force, and torque, and examples of flow are electric current, volume flow, speed, and frequency of rotation. Table 9.1 summarizes efforts and flows and contains further classes of variables: *momenta* defined as time integrals of force, and *displacements* defined as time integrals of flow. Thermal applications will appear in section 3, where both heat flux and entropy flow are taken as flows.

TABLE 9.1. Bondgraph variables in different disciplines, including momenta and displacements.

General	Electric	Hydraulic incompressible	Mechanical rectilinear	Mechanical rotary	Thermal	Chemical
Effort e	Voltage U	Pressure p	Force F	Torque M	Temperature T	Chem pot μ
Flow f	Current i	Volume flow $Q, \dot{V}$	Speed $\dot{x}$	Rotation frequency ω	Entropy flow $\dot{S}$	Molar flow $\dot{n}$
Momentum p	Electric momentum pel	Hydraulic momentum p	Momentum p	Angular momentum L	?	?
Displacement q	Electric charge q	Volume V	Position X	Angle φ	Entropy S	Molar mass n

Real power bonds carry both effort and flow. In addition, we can analyze the flux of energy or power (their product); this gives a simpler, somewhat qualitative model. New insights are gained because of the universal behavior of energy. As an example, the sign of electric current is arbitrary, but the one of power has a fundamental significance because of the laws of thermodynamics. If we assign positive values to the power entering a resistor, then it cannot become negative, because power cannot come out by the second law of thermodynamics. The combination of both types of analysis, effort/flow and power flux is one pillar of strength of BGs.

Power analysis could also be described graphically, perhaps by a notation simplified from a BG. Here we would have accumulators and places where power splits up. The efficiency diagrams of big power plants are a kind of graphical power analysis, as is the reticulation of heat fluxes. In practice, the author uses power analysis frequently for checking computer results. Nevertheless, he has not found a need to formalize it in something like a power flux graph.

Sometimes one variable in a bond can be neglected or ignored, and only the other remains: Then the bond simplifies into a connection in the sense of SFP.

The speed regulator of steam turbines is a good example: Here the regulator closes the steam valve on overspeed. If the required force has no influence (feedback action) on the dynamics of the regulator, it can be ignored: The bond simplifies into a connection. For design, we still need the force in order to select a good size for the physical link.

Neglecting one variable in a bond means that the power flux becomes zero. Hence, power analysis is not possible in a SFP. It follows that BG and SFP are close relatives (as said above) and most BG contain elements of SFP. Furthermore, a BG with all causalities and power directions can always be converted into a SFP, which then contains the same information or system model.

2.2.1. Links, Bonds, and Connections

The term *link* describes a physical connection like a wire, pressure pipe, push rod, or shaft. It connects elements or components of an installation.

A *bond* represents a link in a BG.

A *connection* runs between two blocks of a SFP; it also replaces a bond if one of the signal variables, effort or flow, are neglected.

2.3. Bondgraph Elements

The next step is the study of BG elements and their action. Wishing to bring in some structure, we divide the BG elements into one-ports, two-ports, three-ports, and multiports, according to the number of ports attached. Note that some authors use the term *multiport* for any element with two or more ports. This classification comes from electrical engineering.

Another possible classification is in terms of power (or energy) treatment: Elements can conserve power (energy flux), dissipate or supply power, or, finally, conserve energy. These properties are the base of the power analysis cited in Section 2.2.

A further classification is more related to computation and refers to signal treatment: The output signal is either an algebraic function of the input signal or a function of the integral of it. In linear elements both functions are proportionalities. Functions of the derivative of the input signal should be avoided because they cause computational problems. Curiously, much of classical physics is written in terms of derivatives (Newton's acceleration law) or differential equations.

We use here the term *signal* for the information carried either by effort or flow. Hence, even a one-port can process a signal: In an I-element (inertia), force is mass times acceleration (Newton's law just cited), or, equally, speed is the time integral of force divided by mass. Both statements refer to the same element but to different causalities (Section 2.4).

The above ideas can be combined in a three-dimensional classification, which is another advantage of BGs. We shall discuss BG elements in terms of numbers of ports and mention their other classes.

2.3.1. One-Ports

One-ports comprise electrical capacitors, resistors, and inductors with their equivalents from other disciplines like springs, brakes, and masses. Furthermore, one-ports are the sources that drive the installation by supplying power for normal operation. Table 9.2 displays one-ports in the top half with the BG-symbol at left, name in the middle, and examples at the right.

2.3.2. Two-Ports

Table 9.2 also describes the two kinds of two-ports, the *transformer* and the *gyrator*. In a transformer, output effort is proportional to input effort, and

TABLE 9.2. One-port and two-port elements: Symbols at left, name in the middle, and examples at right.

One ports		
↦ C	C-element	Capacitor, spring
→ R	R-element	Resistor, brake, pressure loss
→⊢ I	I-element	Inductor, mass, fluid inertia
SE →⊢	Effort source	Voltage source, force source, pressure supply
SF ↦	Flow source	Current source, transmission shaft
Two ports		
— TF —	Transformer	Electric TF, lever gear reducer, hydrostatic machine
— GY —	Gyrator	Electric motor (machine)

similarly, input flow is proportional to output flow. In a gyrator, output effort is proportional to input flow, and similarly, input effort is proportional to output flow; therefore, a gyrator is also called an *overcrossed transformer*. The best example is an electric motor with torque proportional to armature current. These two-ports are power conserving; thus input power equals output power in each instant, or in engineering language, they are 100% efficient. The imperfect efficiency of real components comes from parasitic R-elements. A consequence of power conservation is that the constants of proportionality, as just described, are equal.

Note on Table 9.2 that the elements come from electrical engineering, where circuit thinking is developed best. All these elements describe important effects and components in mechanics and (incompressible) hydraulics. Note also that the elements carry preferred power orientations and causalities; see Section 2.4.

For power analysis, C- and I-elements store energy; R-elements dissipate power and transfer it into the thermal domain (Section 3.2). Sources supply power and can absorb it in special circumstances. Transformers and gyrators conserve power.

2.3.3. Three-Ports

Table 9.3 contains the two kinds of three-ports, parallel and series junctions. They appear with three bonds, but can have more. Junctions with only two bonds appear occasionally, but are identities with proper power orientations.

Junctions connect the elements in a BG; they represent essentially the KCL (Kirchhoff Current Law) in parallel junctions and the KVL (Kirchhoff Voltage Law) in series junctions. For a qualitative description,

— in a p-junction all efforts are equal and flows sum to zero (KCL), and
— in an s-junction all flows are equal and efforts sum to zero (KVL).

Junctions have many applications in mechanics and hydraulics. Only the mechanical p-junction seems to be involved. We can say that the relatively

TABLE 9.3. Three-port element (junctions).

		Three ports
— p — |	Parallel junction	Wire connection, mechanical differential gear
— s — |	Series junction	Series wire connection, rigid rotary connection
— 0 — |		
— 1 — |		

Note: Junctions are also denoted by parallel or 0-junction and series or 1-junction

TABLE 9.4. Multiport BG elements.

Multiports		
⊢ C ⊣ ↨	C-field	Capacitor network, moving plate capacitor, gas in thermodynamics
→ R ← ↑	R-field	Resistor network, thermoelectric effect
⊣ I ⊢ ↑	I-field	Inductor network, coupled mass network

complex automobile differential (bevel gears on an axis revolving in space) is needed to realize the conceptually simple p-junction for good curve handling.

With the elements of Table 9.2 and 9.3, most engineering installations and systems can be modeled. The exceptions are systems with compressible mass flow, and heat convection, such as steam turbines. Such convective systems do not fit well into normal bondgraphing. Nevertheless, further BG elements arc convenient.

2.3.4. Multiports

As shown in Table 9.4, it helps to give special symbols and names to networks of capacitors, resistors, and inductors—C-fields, R-fields and I-fields. The suffix *field* is BG terminology and quite different from the field concept in the theory of, say, the electrostatic field (generally of distributed parameter systems). The BG fields appear as three-ports, but they can have any number of bonds. Most frequent arc two-port fields.

Some BG fields describe basic effects of physics, in particular, the moving plate capacitor with attraction force or an ideal gas in thermodynamics (Section 3.1). Consequently, BGs are efficient for teaching basic physics, especially in its qualitative aspects.

2.3.5. Modulated Elements

Table 9.5 contains elements that can be controlled (parameter varied), as indicated by the connections (with the full arrow). With two-ports it is usual but redundant to put the letter M ('Modulated') in front. Parameter variation by connection means that the actuating effort is neglected, as in the steam valve of Section 2.2, which is a modulated R-element. Most modulated capacitors are really two-port C-fields with neglected attraction force. This precludes power analysis, for example, in parametric oscillations produced by periodically varying capacitors (Van der Pol equation).

2.3.6. Carousel of BG Elements

The kind of a BG element depends not on its linearity or otherwise, but on the variables it connects. Figure 9.3 gives a qualitative overview: Power comes

TABLE 9.5. Modulated BG elements.

	Modulated elements	
⊢ C ⤙	Variable, controlled or modulated,	Variable capacitor
→ R ⤙	C-, R-, I-element	Variable resistor
→⊣ I ⤙		Potentiometer
		Variable inductor
⤚ SE →⊣	Controlled	Controlled voltage source
⤚ SF ⊢	effort, flow source	Controlled current source
→⊣ MTF →⊣ ↗	Modulated transformer	Hydrostatic machine with variable displacement
⊢ MGY →⊣ ↗	Modulated gyrator	Electric machine with variable field (excitation)

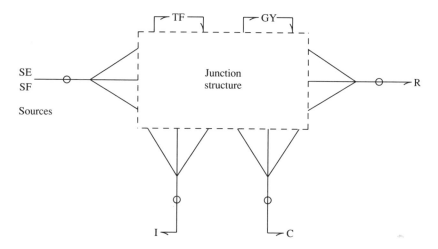

FIGURE 9.3. General structure of a BG with sources (left) and resistors (right). Power flux goes from left to right, but the energy storing elements can shuttle power between them (vibrations).

from the sources at left and finishes in the R-elements at right after passing through the junction structure. Transformers and gyrators on top are similar to junctions in that they transmit power without loss or storage. The energy storing elements, C- and I-, appear below. They can shuttle energy between them during normal operation; this means large, usually objectionable power fluxes in the structure, commonly known as vibration or resonances.

The characteristics of one-ports can be demonstrated by the causality carousel in Figure 9.4, where the kind of variable displacement, effort, momentum, and flow appear on the circle, CCW (Counterclockwise) from the right. Flow and displacement, and effort and momentum are connected through integrations by definition. A C-element implies an algebraic (time-independent) relation between displacement and effort; and an I-element,

FIGURE 9.4. Carousel of displacement, effort, momentum, and flow with the actions of one-ports and integrations between them.

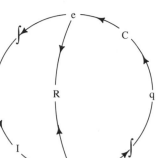

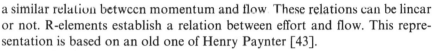

a similar relation between momentum and flow. These relations can be linear or not. R-elements establish a relation between effort and flow. This representation is based on an old one of Henry Paynter [43].

Remarkable from the point of view of physics is that coupling of variables as above always determines the energy properties of the BG elements. There is, for instance, no element that connects effort and flow and is energy conserving. This is certainly a point to ponder in qualitative simulation.

Running around the carousel CCW, we find only integrations; that is, we have integral causalities that are more suitable for computers. R-elements have no preference for resistance or conductance causality in principle. In practice, the difference is important especially with nonlinear R-elements (Section 2.7). Running around CW (Clockwise) instead corresponds to derivative causalities, the way in which most laws of physics are formulated. Causality will be discussed next.

2.4. Causality and Computation

The BG elements of Section 2.3 are the building blocks of a model of engineering systems, similar to (electric) circuits. For getting nearer to the computer, each bond carries two more bits of essential information and a third one for convenience:

1. The half arrows indicate the positive direction of power flux. In normal practice we direct power out of the sources, through transformers and gyrators, and into the one-ports. Power directions on the junctions follow from the physics and are assigned by inspection. Other power directions can be used but require precautions [9, Sect. 2.3].
2. The causality stroke on a bond shows the direction of travel of the effort, in the sense of cause and effect. The flow then travels backward, a process called *handshaking*. It is best to imagine that effort travels on one side and flow on the other side of the bond.
3. As a rule of convenience, flow is considered to travel on the bond side with the half arrow, and effort on the other. This information is useful for Block-BG (Section 2.6).

For details of causality assignment, see [9, sect. 2.3]. Here we say only that C-elements give integrations if flow attacks (acts toward) them and differentiations if effort attacks: integral and derivative causalities, respectively. I-elements are the dual; they give derivative causality if flow, and integral causality if effort attacks them.

Causalities are either desirable or mandatory. Desirable are integrations on energy storing elements (C- and I-elements or -fields). In exceptional cases we can try to program the computer for derivative causalties, overcoming some traps of numerical mathematics [9, sect. 6.4].

If mandatory causalities are violated, the BG is incomputable. Mandatory are the causalities of effort and flow sources. Furthermore, on two-ports and junctions, one causality is free, but once selected the others are mandatory.

In practice, a BG is written without causalities, and then mandatory causalities are applied; whence, some more causalities will become mandatory through two-ports and junctions. Then one desirable causality is applied, and its causal implications are extended (causalities that have become mandadory assigned). The process continues until causalities are complete.

Power directions can be applied independently as recommended above.

The smooth process of causality assignment corresponds to selection of dependent and independent variables of the underlying equations. A BG with all power directions and integral causalities corresponds to a SFP and to the canonical set of state space equations of control engineering. The number of state variables equals the number of C- and I-elements.

The going becomes less smooth if there are conflicts as follows:

— The coupling of C- and I-elements may be such that integral causality is not possible for all of them: Undesirable derivative causalities creep in. In the state space formulation, this means that some variables are algebraically coupled and cannot be independent state variables.
— If mandatory causalities are violated, the BG is incomputable because the underlying equations contradict each other.

There are several remedies for causality trouble, some of them with undesirable side effects, as in medicine. A BG with all causalities, no mandatory one violated, can be programmed using TUTSIM [12] or other programs without writing equations. This greatly facilitates engineering simulation in practice.

Admitting also derivative causalities, different selections are possible. When we transform the BG into a SFP, however, its appearance becomes quite different depending on the selected causalities, whilst in a BG only the cross-strokes change. Thus, BGs are more universal than SFPs or equations.

Causality questions seem to play only a minor role in qualitative simulation, but they are essential for computation. Here BGs have another precious advantage: They allow estimation of eigenvalues and the required time step. Furthermore, we can immediately recognize algebraic loops, which require expensive implicit integration routines. Once recognized, the remedy is usually easy to find [9, sect. 6.5].

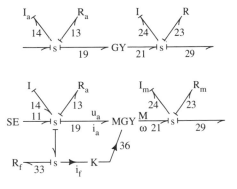

FIGURE 9.5. BG for a (DC) electric motor with constant excitation (top) and with series excited field (bottom).

2.5. Electric Motor Example

The top part of Figure 9.5 displays a simple electric motor with constant magnetic (exciting) field produced normally by permanent magnets. The elements on the electric side (left) are the armature inductance (I14) and armature resistance (R13). The motor action itself take place in the gyrator GY19, 21. At right appear the mechanical effects, shaft inertia I24, and friction R23.

We have here a simple, linear BG with two I-elements that can go into resonance due to the coupling by the gyrator. Note that the the efficiency comes from the the dissipation in R14 and R24. Otherwise, the BG is perfectly reversible and can generate electricity from mechanical power, just as a real electric machine can run either as motor or as generator.

In the lower part of Figure 9.5, the magnetic field comes from a (field) coil in series with the armature and with the coil resistance R33. This is the series excited electric motor used in locomotives and streetcars. The gyrator is now modulated by the field current, and the BG is nonlinear. Parallel excited motors exist also and are modeled by changing the upper left s-junction into a p-junction; here the field coil is in parallel with the armature.

Figure 9.6 shows the simulation of start-up of a series excited electric motor with substantial inertia load like a streetcar. Torque and current show the well-known peaks at the start, and rotation frequency, $\omega 24$, increases smoothly. Engineering design is needed to smooth the peaks, helped by more detailed BG. At the bottom of Figure 9.6 appears the TUTSIM listing.

2.6. Block-Bondgraphs for Nonlinear Systems

Although all BG elements may be nonlinear, it is convenient to include information about the nonlinearity [7]. We use the idea that effort and flow travel (act) on either side of the bond. A block on one side indicates that they encounter a modification like a nonlinearity. Figuratively they hit the side block and must traverse it. This is the block-BG.

Figure 9.7 has on top a simple oscillator with mass, friction, and a spring.

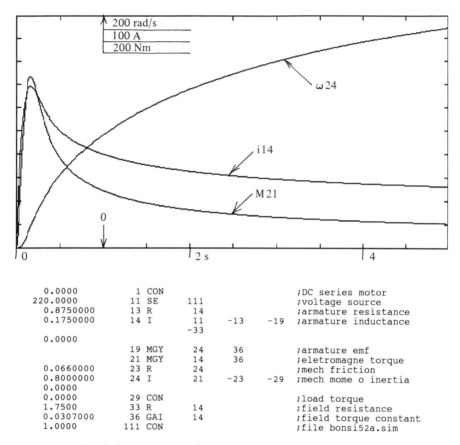

0.0000	1 CON			;DC series motor
220.0000	11 SE	111		;voltage source
0.8750000	13 R	14		;armature resistance
0.1750000	14 I	11	-13 -19	;armature inductance
		-33		
0.0000				
	19 MGY	24	36	;armature emf
	21 MGY	14	36	;eletromagne torque
0.0660000	23 R	24		;mech friction
0.8000000	24 I	21	-23 -29	;mech mome o inertia
0.0000				
0.0000	29 CON			;load torque
1.7500	33 R	14		;field resistance
0.0307000	36 GAI	14		;field torque constant
1.0000	111 CON			;file bonsi52a.sim

FIGURE 9.6. Simulation of start-up of series excited electric motor with TUTSIM listing.

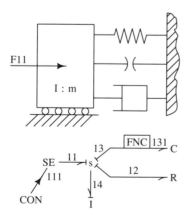

FIGURE 9.7. Oscillator with a single degree of freedom, including a buffer to show a nonlinear spring. Below, the block-BG.

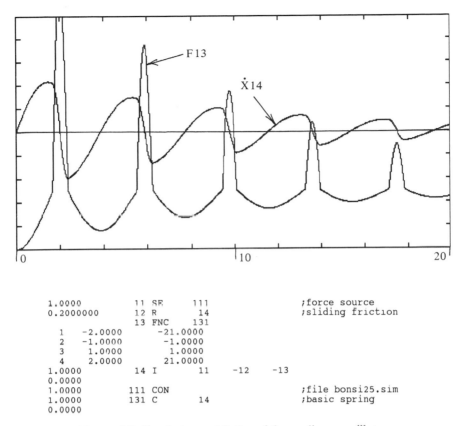

```
1.0000          11 SF      111              ;force source
0.2000000       12 R        14              ;sliding friction
                13 FNC     131
    1   -2.0000       -21.0000
    2   -1.0000        -1.0000
    3    1.0000         1.0000
    4    2.0000        21.0000
1.0000          14 I        11     -12    -13
0.0000
1.0000          111 CON                     ;file bonsi25.sim
1.0000          131 C       14              ;basic spring
0.0000
```

FIGURE 9.8. Simulation and listing of the nonlinear oscillator.

Furthermore, there is a buffer showing that the spring becomes much harder when sufficiently compressed, a frequent nonlinearity. The BG below models the nonlinear spring by the side block on the effort side of C13. The intermediate variable 131 corresponds to the position determined by integration of the flow (speed). The force results from going through the side block, which contains the position/effort characteristics of the spring and buffer; this is indicated by FNC. Any function can be entered into a side block including multiplication by a signal, as in the hydraulic control valve in Section 2.7.

Figure 9.8 gives the simulation result and TUTSIM listing of the oscillator with nonlinear spring. As expected, on hitting the hard part the force peaks and speed changes rapidly. The peaks decay as amplitude decreases due to the friction of R12. With still lower amplitudes, the hard part will no longer be reached, and the oscillator becomes linear, as illustrated in many mechanics textbooks.

2.7. Pressure Regulator Valve

Since a hydraulic pressure regulator appears prominently in the book on qualitative reasoning by Bobrow [1], we shall treat here the quantitative simulation of such a system.

Figure 9.9 is a schematic of the valve embedded between a supply at left and a load at right; both are variable. The task of the valve is to keep the pressure between itself and the load, or downstream, constant.

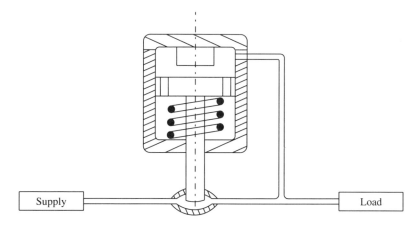

FIGURE 9.9. Pressure-regulating valve between supply and load. It maintains pressure against variations of supply pressure and load.

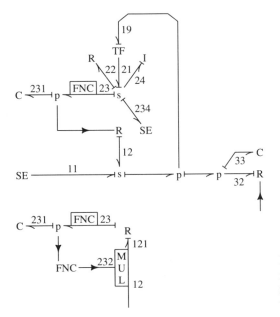

FIGURE 9.10. BG of the pressure-regulating system with side blocks for nonlinear spring and valve throttle. Below, details.

Operation of Fig 9.9 is as follows: In equilibrium, downstream pressure balances the spring force. If this pressure tends to decrease, for instance, by more demand from the load, the piston moves up and opens the throttle further, admitting more fluid; this raises the pressure. Operation depends on the interactions in the complete system, supply, regulator valve, and load; it can be analyzed as nonlinear feedback system. Instability occurs frequently, and the usual compensation methods of control engineering will improve the performance.

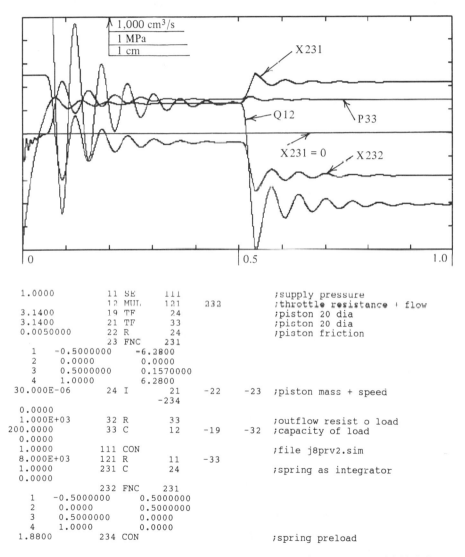

```
1.0000              11 SE      111                  ;supply pressure
                    12 MUL     121      332         ;throttle resistance + flow
3.1400              19 TF       24                  ;piston 20 dia
3.1400              21 TF       33                  ;piston 20 dia
0.0050000           22 R        24                  ;piston friction
                    23 FNC     231
     1   -0.5000000      -6.2800
     2    0.0000          0.0000
     3    0.5000000       0.1570000
     4    1.0000          6.2800
30.000E-06          24 I         21      -22   -23  ;piston mass + speed
                                -234
0.0000
1.000E+03           32 R         33                 ;outflow resist o load
200.0000            33 C         12      -19   -32  ;capacity of load
0.0000
1.0000              111 CON                         ;file j8prv2.sim
8.000E+03           121 R        11      -33
1.0000              231 C        24                 ;spring as integrator
0.0000
                    232 FNC     231
     1   -0.5000000       0.5000000
     2    0.0000          0.5000000
     3    0.5000000       0.0000
     4    1.0000          0.0000
1.8800              234 CON                         ;spring preload
```

FIGURE 9.11. Simulation of the pressure-regulating system from start-up with high flow demand. In the middle, flow demand is reduced by a factor of five.

Figure 9.10 shows on top the BG with the valve in the center, supply at the left, and load at the right. The supply is modeled as controlled pressure source SEll and the load as C33 and R32 at the right. The valve is nonlinear by R12 in the main line, modulated by the position of the piston (TF19, 21). Furthermore, the spring is nonlinear to include the end stops of piston and valve travel.

The lower part of Figure 9.10 contains the detail BG of the nonlinear elements: There is a side block on R12 for multiplication by valve opening. Here R12 should be in conductance causality, as it is. The nonlinear spring with end stops at fully closed or open valve leads to the side block on C23, similarly as in Figure 9.7.

Figure 9.11 contains on top the simulation result and below the TUTSIM listing of the pressure regulating system with start-up from rest (zero initial conditions). Violent and weakly damped oscillations appear. In the middle the outflow through R32 (load flow demand) is set to a much lower level. After the transient, pressure does not change much; this indicates proper function of the pressure regulator.

Let us note that both nonlinearities need to be included to model the three states of operation described in Bobrow [1]: closed, operating, and fully open. Both in closed and fully open position, the piston is held against the hard part of the spring characteristic. We see here the importance of nonlinear effects for qualitative simulation. Of course, the states are reached after violent, dynamic effects, which need the R-elements for decay. We shall return to qualitative simulation in Section 4.1.

3. Bondgraphs in Thermodynamics and Chemistry

3.1. Entropy as Thermal Charge

We come now to the more conceptual and speculative applications of BGs, where quantitative simulation is not often done. Such applications relate mostly to thermal and chemical applications, where the proper efforts and flows are temperature and entropy flow, on the one hand, and chemical potential and molar flow on the other hand; their product is the power flux. For practical thermal simulation, heat flow, not entropy flow, is used for reasons given below. We have then a pseudo-BG, where the product of effort and flow is not a power and has no physical significance.

Thermal BGs hinge on the concept of entropy, about which much nonsense is written. Yet in terms of BGs, it is quite simple: Entropy flow is heat flux divided by (absolute) temperature. Entropy itself is accumulated entropy flow in a thermal C-element or a thermomechanical C-field [6]. Entropy appears as a kind of thermal charge, an analog to electric charge with differences in detail.

The following are the properties of entropy compared to electric charge:

FIGURE 9.12. Fundamental thermal equation, ideal Carnot engine, and Carnot efficiency formula.

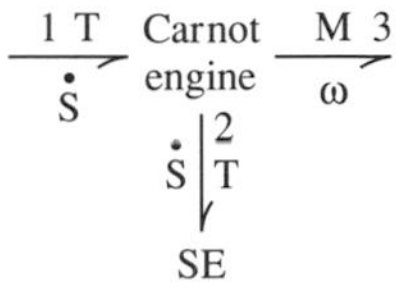

$$\overline{\underset{\dot{S}}{1\ T}}\ \overset{\text{Carnot}}{\underset{\text{engine}}{}}\ \overline{\underset{\omega}{M\ 3}}$$

$$\dot{S}\bigg|^2_T$$

$$SE$$

$$\dot{E}_3 = \dot{Q}_1 - \dot{Q}_2$$

$$\left.\begin{array}{ll}\dot{Q}_1 = T_1 & \dot{S}_1 \\[4pt] \dot{Q}_2 = T_2 & \dot{S}_2 \\[4pt] \dot{S}_2 = \dot{S}_1 \end{array}\right\}\ \begin{array}{l}\text{Fundamental}\\ \text{equation}\end{array}$$

No friction

$$\frac{\dot{E}_3}{\dot{E}_1} = \frac{T_1\dot{S} - T_2\dot{S}}{T_1 S} = \frac{T_1 - T_2}{T_1}$$

1. Both are needed to carry power according to the fundamental thermal equation on Figure 9.12 and its electric equivalent.
2. Both are indestructible and are conserved in frictionless elements or processes.
3. In friction elements (R-elements), electric charge is conserved (current in equals current out in a resistor), but power is not. Thermal charge is generated, and power conserved: This is the entire difference between thermal and electric processes.

An immediate application is the Carnot efficiency formula derived in Figure 9.12. The incoming thermal power brings an entropy flow at high temperature Tl. It must be disposed of at a lower temperature T2, which requires a corresponding power. Only the difference can be converted into mechanical power, even in an ideal frictionless engine. From this the celebrated Carnot [2] formula results. Note that this conversion engine is entirely reversible and used to pump entropy from low to high temperatures in millions of refrigerators and air conditioners. Any kind of loss or irreversibility enters only through the R-elements that produce entropy.

Furthermore, parts of Carnot's book [2] contain the insight that the working fluid behaves like a two-port C-field, with pressure and temperature as efforts and volume and entropy as displacements. He gives an ingenious method to avoid thermal short circuits on switching a parcel of fluid (steam in steam engines) from low to high temperatures and back. The reader will agree that Sadi Carnot was far ahead of his time.

3.2. Entropy Generation

Figure 9.13 describes entropy generation in an electric resistor or R-element. The dissipated electric power, voltage times current, reappears as newly generated entropy flow times temperature: The resistor conserves power and is written as a two-port RS-field (resistor source field). Entropy conduction, or, conventionally, heat conduction, can be reticulated by a similar RS-field

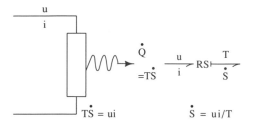

FIGURE 9.13. Entropy generation in a resistor that becomes a power-conserving RS-field when thermal effects are not ignored.

and some junctions. More complex effects of physics, like thermo-electricity or the Peltier effect, require a three-port RS-field.

Let us note some subtle points of thermal BG:

1. In order to relate entropy flow correctly to heat flow in Figure 9.12, the absolute (Kelvin) temperature needs to be used, not a temperature that refers to something as arbitrary as the melting point of ice.
2. The fundamental equation between entropy flow and heat flux is valid only for conduction. For convection, a form factor not much smaller than one needs to added. This is true also for electric and hydraulic convection (transport of accumulators or beer bottles, but of much less practical importance).

Due to the generation of entropy in thermal conduction problems, the entropy flow is not divergence free in the sense of vector field calculus, and would lead to impractically complex differential equations. Heat flow is conserved, hence, divergence free, and leads to the well-known partial differential equation.

3.3. Chemical Reactions and Osmosis

To introduce chemical networks, Figure 9.14 has at left an electric circuit with two capacitors connected by a resistor. Current will flow as long as the voltages are different, and the R-element will dissipate electric power and generate entropy flow. At right appears the BG. All irreversibility lies in the generated entropy.

Figure 9.15 shows a basic chemical network with a reactant in the C-element at the left and the product in the C-element at the right. We have here the chemical potentials and the molar flows of each chemical species or phase as efforts and flows. The reaction will run from higher to lower chemical potential, and the difference will generate entropy in the RS-field below. When the chemical potentials become equal, the reaction stops, all just as in the preceding electrical circuit.

New compared to Figure 9.14 is the concept of entropy stripping: The structural entropy of the reactant is stripped away, as indicated by the transformer. It is used to supply the structural entropy of the product; any difference

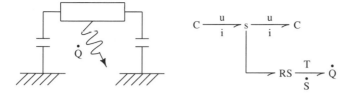

FIGURE 9.14. Electric circuit with two capacitors and a resistor. Current flows as long as voltages are different and power is dissipated in the resistor.

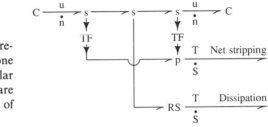

FIGURE 9.15. BG for a chemical reaction with one reactant and one product. The dynamics is similar that in Figure 9.14; what differs are the stripping and unstripping of entropy.

is dumped or sucked in from the environment, where it mixes with the generated entropy from dissipation. The stripping and unstripping process is entirely reversible; it has no influence on equilibrium and reaction dynamics (usually called kinetics). The lack of efforts acting is indicated by the connections, instead of bonds, on the stripping transformers.

The BG of Figure 9.15 explains the existence of endothermic chemical reactions. If the product needs much more entropy for its structure than squeezed out from the reactant, it will take it from the environment. With small dissipation the environment will become colder as it delivers the required entropy, that is; endothermic reaction.

The exchange between water and steam is also an endothermic reaction, reticulated by Figure 9.15, with one reactant (water) and one product (steam). Much entropy is absorbed on evaporation because steam contains much more entropy in its structure than water. This entropy and the corresponding thermal energy come normally from flames or nuclear reactions in a boiler.

More complex reactions are reticulated similarly with transformers for the coupling of different reactants (stoicheiometric equations), together with s-junctions. Some p-junctions appear for competing and parallel reactions. Furthermore, the reactants and products are really contained in three-port C-fields, the chemical port of Figure 9.15, and thermal and hydraulic ports as in the two-port field discovered by Carnot. There is a definite coupling between pressure, temperature, and chemical potential in each species. An extension of Figure 9.15 leads to the reticulation of osmosis, the flow of water through membranes with small pores against a pressure difference [10].

The task of chemical engineering is precisely to choose temperature and pressure such that desired reactions run and undesired parallel reactions do not. The speed of reaction is controlled by chemical potential difference and the parameter of the RS-field; its characteristic is the subject of chemical kinetics.

Chemical BGs are a little more abstract than basic mechanical, hydraulic, and electrical ones. The bonds do not correspond to any physical link, but to interactions of the mixed chemical species or phases.

Concluding this section, we have taken here a phenomenological point of view of entropy, entirely sufficient for engineering. The interpretation of entropy as disorder is a theory of structure not needed here; it requires quantum mechanics to be complete. As a curiosity, there is no structural theory of electric charge: Nobody knows what electricity really is! We can well reason and design with electric current, charge, and voltage, since we know their phenomenological properties. The same is true for entropy.

4. Concluding Observations

BGs are definitely also a qualitative system representation, as seen from our examples. They promote, in general, interpretation, intuition, and invention. BGs become quantitative only when the parameters are added; this is needed for simulation of real systems. Curiously, determination and programming parameters require much more time and introduce many more errors than just writing and programming the BG. So the transition from qualitative to quantitative requires time and effort.

Because of the parameter difficulties, it is good to set all parameters equal to one at first, except the R-elements that get 0.2 for nice curves. This "qualitative" BG is then run on the computer to make sure that the BG is properly connected (no errors in junctions, etc). Furthermore, a BG should be built in pieces and checked out, a practice called "building the BG tree" [8].

Many different BGs are possible for a given installation, depending on the highest signal frequency of interest. In fact, with increasing frequency effects like further resonances become significant. Special are the BGs for zero frequency, where all C- and I-elements become inoperative [9, sect. 6.3]. Used systematically these different BGs should help qualitative simulation.

As a general observation, qualitative simulation uses the concept of state, which is often a gross approximation, as we have seen in the pressure-regulating system. The states required nonlinearities, where, in fact, the closed and fully open state meant squeezes against hard portions of the spring characteristic.

The concept of a state is only well defined in electric circuits like flip-flops and, significantly, in quantum mechanics. So the author would like to conclude by recommending for study the relation between quantum mechanics, flip-flops, and qualitative physics.

References

1. Bobrow, D.G., Ed. *Qualitative Reasoning about Physical Systems*. MIT Press, Cambridge, Mass., 1985.
2. Carnot, S. *Reflections on the Motive Power of Fire*. 1824. Reprinted by Dover Publications, N.Y., 1960.
3. Fishwick, P.A. Qualitative methodology in simulation model engineering. *Simulation 52*, 3 (Mar. 1989), 95–101.
4. Karnopp, D., and Rosenberg, R. *Analysis and Simulation of Multiport Systems*. MIT Press, Cambridge, Mass., 1968.
5. Karnopp, D., and Rosenberg, R. *System Dynamics, an Unified Approach*. Wiley, New York, 1975.
6. Thoma, J.U. Bondgraphs for thermal energy transport and entropy flow. *J. Franklin Inst. 292* (1970), 109–120.
7. Thoma, J.U. Block-bondgraphs for nonlinear systems. *Trans. Soc. Comput. Simul. 2* (1985), 249–255.
8. Thoma, J.U. Simulation, realistic (engineering). *Encyclopedia Phys. Sci. Technol. 12* (1987), 680–698.
9. Thoma, J.U. *Simulation by Bondgraphs*. Springer-Verlag, New York, 1989. Japanese version under preparation by Corona Publisher, Tokyo.
10. Thoma, J.U., and Atlan, H. Osmosis and hydraulics by network thermodynamics and bondgraphs. *J. Franklin Inst. 319* (1985) 217–226.
11. Thoma J.U., and Richter, D.B. Simulation of fluid pipes with modal and segmented methods. *Trans. Soc. Comput. Simul. 3* (1987) 337–349.
12. TUTSIM. Program developed by Vim Meerman. TUTSIM Products, Palo Alto, Calif. or from Meerman Automation, Neede, 1988.

CHAPTER 10

Complex Dynamical Models

Ralph H. Abraham

Abstract

After enthusiastic beginnings during World War II, general systems theory and cybernetics made lasting contributions to the understanding of complex systems, but failed to justify the great hopes of the pioneers. Since the advent of the Chaos Revolution in the 1970s, the dynamic modeling aspect of the theory (system dynamics) has gained greatly in technical power and usefulness to the working scientist, especially in the biological and social sciences. *Complex dynamical systems* (*CDS*) theory denotes this merger of system dynamics with the qualitative theory of dynamical systems (including chaos and bifurcation theories). In this chapter we trace the development of CDS, review its basic concepts and modeling strategies, exhibit some familiar complex systems as exemplary CDS networks, and describe a few subtleties of CDS modeling and simulation.

1. The History of Complex Dynamics

At the turn of this century, vitalism in biology was on its last legs. Mechanism reigned victorious. The story of this paradigm shift is told in full detail in [29]. One of the last of the overt vitalists was Paul A. Weiss (b. 1898), and among his heirs were Kurt Lewin and Ludwig Von Bertalanffy, who, fleeing the last great war, carried the vitalist virus to North America. Kurt Lewin went on to found social psychology [34], while Von Bertalanffy created general systems theory [20, 45]. At the same time, Von Neumann, Wiener, and McCulloch met at the Macy conferences, and cybernetics was born [28]. Gestalt psychology also derived from vitalism and the hermeneutic tradition of German social philosophy. All of these efforts to repair the effects of reductionism in science were derived from vitalism, which may be traced back through Goethe to the Renaissance [7]. And all, after the initial enthusiasm of some of the best

---

Dedicated to Chihiro Hayashi, 1911 to 1987.

scientists, grew into disrepute in the academic environments of Western civilization. This was not so much a *paradigm shift* [32] as a *bifurcation* [3].

The case of general systems theory is particularly important here. While the rejection of Von Bertalanffy's theories by the academic establishment grew, so did the adherents of those theories. Thus was created a kind of intellectual anti-universe. For nearly every department within a normal university, there developed a corresponding department within the general systems anti-university. And each rejected the other, until the intersection became nil. Among these departments numbered mathematics, especially *dynamical systems theory*. Its equivalent field in the general systems anti-university became known as *system dynamics*, with its own journals, international conferences, and so on [40]. Mathematicians speak of *dynamical systems*, while systematicians pronounce it *dynamic systems*. (You can always tell them apart in this way.) The dynamic systems community found a self-support mechanism in industrial therapy, as their theories were fairly successful in the modeling and simulation of complex systems (at least, if chaos was not encountered). Jay Forrester's work [27] and the Club of Rome project [35] exemplified this work. Meanwhile, the dynamical systems community eventually discovered chaos in simple systems, and learned to live with it. Both of these communities had much to gain from the resumption of communications, and gradually, this has occurred [40].

My own involvement in this process came about during the 1970s. After the emergence of *global analysis* as an important branch of mathematics in the turbulent 1960s, and the initial success of its methods applied to dynamical systems theory, there was a period of frustration. The discovery of chaotic attractors challenged the methods of global analysis, and some of us turned to applications and computations in search of guidance. Our efforts to carry out applications in the fields of biological and social sciences were particularly humbling, and the negative reaction of the mathematical and scientific communities to catastrophe theory and its applications brought most global analysts back to pure mathematics on the run. My own attempts [1] to make models for physiological systems proved hard to sell. My vague suggestions provoked serious challenges from scientists. In trying to meet these challenges by constructing explicitly detailed models for particular physiological systems, concepts from the dynamic system anti-establishment spontaneously came into my work, along with similar ideas from nonlinear control theory, and other related engineering disciplines [4, 6, 9, 12, 13]. My first expression of these merged ideas, which I now call *complex dynamical systems theory*, was in a talk in Dubrovnik in 1979 [15]. This theory may be viewed as a qualitative simulation modeling strategy, and that will be our perspective here. The qualitative aspect is based on the *response diagram*, described below. In fact, this aspect is the point at which dynamical systems theory joins and enriches the traditional modeling strategy of system dynamics.

Prior publications may be consulted for additional details and examples of

CDS models, and further references [5, 10, 15]. The present summary is not intended to standardize the definitions, as the subject is still evolving.

2. Complex Dynamical Systems

A complex dynamical system is a network, or directed graph, of nodes and directed edges. The nodes are simple dynamical schemes or dynamical systems depending on control parameters. The directed edges are static schemes, or output/input functions depending on control parameters. These provide the serial coupling from the instantaneous states at one node into the control parameters of another.

2.1. Simple Dynamical Schemes

Definitions. Recall that a *manifold* is a smooth geometrical space, as described in any recent text of differential geometry [17]. Let C be a manifold modeling the control parameters of a system, and S another manifold, representing its instantaneous states. Then a *simple dynamical scheme* is a smooth function assigning a smooth vectorfield on S to every point of C. Alternatively, we may think of this function as a smooth vectorfield on the product manifold, CxS, which is tangent to the state fibers, $\{c\}xS$. For each control point, $c \in C$, let $X(c)$ be the vectorfield assigned by the scheme. We think of this as a dynamical system on S, or a system of first-order ordinary differential equations.

Attractors and basins. In each vectorfield of a scheme, $X(c)$, the main features are the *attractors*. These are asymptotic limit sets, under the flow, for a significant set of initial conditions in S. These initial states, tending to a given attractor asymptotically as time goes to plus infinity, comprise the *basins* of $X(c)$. Every point of S that is not in a basin belongs to the *separator* of $X(c)$. The decomposition of S into basins, each containing a single attractor, is the *phase portrait* of $X(c)$. Attractors occur in three types: *static* (an attractive limit point), *periodic* (an attractive limit cycle, or oscillation), and *chaotic* (meaning any other attractive limit set). The phase portrait is the primary representation of the qualitative behavior of the simple dynamical system and provides a qualitative model for a natural system in a fixed (or laboratory) setting. Its chief features are the basins and attractors. The attractors provide qualitative models for the observed states of dynamical equilibrium of the target system, while the basins model the initial states, which move rapidly to the observed states as startup transients die away.

Response diagrams. For each point c of the control manifold, the portrait of $X(c)$ may be visualized in the corresponding state fiber, $\{c\}xS$, of the product manifold, CxS. The union of the attractors of $X(c)$, for all control points $c \in C$, is the *attractrix* or *locus of attraction* of the scheme. These sets, visualized in the product manifold, comprise the *response diagram* of the scheme. The response diagram is the primary representation of the qualitative behavior of the dynamical scheme, and provides a qualitative model for a natural system in a setting with control variables. Its chief features are the loci of the attractors as they move under the influence of the control variables, and the *bifurcations* at which the locus af attraction undergoes substantial change. The response diagram provides the qualitative model for the dynamical equilibria of the target system, and their transformations, as control parameters are changed. A typical response diagram, for a model with a single control parameter (the stirred fluid system of Couette and Taylor). For a discussion of this diagram, and many others, see the pictorial *Bifurcation Behavior* [14].

2.2. Catastrophes and Subtle Bifurcations

For most control points, $c \in C$, the portrait of $X(c)$ is structurally stable. That is, perturbation of the control parameters from c to another nearby point cause a change in the phase portrait of $X(c)$, which is small and qualitatively insignificant. In exceptional cases, called *bifurcation control points*, the phase portrait of $X(c)$ significantly changes as control parameters are passed through the exceptional point. Many cases, generic in a precise mathematical sense, are known, and the list is growing. These *bifurcation events* all fall into three categories. A bifurcation is *subtle* if only one attractor is involved and if its significant qualitative change is small in magnitude. For example, in a *Hopf bifurcation*, a static attractor becomes a very small periodic attractor, which then slowly grows in amplitude. Other bifurcations are *catastrophic*. In some of these, called blue-sky catastrophes, an attractor appears from, or disappears into, the blue (i.e., from a separator). In those of the third category, called *explosions*, a small attractor suddenly explodes into a much larger one. All of these events are very common in the simplest dynamical schemes, such as forced oscillators. The bifurcations are clearly visualized in the response diagram of a scheme, which is sometimes called the bifurcation diagram. The theory up to this point is adequately described in the literature (see the picture books, and references therein) [14].

2.3. Static Coupling Schemes

Consider two simple dynamical schemes, X on CxS and Y on DxT. The two schemes may be serially coupled by a function that, depending on the instantaneous state of the first (a point in S), sets the controls of the second (a point in D). A static coupling scheme is just such a function, but may also depend on control parameters of its own. Thus, let E be another control manifold, and $g: ExS \to D$. Then the serial coupling of X and Y by the static coupling scheme g is a dynamical scheme with control manifold CxE, and state space SxT, defined by

$$Z((c,e)(s,t)) = (X(c,s), Y(g(e,s),t)).$$

This is the simplest example of a complex dynamical scheme, symbolized in the literature by schematic diagrams such as those shown in Figure 10.2 or

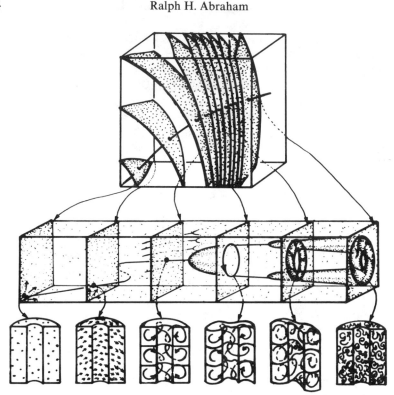

FIGURE 10.1. A typical response diagram.

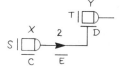

FIGURE 10.2. Static coupling of two simple schemes: Pictorial.

equivalently in Figure 10.3. In Figure 10.2 the bullet icons represent dynamical schemes, with the state spaces, S or T, vertical, and the control spaces, C or D, horizontal. The total spaces of the dynamical schemes are Cartesian product manifolds, for example, $C \times S$. The solid triangle represents a static coupling scheme, g, with its control space, E, horizontal. That is, g is a mapping, $g: S \times E \to D$. In Figure 10.3 the symbols are further abstracted.

2.4. Other Coupling Schemes

Coupling by static functions is the most common device found in applications, but there are others. The most frequent variation is a *delay function*. Thus, the coupling device must remember inputs for a given time (usually fixed), the *lag*, and, at a present time, must deliver a function calculated from past inputs.

FIGURE 10.3. Static coupling of two simple schemes: Schematic.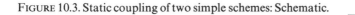

FIGURE 10.4. Multiple couplings.

This uses up memory in the simulation machine, but otherwise is straightforward and familiar. In many applications, delays are unavoidable. One unfortunate aspect of this neccessity is the fact that the completed CDS model is then a dynamical-delay scheme (system of differential-delay equations depending on control parameters), rather than a standard dynamical scheme.

Another coupling variation sometimes encountered in complex systems is an *integral function*. In this case, the coupling device must accumulate inputs over a fixed time, but need not remember the incremental values. This kind of static node can be replaced by a dynamical node, in which the integration of inputs becomes the solution of an equivalent differential equation. Thus, a static node may be regarded as a trivial type of dynamic node, in theory at least.

2.5. Serial Networks

A large number of simple dynamical schemes may be coupled, pairwise, with appropriate static coupling schemes. The result, a serial network, may be symbolized by a directed graph, at least in the simpler cases. The purpose of the CDS, as a mathematical construction, is to create qualitative simulation models for complex dynamical systems in nature [15]. The full-scale complex dynamical system may be symbolized by a graph with two distinct types of directed node, static and dynamic. (A directed node has separate input and output panels.) As controls at a given node or coupling scheme may be segmented (parsed into a product of different control manifolds) and some of these connected to other directed edges, we may have multiple inputs arriving at nodes and at couplings. Multiple outputs from nodes or couplings may also occur. Some examples are shown in Figure 10.4. The edge directions of these graphs of two types of directed nodes may be inferred from the connections because of the rule: Each edge must connect an output panel to an input panel. Furthermore, an edge from a dynamic output may only be connected to a static input.

3. Exemplary Applications

Several pedagogic examples have been presented in the literature listed in the References. We review some of them here.

3.1. Master–Slave Systems

The simplest complex scheme consists of the serial coupling (as illustrated above) of two simple dynamical schemes. The behavior of these simple examples is notoriously complicated. Suppose that the control parameters of the first (or master) system are fixed. After start-up, from an arbitrary initial state, the start-up transient dies away, and the master system settles asymptotically into one of its attractors. We consider the three cases separately.

Static master. If the attractor of the master system is a static (point) attractor and the control parameters of the coupling scheme are left fixed, then the control parameter of the second (slave) system are likewise fixed. Typically, this static control point of the slave system will be a typical (nonbifurcation) point, and the slave system will be observed in one of its attractors (static, periodic, or chaotic).

Periodic master. With fixed controls of the master and the coupling function, a periodic master attractor will drive the slave controls in a periodic cycle. This is the situation in the classical theory of forced oscillation. Experimental study of these systems began a century or so ago, and continues today. Here are the two classic examples:

1. *Duffing systems.* If the slave system is a soft spring or pendulum, the coupled system is the classic one introduced by Rayleigh in 1882, in which Duffing found hysteresis and catastrophes in 1918 [14]. The bifurcation diagram is very rich, full of harmonic periodic attractors and chaos [43].
2. *Van der Pol systems.* If the slave system is a self-sustained oscillator, the coupled system is another classic one introduced by Rayleigh, in which Van der Pol found subtle bifurcations of harmonics and Cartwright and Littlewood apparently found chaos. Both of these classical systems have been central to experimental dynamics, and research continues today.

Chaotic master. This situation, chaotic forcing, has received little attention so far. Many experiments suggest themselves, in analogy with forced oscillations. One situation that has been extensively studied is the perturbation of a conventional dynamical system by noise.

3.2. Chains of Dynamical Schemes

If three schemes are connected in a serial chain by two static coupling schemes (Figure 10.5), a complex system with a very complicated bifurcation diagram may result. If the first pair comprises a periodic master forcing a simple pendulum, as described above, the terminal slave may be either a periodically or chaotically forced system. Of course, if all three systems are pendulum-like (one basin, static attractor) the serial chain is also pendulum-like. But a

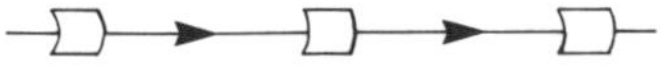

FIGURE 10.5. A chain.

FIGURE 10.6. Bicoupled pair.

FIGURE 10.7. An endocrine system model.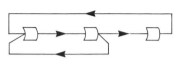

periodic attractor in either the first or second dynamical scheme is adequate to produce rich dynamics in the coupled chain.

3.3. Cycles of Dynamical Schemes

If the directed graph of a complex scheme contains a cycle (closed loop), then complicated dynamics may occur, no matter how simple the component schemes. The minimal example is the serially bicoupled pair (Figure 10.6). Even if the two dynamical schemes are pendulum-like, the complex system may have a periodic attractor. For example, Smale finds a periodic attractor (and a Hopf bifurcation) in exactly this situation, in a discrete reaction-diffusion model for two biological cells [38]. A cycle of three pendulum-like nodes is discussed next, as we turn now to more complex examples.

3.4. Intermittency in an Endocrine System Model

Models for physiological and biochemical systems have a natural complex structure. A recent model for the reproductive system of mammals (hypothalamus, pituitary, gonads) is a very simple network (Figure 10.7) [16]. Although the simple dynamical scheme at each node is a point attractor in a one-dimensional state space, the complex system may have two periodic basins, each containing a periodic attractor. This phenomenon, sometimes called birhythmicity, has also been found in a biochemical model [21]. Small changes in the control parameters of the coupling functions cause intermittent jumps between the two distinct oscillatory states.

3.5. Reaction-Diffusion Systems

An unusual example of serial coupling is provided by the reaction-diffusion model for biological morphogenesis, introduced by Fischer in 1930 (see Section 5 for more history). Given a spatial domain or substrate, D, and a biochemical state space, B, the state space is an infinite-dimensional manifold, F, of functions from D to B. The reaction-diffusion equation may be regarded as a simple dynamical scheme of vectorfields on F, depending on a control space, C. Meanwhile, the spatial substrate is actually composed of biological cells, considered identical in structure. As the reaction-diffusion scheme, the master in this context, determines instantaneous states of biochemical (mor-

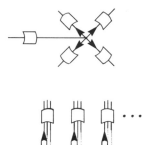

FIGURE 10.8. A star complex.

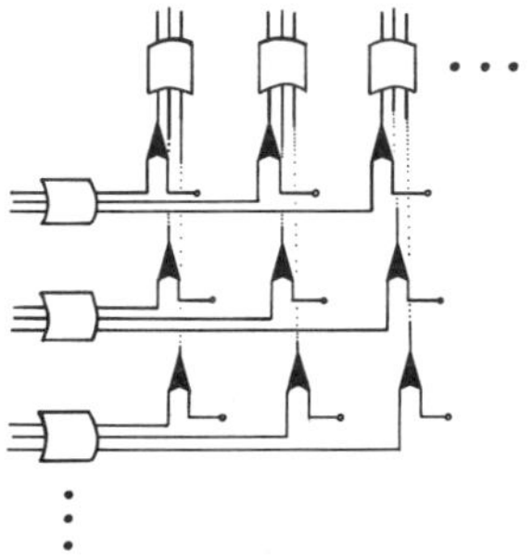

FIGURE 10.9. Neural net.

phogen, or control metabolite) concentrations in the substrate, $f: D \rightarrow B$, the cell at a fixed position in the domain will extract the values of this function at its location, $f(d)$. This is a point of B, which may be regarded as the control space for another simple dynamical scheme, modeling the dynamics within the standard cell. Let $g_d(f) = f(d)$. Then g_d is the static coupling function from master to slave. But there are many slaves, each distinguished by its own location, hence, coupling function. The directed graph is thus a radial spray, or star, of slaves of a common master, as shown in Figure 10.8. If, in addition, each cell may be a source or sink of biochemical (metabolite) controls, then each connection is a bicoupling. A further evolution of this type of system, called a *cellular dynamical system*, is discussed in Section 5.

3.6. Neural Nets

Neural nets may be regarded as a special case of a CDS network. The dynamical nodes are all identical schemes, in which a simple scheme with one dimensional control and state spaces has a single basin of attraction (with a static attractor). The control value adjusts the location of the attractor, and there are no bifurcations. The planar response diagram has an inclined line as attractrix. The coupling schemes are all identical as well and are simple amplifiers, $g(e, s) = es$. All nodes interconnected, as shown in (Fig. 10.9). The intelligence of a neural net depends on the matrix of controls, $E = (e_{ij})$. This strategy, called *connectionism*, may be extended directly to any CDS.

4. Simulation Techniques

After the strategies of complex dynamical systems have been used in an application, the resulting model is simply a large dynamical scheme. That is, a system of coupled ordinary differential equations with free control parameters, or partial differential equations of evolution type (parabolic or hyperbolic) must be explored experimentally. The goal of the exploration is to obtain the response diagram, which is the useful outcome of the qualitative modeling activity. As the exploration of the response diagram is an unfamiliar goal for simulation, we review here some of the strategies used.

4.1. Orbit Methods

When the dynamical scheme consists of a modest number of ordinary differential equations of first order, simulation by the standard digital algorithms (Euler, Runge-Kutta, and so on) or analog techniques provide curve tracing in the bifurcation diagram. A large number of curves, for various values of control parameters and initial conditions, may reveal the principal features of the diagram. Monte Carlo techniques are sometimes used to select the control parameters and/or initial states.

4.2. Relaxation Methods

When partial differential equations (reaction-diffusion, hydrodynamic, plasma, liquid crystal, solid state, elastodynamic, and so on) are part of the model, they may be treated most naturally as dynamical systems by discretization of the spatial variables. Thus, the infinite-dimensional state spaces are projected into finite-dimensional approximations. Finally, these may be treated by orbit methods, to obtain a bifurcation diagram with loci of attraction and separation. This is essentially the relaxation technique of Southwell (method-of-lines).

4.3. Dynasim Methods

Whether small or large, ordinary or partial, the exploration of a bifurcation diagram by analog, digital, or hybrid simulation is extremely time intensive. A considerable gain in speed may be obtained with dynasim methods [2]. Here, special-purpose hardware traces a large number of orbits in parallel. Having thus found all the most probable attractors at once, time is reversed and the basin of each is filled with its own color. This process is repeated (perhaps in parallel) for different values of the control parameters. When dimensions are large, new techniques of visualization may be needed [30].

4.4. Distributed Processing

For the simulation of a complex dynamical model, the static coupling schemes may be implemented by lookup tables or fast arithmetic. It is the dynamical schemes that are FLOP intensive. It makes sense, if distributed processors are available, to devote one to each dynamical node. Thus, the architecture of the simulation device is identical to that of the complex dynamical model and similar to that of the target natural system. Message-passing traffic may be decreased by the following trick, if the model is loosely coupled. This means that although an output may be changing rapidly, the node it controls is only slowly sensitive to the rapid changes. Thus, occasional updates of control may be transmitted in place of rapid ones. Furthermore, if all current states are broadcast on a schedule to the static nodes and controls of the rapid integration routines running in each processor, the node processors may (if they can afford the time) make predictions of the next broadcast. A cheap predictor, such as Euler integration, may be used to change the local controls linearly with each local time step, in ignorance of the real values at the neighboring nodes.

5. Cellular Dynamical Systems

Here we introduce *cellular dynamical systems theory*, a mathematical strategy for creating dynamical models for the computer simulation of biological organs and membranes, and other systems exhibiting natural intelligence. Reaction/diffusion equations were introduced by the pioneers of biological morphogenesis: Fisher (in 1930) [26], Kolmogorov, Petrovsky, and Piscounov (in 1937) [31], Rashevsky (in 1938) [36], Southwell (around 1940) [39], and Turing (in 1952) [42]. Rashevsky introduced spatial discretization corresponding to biological cells. These discretized reaction/diffusion systems are examples of cellular dynamical systems, probably the first in the literature. Further developments were made by Thom (1966 to 1972) [41] and Zeeman (1972 to 1977) [44]. The latter includes a heart model, and a simple brain model exhibiting short and long-term memory. The ideas outlined here are all inspired by these pioneers. The strategy is based on CDS concepts [8].

5.1. Definitions

By *cellular dynamical system* we mean a complex dynamical system in which the nodes are all identical copies of a single dynamical scheme, the *standard cell*, and are associated with specific locations in a supplementary space, the *physical substrate*, or *location space*. Exemplary systems have been developed for reaction/diffusion systems by discretization of the spatial variables. In these examples, pattern formation occurs by Turing bifurcation. One of the most-studied examples of this class is the *Brussellator* of Lefever and Prigogine. Other important examples of this construction are the heart and brain models of Zeeman. These models have something in common with the *cellular automata* of Von Neumann, yet possess more structure. We might call them *cellular dynomata*.

The behavior of a cellular dynamical system may be visualized by Zeeman's *projection method*: An image of the location space (physical substrate) is projected into the response diagram of the standard cell, where it moves about, clinging to the attractrix, or locus of attraction. Alternatively, the behavior may be vizualized by the *graph method*: attaching a separate copy of the standard response diagram to each cell of the location space. Within this product space, the instantaneous state of the model may be represented by a graph, showing the attractor occupied by each cell, within its own response diagram. In either case, the behavior of the complete cellular system may be tracked, as the controls of each cell are separately manipulated, through an understanding of the standard response diagram provided by *dynamical systems theory*: attractors, basins, separators, and their bifurcations.

5.2. Biological Organ Example

Organs typically contain many different types of cells. In the unusual case that there were only one type of cell, one could imagine a model for the organ consisting of a single cellular dynamical system. This is the case with Zeeman's heart model. An explicit cellular dynamical model for the organ will require an explicit model for the standard cell, which (with luck) may be found in the specialized literature devoted to that cell.

However, if there are two distinct cells, then each will give rise to a distinct cellular dynamical model. The model for the organ will then consist of a coupled system of *two cellular dynamical systems*, one for each cell type. More generally, the organ model will consist of a *complex dynamical system*, comprising a network of distinct cellular dynamical models, one for each of the distinct cell types, visualized (intermixed) in a common physical substrate.

Moreover, even if there is only a single cell type in the organ (e.g., a liver cell) a network of cellular models may nevertheless be required. For there are usually at least two important compartments in the organ: the intracellular space and the extracellular space. The concentration of control metabolites or humoral substances (such as the pacemaker substance in Zeeman's heart model) in the extracellular space contributes a second cellular dynamical system to the model. This second system arises through the discretization of the nonlinear Fickian diffusion equation for the perfusion of metabolites through the organ. Even if the substance in the two compartments is the same (e.g., cortisol in the adrenal cortex), there will be two distinct cellular systems in the organ model. The dynamics of the extracellular substance will be modeled by a (discretized) reaction/diffusion system, while the intracellular dynamics may be modeled by reaction kinetics alone.

5.3. Nonlinear Spectroscopy

Even with enormous computers, the simulation of a detailed model of a realistic organ, on the scale of individual cells, may be too slow to be useful. Thus, for models that can interact fruitfully with researchers on the frontiers of science, we must use computational cells larger than a single physiological cell. These computational cells will be assigned average values of the state variables of the individual biological cells (or subcellular units, or extracellular spaces) contained within it. If the size of the computational cell is varied through a sequence of increasing sizes or scales, from a fraction of a single cell to the whole organ or organism, we obtain a family of distinct cellular dynamical models for the same organ. Their spectrum of behaviors comprises the nonlinear spectral analysis of the modeling scheme used to construct the family of models. The shape of this spectrum may be very useful in optimizing a model for a specific purpose, as well as for understanding the physiology of the organ or target system.

5.4. Numerical Methods and Experiments

The destiny of a cellular dynamical model is a computer program for qualitative simulation. Although we may expect someday a theory of these models, it may not replace simulation as the dominant method of science, but only supplement it. Thus, we need a technology of numerical methods adapted to these large-scale simulations. Beyond brute-force integration of thousands of identical copies of the standard dynamical scheme with differing (and slowly changing) values of the control parameters, lookup-table methods might be employed for acceleration or economy. In any case, massively parallel hardware and software will be needed, along with new methods of monitoring large numbers of state variables. Color graphics is the method of choice at the moment, and we may imagine a color movie projected upon a model of the physical substrate of the organ as the monitoring scheme.

The current state of the art seems to be simple experiments with standard cells culled from the literature of the physical sciences, such as the Duffing pendulum, the cusp catastrophe, and so on. From these experiments, we may try to recognize some functions of natural intelligence, such as memory, perception, decision, learning, and the like, as in neural net theory.

6. Netscopy

To create a complex dynamical model for a complex system, it is normally necessary to have a directed graph of the network, a dynamical model for each node, and a coupling function for each directed edge. But, in many applications, the only observable data consist of communications from one node to another. In this situation, the modeler may infer a complex dynamical model for the network without any explicit knowledge of the independent dynamical behavior of the component systems (nodes). Here we present one procedure for this type of modeling problem, inspired by the attractor reconstruction technique of chaos theory [25]. The first part of this procedure consists of a strategy for computer graphic presentation of the interactive dynamics of the complex system (or social network of dynamical schemes) called a *netscope*. We can imagine applications to diverse situations, such as decision groups, management, forecasting, international relations, classroom monitoring, therapy (personal, family, group, etc.), and distributed processors, to name a few [11].

We begin in this section with the first step: the observation of the target system, or creation of a database from the working network. An approach to this problem in a psychotherapeutic context, based on joint work in progress with Marsha Fox and Bob Langs, will be used as a basis for discussion.

6.1. Observation

In a general network, communications between the participants might be written, verbal, nonverbal, video, code, and so on. We consider here only one of these possibilities: verbal communication. Other cases might be handled similarly. Furthermore, to simplify the description we consider only the smallest network: two participants. Remarks on the general case are inserted from time-to-time in italics. Due to the original context (psychotherapy), we call the communicants P (patient) and T (therapist). We now describe the first step in four parts: observation, scoring, superscores, and viewing.

There are two communication channels to monitor: P-to-T and T-to-P. Due to the face-to-face spoken language context of the communication, the two channels are overlapped and are recorded on a single tape. In the future, the whole process might be managed, like simultaneous translation, without recording. But at present, the observation process is based on audio or video tape recordings.

In case of more communicants, each spoken message might be intended for one or more recipients. We might then assume that the sender (speaker) can be identified by voice, but the intended recipients (or the actual recipients) may not be identifiable from the tape recording. With written communications or electronic mail, however, we would have an explicit target list for each communication. We may deal with this by regarding each transmission as a broadcast, for public reception by all participants. In the general context, each message would be identified with one sender and a set of receivers.

Our current context (two people in conversation) is of this type, so we regard each transmission as belonging primarily to the sender. This is compatible with the viewpoint of complex dynamical system theory, in which couplings are expressed in terms of a function from the internal state of the source (sending) node to the control parameters of the target (receiving) nodes. Hence, we will label each transmission by P (rather than P-to-T) or T (rather than T-to-P) to identify the sender.

As we will want to analyze the dynamics of the interactions, we should have a clock in view (in case of video recording) or a prerecorded clock track (in case of audio recording only). This will allow time data to be included in the transcription.

After recording a session of the working network in this way, the recording is transcribed by a typist to a text file on a computer disk or diskette. The communications are broken into *lines* of a more-or-less fixed length. For example, Langs and Fox use a long line length, roughly equivalent to 20 s of normal speech. Each line is labeled with a line number, the clock-time recorded next to its first word, and the identification of the sender (the speaker, P or T). A fictitious example is presented in Table 10.1.

TABLE 10.1. Transcribed data.

Line	Time	Node	Test
1	011500	P	My mother brought me today.
2	011520	T	How nice, I always wanted to meet her.

TABLE 10.2. Scored data.

Line	Time	Node	S1	S2	S3	S4
1	011500	P	1	-3	2	-5
2	011520	T	0	2	-7	-2

6.2. Scoring

The transcription must now be scored. Each line of text must be transformed into numerical values of the observable parameters according to some theory. The procedure is circular, in practice. A list of observables is proposed, with a scoring range for each. Rules are written for the transformation from text into scores. This is called the *scoring manual*. Then, people are trained in the use of the scoring system from the manual, and the transcribed recording is scored. This produces a database file on a personal computer disk or diskette, which will be the basis for the next step. An example, based on Table 10.1 and a fictitious scoring manual with 4 scores, is shown in Table 10.2. This next step is the most important and, in our experience, can profit from several months of iteration: The manual is rewritten, the training is repeated, and the transcribed recording is scored again. With each revision, it seems to grow. The scoring system of Langs and Fox currently records 67 scores for each line of text.

6.3. Superscores

To obtain a simple visualization of the session based on the scores, we must reduce their number. Eventually, the analysis might provide an estimate for the actual dimension of the information, and thus an indication of a good target value for the total number of scores to record for each line [25]. But, at the start, we will be restricted primarily by our cognitive strategies. And, in this project, we will rely on computer graphics to inspect the data. Thus, we must ask the scoring manual experts to indicate which scores might be totally ignored in a preliminary inspection, which might be largely ignored, which are the most important, and so on. Considering our reliance on inexpensive spreadsheet software for personal computers, we might try to find a small number of reduced indicators to reveal graphically the significance of the scores. The method we have used is to combine several scores into a

TABLE 10.3. Superscored data.

Line	Time	Node	S1	S2	S3	S4	U	C
1	011500	P	1	−3	2	−5	0	5
2	011520	T	0	2	−7	−2	5	−2

weighted average or linear combination, which we call a *superscore*. For example, Langsian analysis might make use of two superscores, activity of the conscious (C) and unconscious (U) systems, as we show in Table 10.3. The spreadsheet program may be able to add the superscore columns automatically.

6.4. Viewing

All the scores may be viewed graphically as functions of time (time series) by utilization of the built-in graphing functions of the database manager. But, in the spirit of dynamical systems theory, we want to view trajectories in the state space or response diagram of the various nodes [14]. Here our task is simplified if our network is *symmetric*. By this we mean that the same dynamical scheme appears as the dynamical model for each node. In the present context, this means that we will use the same model (dynamical scheme, i.e., dynamical system depending on control parameters) for the patient (P) and for the therapist (T). And, therefore, we may indicate the data for the entire network within a single portrait or response diagram. For example, if we are satisfied with two superscores and no controls, the common portrait is two-dimensional. In case of two superscores and one control parameter, the common response diagram is three-dimensional. The two participants will each have their own trajectory, say, a blue one (P) and a red one (T). This is not essential, however. We could view the trajectories on separate screens, each screen devoted to a different nodal response diagram.

The observation of a symmetric communications network with several participants in this manner would show several colored trajectories moving about within a common response diagram. We call this strategy of observation (which could conceivably be achieved in real-time with a short delay) a netscope. Each trajectory should advance at the proper time, to represent the true dynamics along the locus of attraction within its own response diagram. For example, we could imagine a two-screen replay of a summit conference. On the left screen, we would see (and hear) the actual negotiations for world peace. And on the right, the simultaneous representation by the trajectories winding around the locus of attraction in contrasting colors. In our case, there would be two dots moving on the right-hand screen, each trailing a trajectory behind. When this can be accomplished in real-time with a brief delay, the discussants might be aided in achieving their goals by watching themselves on the netscope!

7. Construction of the Complex Model

Now we have data from the netscope. The second part of our procedure creates a complex dynamical model from the netscopic data. We give here a concise recipe for this modeling process, in five steps: filtering, smoothing, parsing, interpolating, and embedding. This is also based on joint work with Marsha Fox and Robert Langs.

7.1. Filtering the Data by Sender

Eventually we propose to view each participant as a trajectory moving within a response diagram. At this point, we have data, but no response diagram. To develop this model for the dynamics of each participant, we must treat the data for each sender separately. In our present context (conversation), participants generally take turns sending. Thus, there will be long gaps in each trajectory.

For example, the trajectory of P data has a long gap while the T trajectory moves. During this gap, we assume that the P trajectory continues to move, but we have no data to reveal its motion. When T quits, there may be a pause, then the P trajectory may resume from a new location. Furthermore, it is *only* during this gap, or invisible segment in the P trajectory, that the control parameters of the P model scheme are being changed by the message from T. Thus, what we are missing is the most vital information about the P model, its bifurcation behavior. As we will probably never obtain enough data to fill in the full response diagram, we may eventually have to guess one, taken from an atlas of standard response diagrams (such as DYN, Part Four). This step is reflected in the tabular data by a separation (filtration) into two tables, as shown in Tables 10.4a and 10.4b.

7.2. Smoothing the Data

In our experience, the data obtained by this method are rough. They do not graph well. This is inherent in our discrete scoring method, and the more

TABLE 10.4a. Filtered data: Node P.

Line	Time	Node	S1	S2	S3	S4	U	C
1	011500	P	1	−3	2	−5	0	5
2	011520	T	?	?	?	?	?	?

TABLE 10.4b. Filtered data: Node T.

Line	Time	Node	S1	S2	S3	S4	U	C
1	011500	P	?	?	?	?	?	?
2	011520	T	0	2	−7	−2	5	−2

different scores utilized in the method, the rougher the resulting data. But our dynamical models assume continuous state and control parameters. So, smoothing the data may help in the development of the nodal models. As the gaps are significant and as catastrophic bifurcations (i.e., discontinuities) are expected to occur during these invisible portions, we do not want to smooth the gaps. Our strategy, then, is to smooth the data within each message or speech (i.e., between gaps). This can be done by averaging, splines, least squares, or by any other means.

7.3. Parsing the Data by Control Parameters

If we now plot some superscore trajectories (e.g., U versus C for P only, smoothed as described above), we may expect to see trajectories crossing themselves in a jumble. This is discouraging, as it should not occur in a dynamical system. One of the usual remedies is embedding the data in higher dimensions. We regard this as a last resort, as will be discussed. Now, however, we describe a more fundamental strategy.

We have not yet devoted much discussion to control parameters. Yet state and control parameters are equally basic to a dynamical scheme. Recall that the phase portrait is a visual representation of a dynamical system emphasizing its attractors, basins, and separators. In contrast, the response diagram of a scheme is a visual representation of its locus of attraction, drawn in the response space of both state and control parameters [14]. For each value of the control parameters, we have a different dynamical system in the state space, with its own portrait, attractors, basins, separatrices, and trajectories. Thus, each trajectory data point must be located in the portrait corresponding to its own control parameter values. But what are the controls, in the data obtained by our scoring method, for node P, for example?

In general, the controls of one nodal model are to be determined from the state of other nodal models via coupling functions. Thus, the control parameters for P may be added to our model by hypotheses. We must decide what factors change the dynamics of P, and how these factors depend on the state (i.e., the scores or superscores) of T. These choices are quite arbitrary, depend on the prevailing theory of the modelers, and may be modified many times before a useful model results. In fact, many different models may fit the data equally well (or badly) and may be interchanged at will.

We are going to suggest now the addition to our database of additional columns for control parameters. These may be defined, like superscores, as functions, the *coupling functions.* Superscores are functions of scores, and controls may be functions of superscores. The coupling functions are maps from the state parameters of one node to the control parameters of another. *In general, different control parameters and coupling functions are required for each directed edge* (e.g., separate control columns for P and T in our current example). But, for the present, we may assume the control parameter superscore columns are shared by the P-to-T and T-to-P edges (another aspect of

TABLE 10.5a. Filtered data: Node P.

Line	Time	Node	S1	S2	S3	S4	U	C	A
1	011500	P	1	−3	2	−5	0	5	—
2	011520	T	—	—	—	—	—	—	0.6

TABLE 10.5b. Filtered data: Node T.

Line	Time	Node	S1	S2	S3	S4	U	C	A
1	011500	P	—	—	—	—	—	—	1.0
2	011520	T	0	2	−7	−2	5	−2	—

our symmetry assumption). The control values for node T must be entered in the table of filtered data for node T, during the gaps occupied by the message from node P, and vice versa.

To begin with the simplest possible case, we will try to model these nodes with schemes having two superscores (U and C) and one control parameter (A). We may assume that the coupling function defines A as a superscore obtained from U and C only, for example,

$$A = 0.2*(U + C),$$

which we may call *activation*. This is now added to the database, as shown in Tables 10.5a and 10.5b.

In general, the strength of these couplings may be changed to alter the behavior of the model. This is the connectionist approach of neural net theory. In the asymmetric case, we could have different coupling functions for each directed edge.

Thus in our context, we could have two activation formulas, for example,

$$A = 0.2*(U + C) \quad \text{if} \quad P\text{-to-}T,$$

$$A = 0.4*(U + C) \quad \text{if} \quad T\text{-to-}P.$$

But, for the present, we continue to assume symmetry.

Now, the trajectories (smoothed, but retaining gaps) may be drawn in the 3-D response space of the variables (A, U, C). *We assume that P's control A changes only during a gap, while T is transmitting, and vice versa.* When U, C, and A are properly chosen, we hope that all self-crossings will disappear. Important information may now be obtained by constructing a *response histogram* (i.e., a scatter plot) of all P data points (red) and T data points (blue), plotted within the 3-D response space. In case of multiple scorers, we might try plotting all the data without smoothing. The response histogram (also called the *invariant measure*) is a very important aspect of the nodal scheme. The response diagram is obtained by interpolating the response histogram.

7.4. Interpolating the Response Diagram

Assume that, proceeding as described above, we have obtained trajectories
without crossings. All that remains to complete the nodal models is to smoothly fill in the locus of attraction, using the histogram as a guide. A knowledge
of the atlas of bifurcations will be essential to this task, as data will generally
be sparse.

On the other hand, if crossings remain, then we must increase the number
of state or control variables. One way to accomplish this is to utilize more
superscores of the original scores (if there are lots of them) or to embed the
data (if there few). In our case, the Langs–Fox scoring system provides a large
number (about 67) of scores, so new superscores may be added to the database.
Hopefully, a small number of superscores will suffice to provide useful simple
models [33]. Otherwise, we are in trouble.

7.5. Embedding the Data

In the exceptional case in which only a small number of scores can be obtained
from the data (e.g., we are processing someone else's scores, and the original
data or transcript is unavailable), we may create fictitious supplementary
scores by the embedding procedure. We would just add new columns identical
to the original columns, but slipped up by one or more rows [22].

7.6. Simulating the Complex Model

The complex model now exists. Each node has a model scheme, represented
by the interpolated response diagram constructed above, and the control
parameters and coupling functions are provided by the superscore and coupling formulas. In order to do computer simulation with the model, we need
some mathematical expressions for the dynamical schemes at each node. The
experienced dynamicist should be called at this point, to conjure appropriate
formulas for the schemes. These are generally built from a library of known
models, inherited from the early pioneers. Simulation software [2] and chaotic
measurement tools [37] are then available to study the model and to compare
the simulated data to the experimental data, and so on. Sophisticated programs for obtaining equations from the data [19] or economically generating
additional data [24] may be called upon if needed.

This completes the construction of the working model for the interactive
social network of two participants. Without substantial modification, a model
may be constructed for larger networks, even if asymmetric. The evolution of
the model may be an accomplishment for the social sciences, but the posses-
sion of the model may convey a certain power. For example, crude forecasting
becomes possible, and may enable winning bets, as in a roulette game [18].
Complex dynamical models have also been used in therapy [23].

As we might fairly wish all participants to have equal access to the model,
the possibility must be considered to carry out the simulation on a distributed

network of computer graphic workstations, one for each node. Conceivably, each participant might utilize their own actual self, together with a dynamical model of the other, to rehearse their interactions in advance of an actual interchange.

8. Conclusion

The procedure described here for the construction of a complex dynamical model for a social network entirely from communications data may be easily generalized to asymmetric networks with many nodes, with different schemes at each node. The communications need not be restricted to the verbal.

Models made in this way may play the role, in the social sciences, that Newton's laws played in the history of the physical sciences. The applications are numerous, and not all may be entirely benign. But we hope the stability of the world may be increased by the development of this modeling strategy. We have proposed applications to international political relationships, as well as to group decision processes. Good models, when and if they eventually become available, might be used for education, amusement, the arts, police work, management, decision making, and, in fact, wherever the social sciences are already applied. In sum, it seems that netscopes may function to make the unconscious visible. This may be hard to get used to, but basically evolutionary.

Complex dynamical systems theory is a new development. An outgrowth of nonlinear dynamics, system dynamics, and control theory, it aims to provide complete strategies for modeling and simulation of complex systems, whether in the physical, biological, or social sciences.

Acknowledgments. It is a pleasure to acknowledge the generosity of Nico Kuiper and the Institut des Hautes Etudes Scientifiques, Bill Smith and the University of Guelph, Gene Yates and the Crump Institute of Medical Engineering, Anna Wirz and the University of Basel, Chris Zeeman and the University of Warwick, Rene Thom, Arthur Iberall, Alan Garfinkel, Bob Langs, Marsha Fox, David Loye, and Ervin Laszlo in sharing their ideas and resources. To the late Professor Chihiro Hayashi of Kyoto, I am especially grateful for his kindness and the inspiration of his work.

References

1. Abraham, R.H. Vibrations and the realization of form. In *Evolution in the Human World*, E. Jantsch and C. Waddington, Eds. Addison-Wesley, Reading, Mass., 1976, pp. 134–149.
2. Abraham, R.H. Dynasim: Exploratory research in bifurcations using interactive computer graphics. *Ann. N.Y. Acad. Sci. 316* (1979), 676–684.
3. Abraham, R.H. The function of mathematics in the evolution of the noosphere. In *The Evolutionary Vision*, E. Jantsch, Ed. 1981, pp. 153–168.

4. Abraham, R.H. Dynamical models for physiology. *Am. J. Physiol.* (1983), 467–472.

5. Abraham, R.H. Complex dynamical systems. In *Mathematical Modelling in Science and Technology*, X.J.R. Avula, R.E. Kalman, A.I. Leapis, and E.Y. Rodin, Eds. Pergamon, 1984, pp. 82–86.

6. Abraham, R.H. ENDOSIM: A progress report. In *Mathematics and Computers in Biomedical Applications, Proc. IMACS Symposium, Bathesda, 1984*, J. Eisenfeld and C. DeLisi, Eds. North-Holland, Amsterdam, 1985, pp. 133–136.

7. Abraham, R.H. Mathematics and evolution: A manifesto. *IS Journal 1*, 3 (1986), 14–23.

8. Abraham, R.H. Cellular dynamical systems. In *Mathematics and Computers in Biomedical Applications, Proc. IMACS World Congress, Oslo, 1985*, J. Eisenfeld and C. DeLisi, Eds. North-Holland, Amsterdam, 1986, pp. 7–8.

9. Abraham, R.H. Mechanics of resonance. *Revision 10* (1987), 13–19.

10. Abraham, R.H. Complex dynamics and the social science. *J. World Futures 23*, (1987), 1–10.

11. Abraham, R.H. Netscope: Dynamics from communications data. *J. Soc. Biol. Struct.* (1989).

12. Abraham, R.H., and Garfinkel, A. *Orbital Plots of Dynamical Processes: Application to a Circadian Oscillator Model.* Preprint, Univ. of California, Santa Cruz, Calif. 1985.

13. Abraham, R.H., and Garfinkel, A. CORTISIM: A complex dynamical model of the cortisol regulation system. *Simulation 47* (1986), 199–207.

14. Abraham, R.H., and Shaw, C.D. *Dynamics, the Geometry of Behavior.* Four vols. Aerial Press, Santa Cruz, Calif., 1982–1988.

15. Abraham, R.H., and Shaw, C.D. Dynamics, a visual introduction. In *Self-Organization*, F. Eugene Yates, Ed. Plenum, New York, 1988, pp. 543–597.

16. Abraham, R.H., Kocak, H., and Smith, W.R. Chaos and intermittency in an endocrine system. In *Chaos, Fractals, and Dynamics*, W.R. Smith and P. Fischer, Eds. Plenum, New York, 1985, pp. 33–70.

17. Abraham, R.H., Marsden, J.E., and Ratiu, T. *Manifolds, Tensor Analysis, and Applications.* 2nd ed., Springer-Verlag, Berlin, 1988.

18. Bass, T. *The Eudomonic Pie.* Vintage, New York, 1986.

19. Crutchfield, J.P., and MacNamara, B.S. *Complex Syst. 1* (1987), 417.

20. Davidson, M. *Uncommon Sense: The Life and Thought of Ludwig von Bertalanffy (1901–1972), Father of General Systems Theory.* J.P. Tarcher, Los Angeles, Calif.

21. Decroly, O., and Goldbeter, A. Birhythmicity, chaos and other patterns of temporal self-organization in a multiply regulated biochemical system. *Proc. Natl. Acad. Sci. USA 79* (1982), 6917–6921.

22. Eckmann, J.-P., and Rulle, D. Ergodic theory of chaos and strange attractors. *Rev. Mod. Phys. 57* (1985), 617–656.

23. Elkaim, M., Goldbeter, A., and Goldbeter-Merinfeld, E. Analysis of the dynamics of a family system in terms of bifurcations. *J. Soc. Biol. Struct. 10* (1987), 21–36.

24. Farmer, J.D., and Sidorowicz, J.J. Exploiting chaos to predict the future and reduce noise. In Evolution, *Learning and Cognition*, Y.C. Lee, Ed. World Scientific, Singapore, 1988, 277.

25. Doyne Farmer, J., Ott, E., and Yorke, J.A. Fractal dimension. *Physica D7* (1983), 153.

26. Fisher, R.A. *The Genetical Theory of Natural Selection.* Dover, New York, 1930/1958.

27. Forrester, J.W. *Industrial Dynamics.* MIT Press, Cambridge, Mass., 1961.

28. Gardner, H. *The Mind's New Science: A History of the Cognitive Revolution.* Basic Books, New York, 1985.
29. Haraway, D.J. *Crystals, Fabrics, and Fields: Metaphors of Organicism in Twentienth-Century Development Biology.* Yale University Press, New Haven, Conn., 1976.
30. Inselberg, A. The plane with parallel coordinates. *Vis. Comput. 1* (1985), 69–91.
31. Kolmogorov, A., Petrovski, I., and Piskunov, N. Etude de l'equation de la diffusion avec croissance de la quantite de matiee et son application a une probleme biologique. *Bull. de l'Universite d'Etat a Moscou, Ser. International 1,* A (1937), 1–25.
32. Kuhn, T. *The Structure of Scientific Revolutions.* University of Chicago Press, Chicago, Il., 1962.
33. Langs, R. Clarifying a new model of the mind. *Contemp. Psychoanalysis 23* (1987), 162–180.
34. Loye, D. *The Healing of a Nation.* Dell Books, New York, 1972.
35. Meadow, D.H., Meadows, D.L., et al. *The Limits of Growth: A Report for the Club of Rome's Project on the Predicament of Mankind.* Universe Books, New York, 1974.
36. Rashevsky, N. *Mathematical Biophysics.* University of Chicago Press, Chicago, Il., 1938.
37. Schaffer, W.M. *Dynamical Software.* Dynamical Software, Tucson, Ariz., 1986.
38. Smale, S. A mathematical model of two cells. In *The Hopf Bifurcation and Its Applications,* M. McCracken, Ed. Springer-Verlag, New York, 1976.
39. Southwell, R.V. *Relaxation Methods in Engineering Science.* Oxford University Press, London, 1940.
40. *Systems Dynamics Review.* Special issue on chaos. *Syst. Dynamics Rev. 4,* 1–2 (1988).
41. Thom, R. *Structural Stability and Morphogenesis.* Addison-Wesley, Reading, Mass., 1975.
42. Turing, A. A chemical basis for biological morphogenesis. *Phil. Trans. Roy. Soc. (London), Ser. B 237* (1952), 37.
43. Ueda, Y. Explosion of strange attractors exhibited by Duffing's equation. *Ann. N.Y. Acad. Sci. 357* (1980), 422–434.
44. Zeeman, C. *Catastrophe Theory.* Addison-Wesley, Reading, Mass., 1977.
45. Zeleny, M. Autopoiesis. In *Systems and Control Encyclopedia: Theory, Technology, Applications,* M.G. Singh, Ed. Pergamon Press, New York, 1988, pp. 393–400.

CHAPTER 11

Qualitative Modeling Using Natural Language: An Application in System Dynamics

Wanda M. Austin and Behrokh Khoshnevis

Abstract

System dynamics modeling is a powerful tool for system analysis and decision support. A knowledge-based human-to-computer interface for this modeling framework will enable users to build complex models with fewer errors and in less time. In this chapter we present a methodology for building system dynamics models using a natural language interface. An approach is presented for analyzing natural language descriptions of systems. A methodology for representing systems that is language independent and computationally efficient is developed. This methodology was used to build a prototype system, NATSIM. The design of NATSIM is described and the functionality of the system is demonstrated within the context of the production-distribution domain.

1. Introduction

System dynamics modeling is a powerful tool for system analysis and decision support. A knowledge-based human-to-computer interface for this modeling framework will enable users to build complex models with fewer errors and in less time.

This chapter presents a methodology for building system dynamics models using a natural language interface. The well-established constructs from system dynamics form the basis of a generic but rigorous framework for exploiting natural language for the generation of qualitative models. The methodology for analyzing natural language descriptions of systems and for representing these systems in a language independent form is presented. We implemented a prototype system called NATSIM, predicated on this methodology.

1.1. Problem Description

Simulation is a powerful tool for system analysis and decision support. Given the state of the art in computer technology, a diverse set of simulation tools can be made available to managers and decision makers to provide a fast,

263

sophisticated analysis capability; however, these individuals may only use these tools on an intermittent basis. Simulation models are also frequently built by individuals who are knowledgeable about a specific task domain and familiar with computer concepts but less comfortable with syntactic details. Although simulation languages available on the market today are more user friendly than the standard programming languages, they still require precise syntax and detailed knowledge of constructs and requirements that are unique for each language. This is a serious deterrent for the people who can benefit the most from using simulation.

Problem formulation is recognized as one of the toughest parts of building a simulation model, yet all simulation languages make the assumption that this phase is complete and correct. In addition, novice modelers need assistance with integrating simulation concepts, the modeling framework, the task domain, and the requirements of a specific simulation language. It is only after experience is gained from building many models that these modelers amass a repertoire of aids to help them build models quickly and correctly. Model error reporting is limited to the detection of obvious syntactic errors, and in many instances, the system warns the user that "no errors were detected." This implies that other errors may exist, but the system is limited in its ability to identify them. Users are left to their own devices to detect logical errors or errors that violate basic concepts in simulation.

System dynamics is a computer-based method for qualitative analysis of complex problems that develop or persist over time. The method employs simulation modeling to identify the often hidden sources of dynamic problems and to find robust solutions that approach equilibrium and remain effective over time. System dynamics helps the user to understand the structures that produce undesirable symptoms and to identify the changes in structure and policy that will make a system better behaved. This tool was developed specifically for high-level managers, but it is not readily accessible to them due to the drawbacks associated with simulation modeling previously mentioned.

1.2. Natural Language as a Qualitative Tool

System dynamics modeling is enhanced if the user can access the modeling framework through a natural language interface. This intelligent modeling environment allows the user to focus on problem definition and analysis of results. The knowledge base within this environment is defined so that basic simulation concepts can be inferred and so that user intentions are understood. This is accomplished by taking advantage of the generic and domain-independent structures of the system dynamics methodology. The need for the user to learn the syntax of various simulation languages is also eliminated. The internal formal representation of the system can be used to generate executable code automatically for any of the appropriate continuous system simulation languages. The user is expected to understand basic concepts of simulation modeling, to be knowledgeable in the application domain, and to set the system boundaries by specifying the elements that are endogenous to the problem under study.

If the interface to this intelligent modeling environment is through natural language, the user is not burdened with the need to learn how to use the system. The user provides a natural language description of a system that is, in fact, a qualitative model of the system. A natural language interface is attractive to the experienced, the intermittent, and the novice user because the system builds the model by analyzing the user input. The user should only be given assistance on an as-needed basis. The input must be analyzed for completeness, consistency, and logical conflicts. In this way, the modeling environment is not only user friendly, but sensitive to the competence level of the user.

We present a methodology for transforming the natural language model into a simulation language independent form. With this form it is easy to retrieve the information needed to generate a model in a specific simulation language.

1.3. Theory Versus Reality of Natural Language Systems

NATSIM is a natural-language-based simulation system that transforms qualitative natural language models into simulation code. The specific implementation of NATSIM that is described here generates DYNAMO code. Because of the limitations of natural language parsing systems and the potential for complexities in the structure of real-life problems, the problem context of NATSIM is restricted to production distribution systems. Simulation is a large and complex analysis technique and is still sometimes referred to as an art. If two humans are given an ambiguous system description, they will undoubtedly build two different models. We cannot expect a computer system to do any better than humans. However, given a reasonably well-defined description of a system, within the system dynamics framework, in a prespecified domain, it is feasible to build a system that can automatically generate the correct model.

In this chapter the term *system* refers to feedback systems and, more specifically, to the class of feedback systems that can be studied using system dynamics. System dynamics is the application of feedback control systems principles and techniques to the modeling of managerial, organizational, and socioeconomic problems. The feedback path allows control to be exercised by comparing the difference between the output and some desired result. The aim is to explore the dynamics of feedback systems in terms of their stability and response to external variations.

The phrase *natural language* refers to a comfortable but restricted subset of English within an application domain. It is assumed that this subset can be identified and circumscribed to include all language that is likely to be used by practitioners of that domain.

The prototype system, NATSIM, is a natural language system shell. It is defined by the domain, knowledge bases and target simulation language that support it. It is limited by the size of the lexicon and knowledge bases supporting it. The system uses 40 verbs, 40 nouns, and 200 patterns from the production distribution application domain.

1.4. Chapter Overview

In this chapter we discuss (1) a methodology for analyzing natural language descriptions of systems, (2) a representation of systems that is independent of any specific simulation language and is computationally efficient, and (3) the design of NATSIM, a working prototype. The functionality of these concepts is demonstrated within the context of a real, although limited, domain. By using the well-established constructs from system dynamics, a generic but rigorous framework for exploiting natural language for the generation of qualitative models has been defined. The design creates an intelligent simulation environment that gives modelers every advantage and makes them appear more experienced because of the capability to build more complex models with fewer errors and in less time.

Section 2 briefly reviews the state of the art in each discipline and identifies specific accepted tenets that form the foundation for NATSIM. Section 3 introduces the conceptual framework and methodology for a systematic approach to the model-building process, definition of a representation for the model, and a methodology for processing natural language descriptions that specify the model. The analyses and results presented address the problem generically. Section 4 presents a specific implementation of a software prototype called NATSIM. It includes an overview of the major components of NATSIM, its features, and its limitations. The technical issues encountered in the process of designing and implementing NATSIM are also discussed here. Section 5 contains examples from the production distribution domain and an evaluation of the performance of NATSIM. Section 6 summarizes significant results and offers suggestions for future investigations.

2. Background

Previous work related to this area can be summarized by examining three major topics: intelligent simulation environments, qualitative systems modeling, and natural language processing.

2.1. Intelligent Simulation Environments

Intelligent simulation environments are software environments that have the methodological knowledge of simulation study and simulation software generation. While not all intelligent simulation environments have a capability to generate simulation software, that ultimate goal will be reflected. As a result, knowledge-based simulation and simulation program generators are two areas of interest.

2.1.1. Knowledge-Based Simulation

Knowledge-based simulation makes simulation more effective for system analysis and decision support. The following discussion references many of the recent developments in the field.

A user-friendly front end, ECO, was developed for ecological modeling [23]. It utilizes a task specification as a formal representation of the mathematical structure of the model using a question-and-answer input format. ECO, which uses a system dynamics framework for representing ecological systems, was designed for ecologists with little or no modeling experience. NATSIM focuses on developing a generic systems representation and will not require the user to learn a set of allowable sentence forms. A computer-assisted modeling facility, MODELLER, has been produced for continuous systems simulation [20]. In MODELLER the description of the model and the experiment to be performed are entered by responding to prompts from the software. This facility differs from the proposed study because the user is required to learn the equation syntax, MODELLER, in order to specify a model. Heidorn [12, 13] implemented an automatic programming system that produced GPSS simulation programs from information about queueing problems obtained through natural language dialogue. However, the emphasis was on demonstration of automatic coding, and the system addressed only simple queuing problems. An intelligent interface for design and simulation was developed to simplify the use of large simulation codes used in analyzing and designing weapons [4]. The intelligent interface is used to generate simulation input parameters to an existing model.

Other related efforts are an expert manufacturing simulation system [7] and an expert simulation model builder [16]. Although both efforts focus on discrete system simulation, the former is objective or goal driven with a natural language interface, and the latter uses a graphic interface for model building. The potential for use of knowledge-based techniques in simulation is also demonstrated in the knowledge-based model construction (KBMC) system [24]. It builds SIMAN models of queuing systems by acquiring information from the user in an interactive question/answer dialog.

Consideration must be given to the human-to-computer interface in developing an intelligent simulation environment. Researchers have shown that redesign of the human-to-computer interface can make a substantial difference in learning time, performance, speed, error rates, and user satisfaction [30]. Users view their interactions with the computer in terms of goals rather than system commands [25]. The mental model, which the user forms of the system; the conceptual model, the designer's view of the system; and the system image, which the system presents to the user, must all be reconciled [25]. The methodology for systems representation and the interface must be designed so as not to impede the user in the description of the system. Several studies [17, 25] have gone beyond user-friendly systems to user-centered systems. To minimize ambiguity and circumvention by the user, it is clear from the literature that future efforts must bridge the gap between how the user thinks about a problem and how the problem is represented in the system [14, 15].

2.1.2. Simulation Program Generators

In an intelligent simulation environment, the user needs an intelligent interface between the simulation model and the simulation programming language. Simulation program generators (SPG) provide that function. The purpose of an SPG is to alleviate some of the difficulties experienced by modelers who use either a simulation programming language or a high-level language. The SPG acts as an intelligent interface between the simulation model and the target language and represents the model translation phase of the simulation analysis process. Learning how to use a new language demands an expenditure of time and patience that few are willing to give. Manuals are usually designed for those who are already familiar with the language but simply need a reference guide. Knowledge of other languages is of little help in learning how to use a new one, and it can often be a hindrance because of slight differences in syntax or terminology. Because of these barriers there is a growing interest in improved user interfaces for simulation code generators. Since the program generator can be built by a computer expert, the simulation language can be exploited to its full capability without requiring the user to become familiar with the intricate details of the interaction between the hardware and software. Subsequent upgrades to the simulation language can also be transparent to the user.

A significant conclusion from research on SPGs is that two types of knowledge are required to be coded: simulation modeling knowledge and domain knowledge [1]. In NATSIM the domain and simulation knowledge is used to generate a simulation language-independent formal model. The simulation program generator is domain independent and relies exclusively on knowledge about the syntax and limitation of the target language.

2.2. Qualitative Systems Modeling

Historically, systems modeling has been viewed as an intuitive process. Although intuition and experience play important roles, it has been acknowledged in the literature that many aspects of systems modeling can be made algorithmic [5, 6, 34]. Several approaches to qualitative modeling and detailed discussions on system dynamics have already been presented in this book. Therefore, we only present some of the major considerations and conclusions, relative to systems modeling.

2.2.1. General Systems Problem Solving

An architectural approach to systems problem solving places emphasis on the development of pragmatically sound principles for organizing systems and on capturing a comprehensive view of the systems problem-solving process [18, 19]. This approach has been examined with respect to concepts for the design and implementation of advanced simulation methodologies [26]. It was concluded that the computer offers too little help in developing models and cites inadequate conceptual frameworks as a major cause. Conceptual theories, which are drawn from systems theory, are needed for guiding the practice of modeling. One conceptual framework suggested is the separation of structure and behavior: Separate the specification of the model structure from the specification of experimentation. This approach is unbiased as to whether the variables are quantitative or qualitative and will ultimately reduce simulation costs because it simplifies complex models without invalidating the model.

2.2.2. System Dynamics

System dynamics allows for a systematic construction of qualitative models. The details of system dynamics are presented in another chapter; however, it is an ideal modeling framework for an intelligent simulation environment. In modeling feedback systems, it is important to focus on system structure rather than on specific content [27]. Structure is as important in determining system behavior as the individual components themselves [22]. System dynamics operates on the aggregate level and focuses on the rates of change of populations of entities. The structure defines how variables interact. The content is the meaning of those variables for a specific domain application. Two systems may have similar structure but quite different content. Model building is the process of extracting and defining the system in terms of its structure. Generic structures are feedback mechanisms that are transferable to new situations within a field and/or can be transferred across fields (context independent). Atoms of structure generate primitive feedback loops, which in turn generate the behavior of a basic process. Generic structures provide a more powerful approach than case-specific models and cut across disciplinary boundaries. Studying problems from a systems perspective is critical in identifying reasons for poor system performance.

The computer simulation language, DYNAMO [28], is the target simulation language in NATSIM. Potential users may lack the necessary skills and experience with computers to build models successfully and to perform analyses using DYNAMO. The J, K, L implementation of DYNAMO forces the simulation model to consist of a series of first-order difference equations. They are integrated numerically in DYNAMO by the Euler–Cauchy method. The limitation of the Euler–Cauchy method of integration is that it is highly sensitive to the size of the integration step and it tends to propagate errors.

2.3. Natural Language Processing

Natural language processing is a field within artificial intelligence that potentially will impact the number and nature of computer users and facilitate new areas for computer applications. Two subtopics of natural language processing briefly addressed here are the natural language interface and natural language understanding.

2.3.1. Natural Language Interface

A natural language interface is part of the solution to the problem posed by the continuing increase in the number and sophistication of simulation languages. A natural language interface for simulation has several advantages: It provides the user with an access to computational resources, it is flexible and requires little training, and it can be used to transform a description of what the user wants into a computer program that specifies how to accomplish it. It is important that users assess whether, and to what extent, natural language interface techniques can be used to solve their problems. Natural language and English language are not synonymous. The term *natural language* refers to a subset of the English language. The goal is to ensure that the subset is still very natural and capitalizes on the familiarity and power of the English language. The challenge is to select an appropriate subset.

A significant number of research efforts have used natural language interfaces to facilitate problem solving [7, 8, 11]. In Cleopatra the use of natural language allowed the system to capture the designers' intent, as well as the explicit description of the CAD systems behavior [29]. Mecho is a program that solves a wide range of mechanics problems from statements in both predicate calculus and English [3]. It uses a goal-directed algorithm for equation extraction. Because of the complexities involved in understanding a completely natural language, previous applications of natural language interfaces have been implemented primarily for database retrieval, or they have used constrained vocabularies, natural language menus, or controlled dialogue to communicate with the user.

2.3.2. Natural Language Understanding

The process of understanding language is very complex. Understanding sentences in context, resolving pronoun references or even making simple inferences requires a sophisticated amount of knowledge. Language is far more intricate and subtle than it appears on first inspection. Natural language understanding can be studied as a form of psychological modeling and/or as a means for effective human–computer interaction. In either case, the study of language understanding has led to the identification of fundamental problems of representation and reasoning.

The process of understanding or translating statements from the English subset into a program-specific form that will cause the appropriate actions to be performed is specifically the task of identifying the lexicon, sentence structure, and sentence meaning and resolving any ambiguities or poorly formed inputs. For the construction of operational systems, there are practical limitations on our ability to collect and organize the domain-specific knowledge for any substantial domain. Therefore, it is essential to identify manageable components of this domain-specific knowledge. This helps to construct portable systems, systems that can be readily moved from one domain to another. A description of the structure of information in a domain must be separated from the specific facts about a domain. This serves to rule out incorrect syntactic analyses that are caused by structural ambiguity due to adjunct placement and conjunction and by lexical ambiguity due to homographs [10]. System portability has been enhanced by using information of simple structure that can be isolated from the linguistic processing mechanisms.

These goals can be achieved by using a *sublanguage*. A sublanguage is a subsystem of language that behaves essentially like the whole language. Successful computer processing of natural language requires detailed knowledge at many levels. The sublanguage is clearly systematic in structure and meaning, with properties that have been defined by linguists and computer scientists. Studies reveal the close correspondence between grammatical organization of a sublanguage and the information bearing properties of that same sublanguage [21]. Restrictions on word combinations, that is, sublanguage co-occurrence patterns, help to resolve syntactic ambiguity.

Sublanguage analysis facilitates disambiguation of most polysemous words. Sublanguage structures may also represent patterns that include representation of domain knowledge not explicit in the sublanguage text. Each domain represents a highly circumscribed sublanguage. This makes it possible to obtain correct sentence analysis with high reliability. The necessity for incorporating domain-specific semantic information into natural language processing systems is recognized [9]. A successful understanding system incorporates knowledge about language, grammar, semantics, and the specific domain of the problem.

PHRasal ANalyzer (PHRAN) [32] is an understanding system that incorporates knowledge about language, grammar, semantics, and the specific domain of the problem. It is an approach to language analysis that treats the phrase as the basic unit of language by pairing a pattern and its meaning in a pattern–concept pair. This is a very flexible parsing mechanism that can handle literal phrases, phrases in which order varies, phrases that allow all verb forms, and any combination of these so that implicit and explicit meaning can be captured. PHRAN offers flexibility that supports a complex language interface. The understanding process reads the input text and tries to find the phrasal patterns that apply to it. PHRAN is composed of three major parts: a database of pattern–concept pairs, a set of comprehension routines, and a program that suggests appropriate pattern–concept pairs. It takes English sentences for input and generates output that is similar in format to conceptual dependencies [33].

There are a number of difficulties in natural language understanding that are discussed in the literature but have not been resolved, for example, quantifier scoping, modifier attachment, coercion, ellipsis, and pronoun references. It is clear, nonetheless, that sublanguage analysis can be used as a computational tool.

2.4. Summary

Artificial intelligence and simulation are complementary technologies. Each modeling phase, from problem formulation to code generation to output analysis, can be enhanced by providing intelligent support to the user. An intelligent simulation environment will revolutionize the practice of simulation. Studying modeling from a systems perspective provides insight into better methodologies for computer-assisted modeling. System dynamics provides a framework in which to apply the idea of systems theory to problems. A systems approach emphasizes the connections among the various parts that constitute the whole and cuts across disciplinary boundaries. A natural language interface for simulation modeling is an attractive alternative since it would support the variety and complexity of inputs that would be encountered. Using natural language as the simulation language can be effective for the novice or intermittent user and for the user who has expertise in the task domain, but is less knowledgeable about computer concepts.

NATSIM builds on the aforementioned accomplishments to address some new issues. The specification of a methodology for model building, which can be implemented as a computer algorithm, is a critical step in developing an end-to-end intelligent simulation capability. By providing a natural language interface to this intelligent environment, the number of potential simulation users is significantly increased .

3. Intelligent System Modeling

System modeling is a problem-solving technique that is advocated for the analysis of proposed and existing systems. To provide tools to automate model building, a more comprehensive view of the system modeling process should be taken. Specifically, basic principles of system modeling must be defined, and the system analysis process must be characterized. Our approach was to define a user-friendly interface to support the model-building process, to develop a mechanism for integrating the static and dynamic knowledge bases needed to generate a model of the system, and to define a computationally efficient formalism for representing the model.

Figure 11.1 depicts the functions of a generic intelligent system modeling environment. The human-to-computer interface is through natural language and is supported by an application domain vocabulary and a system dynamics knowledge base. The natural language input is transformed into an internal declarative representation. The model generation function accepts the de-

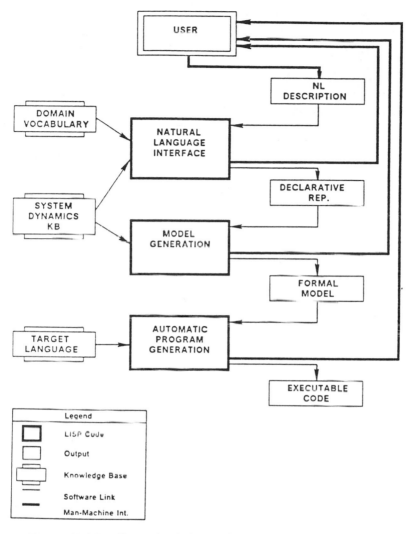

FIGURE 11.1. Intelligent simulation environment system flow diagram.

clarative representation as input, processes it using the system dynamics knowledge base, and generates a formal model. The automatic program generation function translates the formal model into the executable source code for a specific high-order or simulation language. The concepts underlying each function are presented in the following sections.

3.1. A Natural Language Interface for System Modeling

The development of a methodology for building a natural language interface for system dynamics modeling is a significant step. A system description in

English is preferable to conventional input formats because (1) it meets the experienced modeler's requirements for ease of specification, (2) it simultaneously provides novice or intermittent modelers the support and guidance needed, (3) a computer that understands English is more accessible to anyone who speaks English, and (4) it is excellent for describing a problem, as opposed to programming languages that are process oriented, that is, good for describing a method for finding a solution to a problem. A natural language interface is feasible for system dynamics modeling because of the inherent systematic structure of system dynamics models. There are a limited number of objects; the linkages and interrelationships between objects are well defined and limited in number.

Building a natural language interface requires the incorporation of domain-specific knowledge into the understanding system. Two major tasks pursuant to meeting this requirement are (1) development of the domain specific knowledge base and (2) development of a suitable parsing capability using an existing natural language parsing tool. This section addresses each of these tasks separately.

3.1.1. Domain Knowledge Using Sublanguage

In building a natural language interface for system dynamics modeling, two domains must be considered: the simulation or modeling framework domain and the application domain. The descriptions provided by users may use jargon specific to the simulation domain and more than likely will use terminology that has a specific meaning for a specific application domain. As concluded by Grishman [10] and Marsh [21], our ability to collect and organize the domain-specific knowledge for any substantial domain is limited. An alternative approach is to identify significant yet manageable components of this domain-specific knowledge, that is, a sublanguage. The development of the knowledge bases needed for a natural language interface can be enhanced by utilizing sublanguage concepts.

A sublanguage is a comfortable but bounded subset of the English language that behaves like the whole language over the domain in which it is defined. There are numerous advantages in using a sublanguage. The size and complexity of the language understanding problem are significantly reduced. The correspondence between grammatical organization and information supports analysis on the syntactic level. Semantic analysis is aided by reducing the number of possible definitions or interpretations for a given word or phrase. There are some drawbacks to using a sublanguage. It is only a subset of the language and therefore by definition excludes portions of the language. As a result, there are elements that are "unknown" to the sublanguage. There is also the difficulty of defining the sublanguage: what should be included and what should be excluded. Nonetheless, using a sublanguage is a reasonable approach to capturing domain specific knowledge.

To build a natural language understanding capability requires identifying the sublanguage, organizing it, and integrating it into the natural language processing system. Using the discovery procedure for sublanguages presented by Grishman, the information structure is characterized. A set of semantic categories can be defined, and the predicate-argument relationships among members of these categories can be identified. The semantic categories and relationships reflect the simulation domain knowledge, and the specific assignment of words and phrases reflects the application domain knowledge. Both types of knowledge are vital to the success of the understanding process.

3.1.1.1. Simulation Knowledge

The semantic categories and relationships of the sublanguage reflect the simulation domain knowledge. They capture the concepts unique to the system dynamics modeling framework. The semantic categories identified for system dynamics modeling are level, person, physflow, rate, source, and sink. Each noun encountered in the sublanguage can be associated with one of these semantic categories.

The level category is assigned to nouns that have the properties associated with levels in system dynamics. The words in this category are objects that have an ability for accumulation. The semantic category called *person* includes nouns that possess human qualities. This distinction is made because there are functions that people can perform but other physical objects cannot. The physflow category represents the physical objects that have the ability to move. In the system dynamics modeling framework, material flow is represented by the physflow category. The rate category represents nouns that in the context of system dynamics describe how items enter or leave a level. In general, these are nouns that can also be used as adjectives. The source and sink categories are used for nouns that are designated beginning points or end points for material flow. In addition to having other semantic properties, a manufacturer may be designated as a source, and a customer may be designated to be a sink.

The predicate argument relationships for system dynamics are material flow and information flow. These relationships are associated with verbs in the sublanguage. The semantic categories and relationships form the basis for understanding by the natural language processing system.

3.1.1.2. Application-Domain Knowledge

The application-domain knowledge is defined by the specific words and phrases that comprise the sublanguage. The words and terms included in the sublanguage are those that have a specific meaning for the application domain. Nouns are assigned semantic categories, which are used for disambiguation of the input. Each word of the sublanguage is assigned syntactic categories consistent with traditional English grammar. The phrases or idioms unique to the application domain constitute additional knowledge, which is needed to support the natural language understanding function.

The production-distribution domain is a typical application domain for system dynamics modeling. The major activities in this domain can be cate-

TABLE 11.1. Sublanguage.

Nouns	Verbs	Phrases
Customer	Arrive	Backlog
Demand	Leave	Continuous review policy
Distributor	Order	Demand rate
Factory	Receive	Enter the system
Inventory	Reorder	Fixed order quantity
Material	Ship	Lead time
Retailer	Shelve	Raw material
Source	Store	Work-in-process

gorized as the demand for items, the receipt of items, and the review of inventory policies to determine the next appropriate action. Multistage production-distribution systems can be simulated easily using a system dynamics model because of the inherent framework of physical and information flows. Some of the nouns, verbs, and phrases that would be included in a sublanguage for this domain are shown in Table 11.1. Some of the words are specific to the production distribution domain, for example, inventory, fixed order quantity, and reorder. Some of the words have specific meaning in the simulation domain, for example, source, period, and enter the system. Examples of the association of semantic categories with the nouns of the sublanguage are shown in Table 11.2. The singular form of the noun is given, followed by the assigned semantic categories in parentheses. Some nouns are assigned two categories, which indicates that the word can be used in two different ways. For example, demand can refer to the customer demand or to the demand rate. By assigning two different categories, a parser can check which case is appropriate in a given instance.

The same approach can be taken in other application domains. Consider as examples the population and ecological domains. Population dynamics is an area that has been studied extensively using the system dynamics framework. The dynamics of population growth plays a significant role in predator–prey studies, in tracking the spread of disease in different age groups of a population, and in work-force studies.

Ecology is the study of the interaction among animals, plants, and their environment. The nonliving and living parts of the system are constantly interacting. Many problems within this domain can be studied using the system dynamics methodology. Ecological models can be used to test an ecologist's assumptions about how the system works, as decision analysis tools for understanding the potential impacts of various management options, and as tools for prediction in environmental impact assessments.

In each case, the semantic categories and relationships of the sublanguage remain the same. The specific words and phrases that comprise the sublanguage change. The sublanguage defines the domain specific subset of English that must be understood. The semantic categories and relationships provide a mechanism for assigning meaning to the words and phrases in the

TABLE 11.2. Nouns.

Box (physflow)
Customer (person)
Day (time)
Delivery (physflow)
Demand (sink rate)
Distributor (level)
Factory (level)
Goods (physflow)
Inventory (level)
Item (physflow)
Horizon (time)
Level (accumulation level)
Material (physflow)
Month (time)
Order (physflow)
Period (time)
Pool (level)
Rate (rate)
Retailer (level)
Shipment (physflow)
Sink (sink)
Source (source)
Storage (level)
Supply (physflow)
Time (time)
Unit (physflow)
Warehouse (level)
Year (time)

sublanguage that forms the domain-specific knowledge base. The meanings assigned are used to guide and support parsing.

3.1.2. Multiple Sentence Parsing

The most successful implementations of natural language interfaces have been in the area of database retrieval. The user is permitted to formulate short questions, which are parsed by the system, and the required information is retrieved. ADAM [8] is a natural language system designed to understand specifications, but it can only process a single sentence at a time. Although humans, even young children, do it every day, understanding natural language is a complex process even when the context has been established. Researchers continue to investigate different methodologies for language understanding, and many problems remain. In the interim, systems that have been developed have overcome these problems by severely restricting the inputs allowed by the user. This has been accomplished by using natural language menus, constrained vocabularies, constrained input formats, and input limited to a single sentence.

Since simulation models generally cannot be described using a single sentence, it was necessary to develop an approach to natural language processing that would allow multiple sentences to be parsed correctly. System descriptions from several textbooks on simulation modeling were heuristically examined to detect patterns in the way that the information is presented. It was found that elements or relationships that are introduced in one sentence are referenced again, implicitly or explicitly, in subsequent sentences. The latter reference was generally used to supply specific parameter values or other support information. As a result, it was determined that a frame-based approach to knowledge representation would support a multisentence natural language processing system. In reality, verbal descriptions would not be as well organized as the descriptions found in textbooks. People may present the entire system structure before providing specific parameter values. Or, by contrast, the individual may first provide a detailed description of the objects in the system and then specify the relationships between the objects. In either case, a multisentence processing system must parse the input paragraph and store the relevant information in an accessible format.

By using frames, the system can maintain the context of the input description across sentence boundaries. Slots or facets that are not filled in the first sentence can be assigned default values. The default values can be replaced if the information is presented later in the description. Default values can be predetermined or computed, or if necessary, the default can be a flag to the system, to indicate that the user must be prompted to supply this value. This approach allows the maximum flexibility to the user for system description. The input format is unconstrained. The understanding process is aided by the knowledge representation data structure and the specification of the sublanguage.

3.2. A Framework for the Analysis of Feedback Systems

The analysis of feedback systems is simplified by examining the structure of these systems. The concept of a system implies the existence of interaction and interdependence. All relationships in feedback systems can be defined in terms of flows, accumulations, and information links. The variables in the system are either rates, levels, or auxiliaries. Level variables represent the system state. Rate variables represent how fast a level variable is changing. Auxiliary variables are used to simplify computations and/or collect information. Models of systems are formulated using three components: feedback loops, levels, and rates. The feedback loop is a path connecting system state, action, and information. The interrelationships are systematic with a limited number of variations in format.

The following framework for analysis is suggested. The theory for analysis of feedback systems is that the system structure can be determined by a two-phased analysis: analysis of the physical flow of materials and analysis of the flow of information. The methodology for analysis of feedback systems can be specified as

1. identification and analysis of material flow,
2. identification and analysis of primary information flow,
3. identification and analysis of secondary (auxiliary) information flow, and
4. instantiation of the model with the simulation and domain knowledge bases.

The material flow provides the basic structure of the system. When combined with the principles of system dynamics, the material flow can be used to resolve ambiguities in the flow of information. Material flow is the physical movement of material from source to sink. Once the flow path of material is established, objects that represent accumulation are identified as levels. Rates control and decouple levels; hence, their existence is dependent on and defined by the existence of levels. Although the rate relation can take many forms and be quite complex, structurally there are only two possibilities. The first configuration is a rate followed by a level that uses information regarding the state of the level and has a constant as an input. Negative and positive feedback relationships have this structure. The second configuration exists when a level is followed by a rate. The rate in this case may use information related to the state of the level. This structure is seen in relationships that can be represented by exponential decay.

The distinction between primary and secondary information is determined by the source and complexity of the information. Simple constants and information that originates from a level or rate are defined as primary information flows. The secondary or auxiliary information represents combinations of primary information and/or rate information and/or other auxiliary information. The secondary information is used to formulate auxiliary variable relationships. The auxiliary variable establishes relationships between variables using various algebraic and trigonometric functions.

The instantiation process provides the common sense and experimental knowledge to the analysis process. It ensures that the algorithm generates a complete model. It checks for missing information, inconsistencies, and logical conflicts. Although it is incapable of resolving conflict, it will identify problems. To resolve a problem, interaction with the user would be required.

Using these steps, the structure of the feedback system is completely identified and forms a formal model of the system. This methodology can be used in several different ways. Most obviously, it can be used to analyze a model of a feedback system. The same methodology can be used to process natural language descriptions of feedback systems. And finally, the methodology advocated here can be used to generate simulation code systematically.

3.3. Representation of the Formal Model

A representation formalism for the model of systems was developed. A well-defined representation formalism for the model supports a systematic approach to model building. A good formalism simplifies a complex problem because it helps to identify the underlying structures. The formalism must be context free and independent of the target implementation language. The formalism must be suitable for acquiring information during the problem formulation process, should support verification and validation phases, and should not hinder the user during the experimentation phase. The representation of the model must capture the structure of the system.

The knowledge representation formalism chosen for the formal model is a frame system, sometimes referred to as an entity-relationship data structure. Using this data structure, a neutral and computationally efficient representation of the model can be designed. This representation formalism facilitates knowledge retrieval and manipulation. In addition, objects can be defined to have specific properties so that when a specific incidence of the object is encountered it inherits the predefined properties. The existence of an object can also trigger other procedures.

The representation formalism was developed after analysis of the structure of the systems in the class. It was desired to use the same structure for representing objects in the model as for capturing the relations of the model. This makes it easy to retrieve both types of information, add new information as it is obtained or inferred, and continuously check for knowledge-base conflicts and inconsistencies before adding new knowledge. In this section the representation of objects and relations is presented, and examples within each category are explained.

3.3.1. Representation of Objects

Three kinds of objects are defined in the representation structure: levels, rates, and auxiliaries. Levels are defined by the four attributes: name of the level, rates that flow into the level, rates that flow out of the level, and initial accumulation in the level. Figure 11.2 shows an example of a level definition.

In this instance, the level name is *warehouse*, the order rate flows into the level, the shipping rate flows out of the level, and the accumulation in the level when the model is initialized is 500 units. Any of the attributes and their associated values can be asserted onto the knowledge base at any time.

Rates are defined by the three attributes: name of the rate, level it flows into, and level it flows from. Figure 11.3 shows an example of a rate definition. In this instance, the rate name is *order*, and it flows into the level named *warehouse*. The variable *source* indicates that this rate defines the start of the

```
(level   (lname warehouse)
         (ratein order)
         (rateout shipping)
         (initial_level 500) )
```

FIGURE 11.2. An example of a level definition.

FIGURE 11.3. An example of a rate definition.

```
(rate      (rname order)

           (from "source")

           (to warehouse) )
```

FIGURE 11.4. An example of an auxiliary definition.

```
(auxiliary    (aname average_order)

              (to shipping) )
```

material flow in the model. Again, any of the attributes and their associated values can be asserted onto the knowledge base at any time.

Auxiliaries are defined by two attributes: name of the auxiliary and name of the rate or other auxiliary that it supports. Figure 11.4 shows an example of an auxiliary definition. In this instance, the auxiliary name is *average_order*, and it provides information to the shipping rate. Any of the attributes and their associated values can be asserted onto the knowledge base at any time.

3.3.2. Representation of Relationships

The model relationships are also represented using an entity-relationship data structure. Material flow and information flow are captured. In addition, a hierarchical view of all objects in the system is achieved by maintaining a list of all levels, a list of all rates, and a list of all auxiliaries, as shown in Figure 11.5.

Material flow shows the movement of physical objects through the system. This is accomplished by defining, for each object, all sources of material to that object and all destinations of material from that object. A general example is provided in Figure 11.6. Each level can have multiple inflows and outflows. The shipping rate controls the flow of material between the warehouse and inventory. The demand rate controls the flow of material between inventory and the ultimate customer, who is modeled as a sink.

The information flow relationships are captured in a similar manner. Information can originate from any node in the system, but it can terminate only at a rate or auxiliary variable. Therefore, the representation of information flow can be associated with the node at which it terminates, independent of whether it is primary or secondary information flow. This serves two purposes: It provides a unique way to represent all information in the system, and it supports knowledge retrieval and manipulation needed to generate the simulation model. For example, to generate a rate equation, the model-building system must be able to determine all information that flows into that rate. An example of the entity-relationship structure used to represent information flow relationships is given in Figure 11.7.

```
(all_levels   (lname  warehouse)
              (lname  inventory)
                  .
                  .
                  .        )

(all_rates    (rname  order)
              (rname  shipping)
                  .
                  .
                  .        )

(all_auxs     (aname  desired_inventory)
              (aname  average_shipping)
                  .
                  .
                  .        )
```

FIGURE 11.5. Representation of objects.

```
(level    (lname   inventory)
          (ratein shipping)
          (ratein returns)
          (ratein   .  )
          (ratein   .  )
          (ratein   .  )
          (rateout demand)
          (rateout damaged)
          (rateout  .  )
          (rateout  .  )
          (rateout  .  ) )
```

FIGURE 11.6. Representation of material flow.

```
(information     (flows_to shipping)

                 (flows_from warehouse)

                 (life 4) )
```

FIGURE 11.7. Entity-relationship structure.

The first two attributes in Figure 11.7 indicate where the information originates and terminates. The third attribute defines the information, for example, whether it is an algebraic computation involving other variables or a simple constant. In this instance, the information flows from the level *warehouse* and is used to compute the shipping rate. The last attribute, *life*, indicates that the shipping rate has an exponential decay structure. In this case, the attribute *flows–from* and its value, *warehouse*, is redundant information. Given that the shipping rate has an exponential decay structure, information must come from the preceding level, by default.

We have described the representation formalism developed to capture a formal model of systems. The formalism is domain independent and independent of the target simulation language. It provides a description of the model in a form that is easily implemented on the computer, supports symbolic and numeric processing, and stores the model in a format that can be used to generate the corresponding simulation code.

3.4. Automatic Generation of Simulation Code

Simulation program generators are the interface between the model of the system and the target implementation language. The implementation language may be either a conventional procedural language or a simulation language. In the literature, program generators use prewritten code modules and only allow the user to specify required input parameters. Using the methodology presented here, the user specifies the model using natural language, and the code for this model is automatically generated. The input to the program generator is a formally structured representation of the model. This allows the program generator to be suitable for a large class of systems, specifically systems that can be modeled using system dynamics. The program generator relieves the user of the need to learn the syntax of the target language. If developed by a programming specialist, it can be optimized for a specific hardware environment, software upgrades can be integrated independently of the user, and the code generator can be tested and verified.

Since the systems being considered are within the system dynamics world view, an obvious choice for the target language is DYNAMO. DYNAMO was developed specifically for system dynamics modeling and has features that make it a good choice for the target language. There is a one-to-one correspondence between the objects in the formal representation and DYNAMO. Each level in the representation corresponds to a level equation in DYNAMO. The same is true for rates and auxiliaries. Another attractive feature is the fact that DYNAMO is a simulation language and, as such, has built in capabilities specifically designed to support simulation experiments and to generate appropriate output histories. DYNAMO is also flexible because it accepts the model equations in any order. The DYNAMO processor determines the order in which equations should be evaluated.

The major drawback to using DYNAMO is that it uses a method that is based on first-order difference equations and is known to be error prone. The integration method is highly sensitive to the size of the computation interval, DT. The automatic program generator can be developed to address this issue. The program generator can be designed to suggest appropriate values for DT based on the specific parameters of the model. In this way, the program generator is helping the modeler to build a valid model.

However, DYNAMO is a FORTRAN-based language, that is, the DYNAMO statements are translated into FORTRAN statements. This implies that the automatic program generator could be built to generate FORTRAN and to use a different integration method. The disadvantage to this approach is that the other advantages associated with using DYNAMO are lost. The correspondence between objects in the model and objects in the language would no longer exist. FORTRAN is a procedural language and does not correspond directly to the entity-relationship structure used in the model representation. A special output processor also would have to be developed to collect and present the relevant statistics.

Other continuous system simulation languages, for example, SLAM, could also be the target implementation language. In any event, the automatic program generator must be designed to accommodate the specific requirements and constraints of the language chosen.

3.5. Summary

We have presented a methodology for building a natural language interface to system dynamics modeling. To generate a simulation model from a natural language description requires (1) a parsing technique to map the natural language into a declarative representation of the knowledge expressed in the natural language description, (2) an algorithm to map the representation of the input into a formal representation of the model, and (3) a program generator to translate the formal representation into a language-specific simulation code. The parsing technique must process multiple sentence input and be able to resolve ambiguities in context. The algorithm for generating the formal representation must provide the capability to analyze and distinguish between material flow and information flow. The formal representation of the model must efficiently capture the structure of and the relationships among the objects in the system. The program generator translates the formal representation of the model into executable source code.

The approach can be generalized to a broad class of problems. A prototype implementation of these concepts, NATSIM, is presented in Section 4.

4. NATSIM: A Natural-Language-Based Simulation System

A specific implementation of an intelligent simulation environment for system dynamics modeling, NATSIM, is presented. NATSIM is a model development shell that has a natural language interface and is based on the generic and domain-independent structures of the system dynamics methodology. It combines symbolic and numeric processing to generate simulation codes. An overview of NATSIM is provided in Section 4.1. The knowledge bases that support NATSIM are presented in Section 4.2. Examples reflecting the NATSIM capabilities are presented in Section 5.

4.1. NATSIM Overview

The intelligence of NATSIM lies in its knowledge of simulation, system dynamics, the application domain, and the target simulation language. This information resides in knowledge bases that are manipulated using an entity-relationship data-structure model. NATSIM accepts a system description in a comfortable but restricted subset of English text, generates a system representation, and produces executable codes in the target language. All components of NATSIM were written in Franz LISP. It was implemented on a Digital Equipment Corporation (DEC) VAX 11/780 computer under the Berkeley UNIX[1] 4.2 operating system. LISP was chosen as a base for developing NATSIM for a combination of reasons. LISP is extensible, has dynamic storage allocation, and is generally good for symbol manipulation. Excellent LISP programming environments already exist. In addition, the parser used in NATSIM already existed and was developed in LISP. The implementation language is fully transparent to the user.

A primary design goal for NATSIM was to maintain knowledge bases separate from knowledge processing, thereby making the system domain independent. Speed of operation was not a major concern, but the system is designed to run efficiently with reasonable response times. The objective was to evaluate the potential for managers to use such a system, given the limitations of a particular parser or simulation language. The control structure of NATSIM is separate from the knowledge bases so that representational and processing issues can be resolved independently.

---

[1] UNIX is a registered trademark of AT&T Bell Laboratories.

For the purpose of having a practical base for discussion, the production-distribution domain will be used as the application domain. This domain is complex enough to provide substantial subproblems but not so unbounded that a useful working system must include a hopelessly large and unwieldy repertoire of knowledge. It is used to demonstrate a realistic use of natural language, which is participation in a purposive dialogue. Multistage production/distribution systems have been selected to demonstrate the feasibility of using natural language exclusively as an interface for simulation. This particular domain is attractive for study because it represents a large class of operational problems that must be solved. Complex production/distribution systems can be simulated easily using a system dynamics model because of the inherent framework of physical and information flows. Although the prototype system uses a production/distribution domain, NATSIM is methodologically context independent.

Potential users of NATSIM are expected to have varying levels of expertise in the specific domain of application and/or simulation. All users are presumed to have some modeling experience. Although they may not be formally trained in model building, they may have built models informally and should understand the requirements and limitations of the modeling process. Clearly, users who have experience with the systems dynamics methodology will better understand the theoretical concepts that underlie NATSIM. As a result, these users will find it easier to validate the models generated by NATSIM. The prototype system, NATSIM, has limited performance capabilities because of the size of the lexicon and knowledge bases supporting it. The system has 40 verbs, 40 nouns, and 200 patterns for the production-distribution domain. NATSIM users are assumed to have reasonably good typing skills to generate the initial input of the system description. Due to limitations in PHRAN, the user is prohibited from using indefinite articles.

The processing, input, and outputs of NATSIM are depicted in Figure 11.8. The user generates a verbal description of the system under study. This description is processed by a natural language understanding system (NLU). The NLU is a semantic-based parser, PHRAN, with an application-specific vocabulary database and a minimal knowledge base of system dynamics. It uses the pattern–concept pair construct. With each pattern, which may be a word or phrase, it associates a meaning at the semantic and syntactic level by attaching a concept to the pattern. PHRAN reads the sentence from left to right one word at a time. After each word, the knowledge base is examined for patterns that are consistent with the input that has been read so far. The output from NLU is a declarative representation of the meaning of the parsed and processed input statement. This declarative representation is based on the conceptual dependencies and forms the input to the model generator (MG).

The MG uses an extensive knowledge base of system dynamics to draw inferences regarding the system being studied. The MG generates a language-

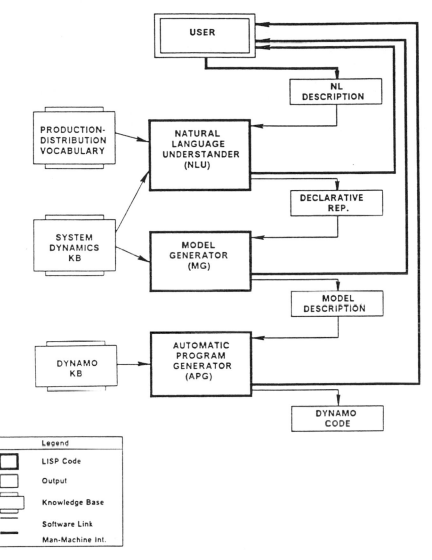

FIGURE 11.8. NATSIM system flow diagram.

independent complete model description. If the MG detects conflicts, in-consistencies, or an incomplete specification, it queries the user for clarifica-tion or additional information. The user's responses are processed directly by the MG (i.e., they are not processed by NLU). The model description is then processed by the automatic program generator. In this implementation of NATSIM, DYNAMO is the target simulation language. DYNAMO was selected because it is a special-purpose language designed for simulating system dynamics models. It also has an advantage in that the statements can be given in any order, since DYNAMO will automatically order equations for the correct computation. The DYNAMO program generator knowledge base is used to formulate the DYNAMO specific syntax and control statement constructs needed to generate an executable simulation code. The program generator will, as much as possible, determine default values for control elements, but also query the user for information such as program name, run length, and output parameters. An example of DPG dialog and output is shown in Figure 11.9.

```
t
- > (progen all_levels all_rates all_auxs)
Please give this program a name test2
The default computation interval is 0.25
   Is that acceptable? (y or n) n
What is the computational interval  2
The default start time is  0
   Is that acceptable? (y or n) n
What is the simulation start time? 25
The default stop time is  65
   Is that acceptable? (y or n) y
ok
The default print period is  2
   Is that acceptable? (y or n) n
What should the print interval be?  5
The default plot period is  2
   Is that acceptable? (y or n) y
ok
 * test 2
NOTE
NOTE  LEVEL  EQUATIONS
NOTE
L lev1.K = lev1.J + DT*(0.0-rate2.JK)
N lev1 = 0
L lev2.K = lev2.J + DT*(rate2.JK-rate3.JK)
N lev2 = 0
NOTE
NOTE   RATE EQUATIONS
NOTE
R rate 2.KL = (10-lev1.K)/2
R rate 3.KL = lev2.K/3
NOTE
NOTE   AUXILIARY EQUATIONS
NOTE
NOTE
NOTE   CONTROL STATEMENTS
NOTE
N TIME = 25
SPEC DT = 2,LENGTH = 65,PRTPER = 5,PLTPER = 2
PLOT lev1 = 1,lev2 = 2
PLOT rate2 = 3.rate3 = 4
PRINT lev1,lev2
PRINT rate2,rate3
RUN   test2
nil
- >  (exit)
```

FIGURE 11.9. DPG dialog and output.

Domain Knowledge Base	NLU (PHRAN)	Model Generator	Dynamo Program Generator	Dynamo Knowledge Base
	System Dynamics Knowledge Base			

FIGURE 11.10. Knowledge-base interfaces for NATSIM.

4.2. Knowledge Bases

The intelligence of NATSIM lies in its knowledge of what is required, what ranges and forms are within limits, and what procedures are followed. This information resides in knowledge bases that are manipulated using an entity-relationship data structure. The knowledge bases that support NATSIM give the system extensive capability and flexibility. The capability is exhibited by the fact that simulation code is generated based solely on a natural language description from the user. NATSIM is extremely flexible because it is data driven and easily portable to other domains. Building a simulation model requires the integration of simulation methodology knowledge and application domain knowledge [1]. To generate the simulation code for that model in a specific language also requires detailed knowledge of that language. The knowledge base interfaces to NATSIM are shown in Figure 11.10. The three knowledge bases underlying NATSIM are the production-distribution domain knowledge base, the system dynamics knowledge base, and the DYNAMO knowledge base.

The first time each knowledge base is built, it requires a significant amount of effort on the part of the designer. The application domain knowledge base is specific to each domain. It should be built to reflect the collective knowledge of the users, thus providing a better knowledge base for each individual user. The system dynamics knowledge base does not change between problems or from one domain to another. It is also independent of the target simulation language. The knowledge base for the APG is only built once for any particular language. It is only modified if the language changes. It is much easier to reflect these changes in the knowledge base than to require high-level managers or intermittent users to keep abreast of these changes. Detailed descriptions of each knowledge base can be found in [2].

4.3. Summary

We presented NATSIM, an intelligent model-development shell. It allows the user to build system dynamics models using natural language. NATSIM accepts a systems description in a comfortable but restricted subset of English text, generates a formal model, and produces executable codes in the target lnguage. The knowledge bases that support NATSIM provide domain knowledge, system dynamics knowledge, and simulation language knowledge. Although the examples provided are drawn from the production/distribution domain, NATSIM is conceptually domain independent.

The major activities in the production-distribution domain can be categorized as the demand for items, the receipt of items, and the review of inventory policies to determine the next appropriate action. Natural language descriptions of these systems can be decomposed to identify the pertinent information in each of these categories. This is one way in which NATSIM uses the domain knowledge to support processing of the natural language input.

5. Model Building with NATSIM

The capabilities and limitations of NATSIM are presented in this section. An example is presented in detail to demonstrate each processing phase. The application domain used is production-distribution systems. The system dynamics and production-distribution knowledge bases provide the domain-specific knowledge needed to support processing by NATSIM. The target simulation language is DYNAMO. In addition to the actual source code generated, intermediate outputs from the natural language understander (NLU) and model generator (MG) are shown.

A general discussion of evaluation issues is presented in Section 5.2. The specific evaluation approach taken is described and the results of an analysis of NATSIM performance is provided. NATSIM is analyzed by examining its performance on a set of carefully selected test cases and by evaluating a representative set of potential users.

The examples and test cases presented are not intended to be all encompassing or extremely sophisticated. NATSIM, as it exists today, could not be put on an analyst's desk. The purpose of the prototype is to show the functionality of the system in the context of a real problem domain. Development of a system that would be appropriate for system analysis and decision support would require a greater number of rate relation structures and a significantly larger vocabulary. Issues relating to the deployment of a system of this type in a real-world setting will be presented as part of the evaluation.

5.1. NATSIM Processing

The major activities in the production-distribution domain can be categorized as the demand for items, the receipt of items, and the review of inventory policies to determine the next appropriate action [31]. Natural language descriptions of these systems can be decomposed to identify the pertinent information in each of these categories. An example from the production-distribution domain is presented to illustrate NATSIM's capability to understand a natural language system description and to generate the corresponding DYNAMO model of the system. The problem description has been adapted from problems found in textbooks. In cases where words had to be

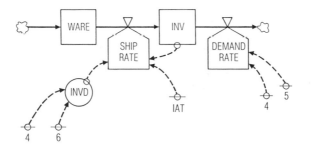

FIGURE 11.11. Example 1 system flow diagram.

added or modified to account for limitations in PHRAN, the changes are enclosed in square brackets.

5.1.1. Example 1

The natural language description for this problem is given below. Figure 11.11 is the flow diagram for this system.

[The] shipments are made out of [the] inventory to [the] customers. As soon as an item is shipped, it [the item] is reordered. The order goes into [the] warehouse. The order arrives into [the] inventory after a delay of four weeks. The demand changes uniformly from 15 to 20 units.

This is a system composed of two levels, warehouse and inventory, and three rates: order, arrival, and shipping. The input is parsed by NLU. Semantic categories are assigned to each word and stored in the knowledge base. Patterns that are recognized trigger the creation of slots to be filled. An excerpt from the output produced by the parser is shown in Figure 11.12. The word *inventory* is recognized as belonging to the semantic category of levels. The PHRAN system generates a token, *inventory2*, which is an instance of the noun inventory. In the model generator (MG), multiple references to the same object are resolved. *Orders* is recognized as being a physflow through the system. *Items* and *shipments* are also physical flows. If the structure detected by the MG indicated disjoint paths, this information would be used to decide which elements were flowing in which structure. The *group* specification indicates that plural forms were used for shipments and customers. The singular form *shipment* is a member of the group, *shipments*, and *customer* is a member of the group *customers*. Information about the rate between inventory and customers is also given. The system recognizes that references to *the demand* means *the customer demand*. The meaning associated with the sentence *As soon as an item is shipped it is reordered* is that a continuous review policy is used.

This declarative representation of the input is then passed to the MG. This

```
((quantity (object units1))
 (measure (object units1))
 (rate (object demand1))
 (sink (object demand1))
 (level (object inventory2))
 (physflow (object order2))
 (level (object warehouse 1))
 (physflow (object order1))
 (physflow (object item2))
 (items (object item2))
 (physflow (object item1))
 (items (object item1))
 (person (object customers1))
 (customer (object customers1))
 (level (object inventory1))
 (physflow (object shipments1)))

(group (object nil) (member shipment))
(group (object nil (member customer))
(group (object nil) (member unit))
(number (group units1) (number 15))
(number (group units1) (number 20))

(rate (rname 'unspecified')
    (from inventory1)
    (physflow shipments1)
    (to customers1)
    (continuous_review_policy))
nil
item2
nil
(rate (rname 'unspecified')
    (from 'unspecified')
    (physflow order1))
    (to warehouse1))
(rate (rname 'unspecified')
    (from 'unspecified')
    (physflow order2)
    (to inventory2)
    (information (delay (amount (time_measure (amount 1.0)
    (units month))))))
(information (demand1 sink) (uniform (15 20 ) )
units1
(284.5 . 97.2)
```

FIGURE 11.12. Example 1 excerpt from NLU output.

function compiles the information from the parser and the system dynamics knowledge base and determines the end-to-end flow of materials and interfaces between rates and levels. It checks for missing information and ensures consistency of the information provided by the parser. In this case, the user is prompted to supply the initial quantities for the two levels in the system. The MG stores a formal representation of the model in its knowledge base. To provide a simple explanation capability, the MG produces output for

MATERIAL FLOW

order ----> warehouse ----> arrival ----> inventory ----> shipment
end of input structure

INFORMATION FLOW

order is of type timesf
(1 shipment) = = = = > order

shipment is of type noisef
(15 20) = = = = > shipment

arrival is of type exp_decay
4 = = = = > arrival < = = = = warehouse

AUXILIARY FLOWS

FIGURE 11.13. Example 1 excerpt from the model generator output.

scrutiny by the user. For this problem, the output produced by the MG is shown in Figure 11.13. The material flow and information flows, as understood by the system, are shown. The levels and rates are named, and parameters and values for the information flows are given. No secondary or auxiliary information flows exist in this problem, and none are detected. The knowledge base can also be queried for additional information. This output is consistent with the original flow diagram.

The knowledge base can now be queried by the automatic program generator to generate executable source code. Figure 11.14 shows a complete listing of the DYNAMO simulation code, which is correctly generated for this problem. NATSIM can be run in a mode whereby the user only gets the source code as output; however, the intermediate printouts are useful in validating the model.

The descriptions used, in this example and other examples that were tried, are representative of descriptions that could be used in a real problem situation. Even though the levels of complexity of the descriptions vary, NATSIM automatically constructed appropriate models and generated source code that is syntactically and logically complete and correct.

5.2. System Evaluation

New approaches and techniques for intelligent simulation environments and specifically for natural language processing are continually being developed. As a result, little attention has been devoted to developing accepted approaches to evaluate their power and performance. Performance evaluation can be used as a tool for system design, as an estimation of future system behavior, or to increase the general body of knowledge of intelligent system design. However, tools that have traditionally been utilized for assessing software quality are limited and insufficient for evaluating a system like

```
NOTE    LEVEL EQUATIONS
NOTE
L inventory.K = inventory.J + DT*(arrival.JK-shipment.JK)
N inventory = 50
L warehouse.K = warehouse.J + DT*(order.JK-arrival.JK)
N warehouse = 500
NOTE
NOTE    RATE EQUATIONS
NOTE
R arrival.KL = warehouse.K/4
R order.KL = 1*shipment.JK
R shipment.KL = 15*noise() + 20
NOTE
NOTE    AUXILIARY EQUATIONS
NOTE
NOTE
NOTE    CONTROL STATEMENTS
NOTE
N TIME = 0
SPEC DT = 1,LENGTH = 20,PRTPER = 1,PLTPER = 1
PLOT inventory = 1,warehouse = 2
PLOT arrival = 3,order = 4,shipment = 5
PRINT inventory,warehouse
PRINT arrival,order,shipment
RUN  testing
```

FIGURE 11.14. Example 1 DYNAMO code.

NATSIM. For example, efficiency, correctness, and reliability have been used as measures of performance. In evaluating the performance of NATSIM, while time and space complexity are of some concern, it is more important to measure how much and how well the system is capable of processing natural language. Measures of correctness are traditionally concerned with checking whether the software does what it was designed to do. In evaluating NATSIM, it is a simple task to discern whether the code generated is correct, but not whether it is the model intended by the user. Traditional approaches for measuring software reliability are concerned with faults due to bad programming of a correct solution. In evaluating NATSIM, it is more important to discover deficiencies due to poor algorithms that have been correctly coded.

In evaluating NATSIM, the goal is to test how well the observable system behavior meets user requirements. A mismatch between user requirements and system behavior can have many causes. Potential sources of problems include poor design, poor implementation, poor system specification of user requirements, and inadequate knowledge bases. Faults or malfunctions that are discovered contribute to the identification of their possible causes at the levels of algorithm design or knowledge-base construction. For these reasons, a qualitative analysis of NATSIM was undertaken. A black-box concept of performance is used so that only the gross system performance is evaluated. Through appropriate experimentation with sample cases and experimentation with potential users, an estimate of global system behavior is inferred.

Insights are gained also as to how restricted the context must be before a reasonable system performance can be achieved.

5.2.1. Test Cases

These cases were selected to show instances where a model is generated, but the model does not reflect the user's intentions. In these cases, information is either missed or misunderstood.

The following system description is similar to the system description given in Example 1.

The shipments are made from the inventory to the customers. When the item is shipped the item is reordered. The order goes into the arrival warehouse. After four weeks, the order arrives into the inventory.

The difference is that the phrase, after four weeks, is at the beginning instead of the end of the last sentence. An excerpt from the NLU output for this description is shown in Figure 11.15. At first glance, the system appeared to process the input correctly. After closer scrutiny, it was discovered that the parser had attached the information about the four-week delay to the wrong rate relation. This occurs because the frame for the arrival rate is not invoked until the system encounters the word *arrives*. The information about the delay is attached to the previous frame, which is for the order rate. A human analyst would not have made this error. This error occurs because the parser is unable to look ahead to the next phrase or to look back at the previous phrase. Thus, code is generated correctly for the incorrect model.

The parser also needs to be robust in handling words or phrases that it has not seen before. Consider the following sentence:

In general, the items flow from the warehouse to the factory.

As shown below, PHRAN does not "know" the word *general*.

 # in general the items flow from the factory to the warehouse
Words processed: 1
Are you sure you meant general?
Type correct word(s), or CR for the previous one >>
2 3 4 5 6 7 8 9 10 11
((*level* (*object warehouse*1))
  (*level* (*object factory*1))
  (*physflow* (*object items*1))
  (*items* (*object items*1)))
(*group* (*object nil*)(*member item*))

(*rate* (*rname *unspecified**)(*from factory*1)(*physflow items*1)(*to warehouse*1))
(49.533 . 21.866)
*

When it encounters a word it does not know, it asks "Are you sure you

```
((level (object inventory2))
 (physflow (object order2))
 (level (object warehouse1))
 (physflow (object order1))
 (physflow (object item2))
 (items (object item2))
 (physflow (object item1))
 (items (object item1))
 (person (object customers1))
 (customer (object customers1))
 (level (object inventory1))
 (physflow (object shipments1))

 (group (object nil) (member shipment))
 (group (object nil) (member customer))

 (rate (rname 'unspecified')
       (from inventory1)
       (physflow shipments1)
       (to customers1)
       (continuous_review_policy))
nil
item2
nil
 (rate (rname 'unspecified')
       (from 'unspecified')
       (physflow order1)
       (to warehouse1)
       (information (delay (amount (time_measure (amount 1.0)
                                   (units month))))))
 (rate (rname 'unspecified')
       (from 'unspecified')
       (physflow order2)
       (to inventory2))
(269.8 . 114.8)
```

FIGURE 11.15. Test case NLU output.

meant "word"." This question is asked to catch any inadvertent misspellings. PHRAN does not allow the user to add new words to the lexicon interactively. It continues to try to parse the sentence and does so successfully because it ignores the prepositional phrase *in general*. In this case the information missed is unimportant to the formulation of the model. In contrast, consider the following:

In general, the flow rate is 10000 *units per month.*

Again, PHRAN would not be able to assign a meaning to the first phrase but would continue processing the sentence. In this case, an important piece of information is lost: the fact that the flow rate is variable.

This points out a significant technical challenge for parsing systems. People frequently use unnecessary words in natural language. These are words or phrases that do not add information, and it would be desirable for the parser to recognize that these phrases do not add information to such phrases. At the same time, the addition of a small word or the absence of a word can greatly alter the meaning of a sentence, and the parser should be able to make this distinction.

5.2.2. Evaluation by Potential Users

Potential users were solicited to use and evaluate NATSIM. Transcripts of the evaluations are provided in open literature [2]. Three categories of users were involved in the evaluation process: those with simulation experience, those with limited experience in the production distribution domain and the simulation domain, and managers who have formal modeling training but are nonetheless responsible for making policy decisions in a production-distribution domain. On an individual basis, each user was given a brief description of NATSIM. No training on how to use NATSIM was provided; however, on request the user was shown a sample of an input description. In each case, the output from NATSIM was compared with a hand simulation of the description. A summary of the comments and recommendations is presented.

Users enjoyed using a natural language interface. All users liked the concept of a system that relieved them of the responsibility for learning a language or interface mechanism to use it. All users also found the output from the system analyzer useful, because it gave them feedback and an opportunity to validate system processing. In a few instances, users assumed that NATSIM has more capability than it has.

All users felt they would benefit from a more interactive dialogue. In particular, users who did not have modeling experience were hindered by the lack of structure and wanted more guidance in building the model. In essence, they wanted the system to ask for what it needed.

Users who did not have formal training in modeling found it very difficult to quantify policy decisions. They rely heavily on rules of thumb and experience over time. In reality, whenever the system has severe problems, these individuals use a predict-and-correct method to try to bring the system back to equilibrium.

In all cases, NATSIM was unable to build correctly a model of the system described by the user. The major problem encountered was language. PHRAN does not have a mechanism for processing words that are not already defined in its lexicon. This represents information that is lost to the system. Even though the overwhelming majority of the words used were understood by NATSIM, it was unable to parse sentences when critical words were not understood. This affected its ability to understand subsequent sentences also. In addition, when the information is not presented in a structure that is captured in the patterns in the knowledge base, NATSIM is unable to relate the objects and information correctly in the system description. The conclusion is that a natural language interface is certainly no better than its

TABLE 11.3. Problems and solutions.

Problem	Solution
Natural language processing	
Misunderstood words	Allow the parser to have a larger frame of reference, i.e., a backward and forward looking capability. Larger knowledge base of words and patterns of words for a given domain.
Inability to recognize new words	Allow the user to define words interactively by associating the word with a known class of words.
Unnecessary words	Define patterns that distinguish between qualitative and quantitative information to decide if words or phrases contain important or unimportant information.
Intelligent modeling environments	
Information elicitation	Make the natural language interface dialog-oriented so that the system can ask and answer questions.
Model validation	Provide a natural language explanation capability.

knowledge base. However, having a large lexicon is not sufficient to handle the variety of natural language formats.

The problems encountered in natural language processing and in building an intelligent simulation environment can be categorized in Table 11.3. Solutions for each class of problem are also suggested.

Additional research is needed in each of these problem areas. This analysis has helped to identify user requirements for an intelligent modeling environment in the context of a real problem domain.

5.3. Summary

The results of a black-box performance evaluation of NATSIM have been presented. The results consist of both successful and unsuccessful attempts to build models from natural language descriptions. As demonstrated in Section 5.1, under certain conditions, NATSIM yields the desired result. The unsuccessful attempts are analyzed to determine how and why they failed to meet user requirements.

6. Conclusions

A survey of the literature in intelligent simulation environments, system modeling, and natural language processing was presented. A review of this material indicated that research efforts to date have only scratched the surface for potential gains in intelligent simulation modeling capabilities. Previous efforts have focused on improving a single phase of the modeling process. The human-to-computer interface for these systems still requires extensive learning on the part of the user. Many researchers have pointed out a need for a more comprehensive and systematic approach to intelligent modeling.

A methodology for building a natural language interface to system dynamics modeling was described. The conceptual framework for a natural language interface is presented. The simulation and application domain knowledge is captured using the accepted techniques of sublanguage analysis. A technique was developed to generalize from single-sentence understanding systems, such as database query systems, to multisentence understanding systems that can interpret text and extended dialogue in context. A framework for analysis of feedback systems was presented that requires analyzing systems in three phases: material flow, primary information flow, and secondary information flow. This results in a model of the system, which can be represented using a computationally efficient data structure. This approach is flexible and copes with the variations in natural language input formats .

Simulation codes can be generated from qualitative natural language models. NATSIM demonstrates how a natural language interface for system dynamics modeling can be implemented, and its potential for application in the production-distribution domain. The use of well-understood ideas from general systems problem solving and system dynamics provides a rigorous and general framework for exploiting natural language for the generation of simulation codes. However, the development of a working system is hindered by the technical problems in building a natural language understanding system.

Suggestions for future areas of study related to the work presented here are considered in three categories: intelligent simulation modeling environments, general problem solving, and natural language systems. The research results can be extended in each of these directions. The conceptual framework and methodology defined can be used to build intelligent front ends to existing systems. As a result, previous work in computer-assisted modeling can be more fully exploited. For example, a natural language interface to STELLA would be an obvious application. Another basic area of research is the investigation of other applications for natural language interfaces to simulation. Natural language can be used for simple input processing, output analysis, or model explanation. The results from analysis and evaluation of the performance of the prototype indicate extensive research is still needed in designing natural language systems. Before natural language can be used exclusively for model specification, a robust parsing capability is needed. Automated procedures are needed so that domain knowledge can be easily specified. A wealth of research problems exists in natural language understanding, including problems in knowledge representation and disambiguation. Since experimentation with new approaches to natural language systems has been preferred to (1) the development of existing systems beyond the level of research prototype and (2) the detailed evaluation of their performance, the evaluation of natural language systems is another basic area for research.

300   Wanda M. Austin and Behrokh Khoshnevis

References

1. Ahmad, A., and Hurrion, R. Automatic model generation using a PROLOG model-base. In *SCS Multi-Conference on AI and Simulation*. Feb. 1988.
2. Austin, W. A methodology for system dynamics modeling using natural language. Ph.D. dissertation, Los Angeles, Calif., Aug. 1988.
3. Bundy, A., Byrd, L., Luger, G., and Mellish, C. Solving mechanics problems using meta-level inference. In *Expert Systems in the Micro Electronic Age*, D. Michie, Ed. Edinburgh, 1979, pp. 50–64.
4. Draisin, W., and Peter, E. An intelligent interface for design and simulation. NTIS-DE-86000762, Los Alamos National Laboratory, Los Alamos, Calif., Apr. 1986.
5. Fishwick, P. Qualitative simulation: Fundamental concepts and issues. In *Artificial Intelligence and Simulation: The Diversity of Applications Proceedings*, T. Henson, ed. SCS Multiconference, 1988.
6. Fishwick, P. Invariance and nominal value mapping as key themes in qualitative simulation. In *Qualitative Simulation Modeling and Analysis*, P.A. Fishwick and P.A. Luker, Eds. Springer-Verlag, New York, 1991. (Chap. 1 of this volume.)
7. Ford, D., Schroer, B., and Johnson, K. An expert manufacturing simulation system. Res. Rep. 485, Univ. of Alabama, Tuscaloosa, Ala., Apr. 1986.
8. Granacki, J., and Parker, A. A natural language interface for specifying digital systems. In *Proceedings of Applications of Artificial Intelligence to Engineering Problems*, D. Sriram and R. Adey, Eds. 1st International Conference, Southampton Univ., U.K., Apr. 1986, pp. 215–226.
9. Grishman, R., and Kittrege, R., Eds. Analyzing language in restricted domains: Sublanguage description. Erlbaum, Hillsdale, N.J., 1986.
10. Grishman, R., Hirschman, L., and Freidman, C. Natural language interfaces using limited semantic information. COLING-82. In *Proceedings of the 9th International Conference on Computational Linguistics*. J. Horecky, Ed. North-Holland, Amsterdam, 1982, pp. 89–94.
11. Grosz, B., Haas, N., Hendrix, G., Hobbs, J., Martin, P., Moore, R., Robinson, J., and Rosenschern, S. Dialogic, a core natural—Language processing system. J. Horechy, Ed. COLING-82. North-Holland, Amsterdam, 1982.
12. Heidorn, G. Natural language inputs to a simulation programming system. NDS-55HD72101A, Naval Post Graduate School, Oct. 1972.
13. Heidorn, G. April 1974. English as a very high level language for simulation programming. In *Proceedings of a Symposium on Very High Level Languages*. *SIGPLAN Noti*. (ACM) *9* (Apr. 1974), 91–100.
14. Henriksen, J. The integrated simulation environment. *Oper. Res. 31* (1983), 1053–1072.
15. Khoshnevis, B., and Austin, W. An intelligent interface for system dynamics modeling. In *AI and Simulation*. Society for Computer Simulation, Jan. 1987.
16. Khoshnevis, B., Austin, W., Chen, A., and Chen, Q. Intelligent simulation environments for systems modeling. In *Proceedings of the IIE Conference*. May 1988.
17. Kieras, D. What people know about electronic devices: A descriptive study. Tech. Rep. 12 (UARZ/DP/TR-82/ONR-12), Oct. 1982.
18. Klir, G. *Architecture of Systems Problem Solving*. Plenum Press, New York, 1985.
19. Klir, G.J. Aspects of uncertainty in qualitative systems modeling. *Qualitative Simu-*

lation Modeling and Analysis, P.A. Fishwick and P.A. Luker, Eds. Springer-Verlag, New York, 1991. (Chap. 2 of this volume.)

20. Luker, P.A. Modeller: Computer-assisted modeling of continuous systems. *Simulation 42-5* (May 1984), 205–214.

21. Marsh, E. General semantic patterns in different sublanguages. In *Analyzing Language in Restricted Domains: Sublanguage Description and Processing*. R. Grishman and R. Kittrege, Eds. Erlbaum, Hillsdale, N.J., 1986, pp. 103–120.

22. Meadows, D., Randers, J., and Behrens, W. *The Limits to Growth*. Potomac Associates, 1972.

23. Muetzelfeldt, R., Bundy, A., Uschold, M., and Robertson, D. ECO—An intelligent front end for ecological modeling. In *AI Applied to Simulation*, Kerckhoffs, Vansteenkiste, and P. Zeigler, Eds. SCS Simulation Series *18-1* San Diego, Calif., 1986, pp. 67–70.

24. Murray, K., and Sheppard, S. Knowledge-based simulation model specification. *Simulation 50-3* (Mar. 1988), 112–119.

25. Norman, D., and Draper, S., Eds. *User Centered System Design*. Erlbaum, Hillsdale, N.J., 1986.

26. Oren, T. Concepts for advanced computer assisted modeling. In *Methodology in Systems Modeling and Simulation*, P. Zeigler, Elzas, G.J. Klir, and T. Oren, Eds. North-Holland, Amsterdam, 1979.

27. Pidd, M. *Computer Simulation in Management Science*. Wiley, New York, 1984, pp. 181–230.

28. Richardson, G., and Pugh, A., III. *Introduction to Systems Dynamics Modeling with DYNAMO*. MIT Press, Cambridge, Mass, 1981.

29. Samad, T., and Director, S. Towards a natural language interface for CAD. In *Proceedings 22nd ACM/EEE Design Automation Conference*, June 1985, pp. 2–8.

30. Shneiderman, B. Designing user interface strategies for effective human–computer interaction. Addison-Wesley, New York, 1987, p. 448.

31. Shtern, V. Validation and verification of inventory control systems using SIMSCRIPT 11.5. In *Simulation in Inventory and Production Control*. Bekiroglu and Haluk, Eds., Jan. 1983.

32. Wilensky, R., Arens, Y., and Chin, D. Talking to UNIX in English: An overview of UC. *Commun. ACM6* (June 1984), 574–593.

33. Winston, P. *Artificial Intelligence*. Addison-Wesley, Redding, Mass., 1984, Chap. 8.

34. Zeigler, B. *Methodology in System Modeling and Simulation*. North-Holland, Amsterdam, 1979.

CHAPTER 12

Natural Language, Cognitive Models, and Simulation

Howard W. Beck and Paul A. Fishwick

Abstract

Models used in qualitative simulation are suitable for use as formal cognitive models, such as those involved in representing language meaning. In a series of examples, we explore the mapping between natural language expressions and formal models used in computer simulation. We present a theoretical representation of categories and word meanings in which cognitive models play an important role. The examples illustrate the use of a model in reasoning and discourse, the expression of temporal relationships, verbal descriptions of mathematical expressions, and the generation of qualitative descriptions of model behavior. This work can be applied in the process of software engineering as natural language specifications are transformed into models, or model results are interpreted and reported by natural language generators. Furthermore, models of various kinds are necessary in systems that use language.

1. Introduction

Cognitive models and methods in qualitative simulation [7] are related when we consider the benefits that each can offer the other. Coarse-grained simulation models offer the benefits of reduced complexity and an increase in model comprehensibility, especially when hierarchically organized with models of a finer grain (such as equational models). A particular model serves to answer a certain class of questions. For instance, a simple finite-state machine, where states are linguistic concepts, can serve as a crude simulation model as long as we are interested in results that can be successfully obtained by simulating that model; in other words, we cannot overstep the "bounds" of what the model is capable of representing. If one's question to a system is "Is the lathe used after the part cleaning process?" (in a manufacturing domain), then an

---

This research was supported in part by grants from the National Science Foundation (Grant IRI-8909152) and the Florida High Technology and Industry Council.

automaton or model in temporal logic may be sufficient. These models, though, are inadequate when used to try to answer questions such as "What is the instantaneous rotation speed 3 s after machine start-up?"

Natural language (NL) serves as an excellent starting point when considering coarse-grained model structures; many system descriptions, problems, and answers are often stated in terms of natural language. The chief problem with natural language, as a simulation modeling language, relates to the lexical ambiguities and incomplete knowledge associated with natural language models. However, this is not a reason to despair and dismiss the study of natural language models. People will continue to think and write system descriptions in natural language whether or not there exists software to manage NL models. It is logical that our everyday language of choice will serve as a vehicle through which we express many rough simulation model structures (at least at the early stages of model development [8]).

What is needed, then, are methods that can help us to deal with the ambiguities and incomplete information in natural language models effectively. In this chapter we first discuss the fundamental process of forming conceptual categories of NL expressions and the important role of cognitive models in this process. It is suggested that qualitative simulations would be generated as a particular kind of cognitive model. Finally, we discuss some examples that we have created to illustrate how to build simulation models in natural language.

2. The Role of Formal Models in Language Understanding

NL expressions have much in common with simulation models. A sentence contains constituent phrases each expressing an idea (submodel), and the phrases are connected by syntax (submodel interaction). One could claim that the language of mathematics is clear, precise, and unambiguous, but it too has a grammar and its symbols are given meaning through conventions set by those using the language. Conventions for algebraic expressions, for instance, take the form of grammars and symbols with well defined semantics necessary for calculating the resulting value of an expression. Language expressions undergo transformation [9]. For example, English sentences are transformed into an internal representation (semantic structures). One such transformation could be into a formal qualitative or quantitative model.

This section explores the relationship between formal models and language. This is an important relationship and sets the stage for formal representations of language meaning. We shall examine some problems with classical representation approaches. We see that theories of categorization play a central role in representing word meanings. Word meanings are by no means simple, but rather are created from complex, interrelated clusters of concepts. In current theories of categorization, such clusters evolve from conflicts between models of the world, and empirical case-based observation. This is the same relationship as that between scientific theory and experimental data.

We suggest that qualitative models can be used as cognitive models for representing natural language meaning and reasoning. Qualitative models are special cases of cognitive models. In order to understand the role of qualitative models in language understanding, we first examine the role of cognitive models in category theory.

2.1. The Classical View of Categorization

Structured knowledge representation languages such as frames, semantic networks, and conceptual dependencies have long been used for representing language meaning. In these systems, classes of structured objects are created by establishing relationships (through slots or links) between entities represented by symbols. The meaning of a natural language expression is represented by combining smaller structured objects representing words and phrases together into larger groups representing entire expressions.

Our departure from traditional knowledge representation approaches has to do with the role of models, theories, rules, and abstract objects in representing word meaning. Essentially, the meaning of a word cannot be represented by a simple definition in the form of a propositional statement. The notion that dictionary definitions are sufficient to represent word meanings is too simple. This is because such definitions do not contain enough information to represent the diversity of ways in which a particular word may be used.

The problem of categorization, of how people place objects into classes, generalizes and illustrates the difficulty. In most representation systems used in artificial intelligence, categories are defined by formal propositions that state necessary and sufficient conditions for category membership. This is evident, for example, in term subsumption languages such as KL-ONE [3]. An instance is a member of a category (KL-ONE Concept node) if it satisfies the restrictions specified by the Concept node. In machine learning, algorithms such as ID3 [20] and CLUSTER [25] automatically generate classification schemes by examining the attributes of sets of instances. The result is a decision tree in ID3 that is traversed to determine class membership of a new instance, or a class description in CLUSTER that states the properties an instance must have to be a member of a class. Although these systems represent the first attempts at generating categories through machine learning, the resulting categories are primitive and do not always match with culturally accepted natural categories such as those that determine word meaning. Expert systems are equally rigid since a fixed rule is used to determine what is the case. The problem is that rules *have exceptions*. Categories based on necessary and sufficient conditions do not accurately represent real categories.

In the case of a word, it is not possible to give simple definitions in the form of necessary and sufficient conditions. The multiple ways in which a word can be used form a category, but it is difficult to say what all the members of this category have in common. Rather, the association results from an almost intangible similarity among the members. This is the "family resemblance" problem identified by Wittgenstein [26]. Considerable research has been conducted in psychology since the mid 1970s that has supported and elaborated this view [14, 19, 21].

Other classical approaches to forming categories, such as distance in feature space, or specification of an exemplar or prototypical class member, are also too simple to be functional. In the case of feature space, an arbitrary threshold inevitably is needed to identify borderline cases. Specification of a prototype does not help in deciding how much like the prototype an instance must be. Canceling of default values specified by the prototype leads to incoherent systems of reasoning.

The difficulty of using necessary and sufficient propositions for determining category membership is that they cannot deal with exceptions. A simple definition does not capture the tremendous diversity in the number of ways a single word can be used. Furthermore, any language processing system must have the capacity to learn, to acquire new word senses since (1) language is constantly changing and (2) the enormous job of knowledge acquisition needed to build robust language processing systems cannot be done entirely by hand.

The classical theory is not a complete theory of categorization because it cannot deal with exceptional cases. Classical knowledge representation techniques are brittle; they cannot deal with any situations that go beyond their boundaries. Yet humans form categories with highly diverse elements and can easily recognize borderline cases.

2.2. Modern View

2.2.1. Case-Based Reasoning and Large-Scale Memory Organization

Moving beyond the classical view requires lowering the status of rules, definitions, and conditions. Understanding a particular situation depends not just on how that situation conforms to preexisting ideals, but on the details and unique features of the situation. The *particulars* of the case are just as important.

The movement away from theory toward the study of individual instances is the main theme in the field of case-based reasoning [12]. For example, the difficulty of extracting rules from experts may be because experts do not operate from rules. Instead, experts have an enormous body of experience in the form of cases. When faced with a new problem, the expert retrieves one or more cases that are similar to the new problem and applies previous solutions as appropriate. Thus, the new situation is compared to previous situations, not to a general rule.

In terms of categorization, new instances are not compared to a generalized class definition, but rather to other instances. Thus, instances are clustered together because they have similar properties, even though there may be nothing in common among all instances in the class.

This approach depends on a memory organization that is capable of storing and retrieving large numbers of cases. The trend towards such large-scale knowledge bases is evident in a number of techniques such as memory-based parsing [24] and Minsky's Society of Mind [17]. In these systems, the ability to reason about new and unusual situations is a result of the vast number of cases available.

2.2.2. Problems with the Similarity-Based Approach

If categories are to be formed on the basis of matching instances with similar features, there is now the problem of what counts as being similar. Descriptions of two instances must be compared. But how can a description of an instance be created in the first place?

Basic building blocks are needed for forming descriptions. Some relationships may exist as epistemological primitives. Object, ISA, part-of, related-to, instance-of, and time/space relationships may be given as part of an a priori vocabulary for building descriptions. But these cannot explain the formation of higher-level concepts. It is not fair to say that feathers, beak, and wings are independent properties that constitute bird, since these concepts have meaning only within the concept of bird [15]. That is, they must be connected within a bird structure. For example, part of what makes a wing a wing is that it is part of a bird. Thus, it is begging the question to define a bird in terms of these constituent parts. In many cases, properties are correlated, such as "swims/webbed feet." Seeing the correlation requires an understanding beyond comparison of common features.

The very notion of similarity implies that we recognize objects that have features in common. The problem is that *features are themselves products of theories*, of our preconceived views of the world. They are not independent properties existing objectively apart from the observer.

2.2.3. Cognitive Models and Explanation-Based Reasoning

Just as reasoning from theory without cases is infexible, it appears that cases cannot exist without theory or models. Cognitive models represent our view of the world. They are theories about the nature of things. They are the basis upon which we perceive things, and, according to current views, play a major role in categorization. Instances form categories because they conform to cognitive models of the category.

In case-based reasoning, a cognitive model appears in the form of explanation-based learning [4]. For example, analysis of cases in which a machine malfunctions along with symptoms are compared with a causal model of how the machine works [11]. The causal model explains the relationships between symptoms and problem and could be use to weight the symptoms as being very important (such as smoke in the exhaust of a gasoline engine) or unimportant (scratched paint). Note that without the model it is difficult to correlate the features of the situation or to assign significance to features.

Categorization can be viewed as resulting from an interaction between theories and observations. That is, case-based reasoning is combined with explanation-based reasoning. This trend is evident in recent work in machine learning in which empirical-based approaches are being merged with explanation-based learning [22]. This situation is exactly like that of the relationship between scientific theory and experimental data. Empirical observations suggest theories. Theories tell what data to observe. Observations confirm or contradict theories. Such an approach is marked by continuous anarchy and revolution, characteristic of shifts in scientific paradigm [13].

2.3. Formalizing the Notion of Cognitive Models

If cognitive models play such a strong role, if not a determining role, in categorization, then it would be important to formalize these models. Unfortunately, the cognitive psychologists appear to have only a general notion of the nature of these models. In few cases have any models actually been formally "written down." Although the major representational techniques (Frames, Scripts, Semantic Networks, and Conceptual Dependencies) have been suggested as being like cognitive models, there appears to be some caution in fully endorsing these as formal representations of cognitive models.

The notion of cognitive model must be formalized. But what form should this notation take? A formal cognitive model in symbolic notation such as a qualitative simulation would have the same properties of the original classical theory and, hence, return to all the original problems. Any particular model is capable of accounting for only a specific domain of instances. There are always exceptions and limits to what any model is capable of describing.

The mistake is to give too much authority to the work performed by a model, and the solution to this dilemma, if any, is to view a model not as "the" model, not the ultimate view, but as only a theory, one of many possible theories. For there are many models for representing any concept or situation, and one or more of them may be appropriate for explaining or reasoning in any particular instance. Even for simple concepts, a vast number of models are involved at various levels of resolution and complexity [5, 27, 28]. We also borrow from the theme in case-based reasoning in that the memory organization includes a vast number of models, clustered around concept categories. In addressing a new problem, we have to select from among many possible models that are most suitable, and this process parallels the selection of previous cases that may have a bearing on the problem.

Such a memory organization would be capable of explaining variation and exceptions. With many models and cases to choose from, the suitable model for describing an unusual situation can be retrieved and adapted. An exception to one model would be explained by another, different model.

2.4. Example: *Grow*

A simple example of a model-based approach to representing word meaning is shown in Figure 12.1, which contains two models for the word *grow*. Add to these simple models additional relationships for time and causality, and a good deal more detail, and it is possible to represent more complex types of models suitable for simulation.

These simple models capture aspects of the event nature and dynamic nature of the concept *grow*. In Figure 12.1a, *grow* is a type of Action that implies that it takes place at a particular time and location. There may be an Agent involved in the growing, and (in the transitive form of the verb) an Object, which is the thing being grown. For example, "A person grows a plant." This model will suffice, and indeed would be required, for understanding phrases such as the following:

grow actively
grow tall
grow in the field
grow flowers in clusters
grow best

Since this model inherits relationships of Actions, it can also account for phrases such as

Grow

    ISA: Action
    Agent: <Person,Plant>
    Object: <Plant>
    Height: <Numerical Value,Short,Tall>
    Pattern: <Cluster,Row,Alone>
    Rate: <Slow,Fast>
    Quality: <Good,Bad>

(a)

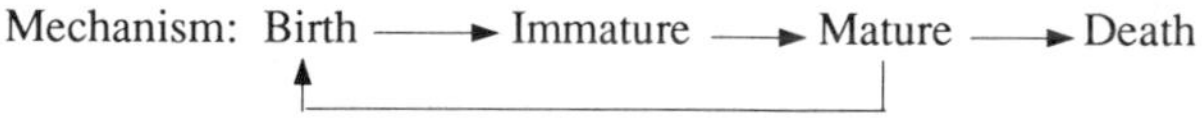

Mechanism: Birth ⟶ Immature ⟶ Mature ⟶ Death

(b)

FIGURE 12.1. Two models for representing the word *grow*. (a) *grow* as an Action. (b) *grow* as a dynamic process.

grow in the spring

which introduces an inherited temporal aspect.

A crude description of the mechanism of growing captures dynamic relations (Figure 12.1b). The mechanism model is needed to interpret phrases that refer to dynamic processes such as the following:

seedlings grow into trees
grow to maturity
grow up

The model fails to account for phrases such as the following:

grow new roots

To accept this, the domain of the Object attribute of *grow* (Figure 12.1a) must be diluted to include plant parts in addition to plants. This dilution effect, that the model becomes less specific as more instances are encountered, is a clear result of the family resemblance principle.

Another failure is illustrated by the following:

grow tired
grow hungry

These metaphors can be understood by extending existing cases (⟨become tired⟩, ⟨grow larger⟩) and mapping to a modified version of the existing dynamic model (growth is a dynamic process of gradual change from state to state), as in the following example:

```
                                        grow over 10 feet tall
                                        grow larger than 25 feet
                     size
                                        grow to be 4 inches

                                        grow several feet long

                     pattern            grow in clusters
grow                                     grow by itself

                                        grow rapidly
                                        grow fast
                                        grow vigorously
                     rate
                                        grow poorly

                                        grow in tropical climates
                                        grow in Florida
                     location
                                        grow inland
```

FIGURE 12.2. A family portrait showing various usages of the word *grow*.

the lights grow dimmer
the lights grow out

The reason the second phase sounds awkward is because it does not describe a gradual process.

With additional instances of *grow*, the complex cluster of meanings begins to emerge. A "family portrait" for "*grow*" is outlined in Figure 12.2. These instances were taken from a corpus of text comprised of technical literature on ornamental plants. We are studying such text examples as an approach to automating lexical acquisition [2]. Overall, the instances shown in the figure have little in common. Yet the instances are not mutually exclusive. Instances are grouped together by their similarity. They are similar in the precise sense that they have some common structural features. For example, the first cluster of instances describes growth in excess of a particular height.

2.5. Summarizing the Role of Models

The evolution of category theory can be briefly summarized as follows:

1. The classical view specifies necessary and sufficient conditions for category membership.
2. Similarity and case-based reasoning build categories by comparing instance descriptions.
3. Cognitive models are needed to describe instances in the first place and determine what similarity is important.
4. The concept of cognitive model needs to be formalized. There is in fact a large number and diversity of models on any particular subject.

The organization of memory is characterized by a large number of models and instances. Models "compete" through their ability to explain the characteristics and similarities of instances. Still, there will always be one or more instances that are exceptions to a particular model. New models are generated to explain the exceptions, but this is a never ending process.

Notice the relevance of these points to simulation. Item 1 above is violated whenever it is supposed that there is just one model of the domain and that it completely describes the domain. Item 2 is the system identification process. Even the collection of empirical data must conform to Item 3 since the data would have no meaning without a model of how the data are collected and a description of what the numerical values mean. Much work is needed for Item 4, and we are proposing that qualitative models may address part of the need.

In the remainder of this chapter, a number of qualitative models will be examined to illustrate the close connection between natural language and models. The purpose of this section was to illustrate general issues involved in representing language meanings. The diversity in language usage requires a corresponding diversity in models. There remains much to be done in formalizing the notion of cognitive model and building systems capable of managing the resulting large-scale memory organization.

3. Language Descriptions Involving Spatial Reasoning

This example shows how a qualitative model is needed both in understanding and in reasoning about a paragraph describing a simple physical system. The following description of a sundial is taken from a children's book on elementary science [23]. As in all the examples, considerable prior knowledge about the physical system, in this case knowledge about movement of the sun and shadows, is needed to understand the passage. These two sentences describe the components of the sundial:

> Sundials are flat, circular plates marked off into hours. A metal stick, called a gnomon, points towards the North Pole. [23].

It is not clear that these sentences can be understood without a visual image of the sundial (which is provided in the book). The following structural description can be built from the literal interpretation of the sentences by using a natural language processor. The exact relationship between the gnomon and plate is unclear:

Sundial
   Components: Plates
               Shape: Flat, Circular
               Markings: Graduated
                     Unit: Hours
           Gnomon
               Shape: Stick
               Material: Metal
               Orientation: Point To
                     Entity: North Pole

Since this example relies heavily on visualization, a representation that captures the spatial aspects must be used. For this, we adapt an image-schema notation developed by Lakoff [14]. Building the image-schema based only on the literal interpretation of the first two sentences (Figure 12.3), we have only the metal plate and the gnomon pointing to the North Pole. The precise relation between the gnomon and plate is ambiguous.

The next sentence elaborates both the structural and dynamic components:

> When the sun shines on the sundial, the gnomon makes a shadow on the plate [23].

Now there is a constrained relationship between the gnomon, plate, and sun dictated from knowledge of shadows:

Shadow
   Light Source: Sun
   Block: Gnomon
   Falls On: Sundial

And the visual image corresponds to Figure 12.4.

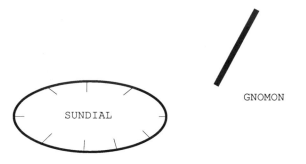

NORTH POLE

GNOMON

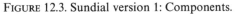

SUNDIAL

FIGURE 12.3. Sundial version 1: Components.

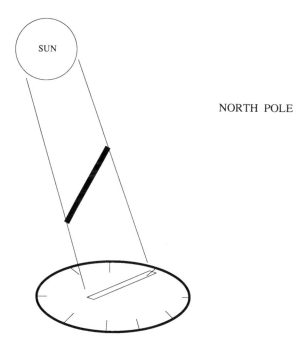

SUN

NORTH POLE

FIGURE 12.4. Sundial version 2: Introducing the shadow.

Now the time-varying component is created by the earth's rotation:

> As the earth turns, the shadow moves from one mark to the next on the plate, telling what hour it is [23].

Understanding this requires the causal connection between the earth's rotation, the angle of the sun, and position of shadows. This can be expressed in

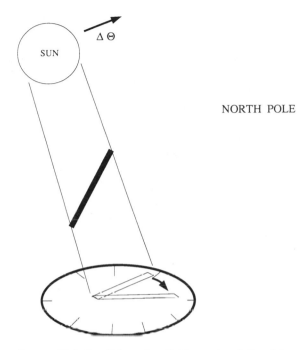

FIGURE 12.5. Sundial version 3: Dynamic relationships.

a mathematical relationship:

$$\Delta\theta(Earth) = C_1 \cdot \Delta\theta(sun) = C_2 \cdot \Delta\theta(shadow).$$

However, this is not likely to be the way small children would reason about such a phenomenon. Rather, a time-varying component can be added to the visual schema. Namely, a change in the position of the earth causes a change in the position of the sun, which causes a change in the position of the shadow (Figure 12.5).

Thus far, the qualitative model has been used to interpret the sentences. The proof lies in being able to reason by using the model:

> Sundials were helpful, but they could not be used on cloudy days or at night.... [23]

So why can't sundials be used on cloudy days or at night? The explanation can be derived from the image-schema, superimposing the image-schema for cloudy days, or by running the model until sunset results in a breakdown of the mechanism shown in Figure 12.5. Without the image-schema, an explanation would be difficult to obtain. Interestingly, the text explicitly stated this explanation, indicating that small children should not be expected to understand such advanced reasoning. The passage concludes:

> ... because there weren't any shadows then! [23]

4. Models Capturing Temporal Relationships

This example attempts to represent temporal events without using mathematical relationships, just by using qualitative relationships expressed in a natural language text. There is a considerable amount of work on temporal reasoning that can be used for this purpose [1, 18]. In this example, statements about properties and time appearing in a natural language text description of time-varying events are mapped to a simple model of the temporal relationships among the events. Properties associated with the entities participating in these events are also extracted and represented explicitly along with the temporal information. This could be the first stage in building a mathematical model.

The analysis is performed on the following paragraph, which describes the life history of a parasite (*Tetrastichus julis*) that attacks an insect pest (cereal leaf beetle) that feeds on grain crops:

> Adults parasitize cereal leaf beetle larvae feeding on the leaves of small grains. Late instar larvae of *T. julis* overwinter in the soil within cereal leaf beetle pupal cells formed in late June. An average of 5 parasite larvae can be found within each pupal cell. In late May *T. julis* larvae complete their development and the adults chew through the pupal cell and make their way to the soil surface where they mate and disperse to grain fields. At this time, *T. julis* can be seen searching the upper surface of spring grains for cereal leaf beetle larvae. [10]

It is possible for a natural language processor to analyze this text and construct representations for both factual and temporal information directly from the words and grammatical structure of each sentence. For example, the first sentence

> Adults parasitize cereal leaf beetle larvae feeding on the leaves of small grains. [10]

can be analyzed at a syntactic level, resulting in a parse tree (Figure 12.6).

The surface semantics of this sentence is represented by a predicate that is constructed by the language processor:

Parasitize(Adult T. julis,
        Larvae [Cereal leaf beetle,
            Feeding[Leaves[Grain[Small]]]]])

which takes the main verb *Parasitize* as the main predicate, and the subject *Adults* and object *Larvae* as arguments. The modifiers (in brackets) *Cereal leaf beetle* and *feeding on the leaves of small grains* are structurally attached to the object. The reference that *Adults* refers to the adults of *T. julis* must be inferred from the context of the paragraph.

The predicate is used to instantiate the generic concept *Parasitize*. Prior knowledge of this concept is needed to interpret the sentence. The generic concept is represented by the object:

```
SENTENCE
   NOUN PHRASE
      NOUN - Adults
   VERB PHRASE
      VERB - Parasitize
      NOUN PHRASE
         NOUN PHRASE
            PROPER NOUN - Cereal Leaf Beetle
            NOUN - Larvae
         GERUND PHRASE
            GERUND - Feeding
            PREPOSITIONAL PHRASE
               PREPOSITION - On
               NOUN PHRASE
                  NOUN PHRASE
                     DETERMINER - The
                     NOUN - Leaves
                  PREPOSITIONAL PHRASE
                     PREPOSITION - Of
                        NOUN PHRASE
                           ADJECTIVE - Small
                           NOUN - Grains
```

FIGURE 12.6. Parse tree for "Adults parasitize cereal leaf bettle larvae feeding on the leaves of small grains."

Parasitize
    SUPERCLASS: Action
    ATTRIBUTES
        Parasite: SOME Organism
        Host: SOME Organism

which means that *Parasitize* is an Action involving a Parasite and a Host, both of which are Organisms. Given this object, the action of parasitism expressed in the first sentence can be used to form the following instance:

Parasitize
    SUPERCLASS: Action
    ATTRIBUTES
        Parasite: Adult T. julis
        Host: Cereal leaf beetle
            ATTRIBUTES
                Growth Stage: Larva
                Habitat: Small Grains
                Feeding_Site: Leaves

Information about cereal leaf beetle larvae is also embedded within this object and is obtained by instantiating the generic concept for *Larva*.

Temporal relationships concerning the life stages of the insects are implicit in this sentence. Specifically, it is the adult developmental stage of *T. julis*, rather than some other stage such as eggs or pupae, which does the parasitizing of the larvae. It is the larval stage of cereal leaf beetle, rather than some other stage, which is attacked. Background knowledge about the life history of insects is needed to understand these relationships. Specifically, all insects begin as eggs, eggs hatch into larvae that progress through several stages or instars, and then enter a pupal stage, after which adults emerge and eventually lay eggs.

In a similar fashion, other factual and temporal information described in the paragraph can be represented in predicate form:

Overwinter(Larvae, In Soil)
    (In Cereal leaf beetle Pupae)
Be_in(5 parasite larvae, One Cereal leaf beetle Pupa)
Begin(Life, Cereal leaf beetle Pupa)
    (Time(Late June))
Become(T. julis Larvae, T. julis Adults)
    (Time(Late May))
Emerge(Adult T. julis, From Pupa, From Soil)
    (Time(Late May))
Disperse(Adult T. julis, To Grain Fields)
    (Time(Late May))
Search_for(Adult T. julis, Cereal leaf beetle)
    (Location(Spring Grains))

Notice that factual information such as "5 parasite larvae per pupae" is directly associated with other information. Properties associated with each concept are connected structurally, and these properties can include both factual and temporal relationships. For example, all the information associated with the adult *T. julis* can be expressed by the object:

T. julis
  SUPERCLASSES: Insect, Parasite
  ATTRIBUTES
    Growth Stage: Adult
    Host: Cereal leaf beetle
    Behavior: Emergence, Mating, Dispersion, Searching,
        Parasitize, Oviposition

where *Insect, Parasite, Adult, Cereal leaf beetle, Emergence*, etc., are also complex objects.

Since the objects associated with Behavior are actions and events, and therefore occur in time, the temporal events can be highlighted as shown in Figure 12.7, which emphasizes the dynamic processes that are occurring. This resembles a state diagram, except that the objects not only represent state variables but also contain all the information associated with each concept.

Notice that time is being represented as multiple states by using different

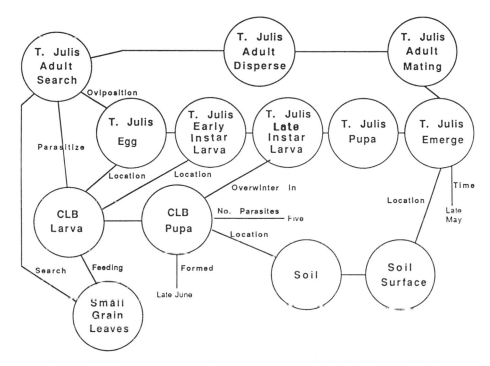

FIGURE 12.7. Semantic network for temporal events in the life history of *T. julis*.

objects. Thus, several objects are used to represent the life stages of each insect. There are three different objects for representing *T. julis* adults. One object represents the newly emergent adult, which is in the mating stage, another represents an adult that is exhibiting dispersion activity, and another represents a later stage for ovipositing adults. This notion of time involves objects "predicting" their next state by pointing to another object. Although it is based only on the information expressed in the natural language description, this way of expressing temporal relationships is consistent with later stages of modeling in which each life stage is represented by a state variable, and difference equations represent the time progression of the insect population through life stages.

Even with the crude model of Figure 12.7, which contains only structural relationships and no quantitative information, questions such as "When will *T. julis* emerge?" or "When will cereal leaf beetle pupate?" or "How many parasites are there per pupae?" can be answered. More specific answers can be given as more detailed knowledge is added, but this is a natural result of refining the model.

Model refinement [6] occurs as more information is added to the representation. For example, experiments were conducted to determine the rate of development of *T. julis* larvae as a function of temperature. Again, background knowledge of insect development reveals that development rate is a linear function of temperature above some minimum threshold. Suppose it is learned that

> a developmental threshold was estimated from data using regression to determine the threshold,

and as a result of the experimental data and regression analysis, the following equation for development was obtained:

$$y = \begin{cases} -12.8 + 0.27x & \text{if } x > 48, \\ 0 & x \le 48. \end{cases}$$

This information can now be associated with *T. julis* larva by attaching it to the object:

```
T. julis
    SUPERCLASSES: Insect, Parasite
    ATTRIBUTES
      Development Stage: Larva
      Host: Cereal leaf beetle
      Development Rate:
        Threshold-Proportional
            Var1: Y
                    Represents: Development Rate
            Var2: Sum
                    Offset: − 12.8
                    Multiply
                      Var1
                        Constant: 0.27
                    Var2: X
                            Represents: Temperature
            Threshold: Value: 48
                Variable X
                    Represents: Temperature
```

where the equation has been converted to an object, Threshold-Proportional. Such information could be used to reason more precisely about when events in the life history of *T. julis* will occur. The utilization of quantitative information is examined in more detail in the next section.

5. Models Capturing Quantitative Relationships

Another example comes from a one-paragraph description of a nanoplankton respiration model taken from a textbook on biological control systems:

> The sunlight is the input to the system and is represented by a battery of voltage e_b. The production rate f of material by photosynthesis is proportional to the difference between e_b and a "backup" potential e, of material in the system, with the constant of proportionality being looked upon as

the battery conductance $1/R_b$. The community respiration rate f_r is assumed proportional to the potential e, and the storage rate f_c proportional to the rate of change of potential in the community cellular storage capacity C. Finally, the total production rate f must equal the sum of respiration and storage rates. [16]

We have constructed a system called NATSIM that can generate mathematical equations based on the descriptions given in this paragraph. For example, the sentence

The community respiration rate f_r is assumed proportional to the potential e. [16]

has the following predicate form:

proportional[assumed, to(e [potential])]
        (fr ⌈rate [respiration [community]]])

The predicate is used to instantiate the concept *Proportional*:

Proportional
  SUPERCLASSES: Equal
  ATTRIBUTES
    Var1: Variable
        Symbol: fr
        Represents: Rate
                Type: Respiration
                    Of: Community
    Var2: Multiply
        Var1: Constant
                Symbol: C1
        Var2: Variable
                Symbol: e
                Represents: Potential

Here the generic notion of *Proportional* implies that a variable is *equal* to the product of a constant (the constant of proportionality) by another variable. *Multiply* is a binary relationship between two variables. Notice that as in the previous example additional information is associated with the mathematical terms, namely, that f_r represents the rate of community respiration and that e is a potential.

The background knowledge needed to understand this paragraph is shown in the concept generalization hierarchy of Figure 12.8. Notice that certain classes represent mathematical operations. For example, *Proportional* is a special case of *Equal*. That is, an equation of proportionality is a special kind of equation. In addition, there are classes describing electrical components and power sources. These are used, for example, to understand the analogy between a battery and sunlight. Also, concepts dealing with biological processes such as photosynthesis and respiration are needed to understand the references in the paragraph.

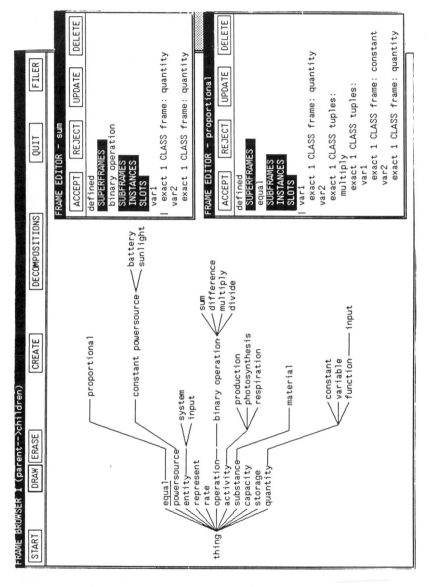

FIGURE 12.8. Concept generalization hierarchy showing sample objects.

The generation of mathematical equations is treated as a language translation problem. Just as objects are created through parsing English sentences and instantiating generic concepts, sentences in any language can be generated by a reverse process. We used a simple context free grammar for generating mathematical equations from objects of class Equal:

Equal → exp = exp.
exp → exp + exp.
exp → exp − exp.
exp → exp exp.
exp → exp/exp.
exp → d exp/d var.
exp → (exp).
exp → var.
exp → numb.

For example, the object for *Proportional* given earlier can be used to derive an equation:

Proportional →
exp = exp →
var − exp →
fr = exp →
fr = exp × exp →
fr = var × exp →
fr = C1 × exp →
fr = C1 × var →
fr = C1 × e.

which is the equation form for the sentence about community respiration rate.

Once the equations have been produced, behavioral analysis can be conducted with the help of a natural language query to answer questions such as "Is this a stable system?" or "What is the time constant for the transient behavior?" These can be answered by sending the system equations to a simulator. The simulator could be coupled with a control systems analysis expert system [16].

This example illustrates that mathematical expressions can merge directly with natural language expressions. Once again, background knowledge needed to fully understand the system under study must be explicitly represented. In this example the mechanics of solving the equations still had to be handled by an external process.

6. Natural Language Generation

There are many situations in which a qualitative, natural language description of simulation behavior and results is highly desirable. This is especially true at run-time where simulation users are decision makers that are unconcerned

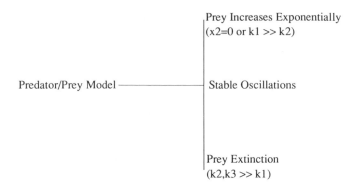

FIGURE 12.9. Category structure for the predator–prey model.

or not knowledgeable about model details. Generating such descriptions is the reverse of the NL understanding process.

Consider the predator–prey model,

$$dx_1/dt = k_1 x_1 - k_2 x_1 x_2,$$

$$dx_2/dt = k_3 x_1 x_2,$$

where x_1 is the prey population density, x_2 is the predator, k_1 and k_3 are the prey and predator population growth rate, respectively, and k_2 is the predation rate. The basic model along with several modes of behavior are represented by the category structure shown in Figure 12.9.

An example of a class description that would be included in the "prey increases exponentially" category would be the following:

Prey_Increases_Exponentially
  SUPERCLASSES: Population Explosion, Exponential Growth
  SUBCLASSES: Predator Extinct, Predator Present at Very Low Levels
  ATTRIBUTES
  Quantitative Parametric Condition: K1 >> K2
  Qualitative Condition: Prey Population Growth Rate >> Predation Rate
  Dynamic Behavior: Rapid Increase (X1)

Naturally there could be many other classes representing the different types of predator–prey models, different qualitative behaviors, and different explanations for observed population dynamics.

A particular simulation run would automatically be classified below one of the classes in Figure 12.9. Once the behavior has been classified, it can be summarized and explained to the user at several levels. Certainly, the raw simulation output or an analytical solution could be displayed. But, in their pure mathematical form, these would not include any interpretation. Another possibility is a template response:

The prey population X1 is exploding because:
  a⟩ The predation rate of $X1 * X2$ is too low
  b⟩ The predator population X2 is too low
  c⟩ The predator population X2 is extinct.

where actual descriptors for $X1$ and $X2$ would be filled in depending on the particular system under study, and a, b, or c would be selected based on further classification of the simulation results.

In more complex situations, a more general natural language generation system would be required. Consider the following observation:

Variable X2
  Represents: Predator Population Level
  Value at T = 35: 1.5
  Value at T = 40: 0

A number of summarizing statements may be made about this situation. The most literal statement is generated from an exact interpretation:

Variable X2 have value at T = 35 of 1.5, and value at T = 40 of 0.

Such a statement is generated by a mapping of the semantic structure down thorough grammar rules. For example, the verb *have* is a linking verb connecting an entity with its properties:

⟨*Entity*⟩ *have* ⟨*Property*1⟩ [*, and* ⟨*Property*2⟩]*

Now other interpretations can be substituted since a mathematical variable in a simulation has an interpretation as representing some entity. The entities can be substituted for the variables:

Predator population level have a value at 35 weeks of 1.5,
and value at 40 weeks of 0.

Now this phrase can be subsumed by a category that contains situations in which some value is decreasing to zero, enabling the substitution:

Predator population level decrease to zero at 40 weeks.

Also, since this form of "level decreasing to zero" is for a particular entity, namely, a population, it is subsumed by the concept extinction:

Predator population become extinct at 40 weeks.

The remaining step is to clean up this expression. One approach is to appeal to rules for grammatical form, such as subject/verb agreement and tense. Thus, *become* is switched to *became*. Although this fixes the grammar, the sentence could be made even smoother by appealing to the case-base of expressions, in which it is discovered that it is more common to say

The predator population became extinct at 40 weeks.

7. Conclusions

These examples have illustrated the importance of models in understanding language expressions. The examples covered use of models for spatial and temporal reasoning, understanding quantitative relationships, and interpreting model behavior through language generation. Through stepwise transformation, natural language expressions are mapped into formal models, and vice versa.

Notice in these examples that the natural language system is tightly coupled with the simulation. In order to generate richness of expression and interpretation, the structures used for representing the simulation must be fully compatible and directly integrated with the structures for representing language semantics. Thus, coupling natural language with simulation is not viewed as an interface problem. Loosely coupled approaches are also possible, but would not be capable of the same level of reasoning.

The importance of categories and the role of models in forming categories have also been illustrated. In the examples, the hierarchical structure of the model base is seen to facilitate reasoning. Qualitative simulation models and their components act as cognitive models for determining the membership of model instances and experimental observations, and interpreting natural language expressions. The examples do not show the use of category theory for dealing with exceptions and explaining new and unusual experimental observations. This is directly related to scientific discovery, and is an area that shows potential for future exploration.

References

1. Allen, J.F. Maintaining knowledge about temporal intervals. *Commun. ACM 26*, 11 (Nov. 1983), 832–843.
2. Beck, H.W. A lexicon design based on theories of categorization. In *Proceedings of the 1st International Workshop on Lexical Acquisition*. AAAI Press, 1989.
3. Brachman, R.J., and Schmolze, J.G. An overview of the KL-ONE knowledge representation system. *Cog. Sci.* 9 (1985), 171–216.
4. DeJong, G., and Mooney, R. Explanation based learning: an alternative view. *Mach. Learning 1* (1986), 145–176.
5. Fishwick, P.A. The role of process abstraction in simulation. *IEEE Trans. Syst., Man, Cybern. 18*, 1 (Jan./Feb. 1988), 18–39.
6. Fishwick, P.A. Automating the transition from lumped models to base models. In *Proceedings of the SCS Eastern Simulation Conference* The Society for Computer Simulation, Apr. 1988, pp. 57–63.
7. Fishwick, P.A. Qualitative methodology in simulation model engineering. *Simulation 52*, 3 (Mar. 1989), 95–101.
8. Fishwick, P.A. Toward an integrated approach to simulation model engineering. *Int. J. Gen. Syst.* To be published.
9. Fodor, J.A. *The Language of Thought*. Harvard University Press, Cambridge, Mass., 1975.

10. Gage, S.H., and Haynes, D.L. Emergence under natural and manipulated conditions if *tetrastichus julis*, an introduced larval parasite of the cereal leaf beetle, with reference to regional population management. *Environ. Entomology 4*, 3 (1975), 425–434.
11. Hammond, K.J., and Hurwitz, N. Extracting diagnostic features from explanations. In *Proceedings of a Workshop on Case-Based Reasoning*, J. Kolodner, Ed. Morgan Kaufmann, 1988, pp. 169–178.
12. Kolodner, J., Ed. *Proceedings of a Workshop on Case-Based Reasoning*. Morgan Kaufmann, 1988.
13. Kuhn, T.S. *The Structure of Scientific Revolutions*. The University of Chicago Press, Chicago, Ill., 1970.
14. Lakoff, G. *Women, fire, and dangerous things*. University of Chicago Press, Chicago, Ill., 1987.
15. Medin, D., and Wattenmaker, W.D. Category cohesiveness, theories, and cognitive archeology. In *Concepts and Conceptual Development: Ecological and Intellectual Factors in Categorization*, U. Neisser, Ed. Cambridge University Press, 1987, pp. 25–62.
16. Milsum, J.H. *Biological Control Systems Analysis*. McGraw-Hill, New York, 1966.
17. Minsky, M.L. *The Society of Mind*. Simon and Schuster, 1986.
18. Moszkowski, B. *Executing Temporal Logic Programs*. Cambridge Press, Cambridge, 1986.
19. Neisser, U., Ed. *Concepts and Conceptual Development: Ecological and Intellectual factors in Categorization*. Cambridge University Press, 1987.
20. Quinlan, J.R. Induction over large databases. Tech. Rep. HPP-79-14, Stanford Univ., Stanford, Calif., 1979.
21. Rosch, E., and Mervis, C.B. Family resemblances: Studies in the internal structure of categories. *Cog. Psycho. 7* (1975), 573–605.
22. Segre, A.M., Ed. *Session on Combining Empirical and Explanation-Based Learning*. Morgan Kaufmann, 1989.
23. Smith, K.B. *How?* Ottenheimer Publishers, Inc., 1985.
24. Stanfill, C., and Waltz, D. Toward memory-based reasoning. *Commun. ACM 12*, 12 (Dec. 1986.), 1213–1228.
25. Stepp, R.E., and Michalski, R.S. Conceptual clustering: Inventing goaloriented classifications of structured objects. In *Machine Learning: An Artificial Intelligence Approach (Vol. 2)*, R.S. Michalski, J.G. Carbonell, and T.M. Mitchell, Eds. Morgan Kaufmann, 1986, pp. 471–498.
26. Wittgenstein, L. *Philosophical Investigations*. Macmillan, 1953.
27. Zeigler, B.P. *Theory of Modelling and Simulation*. Wiley, New York, 1976.
28. Zeigler, B.P. *Multi-Facetted Modelling and Discrete Event Simulation*. Academic Press, New York, 1984.

Biographies

Paul A. Fishwick (Editor) is an Assistant Professor in the Department of Computer and Information Sciences at the University of Florida. He received a B.S. in Mathematics from the Pennsylvania State University, an M.S. in Applied Science from the College of William and Mary, and a Ph.D. in Computer and Information Science from the University of Pennsylvania in 1986. He also has six years of industrial/government production and research experience working at Newport News Shipbuilding and Dry Dock Company (doing CAD/CAM parts definition research) and at NASA Langley Research Center (studying engineering database models for structural engineering). His current research interests are in computer simulation modeling, systems science, artificial intelligence, and scientific visualization. He has published a number of journal articles in the topics of process abstraction in modeling, the use of natural language as a simulation modeling medium, and qualitative simulation. He is a member of the IEEE, the IEEE Society for Systems, Man and Cybernetics, the IEEE Computer Society, The Society for Computer Simulation, the ACM, the AAAI, and the IMACS. Dr. Fishwick was chairman of the IEEE Computer Society Technical Committee on Simulation (TCSIM) from 1988 to 1990, and he is on several journal editorial boards including *ACM Transactions on Modelling and Computer Simulation* and the *Transactions of the Society for Computer Simulation.*

Paul A. Luker (Editor) has been a Professor of Computer Science at the California State University, Chico, since 1985. He was formerly a Lecturer in Computer Science at the University of Bradford, Yorkshire, England. He has a bachelor's degree from the University of London in Electrical Engineering, and a master's degree and a Ph.D. in Computer Science from the City University and from the University of Bradford, respectively. He has been interested in and working with simulation since 1966. This interest led to his first appointment, as a systems engineer designing avionics systems for Elliott Flight Automation (now Marconi) in 1968. Paul Luker is an active member of the Society for Computer Simulation. He is currently Editor-in-Chief of the Society's journal *Transactions of the Society for Computer Simulation.*

326

Ralph H. Abraham is a Professor of Mathematics at the University of California at Santa Cruz. He received a Ph.D. in Mathematics at the University of Michigan in 1960, and taught at Berkeley, Columbia, and Princeton before moving to Santa Cruz in 1968. He has held visiting positions in Amsterdam, Paris, Warwick, Barcelona, and Basel, and is the author of *Linear and Multilinear Algebra, Foundations of Mechanics* (with J.E. Marsden), *Transversal Mappings and Flows.* (with J. Robbin) *Manifolds, Tensor Analysis, and Applications* (with J.E. Marsden and T. Ratiu), and *Dynamics, The Geometry of Behavior* (four volumes, with C.D. Shaw). He has been active on the research frontier of dynamics—in mathematics since 1960, and in applications and experiments since 1973. In 1975 he founded the *Visual Mathematics Project* at the University of California at Santa Cruz, to explore the use of interactive computer graphics in teaching mathematics.

Wanda H. Austin has twelve years of industrial experience in systems engineering, software engineering, and system simulation. She received a B.A. in Mathematics from the Franklin and Marshall College, and a M.S. in Mathematics and a M.S. in Systems Engineering from the University of Pittsburgh. Her Ph.D. is in Industrial and Systems Engineering from the University of Southern California, where she also taught system simulation. The research reported in this volume was performed while she was at U.S.C. Her current position with the Aerospace Corporation is Manager, System Engineering, Satellite Communications Program Office.

Howard W. Beck is an Assistant Professor in the Department of Agricultural Engineering at the University of Florida. He holds a bachelor's degree and master's degree in Electrical Engineering from the University of Illinois and the Ph.D. in Computer and Information Science from the University of Florida. He is also employed by the Florida Cooperative Extension Service, where he has been working on large-scale information-retrieval systems and simulation of agricultural systems. His current research involves incorporating natural language processing into semantic data models, knowledge-based simulation, lexical acquisition, and information-retrieval systems.

François E. Cellier received his B.S. degree in Electrical Engineering in 1972, his M.S. degree in Automatic Control in 1973, and his Ph.D. in Technical Sciences in 1979, all from the Swiss Federal Institute of Technology (ETH) Zürich. Following his Ph.D., Dr. Cellier worked as a Lecturer at ETH Zürich. He joined the University of Arizona in 1984 as an Associate Professor. Dr. Cellier's main scientific interests concern modeling and simulation methodology, and the design of advanced software systems for simulation, computer-aided modeling, and computer-aided design. He has designed and implemented the GASP-V simulation package, and he was the designer of the COSY simulation language, a modified version of which under the name of SYS-MOD has meanwhile become a standard by the British Ministry of Defence. Dr. Cellier has authored or coauthored more than forty technical

publications, and has edited two books. He served as a chairman of the
National Organizing Committee (NOC) of the Simulation '75 conference and
as a chairman of the International Program Committee (IPC) of the Simulation '77 and Simulation '80 conferences, and he has also participated in
several other NOCs and IPCs. He is Associate Editor of several simulation-
related journals, and he served as Vice-Chairman of two committees on
standardization of simulation and modeling software. Memberships include
SCS and IMACS.

Leo C.M.M. van Geffen (born in 1952) received his M.S. degree in Mechanical
Engineering from the Eindhoven University of Technology. His specialization
was in Technical Systems Science. He worked for the Netherlands Organization for Applied Scientific Research (TNO) in a project on Flexible Manufacturing Systems and was a coauthor of the book *The Flexible Corporation*.
Currently he is a Lecturer at the University of Twente, Faculty of Mechanical
Engineering, Engineering Design Section. He is teaching a course on "Analysis
of Technical Systems" and is setting up a course on "Creativity and Engineering Design." He wrote a report on the establishment of a long-term research
program into the "Development of Design Methods" and is conducting
Ph.D.-research on "Computer Assistance in the Conceptual Phase of Engineering Design." He made contributions to international conferences on these
topics. He is also currently working as an independent Engineering Consultant, specialized in the application of Creativity Techniques in Engineering
Design.

Clark Glymour took undergraduate degrees in Chemistry and Philosophy at
the University of New Mexico and a doctorate in History and Philosophy of
Science from Indiana University, where he also pursued minors in Mathematics and Chemical Physics. He is the author of *Theory and Evidence*
(Princeton University Press, 1980), an editor of *Foundations of Space-Time
Theories* (University of Minnesota Press, 1981), and a coauthor of several
historical studies on the development of modern physics and several articles
on induction and machine learning. He is presently Alumni Professor of
Philosophy at Carnegie Mellon University, and Adjunct Professor of History
and Philosophy of Science at the University of Pittsburgh.

Peter M.A.L. Hezemans (born in 1934, deaf) is an Associate Professor of
System Engineering for Power Transmissions at the Faculty of Mechanical
Engineering, Eindhoven University of Technology, Eindhoven, The Netherlands. Peter Hezemans was the Project Manager for the dynamical analysis
of the hydraulically moving floodgates of the riverarm "Oosterschelde" (Eastern Scheldt, The Netherlands) and was involved in several industrial projects
such as the feasibility study/dynamical analysis of the hydraulic rudder-system
of "multipurpose" frigates of the Royal Navy; the dynamical system design of
a 900-kW hydro hammer; the dynamical analysis of the pitch-controlled lips
ship propeller for Mammouth tankers; dynamical analysis/trouble shooting

of the drill string compensator of the drilling derrick, Ecofisk/Norway; and many other projects. Mr. Hezemans is the author of the book *"Fluïdica"* = *Fluidics*, four syllabi, and approximately thirty technical articles, and he has made a contribution to the Dutch "Winkler Prins" Technical Encyclopedia.

Yumi Iwasaki is currently a Research Associate in the Knowledge Systems Laboratory at Stanford University. She received a B.A. in Mathematics from Oberlin College, an M.S. in Artificial Intelligence from Stanford University, and a Ph.D. in Computer Science from Carnegie Mellon University. She also has worked as a Knowledge Engineer at Teknowledge, Inc., building custom expert systems. She is currently involved in a research project to build a model-based reasoning program to reason about the behavior of subsystems of the Hubble Space Telescope. The project also involves building a knowledge base rich in both general physics principles and device-specific knowledge. Her research interests include causal reasoning, model construction, and reasoning about physical systems using both qualitative and quantitative methods.

Behrokh Khoshnevis is an Associate Professor in the Industrial and Systems Engineering Department and is the Associate Director of the Manufacturing Engineering Program at the University of Southern California. He joined U.S.C. in 1983. He has also taught at Ohio University and at Oklahoma State University, where he received his M.S. (1975) and Ph.D. (1979) degrees in Industrial Engineering. His B.S. degree, also in Industrial Engineering, is from Tehran University of Technology (1974). Dr Khoshnevis's major research and teaching interests are in simulation, computer automated manufacturing, and computerized production planning and control systems. He has successfully directed the development of several intelligent simulation systems.

George J. Klir is a Distinguished Professor of Systems Science and Chairman of the Department of Systems Science, Thomas J. Watson School of Engineering, Applied Science and Technology, State University of New York, Binghamton. Department of Systems Science, Thomas J. Watson School of Engineering, State University of New York, Binghamton, NY 13901, USA. He received an M.S. degree in Electrical Engineering from the Prague Institute of Technology in 1957, and a Ph.D. in Computer Science from the Czechoslovak Academy of Sciences in 1964. He is also a graduate of the IBM Systems Research Institute in New York. Before joining the State University of New York, Dr. Klir had been with the Computer Research Institute and Charles University in Prague, the University of Baghdad, the University of California at Los Angeles, and Fairleigh Dickinson University in New Jersey; he has also worked part-time for IBM and Bell Laboratories, and taught summer courses at the University of Colorado, Portland State University in Oregon, and Rutgers University in New Jersey. During the academic years 1975 to 1976 and 1982 to 1983, he was a Fellow at the Netherlands Institute for Advanced Studies in Wassenaar, Holland, and in 1980 he was a fellow of the Japan

Society for the Promotion of Science. Dr. Klir's main research activities have been in general systems methodology, logic design and computer architecture, switching and automata theory, information theory, expert systems, and the philosophy of science. He is the author of over one hundred articles published in various professional journals and holds a number of patents. He is an author or editor of fifteen books, among them *Cybernetic Modeling* (Iliffe, London, 1967), *An Approach to General Systems Theory* (Van Nostrand Reinhold, New York, 1969), *Trends in General Systems Theory* (John Wiley, New York, 1972), *Methodology of Switching Circuits* (Van Nostrand, New York, 1972), *Architecture of Systems Problem Solving* (Plenum Press, New York, 1985), and *Fuzzy Sets, Uncertainty, and Information* (Prentice-Hall, Englewood Cliffs, N.J., 1988). Dr. Klir has been Editor-in-chief of the *International Journal of General Systems* since 1974. He was President of the Society for General Systems Research in 1981 to 1982 and President of the International Federation for Systems Research (IFSR) in 1980 to 1984. He is currently Editor of the *IFSR Book Series on Systems Science and Engineering* and a member of Editorial Boards of thirteen journals. He is a senior member of the IEEE and a member of SGSR, AAAS, and PSA.

Richard Levins is John Rock Professor of Population Sciences at the Harvard School of Public Health. His research is in the mathematical analysis of complex systems with applications in applied ecology, biological control in agriculture, social epidemiology, and public health. Dr. Levins has published in areas of genetics, evolution, ecology, agriculture, and mathematical methods. He developed the use of signed-digraphs for applications in ecology and has investigated problems in theoretical ecology. Dr. Levins is the author of the book *Evolution in Changing Environments* and is coauthor of the books *Qualitative Modeling of Complex Systems* and *The Dialectical Biologist*. Dr. Levins has a long-time interest in the ecology of ants, their use in biological control and differential/difference equations, and their applications to ecological problems.

Charles J. Puccia has been a Research Associate in Marine Ecology and Complex Systems at the Harvard School of Public Health for ten years. He has also been a researcher at the Centre d'Etudes Phytosociologiques et Ecologiques Louis Emberger, CNRS, Montpellier, France; a visiting scientist at the Università di Messina, Messina, Italy; and a lecturer in the Venice Summer School on Environmental Dynamics. Dr. Puccia conducts research in the development and application of modeling methods to applied ecology, environmental analysis, and assessment. He has furthered the method of qualitative analysis for application to problems in ecology. He has published in areas ranging from marine ecology, desertification processes in an arid environment, and the impact of tourists on small islands. Dr. Puccia is the coauthor of the books *Qualitative Modeling of Complex Systems* and *Modellizzazione di Ecosistemi Complessi: Modelli Qualitativi e Simulazioni di Ambiente Acquatici*. His work in environmental areas includes studies in oil pollution in the marine environment, effects of heated discharge to coastal waters from power generation, and the use of qualitative models to understand benthic disturbance from scallop and mussel drags.

George P. Richardson is Associate Professor in the Rockefeller College of Public Affairs and Policy at the State University of New York at Albany, and Executive Editor of the *System Dynamics Review*. At SUNYA, he serves as Director of the certificate program in Advanced Planning and Policy Analysis and as Acting Director of the masters program in Public Policy. He has an A.B. in Mathematics from Harvard College, an M.A.T. in Mathematics from the University of Chicago, and a Ph.D. in System Dynamics from the Sloan School of Management at M.I.T. He is the author of *Introduction to System Dynamics Modeling with Dynamo* and has recently completed a study of the intellectual history of feedback thought in social science. His current research interests center on dynamic problems and decision support in public policy.

Richard Scheines received his Ph.D. in History and Philosophy of Science at the University of Pittsburgh. He is currently a special faculty member in the Philosophy Department at Carnegie Mellon University, and he maintains close ties with the Center for Design of Educational Computing, also at Carnegie Mellon. Besides his work on the the TETRAD project, Dr. Scheines designs and supervises the implementation of an intelligent computer tutor for mathematical logic. He is also the Men's Varsity Tennis Coach at CMU.

Peter Spirtes took degrees in Physics and in Philosophy at the University of Michigan, and both a doctorate in History and Philosophy of Science and a master's degree in Computer Science from the University of Pittsburgh. Formerly Research Programmer in the Laboratory for Computational Linguistics, and Research Scientist in the Department of Philosophy at Carnegie Mellon, he is now Assistant Professor of Philosophy at Carnegie Mellon. Peter recently appeared on the game show "Jeopardy" and was Champion for a day.

Jean U. Thoma (born in 1927) has a diploma in Quantum Mechanics and a Ph.D. in Semiconductor Physics from ETH Zurich, Switzerland. He designed an axial piston hydrostatic machine with variable displacement for fluid power applications, an MTF (modulated transformer) in BG terms. This pump is manufactured in Italy and Japan, and since then he has for many years been Consultant for hydraulic systems that for the most part include this pump. In Italy he is Resident Consultant with C. Galdabini Spa, Gallarate, near Milan, responsible for new electronic presses and testing machines. On the academic side, he was visiting professor at several American universities including M.I.T., where he was introduced to the BG method in 1966. Since 1978 he has been at the University of Waterloo, Canada, first visiting, then full-time, and since 1988, Adjunct Professor for Mechanical Engineering. He has written books on hydrostatic transmissions, oilhydraulic engineering, thermodynamics, and bondgraphs. His newest book is *Simulation by Bondgraphs* (Springer-Verlag New York, Inc., 1989).

Index

BETHANY
COLLEGE
LIBRARY

DISCARD